A Canonical Exegesis of the Eighth Psalm

Journal of Theological Interpretation Supplements
MURRAY RAE
University of Otago, New Zealand
Editor-in-Chief

1. Thomas Holsinger-Friesen, *Irenaeus and Genesis: A Study of Competition in Early Christian Hermeneutics*
2. Douglas S. Earl, *Reading Joshua as Christian Scripture*
3. Joshua N. Moon, *Jeremiah's New Covenant: An Augustinian Reading*
4. Csilla Saysell, *"According to the Law": Reading Ezra 9–10 as Christian Scripture*
5. Joshua Marshall Strahan, *The Limits of a Text: Luke 23:34a as a Case Study in Theological Interpretation*
6. Seth B. Tarrer, *Reading with the Faithful: Interpretation of True and False Prophecy in the Book of Jeremiah from Ancient Times to Modern*
7. Zoltán S. Schwáb, *Toward an Interpretation of the Book of Proverbs: Selfishness and Secularity Reconsidered*
8. Steven Joe Koskie Jr., *Reading the Way to Heaven: A Wesleyan Theological Hermeneutic of Scripture*
9. Hubert James Keener, *A Canonical Exegesis of the Eighth Psalm: Y<small>HWH</small>'s Maintenance of the Created Order through Divine Intervention*

A Canonical Exegesis of the Eighth Psalm

Y<small>HWH</small>'s Maintenance of the Created Order through Divine Intervention

H<small>UBERT</small> J<small>AMES</small> K<small>EENER</small>

Winona Lake, Indiana
E<small>ISENBRAUNS</small>
2013

Copyright © 2013 Eisenbrauns
All rights reserved.

Printed in the United States of America

www.eisenbrauns.com

Library of Congress Cataloging-in-Publication Data

Keener, Hubert James.
  A canonical exegesis of the eighth Psalm : YHWH's maintenance of the
    created order through divine reversal / by Hubert James Keener.
      page cm. — (Journal of theological interpretation supplements ; 9)
  Includes bibliographical references and index.
  ISBN 978-1-57506-708-7 (pbk. : alk. paper)
  1. Bible. Psalms, VIII—Criticism, interpretation, etc.   I. Title.
  BS1450 8th .K44 2013
  223'.206—dc23
                                                          2013040737

The paper used in this publication meets the minimum requirements of the American National Standard for Information Sciences—Permanence of Paper for Printed Library Materials, ANSI Z39.48-1984.♾™

Dedication

To Jennifer
היפה בנשים

To my children Dorea Grace, Jameson Noble, and Cooper Augustine
נחלת יהוה

TABLE OF CONTENTS

LIST OF FIGURES — X

ACKNOWLEDGMENTS — XI

I. **The Canon-Exegetical Approach** — 1
  1. Introduction — 1
  2. A Survey of Literature on Canonical Exegesis — 3
    2.1 Brevard Childs — 3
    2.2 Barr and the Defense of "Biblical Criticism" — 6
    2.3 Mark Brett: The Case for a Pluralistic Approach — 13
    2.4 The Continuation of the Canonical Approach — 16
      2.4.1 Paul Noble — 16
      2.4.2 Christopher Seitz — 17
      2.4.3 On inspiration: Chapman, Vanhoozer, and others — 17
      2.4.4 Evangelical canonical exegesis — 19
      2.4.5 Daniel Driver — 19
      2.4.6 An emerging consensus and open questions — 21
  3. The Canonical Approach in Dialogue with *De Doctrina Christiana* — 23
    3.1 The Hermeneutic of *De Doctrina Christiana* — 25
    3.2 *De Doctrina Christiana* and Canonical Exegesis — 27
  4. Current Scholarship on Psalm 8 — 35

II. **Reading Psalm Eight as a Discrete Unit** — 39
  1. Reading the Eighth Psalm — 39
    1.1 Translation — 39
    1.2 Some Text-Critical and Translational Concerns — 41
    1.3 Date and Setting — 45
    1.4 Themes and Motifs — 46
    1.5 A Close Reading of Psalm 8 — 47
      1.5.1 An initial skeletal framework: Analyzing the topical presentation — 47
      1.5.2 Babies and sucklings/enemy and avenger — 52
      1.5.3 Tying it all together — 57
      1.5.4 Encountering the *res* and engendering *caritas* — 59
  2. Tracing Trajectories for Canonical Exegesis — 60
    2.1 YHWH's majestic name — 61
    2.2 The created order — 62
    2.3 The role of humanity — 62

		2.4 The reversal motif	64
	3.	Selecting Passages for Canonical Exegesis	64
III.	**Psalm 8 in the Context of the Psalter**		**66**
	1.	Psalm 8 in the Context of Psalms 7-9/10	67
	2.	Psalm 8 in the Context of Psalms 1-14	73
	3.	Psalm 8 in the Context of Book One of the Psalter	76
	4.	Psalm 8 in the Context of the Entire Psalter	81
		4.1 An Overview of the Shape of the Psalter	81
		4.2 Psalm 8 and the Shape of the Psalter	82
	5.	Summary	89
	6.	Encountering the *res* and engendering *caritas*	90
IV.	**Psalm 8 in the Context of the Old Testament**		**92**
	1.	The First Creation Account and Psalm 8	94
		1.1 Reading Genesis 1:1-2:3 "In Itself"	94
		1.2 Genesis 1 and Psalm 8	98
		1.2.1 Literary dependence	99
		1.2.2 Reading Psalm 8 in light of Genesis 1	101
	2.	Reading Psalm 8 in Light of Job 7	110
		2.1 Job 7:17-18	111
		2.1.1 Reading Job 7:17-18 "in itself"	111
		2.1.2 The Broader Literary Contexts (Job 4-7 and the Book of Job)	111
		2.1.3 The Nearer Literary Contexts (Job 6-7 and Job 7:17-21)	114
		2.2 Job 7:17-18 and Psalm 8	115
		2.2.1 Literary dependence	115
		2.2.2 Reading Psalm 8 in light of Job 7:17-18 and the book of Job	117
	3.	Reading Psalm 8 in Light of Psalm 144	120
		3.1 Reading Psalm 144:3-4 "in itself"	120
		3.2 Psalm 144:3-4 and Psalm 8	122
		3.2.1 Literary dependence	122
		3.2.2 Reading Psalm 8 in Light of Psalm 144	126
	4.	Reversing the Dialectic: Reading the Old Testament in Light of Psalm 8; Encountering the *res* and engendering *caritas*	127
V.	**Psalm 8 and the New Testament**		**132**
	1.	Matthew 21:14-17 and Psalm 8	133
		1.1 Reading Matthew 21:14-17 "In Itself"	133
		1.1.1 The broader context: The Gospel of Matthew	133
		1.1.2 The nearer context: Matt 21:1-17	135
		1.1.3 The use of Psalm 8:3 in Matthew 21:16	139
		1.2 Reading Psalm 8 in Light of Matthew 21:1-17	142
	2.	1 Corinthians 15:25-28 and Psalm 8	145
		2.1 Reading 1 Corinthians 15:25-28 "In Itself"	145
		2.1.1 The broader context: 1 Corinthians	145

		2.1.2 The nearer context: 1 Corinthians 15 and 1 Corinthians 15:20-28	146
		2.1.3 The use of Psalm 8:7 in 1 Corinthians 15:27	151
	2.2	Reading Psalm 8 in Light of 1 Corinthians 15:27	154
3.	Ephesians 1:15-22 and Psalm 8		158
	3.1	Reading Ephesians 1:15-22 "In Itself"	158
		3.1.1 The broader context: the Epistle to the Ephesians	158
		3.1.2 The nearer context: Ephesians 1 and Ephesians 1:19-23	161
		3.1.3 The use of Psalm 8:7 in Ephesians 1:22	165
	3.2	Reading Psalm 8 in Light of Ephesians 1:19-23	168
4.	Hebrews 2:5-9 and Psalm 8		169
	4.1	Reading Hebrews 2:5-9 "In Itself"	169
		4.1.1 The broader context: the Epistle to the Hebrews	169
		4.1.2 The nearer context: Hebrews 1:5-2:18 and Hebrews 2:5-9	173
		4.1.3 The use of Psalm 8:5-7 in Hebrews 2:5-9	176
	4.2	Reading Psalm 8 in Light of Hebrews 2:5-18	180
5.	Psalm 8 in Dialogue with the New Testament: Encountering the *res* and engendering *caritas*		183

VI. Summary and Conclusions — **185**

Bibliography — 191

Index of Biblical Citations — 209

Index of Authors and Subjects — 215

List of Figures

Figure 1: The structure of Genesis 1:1-2:3   98

Figure 2: The structure of 1 Corinthians 15:20-28   149

Figure 3: Internal movement within Hebrews 1:5-10:18   176

Acknowledgments

This book is a revised version of my dissertation, written under the direction of William H. Bellinger at Baylor University. All of the members of my dissertation committee deserve special thanks. Dr. Bellinger was a fantastic advisor, not only as an insightful and wise scholar, but also as a patient guide. Lidija Novakovic's careful and insightful input has strengthened the work tremendously. Phillip Donnelly went well above and beyond the duties associated with a third dissertation reader and exemplified Augustinian *caritas* for me in his daily life. James Nogalski and Ralph Wood, who rounded out my examination committee, also deserve special thanks. Dan Williams also deserves my gratitude; his role in helping me to think through the nature and relevance of the hermeneutic of *de Doctrina Christiana* was essential to the study presented here.

The very first iteration of what was to germinate and, perhaps, eventually mutate into this book-length study was written at Pittsburgh Seminary in a course on the book of Psalms under Jerome Creach, whose encouragement and guidance through the years have been invaluable. My first academic foray into the book of Psalms came many years ago as an undergraduate student at Moody Bible Institute under then doctoral candidate Andrew Schmutzer, and our paths have crossed again more recently as my work has appeared in connection with conference sessions chaired by Dr. Schmutzer twice now. Kevin Vanhoozer has also graciously examined my manuscript at several stages in the process, suggesting revisions that have made their way into the final form. All three of these esteemed and value colleagues deserve special thanks.

During the final stages of manuscript preparation, many people here at Wheaton College have been helpful and encouraging. Two of these deserve special mention. Jon Sumulong, my TA, has provided assistance with the development of my Scripture index, and Matthew Patton has taken the initiative in sharing his Elementary Hebrew course materials with me, freeing up valuable time for me that I have been able to spend formatting the book, rather than producing Hebrew course materials whole-cloth on my own.

Of course, my patient and supportive family deserves more than mere words of gratitude. My wife, Jennifer, and three children, to whom this book is dedicated, have all shown patience and love beyond measure. They give my life meaning. My mother, Joan Noble Keener, father, Hubert Lee Keener, mother-in-law, Virginia Lee Cooper, and cousins Carole and Lowell Nafziger all deserve much gratitude; their hospitality and support have meant much. Finally, I would like to acknowledge my deceased grandfather, John Noble, the gas company meter reader who was known to quote Augustine frequently and owned a theological library that would put some pastors to shame. He is the one who inspired me to take advantage of the educational opportunities that were not available to him. I pray that I have made him proud.

These individuals and others too numerous to mention have had some hand in shaping this book. Any errors that remain are, of course, my own and have persisted in spite of, and not because of, their influence.

1

THE CANON-EXEGETICAL APPROACH

1. Introduction

Since Brevard S. Childs first introduced it as a "fresh approach" in the late 1960's,[1] canonical exegesis has grown into a widely discussed and developed program as Childs has fleshed out his own thought in greater detail[2] and many scholars have continued to carry his work forward.[3] Now after Childs's passing

---

[1] Childs began developing his exegetical program in articles ("Interpretation in Faith: The Theological Responsibility of an Old Testament Commentary," *Interpretation* 18 [1964]: 432-49; "Psalm 8 in the Context of the Christian Canon," *Interpretation* 23 [1969], 20-31; "Karl Barth as Interpreter of Scripture," in *Karl Barth and the Future of Theology: A Memorial Colloquium Held at Yale Divinity School January 28, 1969* [ed. D. L. Dickerman; New Haven: Yale Divinity School Association, 1969], 30-39). Earlier works, such as *Myth and Reality in the Old Testament* (SBT 27; London: SCM, 1960), a revision of Childs's Th.D. dissertation at Basel, contained hints of the early struggle to "recover the Old Testament for the Christian church" that would germinate into the canonical approach. Nevertheless, the canonical approach does not really begin to emerge until the late 1960s. See Daniel R. Driver, *Brevard Childs, Biblical Theologian: For the Church's One Bible* (Grand Rapids, MI: Baker Academic, 2012), 14-20.

[2] Some important works among Childs's impressive corpus include *Biblical Theology in Crisis* (Philadelphia: Westminster, 1974), *Introduction to the Old Testament as Scripture* (Philadelphia: Fortress, 1979), *The New Testament as Canon: An Introduction* (Philadelphia: Fortress, 1984); *Old Testament Theology in a Canonical Context* (Philadelphia: Fortress, 1985); *Biblical Theology of the Old and New Testaments: Theological Reflection on the Christian Bible* (Minneapolis: Fortress, 1993); *The Canonical Shape of the Pauline Corpus: The Church's Guide for Reading Paul* (Grand Rapids: Eerdmans, 2008). He also put his approach into practice in commentaries (*The Book of Exodus: A Critical, Theological Commentary* [OTL; Philadelphia: Westminster, 1974]; *Isaiah: A Commentary* [OTL; Philadelphia: Westminster, 2001]).

[3] Works responding positively to Childs include Driver, *Brevard Childs*; Mark G. Brett, *Biblical Criticism in Crisis? The Impact of the Canonical Approach on Old Testament Studies* (New York: Cambridge University Press, 1991); Paul R. Noble, *The Canonical Approach: A Critical Reconstruction of the Hermeneutics of Brevard S. Childs* (BIS 16; New York: E. J. Brill, 1995); Craig G. Bartholomew, Scott Hahn, Robin Parry, Christopher Seitz, and Al Wolters, editors, *Canon and Biblical Interpretation* (SHS 7; Grand Rapids, MI: Zondervan, 2006); Charles J. Scalise, *Hermeneutics as Theological Prolegomena: A Canonical Approach*, (SiABH 8; Macon, Georgia: Mercer University Press, 1994); and G. Michael O'Neal, *Interpreting Habakkuk as Scripture* (SiBL 9; New

it is appropriate to speak of a canon-exegetical school that emphasizes the role of the canon as the central context for interpretation of the Christian Scriptures. Nevertheless, the canonical approach has not been without its critics,[4] and practitioners of the canon-exegetical approach still grapple with the methodological questions that, to quote Paul Noble, "are unlikely to develop fruitfully unless they are conducted in the context of concrete . . . exegetical work."[5] This book will contribute to the ongoing efforts to construct a workable canon-exegetical approach by presenting a canonical exegesis of Psalm 8. The aim will be two-fold: 1) to demonstrate that a canonical exegesis is tenable if one can approach the task with clarity regarding the theological foundation of the approach, and 2) to utilize the approach in order to address the often difficult questions related to the interpretation of Psalm 8 as Scripture.

Psalm 8 is well suited to serve as a test case for a canonical exegesis, and the canonical approach is well suited to address the issues involved in the theological interpretation of Psalm 8. Childs's early article on Psalm 8 represents his first attempt to demonstrate a canonical approach to exegesis.[6] Thus, Psalm 8 provides a basis for assessing his early thought and demonstrating how more recent advances in scholarship enable an expansion and clarification of the canonical approach. Furthermore, Psalm 8, in light of its many intertextual connections with the rest of the Bible and debates concerning its pre-canonical form, offers a helpful vantage point for considering some of the thornier issues involved in the practice of canonical exegesis. Conversely, a thoroughgoing canonical approach can help to clarify many open questions concerning Psalm 8, including questions about Psalm 8's structure and meaning and its use by New Testament authors.

Chapter one will address the literature on canonical exegesis in order to clarify some outstanding questions facing attempts to employ the canonical approach. This chapter will consider the literature addressing the canonical approach, beginning with a brief survey of Childs's articulation of the approach; there I will a) argue that the canonical approach is the best candidate available for theological ecclesiastical exegesis, and b) highlight some of the salient theoretical and theological assumptions that the present work must tend to if it is to make a substantive contribution to canonical exegesis. Next, I will attempt to clarify the theological underpinnings of the approach as it is taken in the present work through an engagement with the theological hermeneutic that is articulated

---

York: Peter Lang, 2007). See also Paul R. House, *Old Testament Theology* (Downers Grove, IL: InterVarsity, 1998) and John H. Sailhamer, *Introduction to Old Testament Theology: A Canonical Approach* (Grand Rapids, MI: Zondervan, 1995).
[4] Childs's most prominent critic is James Barr, who attacked Childs's approach at length in *Holy Scripture: Canon, Authority, Criticism* (Philadelphia: Westminster, 1983).
[5] Noble, *The Canonical Approach*, 370.
[6] Brevard S. Childs, "Psalm 8," 20-31.

in Augustine's *De doctrina Christiana*.⁷ Finally, this chapter will survey the scholarly literature on Psalm 8 to show 1) how the current state of scholarship makes Psalm 8 especially well suited to serve as a test case for canonical exegesis and 2) how the canonical approach is well suited for addressing questions germane to the interpretation of Psalm 8. The chapter will then conclude by outlining the rest of the book.

At the outset, the reader must bear in mind the scope and limitations inherent in the agenda set forth for this opening chapter. In the first place, while Childs is by far the most significant figure in the discussion, the ultimate focus here is canonical exegesis; this chapter will set forth neither an *apologia* for Dr. Childs nor a corrective to Childs's work nor even the advancement of a particular interpretation of the (sometimes debated) meaning of Childs's voluminous literature.⁸ Furthermore, this chapter cannot address every issue raised in the sizeable body of literature on canonical exegesis; capable hands have attended to these issues already. Rather, the purpose here is to situate the current work within that larger body of literature, concisely arguing for the reasonableness of both the canonical approach in general as well as the version of the canonical approach taken in this study. In order to lay the foundations for what follows, several tantalizing issues and areas of interest will arise (the thought of Childs, Augustine's hermeneutics, the relationship between canon and inspiration, etc.). Addressing each issue in extensive detail, however, could require several monographs; at the very least it would derail the book from its stated aim—that of putting the approach into action for a sustained and extended consideration of a single text.

2. A Survey of Literature on Canonical Exegesis

2.1 Brevard Childs

Childs began to formulate his canonical approach in the late 1960's in journal articles, including "Psalm 8 in the Context of the Christian Canon."⁹ Expressing discontent with the contemporary approach to biblical commentary, Childs suggests a new approach to exegesis.¹⁰ His article on Psalm 8 touches on three seminal emphases that have come to characterize the program of canonical

---

⁷ Saint Augustine, *Teaching Christianity: De Doctrina Christiana. The Works of Saint Augustine: A Translation for the 21'st Century, part I, vol. 11* (Edmund Hill, O. P., trans.; Hyde Park, NY: New City, 1996).

⁸ For a thorough, up to date, and careful survey of the secondary literature on Childs, see Driver, *Brevard Childs*, 35-102.

⁹ In addition to "Psalm 8," Childs's articles "Interpretation in Faith" and "Karl Barth as Interpreter of Scripture" both hinted at some seminal concerns that would drive Childs throughout his career.

¹⁰ While Childs hinted at the need to replace current approaches to the Bible with a canonical model in these articles, his first full argument for a new canonical approach was in *Biblical Theology in Crisis*.

exegesis: 1) Childs wants to move beyond "the descriptive task and speak of theological reflection."[11] 2) Childs attempts to relate "the way in which a text may once have functioned historically and its later distinctive role in the Christian faith."[12] In his view, scholarly approaches to the text through the middle of the Twentieth Century had struggled to produce results theologically relevant to the twentieth-century Church because they have focused their attention solely upon reconstructing hypothetical historical origins for the text. 3) Perhaps most importantly, Childs seeks to develop "a concept of interpretation which attempts to deal seriously with the whole Christian canon."[13] By treating the canon as the context for conducting the exegesis of Christian Scripture, Childs believes that interpreters can rectify the shortcomings of contemporary biblical scholarship without lapsing into pre-critical *naïveté*.[14]

This third emphasis has special significance for Childs, who has built his hermeneutical approach on the acceptance of the final form of the text as canonical and exegetically determinative for the Church.[15] In subsequent works, Childs makes the case for his "fresh approach."[16] In these later works, he continues to maintain that, by attending to the final form of the text rather than exclusively limiting one's focus to "the history of the development of the Hebrew literature,"[17] one can better understand the literature itself in its shape and scope and can also better relate the text to the community of faith which had for centuries understood it as "an authoritative body of Scripture."[18]

The "canon-critical" approach employed by James Sanders bears strong similarities with Childs's approach.[19] Yet, whereas Childs's approach aims at producing an exegesis for the Church of today, Sanders's aim seems to be "to reconstruct the prehistory of the canon with historical-critical interests and

---

[11] Childs, "Psalm 8," 20.
[12] Childs, "Psalm 8," 20.
[13] Childs, "Psalm 8," 21.
[14] See also Seitz, "The Canonical Approach and Theological Interpretation," in *Canon and Theological Interpretation*, 59.
[15] See, for example, Childs's introduction to *Exodus*, especially xiv-xvi.
[16] In 1970 he gave a full statement of his concerns with the current state of scholarship and his proposal for a new approach in the book *Biblical Theology in Crisis*. There, he made a compelling case that the exegetical approach of the "Biblical Theology Movement," which had been the reigning model among American Protestant academics, was failing as a theological enterprise, and that his own canon-exegetical approach was a theologically productive way forward.
[17] In 1979, Childs would maintain that approaches to the text prevalent at that time had attempted to limit themselves to addressing the history of the development of the text, and had thus failed to fully "understand the peculiar dynamics of Israel's religious literature" and "to relate the nature of the literature correctly to the community which treasured it as Scripture" (*Introduction to the Old Testament*, 39-41).
[18] Ibid., 51.
[19] James A. Sanders, *Canon and Community: A Guide to Canonical Criticism* (Philadelphia: Fortress, 1984); *From Sacred Story to Sacred Text: Canon as Paradigm* (Philadelphia, Fortress, 1987); *Torah and Canon*, 2nd edition (Eugene, OR: Cascade Books, 2005).

tools."[20] As Seitz says, "it would be unfair to compare the two models [of Sanders and Childs] or evaluate the merits of the two terms [canonical criticism vs. canonical approach]."[21] As a result, the following will focus upon works carrying forward the emphases put forth in Childs's program (hereafter "canonical exegesis" or "the canonical approach [to exegesis]"), recognizing that the aims of Sanders (hereafter the "canon-critical approach") constitute a distinct, although similar, enterprise.

Other literature responding to the canonical approach has tended to proceed along one of three lines: 1) James Barr and some others argue that the canon-exegetical program is dangerous and that biblical scholars ought rather to carry forward a program of "modern biblical research" or "biblical criticism."[22] 2) Several scholars, including Mark Brett, are amenable to the canon-exegetical approach yet seek to bolster its theoretical basis in some manner, perhaps by coupling it with literary theory.[23] 3) Other scholars carry forward the canonical approach as Childs articulates it, without linking it to external epistemic assumptions; some of these scholars still feel the need to address perceived shortcomings in Childs's program (so Paul Noble), while others argue that Childs's program as it stands already exhibits a high degree of inner coherence (so Daniel Driver and Christopher Seitz).[24] I shall consider each of these lines of response before proposing a way forward.

2.2 Barr and the Defense of "Biblical Criticism"

Among Childs's critics, James Barr[25] deserves special attention as his attacks on the canonical approach have been particularly influential.[26] In light of

---

[20] Brett, *Biblical Criticism in Crisis?* 121. Childs rightly distinguished Sanders's approach from his own ("Canonical Shape of the Prophetic Literature," *Interpretation* 32 (1978): 54).
[21] Seitz, "The Canonical Approach," 59.
[22] Barr, *Holy Scripture*; idem, *The Concept of Biblical Theology: an Old Testament Perspective* (London, UK: SCM, 1999). See also Samuel Cheon, "B. S. Childs' Debate with Scholars about His Canonical Approach," *AJT* 11 (1997): 343-357; John C. Poirier, "The Canonical Approach and the Idea of 'Scripture,'" 11 (2005): 366-370.
[23] Brett, *Biblical Criticism in Crisis*; Georg Steins, *Die Bindung Isaaks im Kanon, Gen 22: Grundlagen und Programm einer Kanonisch-Intertextuellen Lektüre: Mit einer Spezialbibliographie zu Gen 22* (Freiburg: Herder, 1999); George Lindbeck, "Postcritical Canonical Interpretation: Three Modes of Retrieval," in *Theological Exegesis: Essays in Honor of Brevard S. Childs* (Grand Rapids: Eerdmans, 1999), 26-50.
[24] Noble, *The Canonical Approach*; Driver, *Brevard Childs*; Seitz, "The Canonical Approach;" see also Scalise, *Hermeneutics as Theological Prolegomena*; and O'Neal, *Interpreting Habakkuk as Scripture*.
[25] Barr, *Holy Scripture*; idem, *The Concept of Biblical Theology: an Old Testament Perspective* (London, UK: SCM, 1999). Unlike *Holy Scripture*, *The Concept of Biblical Theology* does not focus exclusively upon the canonical approach. Moreover, Barr's critique of Childs (and others) in the latter is essentially a re-articulation and entrenchment of the views already articulated in *Holy Scripture*. Among the various works that already defend the canonical approach against Barr's critique, see Childs,

Barr's writings, proponents of the approach have felt the need either to modify the approach to rectify its putative flaws[27] or to give a sustained and thoughtful defense of Childs's program that directly addresses Barr's critique.[28] Barr's wide ranging and sustained attack can be distilled into three main allegations: 1) that the canonical approach to exegesis is inconsistent, particularly in the way in which it uses terms such as "canon" and "canonical;"[29] 2) that it is theologically and philosophically unsound, running counter to the "spiritual and intellectual basis of modern biblical research;"[30] and 3) that it is historically untenable, built upon concepts of Scripture and canon that are foreign to the biblical text itself.[31] I will address each of these allegations in turn.

1) Barr argues that Childs fails to distinguish between canon as a list of received books, canon as an emphasis upon the final form of the text, and canon as an impulse towards holistic readings of the text.[32] At this point, those who would defend the canonical approach are split. On the one hand, some believe that Barr puts his finger on a real problem that hinders Childs's ability to employ the canonical approach clearly and consistently.[33] On the other, Childs charges Barr and other critics of being overly simplistic (he says they are "asking for an

---

Review of James Barr, *Holy Scripture: Canon, Authority, Criticism*, 66-70; idem, "Response to Reviewers of the Introduction to the OT as Scripture," *JSOT* 16 (1980): 52-60; Iain Provan, "Canons to the Left of Him: Brevard Childs, His Critics, and the Future of Old Testament Theology," *SJT* 50 (1997): 1-38; Brett, *Biblical Criticism in Crisis?* 118-148; Richard Topping, "The Canon and the Truth: Brevard Childs and James Barr on the Canon and the Historical-Critical Method," *TJT* 8 (1992): 239-260.

[26] For a discussion of the impact that Barr has had on subsequent readers of Childs in the English speaking world, see Driver, *Brevard Childs*, 41-58.

[27] So Brett, *Biblical Criticism in Crisis?*

[28] For example, Childs, "Response to Reviewers;" Seitz, "The Canonical Approach," 68-72, Provan, "Canons to the Left of Him," 1-38.

[29] This line of assault is especially prominent in the chapter of *Holy Scripture* entitled "Further Adventures of the Canon," 75-104.

[30] Barr develops this critique in his concluding chapter of *Holy Scripture*, "The spiritual and intellectual basis of modern biblical research," 105-129. See also idem, *Biblical Theology*, 401-438.

[31] See especially Barr, *Holy Scripture.*, 50-66.

[32] Barr, *Holy Scripture*, 75-82; c.f. *The Concept of Biblical Theology*, 602. Barr would eventually despair of any meaningful use for the term or concept of canon, alleging that "[t]here is no such thing as 'the' Christian canon, except in so far as we take 'canon' in a rather vague and imprecise sense," *The Concept of Biblical Theology*, 579.

[33] Addressing "the relation between diachronic and synchronic interpretation in [Childs's] *Exodus* commentary," Brett concludes that "Childs's actual exegetical practice is at times marred by conceptual confusion" (*Biblical Criticism in Crisis?* 52). See also Paul D. Wegner, review of Brevard S. Childs, *Isaiah: A Commentary*, *JETS* 45 (2002), 692-694 and Reed Lessing, review of Brevard S. Childs, *Isaiah: A Commentary*, *CJ* 28 (2002), 470. Similarly Georg Steins, who is arguably more sympathetic to Childs than Brett, divides Childs's use of canon into five different but related categories (Georg Steins, *Die Bindung Isaaks im Kanon*; see also Driver, *Brevard Childs*, 145).

algebraic solution to a problem requiring calculus"),[34] and Seitz and Driver argue that Childs's broader definition of canon is not only internally coherent but also advantageous on several levels.[35]

However one resolves the question of the role of pre-canonical forms of the text, it bears emphasizing that all proponents of canonical exegesis can agree that the final form of the text has authority for the believing interpreter. As Childs says in responding to Barr, the focus upon the canon as the context for exegesis proceeds from the recognition that "the process of religious interpretation by a historical faith community left its mark on a literary text which did not continue to evolve and *which became the normative interpretation of those events to which it bore witness*."[36] Of course, the canonical process and other concerns related to the final form become of interest to a canon-exegetical approach, but the assertion that the final form is authoritative constitutes the driving principle behind the approach.

In terms of assessing Barr's critique of the canonical approach, the key question is not whether Childs himself was consistently committed to this driving principle. Nor is the key question how the canonical process and final form are to be understood. Rather, the key question is whether or not this driving principle is untenable, as Barr alleges.

2) Is Barr correct, then, when he argues that the canonical approach is theologically and philosophically problematic, despite having a superficial "sense of religious satisfaction"?[37] Barr argues that the canonical approach (which he labels "canon criticism") entails a "conception of exegesis as a *purely* theological undertaking," and thus violates Barr's canons of modern biblical research.[38] For him, "modern biblical research" or "biblical criticism" is "a literary mode of operation, which carries with it historical consequences," within which "the standard and criterion for judging the validity of exegesis lies no longer in church doctrine, but in research;"[39] it "requires freedom of thought," entailing a "creative prejudice" resulting in "a considerable degree of scientific objectivity" that produces "more 'scientific'" results than theology is able to provide.[40]

At first glance, this seems a curious line of attack; Barr criticizes the canonical approach for not doing modern biblical research (as Barr defines it), when the canonical approach does not claim to undertake Barr's "modern biblical research." The canonical approach allows, engages with, encourages, and utilizes "biblical criticism" as a means to the end of answering historical questions. Yet, when a canonical approach engages in its own exegesis the explicit goal is the appropriation of the text by the Church of today, not the

---

[34] Childs, "Response to Reviewers," 52.
[35] Seitz, "The Canonical Approach," 68-72; Driver, *Brevard Childs*, passim.
[36] Childs, Review of James Barr, *Holy Scripture: Canon, Authority, Criticism*, 68; emphasis mine.
[37] Barr, *Holy Scripture*, 104.
[38] Barr, *Holy Scripture*, 118.
[39] Barr, *Holy Scripture*, 105, 108.
[40] Barr, *Holy Scripture*, 109.

reconstruction of historical events. Thus, it does something decidedly different from Barr's "biblical criticism." It would be more accurate, therefore, if Barr characterized the canonical approach as entailing a "conception of exegesis" *for the Church* that is a "theological undertaking;" a canonical approach allows for and even draws upon other modes of exegesis with other ends, but, for its own part, focuses upon bringing the Church into a fresh encounter with God through the text.

Barr's argument is convincing, however, if one shares Barr's a priori epistemic presuppositions. Throughout, Barr's critique consistently relies upon a positive evaluation of the Enlightenment resulting in a self-conscious commitment to an epistemic framework wherein humans, as free rational agents, are able to ascertain truth independent of any faith commitments or of any a priori theological presuppositions. Barr describes how, through the rigorous intellectual pursuit of truth, rational humans are able to ascertain the various facts necessary for the construction of theology. For Barr, theology does not come through revelation from above. Rather it moves inductively[41] and comes through discovery from below in the assembly of data derived via "sub-theological disciplines."[42]

Given such a view of knowledge, Barr concludes that the canonical approach is simultaneously theologically unnecessary and epistemologically dangerous, as it militates, says Barr, against "freedom."[43] Yet, as Iain Provan asks of Barr:

> Is the Enlightenment's polarization of authoritative tradition and the freedom of reason at all adequate? With Gadamer and others, I should have thought the answer is clearly "no." . . . [D]escription of a given object always presupposes a prior construction of that object in terms of a given interpretative paradigm.[44]

Barr's view of knowledge is epistemologically and theologically problematic in several regards. Barr a) ignores the situatedness of finite human interpreters and b) presumes that such a finite interpreter, via the collation and organization of

---

[41] *Holy Scripture.*, 22. See also *Biblical Theology*, 205-208.

[42] "Theology may be pictured as the apex of a pyramid, the lower levels of which consist of non-theological, or semi-theological, bodies of fact, and are controlled by non-theological, or semi-theological, disciplines; and what is decided at the ultimate theological level is in many respects dependent upon what is judged to be possible at these lower, not fully theological levels" (*Holy Scripture*, 117).

[43] *Holy Scripture*, 123-125.

[44] Provan continues: "To assert that this 'freedom to follow critical methods wherever they lead' actually exists in any absolute sense, then, is either to display signs of self-delusion or to suggest a conscious ideological move" ("Canons to he Left of Him," 23-24; see also Topping, "The Canon and the Truth," 248-251).

finite facts and empirical data, can attain knowledge of a God who is infinite, transcendent, and non-empirical.[45]

Childs's approach moves along quite different lines. In one of his several responses to Barr, Childs gives a summation of his method that is worth quoting at length:

> [T]he acceptance of the canon as normative does not function initially as a derivative of reasoned argument. The canon is the deposit of the religious community's sacred tradition which one receives as a member of that body . . . Does this mean that the relation to the canon is irrational and beyond the scope of all reasoned argument? Certainly not . . . The testimony of faith and not reason establishes the canon. Yet there is an internal logic of faith within the framework of the confession. The exact nature of the canon's authority must be an object of constant critical reflection within the community.[46]

Therefore, unlike Barr's approach, the theological method of the canonical approach a) acknowledges the limits of human reason and the situatedness of the individual and b) does not presume that knowledge of the infinite and transcendent divine may be ascertained inductively through the careful examination of the finite cosmos; it leaves room for faith. And yet, it seeks to avoid fideism by engaging in the classic Anselmian method of *"fides quaerens intellectum."*[47] If, however, Barr's allegation that the canonical approach runs against the historical data is correct, then the canonical approach is mere fideism in that it proceeds from a faith claim that is historically erroneous. I turn, then, to consider Barr's historical objection to the approach.

3) Barr avers that the Old Testament does not exhibit self-awareness as Scripture, i.e. authoritative religious literature, until very late, and that the concept of canon, i.e., a limited collection of authoritative books, is nowhere to

---

[45] Barr's own use and description of "freedom" is inconsistent and problematic. In one paragraph, Barr states that "biblical research" encompasses "the entire universe of discourse in which scholarly knowledge of the Bible is advanced and maintained," and thus entails "much scholarship which feels itself bound to reach the results required by this or that religious tradition and which in this sense is not critical" (*Holy Scripture*, 107-108). On the next page, however, Barr says that "research requires freedom of thought" (109-110). Then, a few pages later, Barr attempts to preempt potential criticism of "modern biblical research" on the ground that all research entails presuppositions (presuppositions which, presumably, are binding and somehow limit "freedom"); "critical scholars," he says, "were if anything too much guided by" theological forces, yet still produced salutary work (113). Then, Barr concludes his book with an appeal for the preservation of enlightenment rational freedom through a brief reflection upon the Edict of Religious Toleration and the Declaration of Independence (123-125).

[46] Childs, "Response to Reviewers," 56.

[47] See St. Anselm, *Proslogion: With the Replies of Gaunilo and Anselm* (Thomas Williams, trans.; Indianapolis, IN: Hackett, 2001); Karl Barth, *Fides Quaerens Intellectum: Anselm's Proof of the Existence of God in the Context of his Theological Scheme* (Ian W. Robertson, trans.; Richmond, VA: John Knox, 1960).

be found in the Bible.⁴⁸ If, for the sake of argument, one accepts Barr's definition of "canon" as a closed list of books, then it is mere tautology to aver that the canon did not exist until it was closed; a canonical hermeneutic that presupposes a closed canon of books that are authoritative for the believer today is in no way threatened by the acknowledgement that, at one time, these books did not yet constitute a completed and closed canon.⁴⁹ It is questionable then whether distinguishing between Scripture and canon in this way is helpful at all.⁵⁰ If Barr means to say that the biblical books themselves exhibit absolutely no awareness of a movement towards inclusion in an authoritative collection at any stage, then this claim could be somewhat more problematic (though not decisive) for the canonical approach.

Yet, it increasingly appears that such is not the case, with a growing group of scholars arguing for what Zipora Talshir calls "closing phenomena" in Old Testament texts revealing a self-awareness of the final stages of the canonical process.⁵¹ Such closing phenomena are in keeping with Childs's view: "[T]he concept of canon was not a late, ecclesiastical ordering which was basically foreign to the material itself, but . . . canon-consciousness lay deep within the formation of the literature."⁵² A full analysis of the evidence, which runs through the canon from Deuteronomy to the books of Chronicles and on into the New Testament, lies beyond the scope of this study.⁵³ For now it suffices to note that there is evidence to be marshaled in support of Childs's formulation of

---

⁴⁸ "There is thus a great difference between the religion of the Old Testament as it was for those who lived by it, and a religion controlled by Scripture" (*Holy Scripture*, 6. See also *The Concept of Biblical Theology* 563-580).

⁴⁹ See Brett, *Biblical Criticism in Crisis?* 118-122. See also Childs, *Introduction to the Old Testament*, 62-67.

⁵⁰ Barr does not contest the claim that, after the closure of the canon, the Church accepted the closed canon as the source of orthodox doctrine, Barr, *Holy Scripture*, 2-3.

⁵¹ Zipora Talshir, "Several Canon-Related Concepts Originating in Chronicles," *ZAW* 113 (2001): 386-403. As Talshir points out, "[a]ctual examples . . . include the final editing of Psalms, which regarded the book as authoritative, and appended it to the Torah and the Prophets . . . the conclusion of Ecclesiastes . . . and, finally, Chr itself" (402). See Talshir's article for other recent scholarship that views I and II Chronicles as containing strong signs of "closing phenomena" and canon consciousness. In a similar vein, several scholars have argued that there are intertextual links at the seams of the Tanakh indicating canon-consciousness at the macro level (so Stephen G. Dempster, "An 'Extraordinary Fact:' *Torah and Temple* and the Contours of the Hebrew Canon," *TB* 48 [1997]: 23-53, 191-218, idem "Canons on the Right and Canons on the Left: Finding a Resolution in the Canon Debate," *JETS* 52 [2009]: 69-71, Joseph Blenkinsopp, *Prophecy and Canon: A Contribution to the Study of Jewish Origins* [Notre Dame, IN: Notre Dame University Press, 1977], 85-88, 120-123, and Sailhamer, *Introduction to Old Testament Theology*).

⁵² Childs, *Biblical Theology*, 70.

⁵³ For literature presenting evidence for a canon-consciousness within the biblical literature itself, in addition to the works surveyed in Talshir and cited in note 51 above, see Childs, "The Canon in Recent Biblical Studies: Reflections on an Era," *Canon and Biblical Interpretation*, 45-48.

canon-consciousness, such that the canonical approach is not based upon an irrational view of canon that is clearly contradicted by the data, as Barr would have it.

What, then, of Barr's allegation that the earlier biblical texts do not even exhibit *scriptural* self-awareness until late, and that, even then, the extent of the authority ascribed to Scripture is limited?[54] To quote Provan,

> [i]t is not at all clear . . . where the hard evidence lies that necessitates the view that texts later regarded as having special status as scripture were once not so regarded . . . It seems intrinsic in the careful preservation and passing on of prophetic traditions, for example, that these traditions were already regarded at the point of origin as specially important.[55]

Provan notes that, in order to support his claim, Barr must dismiss the "multitude of cross-references" between Old Testament texts as merely reflecting "a loose relation between books and traditions," not any acknowledgement of scriptural authority.[56] Yet when the vast range of inner-biblical allusions are read more carefully than Barr allows a very different picture emerges wherein such intertextual references imply a self-portrayal of the Scriptures as authoritative texts throughout the Old Testament.[57]

Moreover, the canonical approach is concerned with the faith claim that the text of Scripture is authoritative for the Church today, and the question of whether or not it was considered authoritative by all members of its original audience is only of secondary concern. An "original" audience may have failed to feel the full authoritative force of a text, oracle, or tradition that the later faith community came to rightly recognize as authoritative. As Brett points out, "some Israelite communities would have known, say, prophetic oracles, before they had actually acquired an authoritative status . . . [I]s this really a controversial point? The biblical texts concerned with true and false prophecy provide evidence enough for this kind of situation."[58] In fact, Isaiah is told to

---

[54] Barr, *Holy Scriptures*, 3-23. Barr writes: "The idea of the near-absolute scriptural *control* of faith is a quite foreign conception, based on a quite different construct of problems, and read into the New Testament statements about Old Testament scripture by a later generation" (ibid., 14).

[55] Provan, "Canons to the Left of Him," 8.

[56] Ibid., 9.

[57] Quoting Provan again, "the level of intertextuality among [OT texts] is extraordinarily high. It is not a trivial or marginal matter, this reality of cross-referencing. It is, rather, a central matter. It is, for example, an intrinsic feature of the nature of our OT narrative texts that they have come into their present form in relationship with each other and with torah and prophetic texts, the very form in which they are written inviting reference time and time again to these other scriptural texts" ("Canons to the Left of Him," 8). OT texts at various stages reference other OT texts in a way that betrays an awareness of the authoritative status of the texts referenced (for example, Psalm 8's presupposition of a creation account very much like the account of Genesis 1), even if the purpose of the reference seems to be to reevaluate or call into question that authoritative status (for example, Job's allusion to Psalm 8 in Job 7:17-18).

[58] Brett, *Biblical Criticism in Crisis*, 120.

preach in such a way that the original audience will not acknowledge his message, though it is a divine message (Isa 6:9-10). Thus, the canonical approach may rest on a faith claim, but it is a faith claim that is consonant with the claims made by the biblical text itself. Such a faith claim poses no problem if the purpose of interpretation is to address an ecclesial body that already accepts the text as authoritative.

Therefore, there is much to commend a canonical approach as uniquely well suited for doing exegesis within the context of the Church. The claim for the authoritative status of Scripture presupposed by the canonical approach is consonant with the hermeneutical claims of many Christian interpreters from diverse traditions and times, as Childs is at pains to show and as Barr never contests,[59] and it is also consonant with the Scriptures' own self-presentation.[60] Furthermore, the faith claims that a canonical exegesis presupposes are no less compelling than the Enlightenment claims presupposed by Barr. The canonical approach recognizes the situatedness of the interpreter, acknowledges the epistemic limits of the individual, and seeks to speak to the community of faith from within the community of faith. With Seitz I affirm that "the canonical approach offers the most compelling, comprehensive account of biblical interpretation and theology presently on offer."[61]

This book, then, seeks to articulate a hermeneutic that embraces the faith commitment that underlies the canonical approach, but it does not seek to argue rationalistically for such a faith claim. One might object that such a study will only be of parochial interest. Yet, as I shall argue below, a canonical approach need not silence all other voices. Rather, on the one hand, a canonical approach seeks to glean insight from other approaches to the text, even if such approaches do not share the same aims and presuppositions as the canonical approach; on the other hand, a canonical approach will, in turn, yield insights of interest to practitioners of other approaches, as Barr himself acknowledges.[62] Additionally, the canonical approach is of special interest to one specific group—those believers who share a faith commitment to the authoritative status of the canonical literature. I turn now, therefore, to consider some works of others who, unlike Barr, see the canon-exegetical approach as a worthwhile undertaking.

---

[59] Childs, *Biblical Theology*, 30-69.
[60] "Childs is right when he claims that canon does not represent an arbitrary and late imposition on the OT texts, but is rather intrinsically bound up with the OT texts as we have them" (Provan, "Canons to the Left of Him," 11).
[61] Seitz, "The Canonical Approach," 63.
[62] See Leo G. Perdue, *The Collapse of History: Reconstructing Old Testament Theology* (Minneapolis: Fortress, 1994); *Reconstructing Old Testament Theology: After the Collapse of History* (Minneapolis: Fortress, 2005).

2.3 Mark Brett: The Case for a Pluralistic Approach

While many theological approaches to the text have gained traction in various circles in recent decades with none gaining ascendancy,[63] a substantial body of literature has carried forward the canonical approach to exegesis. Much of this literature advances the view that, while the canonical approach has produced exegetical insights, Childs's work has left many questions unanswered regarding both the precise nature of the philosophical or theological basis for the approach and the implementation of it in practice.[64] For example, Mark Brett sees Childs as inconsistent, sometimes exhibiting a "totalitarian tendency," or a "hermeneutical 'monism,'"[65] while sometimes exhibiting a "hermeneutical 'pluralism.'"[66] In Brett's view, Childs is at his best when his hermeneutics are pluralistic, and a successful canonical approach will consistently embrace pluralism over monism.[67] "Childs," he writes, "wants to put all our theological eggs in one basket—the canonical approach. It would be more responsible, on the pluralist argument, to distribute them widely."[68] In Brett's view, canonical exegesis is best understood in light of its affinities with various forms of literary theory.[69]

Brett is not alone in attempting to construct a canonical approach upon external "schools of thought" to provide a new "theoretical underpinning" for canonical exegesis,[70] often drawing upon literary theory or some type of narrative approach. Georg Steins, for example, articulates a "kanonisch-intertextuelle Lektüre" on the basis of the textual theories of Kristeva and Bakhtin.[71] Similarly, George Lindbeck argues that Childs's approach would work best within the context of Lindbeck's own cultural linguistic model.[72] A

---

[63] See, for example, Perdue, *Collapse of History* and idem, *Reconstructing*.

[64] In 1995 Paul Noble summed up much of the secondary literature on Childs of that time as follows: "One important theme that keeps recurring . . . is that Childs' own methodological foundations are insufficient for the superstructure he wishes to build upon them; and this has naturally led to various thinkers and schools of thought being suggested as providing the theoretical underpinning which Childs' work needs" (Noble, *The Canonical Approach*, 6).

[65] Brett, *Biblical Criticism in Crisis*, 11, 41.

[66] Ibid., 41-42.

[67] Brett says of Childs's *Exodus* commentary that "[t]here seem to be two competing attitudes . . . The coherent attitude I shall characterize as hermeneutical 'pluralism,' and the incoherent one, hermeneutical 'monism.'" Brett laments that "[u]nfortunately, Childs is more often a hermeneutical monist," and then goes on to examine some "less happy examples" of Childs's monistic tendencies, concluding that Childs's approach fails when he adopts the monistic attitude (*Biblical Criticism in Crisis*, 41-47).

[68] Brett, *Biblical Criticism in Crisis*, 167.

[69] It is worth pointing out, however, that some of the thinkers that Brett draws upon to construct a theoretical basis for Childs's approach—such as Gadamer (135-148) and Childs's colleagues Frei and Lindbeck (156-164)—are not necessarily thoroughgoing pluralists in their approach.

[70] Noble, *The Canonical Approach*, 6.

[71] Steins, *Die Bindung Isaaks im Kanon*.

[72] Lindbeck, "Postcritical Canonical Interpretation."

full assessment of each alternative proposal is beyond the scope of this book, and Daniel Driver (discussed in section 2.4.5 below) has recently dealt adequately with the points of contact and divergence between Childs, Brett, Steins, Lindbeck, Frei, and others, demonstrating both the internal coherence and the salutary nature of the approach as Childs articulates it.[73] I have chosen Brett here as a convenient interlocutor because an assessment of his view enables us to consider briefly two important questions: 1) What is the proper role for integrating external hermeneutical or epistemic systems into the approach? 2) Ought a canonical approach to proceed along "totalitarian" lines, "pluralistic" lines, or in some other manner altogether?

1) On the first front, the answer presupposed in the present work is one of nuance and caution. On the one hand, bringing the canonical approach into dialogue with other work—whether that be Gadamer's discussion of the "classics," as per Brett, or Lindbeck's cultural linguistic model[74]—can yield profitable results. Brett's appropriation of "Gadamer's philosophical discussion of the classic"[75] to the canonical approach has provided a helpful framework within which to understand how and why a community of faith can justifiably focus its attention on the final form of the canonical text. Furthermore, Brett has reminded practitioners of the canonical approach that they need not dismiss out of hand all other approaches to the text as irrelevant and unable to produce theological insight.

On the other hand, given the complexities of the issues involved, we must be careful to avoid importing foreign categories that subtly militate against the task of discerning God's voice for the believing community. For his part, Childs expresses appreciation for the insights of contemporary literary theory and narrative approaches, but he rightly emphasizes the theologically oriented distinctives that make the canonical approach something more than the esthetic appreciation of a literary text.[76] Childs insists that his canonical approach has a fundamentally different "theological understanding of the nature and function of scripture" from "many modern literary proposals, which are theologically inert at best, and avowedly agnostic at worst."[77] Perhaps Childs is wise to eschew narrative approaches such as Lindbeck's (although Lindbeck is neither "theologically inert" nor agnostic) in favor of "traditional categories like *sensus literalis* and *regula fidei*."[78] In any case, the key point here is that literary theory, narrative approaches, etc., may be used profitably within the context of a

---

[73] Driver, *Brevard Childs*, 49-52 (regarding Brett); 139-143, 154-156 (regarding Frei, Lindbeck, and the "Yale School"); and 72-79, 140-154 (for various treatments of Steins and Childs).
[74] See, for example, Kevin Vanhoozer, *A Canonical-Linguistic Approach to Christian Theology* (Louisville: WJK, 2005).
[75] Brett, *Biblical Criticism in Crisis*, 6.
[76] See especially Brevard S. Childs, "Critique of Recent Intertextual Canonical Interpretation," *ZAW*, 115 (2003), 173-184.
[77] Childs, *Isaiah*, 4.
[78] Driver, *Brevard Childs*, 140.

canonical approach, but they must be used with care, so that the nature of the approach as a theological exegesis for the Church is in no way obscured.

2) What, then, of Brett's discussion of whether a canonical approach is best served by adopting a "monistic" or a "pluralistic" orientation? As Childs insists nearly a decade after Brett's analysis (although he is more directly addressing Steins, not Brett), "a canonical approach" ought not "simply be relegated to one option within a pluralistic menu."[79] Pluralism as Brett construes it goes too far if it intends to eliminate the normative status that the canonical text plays within the canonical approach itself. When it does so, Brett's proposal fails to do full justice to canonical exegesis epistemologically and theologically.

Considering Barr's treatment and Brett's treatment in tandem is instructive at this point. For all of their differences, Barr and Brett are agreed in presupposing the existence of only two diametrically opposed epistemologies, which Barr describes as "modern biblical criticism" on the one hand and "relativism" on the other, and Brett describes as "totalitarianism" or "monism" on the one hand and "pluralism" on the other.[80] The difference, of course, is that Barr sides with modern biblical criticism (which resembles the "totalitarianism" that Brett disparages), while Brett sides with pluralism (which resembles the "relativism" that Barr criticizes); presupposing such a dichotomy forces Brett to imply that a canonical approach cannot co-exist alongside other approaches and engage in fruitful dialogue with them without abandoning its core claim that the canon has an authoritative status for the faith community.

The canonical approach, as it is conceived in this work (and, I would argue, in the works of Provan, Seitz, Childs, and others) differs from both the modern/totalitarian view and the relativist/pluralist view. While affirming the belief that there is a meaning in the text and that the text is authoritative for faith within the community of believers, such a view acknowledges that these claims are faith claims, and not claims made solely on the basis of rationalistic argumentation.[81] On the one hand, such an understanding acknowledges the interpreter's situatedness. Yet, on the other hand, it avoids asserting that objective reality is not knowable. Furthermore, while canonical exegesis finds the idea "that there is only one fixed, 'objective' meaning to a given text which only needs to be critically excavated" to be problematic, this does not mean that it completely relativizes the text's meaning.[82]

---

[79] Childs goes on to say that the canon's "function as scripture is to point to the substance (*res*) of its witness, to the content of its message, namely to the ways of God in the world ("Critique," 176)."
[80] Barr argues that, in introducing a distinction between the meaning of the text for the people of the biblical era and the meaning of the text for the Church of today, a canonical approach is "in tune with the rather radical thinking associated with 'cultural relativism.'" Such a view, Barr says, brings about "a much more serious breach with traditional Christianity than anything that biblical criticism brought about" (*Holy Scripture* 64-65).
[81] See, for example, Kevin J. Vanhoozer, *Is There Meaning in This Text?* (Grand Rapids: Zondervan, 1998), especially pages 455-457.
[82] "The entire OT," Childs says, "is consistent in confessing that there is a divine address in Scripture," and "both synagogue and Church assigned a unique value to the text's plain

Thus, while Brett's insights may help to clarify canonical exegesis, if Brett's "pluralism" is applied in a sweeping fashion so that the interpreter may not acknowledge the authoritative status of the canonical text, then Brett's proposed modifications run against the claims of the canonical approach. For those who share the faith commitment that the canonical text plays an authoritative role for faith and practice and embrace the canonical approach, Brett has offered valuable insights. Yet they must be applied with caution.

2.4 The Continuation of the Canonical Approach

A significant number of other scholars attempt to carry forward the canon-exegetical enterprise in a way that is more in keeping with Childs's emphases.[83] While some simply move forward in applying the canonical approach either to exegesis or to constructive theology, others address the approach on the theoretical level. This book situates itself within this growing school and hopes to contribute to it. It will be helpful, then, to survey briefly a few representative works attending closely to theoretical questions.

2.4.1 Paul Noble. Noble sees Childs as falling short in terms of addressing directly the theoretical underpinnings of the canonical approach.[84] Even so, he attempts to rectify this putative shortcoming in a way that does justice to an understanding of Childs on his own terms without superimposing an alien framework upon the approach.[85] Noble proposes eight helpful methodological alterations to the approach of Childs, resulting in a treatment that is often balanced and insightful.[86] Noble advances the discussion in two helpful ways: 1) He highlights two methodological convictions which are necessary for a canon-exegetical approach yet stand in tension with one-another: the recognition

---

sense," implicitly maintaining "some form of authorial intent." Thus, "When Steins' theory of intertextuality eliminates the privileged status of the canonical context and removes all hermeneutical value from any form of authorial intent, an interpretive style emerges that runs directly contrary to the function of an authoritative canon which continues to serve a confessing community of faith and practice" ("Critique," 176-177).
[83] Noble, *The Canonical Approach,* Scalise, *Hermeneutics as Theological Prolegomena,* and O'Neal, *Interpreting Habakkuk as Scripture.*
[84] Noble astutely observes that, "[a]lthough, officially, 'canonical context' is the fundamental principle of [Childs's] approach, what often seems to be doing the real work (although from just below the surface) is a belief in the 'inspiration' . . . of the canonical text . . . In other words, granted a suitable doctrine of inspiration, the rest of Childs' programme flows naturally from it" (*The Canonical Approach*, 30-31). Whether or not one agrees with Noble's choice of the phrase "doctrine of inspiration" here, Noble is correct that Childs's theological presuppositions are "just below the surface," and in need of a full articulation if a canonical exegesis is to succeed.
[85] Noble, *The Canonical Approach.*
[86] Noble, *The Canonical Approach,* 368-370. Noble's response contrasts with Brett's post-modern response, yet does not represent a complete return to a modernistic epistemology.

of intentionality as an exegetical criterion and the allowance for textual multivalence.[87] 2) He provides a way to keep these two convictions in fruitful tension by suggesting the adoption of a formal, but not material, model of inspiration.[88]

2.4.2 Christopher Seitz. Seitz, a student of Childs's, has also carried forward the canonical approach in several works.[89] Seitz is less critical of Childs than Noble, arguing for greater consistency across Childs's works than Noble seems to recognize.[90] Yet our concern is not a proper reading of Childs, but a clear articulation of the canonical approach. In this regard, Seitz, with Noble, insists that the canonical approach must not, on the one hand "detach itself from a view of human or authorial intentionality" (*contra* critics who allege that it does just that).[91] On the other hand, a canonical approach is concerned to move beyond the level of the historical human author to find meaning, for example, "in the present structure and presentation of the Book of the Twelve."[92] And, with Noble, Seitz sees these two elements as being held together by a conviction that "[t]here is an inspired and coherent Word of God to Israel and to the world, that in turn uses the historical speech of Amos and Hosea, in the canonical form of the Twelve."[93] While Noble and Seitz may disagree about whether or not these themes were articulated robustly enough in the corpus of Childs, this question is beside the point for our purposes. It suffices to note here that this book is based upon an agreement with both Seitz and Noble that three concepts must be held together within the approach: a) a concept of intentionality; b) a concept of canonical multivalence; and c) a concept of inspiration.[94]

2.4.3 On inspiration: Chapman, Vanhoozer, and others. Another practitioner of the canonical approach, Stephen Chapman, also agrees with Noble and Seitz that a concept of inspiration is a necessary part of canonical exegesis.[95]

---

[87] Noble, *The Canonical Approach*, 368-370.
[88] Noble, *The Canonical Approach*, 340-350.
[89] Seitz, *Word Without End: The Old Testament as Abiding Theological Witness* (Grand Rapids: Eerdmans, 1998); *Figured Out*; "The Canonical Approach;" *The Goodly Fellowship of the Prophets: The Achievement of Association in Canon Formation* (ASBT; Grand Rapids, MI: Baker Academic, 2009).
[90] Seitz, "The Canonical Approach," 59.
[91] Seitz, "The Canonical Approach," 97.
[92] Seitz, "The Canonical Approach," 98.
[93] Ibid. See also idem, *The Goodly Fellowship*.
[94] Seitz's work is also helpful in dealing with the question of which canon forms the basis of the approach (Greek, Hebrew, or something else). Since the discussion of Augustine below necessarily brings this question to the foreground, I will return to address it there. See Seitz, "Canonical Approach," 92-93.
[95] Stephen Chapman, "Reclaiming Inspiration for the Bible," in *Canon and Biblical Intepretation*, 167-200. Chapman argues that a conception of inspiration is more evident already in Childs than Noble and others allow, even though he admits that it is only there implicitly and the term "inspiration" itself is avoided by Childs ("Reclaiming Inspiration,

Chapman attempts to provide a precise articulation of what a "canonical account of inspiration" ought to look like through dialogue with incarnational, Trinitarian, and evangelical models of inspiration, each of which he finds wanting.[96] Chapman's discussion on this point highlights the consensus and diversity that exists within those advancing the canonical approach. While Noble, Seitz, Chapman, and others agree upon the importance of a doctrine of inspiration, there is diversity concerning the way in which this is understood. Practitioners of the canonical approach may ask which model of inspiration is to be preferred: Noble's formal/material proposal,[97] Chapman's own "canonical account,"[98] the incarnational model,[99] one of the various evangelical views that Chapman surveys,[100] or something else.

On the one hand, this book aims to emphasize points of agreement among practitioners of the approach and proffer an exegesis that is of broad interest and benefit. It is possible to forge an exegesis that proceeds from the consensus assumption that "[t]here is an inspired and coherent Word of God . . . that in turn uses the historical speech"[101] of the biblical authors on multiple canonical levels. The primary focus of this work is not an extensive evaluation of the precise articulation of that belief in divine authorship, which is more contested.

On the other hand, it is fair to the reader that I provide some brief account of how I conceive of inspiration. Succinctly: I am sympathetic to the articulation given by Kevin Vanhoozer in his discussion of "The Canon as Spirited Practice." As Vanhoozer writes:

> The Scriptures are the Spirit's work from first to last. The Spirit is involved in Scripture in the very messy historical process of producing Scripture—prompting, appropriating, and coordinating human discourse to present God's Word—as well as in the process of bringing about understanding of Scripture among present-day readers. The traditional names for these modes of participation are *inspiration* and *illumination*, respectively.[102]

This traditional understanding of inspiration and illumination as rooted in the Spirit's work grounds canonical interpretation. "The doctrine of inspiration," writes Vanhoozer, "is what justifies the canonical practice of reading the Bible to hear the Word of God."[103] The dialogue between the canonical approach and the hermeneutic of *De doctrina Christiana* below should clarify the discussion further.

172-173). See also idem, *The Law and the Prophets: A Study in Old Testament Canon Formation* (Tübingen: Mohr Siebeck, 2000).
[96] Chapman, "Reclaiming Inspiration," 170-198.
[97] Noble, *The Canonical Approach*, 340-350.
[98] Chapman, "Reclaiming Inspiration," 199-200.
[99] Chapman, "Reclaiming Inspiration," 190-193.
[100] Chapman, "Reclaiming Inspiration," 174-189.
[101] Seitz, "The Canonical Approach," 98.
[102] Vanhoozer, *Drama*, 226.
[103] Ibid., 230.

2.4.4 Evangelical canonical exegesis. Chapman's discussion of inspiration highlights another important trend: "Canonical" language has been embraced and utilized by many theologians and biblical scholars who identify themselves as evangelicals, and Chapman engages with several of them. As early as 1980 Bruce Waltke interacted positively with Childs's program (with caveats), arguing for "a canonical process approach to the Psalms."[104] In his view, the "text's intention became deeper and clearer as the parameters of the canon were expanded."[105] He based this view upon the conviction that "God is the ultimate author of the progressively developing canon."[106] These convictions are evident in Waltke's recent *Old Testament Theology: An Exegetical, Canonical, and Thematic Approach.*[107]

John Sailhamer takes a similar approach, which Chapman evaluates somewhat favorably.[108] "In fact," notes Chapman, "scholars such as Robert Dick Wilson, E. J. Young, Merril F. Unger, Bruce Waltke, Ronald Youngblood, Herbert Wolf and Duane Garrett have all sought to" forge a canonical hermeneutic that allows "for some degree of inspired 'updating' of the biblical books."[109] Even more names could be added to this list of canonically oriented scholars who use the label "evangelical" to describe their position.[110] It is hoped that this book will present a canonical exegesis that will be informative to such scholars interested in contributing to the canonical school.

2.4.5 Daniel Driver. I conclude this survey of the canon-exegetical school with the most recent and arguably most significant work on Childs to date: a modified dissertation by Daniel Driver, originally written under Richard Bauckham at Saint Andrew's University while Seitz was on faculty there.[111] Driver situates Childs in his context, and the book provides a thorough accounting of both a) Childs's development across time and b) the secondary literature on Childs. The work is comprehensive, careful, and nuanced. Driver

---

[104] Bruce K. Waltke, "A Canonical Process Approach to the Psalms," *Traditions and Testament: Essays in Honor of Charles Lee Feinberg* (Chicago: Moody, 1981), 3-18.
[105] Waltke, "Canonical," 7.
[106] Waltke, "Canonical," 10.
[107] Waltke with Charles Yu, *An Old Testament Theology: An Exegetical, Canonical, and Thematic Approach* (Grand Rapids, MI: Zondervan Academic, 2007). To cite but one example, Waltke argues that the book of Deuteronomy reached its final form during the exile and he considers how such a view has theological implications for the book of Deuteronomy, the Torah, the "Primary History," and the Tanakh as a whole (Waltke, *Old Testament Theology*, 57, 502-503).
[108] Sailhamer, *Introduction*, especially 86-113, 253-311; Chapman, "Reclaiming Inspiration," 182.
[109] Chapman, "Reclaiming Inspiration," 181. The full quote reads: " . . . and Duane Garrett have all sought to resolve the difficulties of an exclusively author-centered hermeneutic by allowing for some degree of inspired 'updating' of the biblical books."
[110] House, *Old Testament Theology;* idem, *The Unity of the Twelve* (BLS 27; Sheffield, UK: Sheffield Academic, 1990); Vanhoozer, *Drama of Doctrine.*
[111] Driver, *Brevard Childs.*

offers a sustained and persuasive argument that Childs's oeuvre does indeed have "a logic of its own."[112] With the exception of one shift in Childs's thinking,[113] Driver, with Seitz, sees Childs's post-1970 work as being marked by consistency, coherence, and growth, *contra* Barr and others.[114] Driver has done much to counterbalance what he calls the "caricature" of Childs advanced by Barr and others that has gained a wide hearing.[115]

Furthermore, Driver offers an *apologia* for Childs's allegedly inconsistent definition of the term "canon."[116] "Childs," writes Driver, "actively exploits the polyvalence of the word canon, which for him is an expansive cipher."[117] For Childs,[118] there is no clear distinction between Scripture and Canon, so that "[t]he Christian church was never without a canon."[119] According to Driver, Childs is able to make this move from canonical process to final form, all under the same cipher by using the term "canon" in a way that encompasses rather than fragments the development of the term in the early church. "[T]he second century sense of canon as a rule of truth or faith dominates in Childs' thought," writes Driver, "but this contains rather than rivals fourth century and other subsequent senses of canon [as a closed body of authoritative literature]."[120] While determining the correct understanding of Childs's oeuvre is a peripheral concern for the present work, understanding the interrelationship between canonical process and final form is central. As this question requires special attention, I will take it up again later in the chapter.

Another salient element of Driver's treatment is his emphasis upon the way in which Childs construes the (especially intertextual) nature of the approach by

---

[112] Driver, *Brevard Childs*, 59.

[113] Driver discusses two shifts in Childs's thinking: 1) The first comes after Childs's very early works (his Basel dissertation, *Myth and Reality,* etc.) and prior to Child's seminal writing on the canonical approach (Childs, "Interpretation in Faith," "Psalm 8," *Biblical Theology in Crisis*, etc.). This is the shift "from form to final form," and this shift gives rise to the canonical approach (Driver, *Brevard Childs*, 30). 2) The second shift comes later. According to Driver, while Childs at first saw midrash as a promising way to understand biblical intertextuality, he later moved away from midrash toward a deictic approach (*Brevard Childs*, chapters four and five).

[114] In his conclusion, Driver writes that, *contra* Childs's critics, "[t]he contours of Childs work are better described as a long process marked by struggle, discipline, and care. Through each adjustment persists a remarkable consistency" (*Brevard Childs*, 286). See also Seitz, "Canonical Approach," 59.

[115] Driver, *Brevard Childs,* 43.

[116] Driver, *Brevard Childs,* 21-29, 229-252, *passim*.

[117] Driver, *Brevard Childs*, 27.

[118] And, Childs would say, for most of German scholarship (Childs, "The Canon in Recent Biblical Studies," 43-48).

[119] Brevard S. Childs, *The Church's Guide for Reading Paul: The Canonical Shaping of the Pauline Corpus* (Grand Rapids, MI: Eerdman's, 2008), 61; see also Driver, *Brevard Childs*, 28. Contra Barr, the Canon is an authoritative rule for the believing community even before its closure.

[120] Driver, *Brevard Childs*, 28.

emphasizing "the centering function of the *res*" in the canonical approach.[121] On this point, Driver's discussion of Childs's works has yielded two salient insights that can be of service in articulating a canon-exegetical approach: 1) He highlights the significant role that concepts drawn from the early Church play in Childs's canonical approach and the intertextual element within it; "Canon, *res*, scope," he writes, "all such language issues from a reading of the Fathers."[122] In particular, Driver carries forward an interesting comparison of Augustine and Childs on Psalm 102.[123] 2) Among these concepts deriving "from . . . the Fathers," the understanding that Scripture is to be read as pointing to a divine reality (the centering *res*; Driver calls this view deictic, rather than midrashic), may prove especially helpful in dealing with several of the thornier issues practitioners of the canon-exegetical approach must address. These considerations gesture towards a fruitful path that this introductory chapter will take as I strive to articulate concisely the theological frame that grounds the exegetical study that follows: I will turn to the hermeneutic articulated by Augustine in *De doctrina Christiana* and bring it into dialogue with the canonical approach.

2.4.6 An emerging consensus and open questions. One could multiply this survey to consider other scholars who have responded positively to the canonical approach, agreeing with the vision and main emphases put forth by Brevard Childs. R. W. L. Moberly has developed his own canonically oriented theological take on exegesis across several works.[124] For example, in *The Bible, Theology, and Faith,* Moberly interprets Genesis 22 from a Christian perspective in its canonical context (including the New Testament).[125] Among others "sympathetic to Childs' articulation of his approach," Driver lists "Sheppard . . . Ellen Davis, Robert Wall and Kavin Rowe . . . Nathan MacDonald, [and] Neil MacDonald."[126] Again, even more names could be added than these.[127] Thus, the canonical approach in the spirit of Brevard Childs is alive and well.

Yet difficult questions remain that any contribution to the canonical approach must address if it is to be implemented successfully, and the complexity of the task demands that responses to these questions be framed with care.

---

[121] Driver, *Brevard Childs*, 101.
[122] Driver, *Brevard Childs*, 285. See also Ibid., 250-252.
[123] Driver, *Brevard Childs*, 265-278.
[124] R. W. L. Moberly, *From Eden to Golgotha: Essays in Biblical Theology* (SFSiHJ 52; Atlanta: Scholars, 1992); *The Theology of the Book of Genesis* (OTT; New York: Cambridge University Press, 2009); *The Bible, Theology, and Faith: A Study of Abraham and Jesus* (Cambridge: Cambridge University Press, 2000.
[125] Moberly, *Bible*.
[126] Driver, *Brevard Childs*, 59; I have omitted here names from the list that appear in the discussion above.
[127] Jochen Teuffel, "Fate and Word: The Book of Esther as Guidance to the Canonical Reading of Scripture," *CTM* 36 (2009): 26-31; Jon M. Isaak, "Hearing God's Word in the Silence: A Canonical Approach to 1 Corinthians 14.34-35," *Direction* 24 (1995): 55-64; and, with qualifications, Rolf Rendtorff, *The Canonical Hebrew Bible: A Theology of the Old Testament* (Leiden: Deo, 2005).

First of all, while Childs, Seitz, and Driver have done much to show the value of an extended, dynamic definition of canon, I must nevertheless express my own understanding of the nature of the relationship between diachronic and synchronic interpretations of a canonical text carefully. How, then, will this work attempt to articulate the interpretive relationship between the pre-canonical forms of the text and the final form? Similarly, how is one to navigate the relationship between the Old and New Testaments in a canonical program?[128] A related question pertains to the role of the authority of the Church. The canon (not the Church) sets the normative context for exegesis, yet the canon is the collection of texts that the Church has received. Where does this put the authority of Church teaching and tradition?[129] And what role ought the history of exegesis to play in a canonical approach?[130]

In sum, on the one hand there is a broad outline of consensus among practitioners of canonical exegesis about the nature and framework for the approach, and this study of Psalm 8 situates itself within this framework. On the other hand, a carefully deployed canonical exegesis must attend to several intricate questions with care. In what follows, I will show how I intend to address some of these questions by bringing the canonical approach into dialogue with the hermeneutical theory of *De doctrina Christiana*. The aim will not be to settle every issue exhaustively and definitively. Rather, the goal is to set in place the

---

[128] Noble singles out Childs's inability to articulate clearly the relationship between the testaments as especially problematic. Noble argues that, despite Childs's claim to read both testaments as bearing witness to Christ, Childs's *Old Testament Theology* is almost devoid of references to Christ, and his *Biblical Theology* is unconvincing in its Christological reading of the Old Testament, (*The Canonical Approach* 65-76). In contrast to Noble's assessment, Walter Brueggemann says that "the Old Testament is enveloped in New Testament claims and nearly disappears" in the second part of Childs's *Biblical Theology of the Old and New Testaments* (*Theology of the Old Testament: Testimony, Dispute, Advocacy* [Minneapolis: Fortress, 1997], 731). The conflicting assessments of Noble and Brueggemann highlight the confusion that scholars express in understanding how, exactly, Childs expects to hear the distinctive voice of each testament and at the same time understand both testaments as speaking of Christ.

[129] For example, Barr alleges (erroneously) that the canonical approach to exegesis entails "in effect a sharing of authority between scripture and the patristic period" (*Holy Scripture*, 66). Ongoing work on the canon-exegetical approach must both address this claim at the theoretical level and also work out the proper role for Church teaching and tradition in exegetical practice.

[130] Brett, *Biblical Criticism in Crisis?* 57. The omission in his *Isaiah* commentary of a section on the history of exegesis (which he included in his *Exodus* commentary) may reflect a shift in Childs' thinking. Nevertheless, Childs has not explicitly stated why he omitted the history of exegesis section in *Isaiah*, leaving readers to guess as to how, if at all, the history of interpretation is to function in a canonical exegesis. The fact that Childs published *The Struggle to Understand Isaiah as Christian Scripture* (Grand Rapids: Eerdmans, 2004), which selectively treats the history of interpretation of Isaiah, a few years after the publication of his *Isaiah* commentary should guard anyone against assuming that Childs's later works abandon any interest in the history of interpretation.

framework for the study that follows, where I will attempt to advance the approach "in the context of concrete . . . exegetical work."[131]

3. The Canonical Approach in Dialogue with *De Doctrina Christiana*

One reasonable way to advance the canon-exegetical program is to look for someone who has clearly articulated a theological foundation for exegesis and, through careful interaction with their work, address the questions facing canonical exegesis. Many theological works, including some recent literature, address the theological basis for exegesis in a way that resonates with the canonical approach.[132] Therefore, canonical practitioners would be wise to interact with a broad array of works dealing with theological hermeneutics. Nevertheless, in order to achieve lucid brevity, I will select one primary interlocutor representing a thoroughgoing theology of exegesis—Augustine's *De doctrina Christiana*—to bring into dialogue with the canonical approach.

The concise treatise *De doctrina Christiana* is especially well suited to aid in bringing clarity for several reasons. First of all, Augustine has been influential throughout Western Christendom, and his hermeneutical thought is no exception. Thus, choosing Augustine as an interlocutor has the benefit of 1) broadening the discussion beyond the parochial limitations of Reformed Protestant thought to include other Christians in the discussion while 2) honestly highlighting the Protestant distinctives that underlie the canonical approach. Among Augustine's variegated works,[133] *De doctrina Christiana* commends itself as the source for Augustinian hermeneutical theory and method best suited for the present purposes in that it concisely articulates a Scriptural hermeneutic[134] that reflects both the early stages and the mature development of Augustine's exegetical theory,[135] and it has had "an extraordinarily fruitful history of influence, which has continued for many centuries."[136]

---

[131] Noble, *The Canonical Approach*, 370.

[132] In addition to Scalise (*From Scripture to Theology*), who applies the canonical approach to constructive theology, Kevin Vanhoozer also approaches theology in a canonical fashion that resonates partly with the canon-exegetical approach outlined in this chapter in *The Drama of Doctrine*.

[133] As Van Fleteren puts it, "Augustine's hermeneutic is difficult to study," and "while most of [his] scriptural themes are constant, they evolve over the years;" the difficulty is exacerbated by the fact that "Augustine's axioms of biblical interpretation are scattered throughout his works." ("Principles of Augustine's Hermeneutic: An Overview," in *Augustine: Biblical Exegete* [New York: Augustinian Historical Institute at Villanova University, 2001], 2).

[134] See James J. O'Donnel, "*Doctrina Christiana, De*," in *Augustine Through the Ages: An Encyclopedia* (Grand Rapids: Eerdmans, 1999), 278.

[135] While Augustine began *De doctrina Christiana* early in his bishopric, he completed it later in his ministry, endorsing the earlier sections without altering them. "The circumstances of composition are imperfectly known, but are clearly tied up with Augustine's understanding of his own position as a bishop at the outset of his Episcopal career (roughly 395/6). What we know comes from the note in the *Retractiones* (2.4) which

Furthermore, *De doctrina Christiana* addresses questions especially germane to a canon-exegetical approach to Scripture, and it does so from a theological orientation compatible with that of the canonical approach. Augustine addresses both the hermeneutical role that the tradents who pass on the Scriptures play, and the hermeneutical role that the Scriptures themselves play, and he addresses these roles within the context of a theological framework. Also, as I have shown above, canonical exegesis does not fit easily into either a modern/totalizing or a pluralist/relativist epistemic framework; similarly, *De doctrina Christiana* articulates a hermeneutic of *fides quaerens intellectum* which, on the one hand, recognizes the situatedness of the reader while, on the other hand, is not epistemically nihilistic. This is of special interest in light of the appropriation of Augustine by literary theorists;[137] *De doctrina Christiana* may provide a means of incorporating some insights of literary theory into canonical exegesis without adopting the pluralist epistemic framework that Brett insists upon.[138]

In light of these considerations, the following section will survey Augustine's hermeneutic, giving special attention to the theological framework, the role of the rule of faith, and the role of the self-interpretation of Scripture (the "analogy of Scripture").[139] Next, I will clarify some of the theological questions lying at the foundation of the canonical approach by bringing Augustine's hermeneutic into conversation with the canonical approach. The reader must bear in mind, however, that what follows does not purport to be a wholesale acceptance of either Childs or Augustine. Rather, I will argue for a canon-

---

places the work at the outset of his bishopric but tells us that he left it incomplete and finished it at about the time he wrote the *Retractiones*" (O'Donnel, "*Doctrina Christiana, De*," 278).

[136] Christof Schäublin, "*De doctrina christiana: A Classic of Western Culture?*" in *De doctrina Christiana: A Classic of Western Culture* (ed. Duane W. H. Arnold and Pamela Bright; Notre Dame, IN: University of Notre Dame Press, 1995), 48. For a collection of essays on the influence of *De doctrina* in the middle ages, see *Reading and Wisdom: The De doctrina Christiana of Augustine in the Middle Ages* (ed. Edward D. English; Notre Dame, IN: University of Notre Dame Press, 1995). See also Duane W. H. Arnold, "To Adjust Rather than to Reconcile: *De doctrina Christiana* and the Oxford Movement," in *De doctrina Christiana: A Classic of Western Culture*, 207-216.

[137] Cyril O'Regan, "*De doctrina Christiana* and Modern Hermeneutics" in *De doctrina Christiana: A Classic of Western Culture*, 217-243; Phillip J. Donnelly, *Rhetorical Faith: The Literary Hermeneutics of Stanley Fish* (ELMS 84; Victoria: English Literary Studies, 2000).

[138] See Frances M. Young, "Augustine's Hermeneutic and Postmodern Criticism," in *Interpretation* 58 (2004) 42-55.

[139] I am well aware that this term "analogy of Scripture" is an anachronistic way to describe Augustine's thought. Following Prosper Grech, who uses the phrase to put Augustine's thought "into modern terms," I will use the phrase "analogy of Scripture" as short hand for the instrumental use of Scripture in the process of the interpretation of Scripture ("Hermeneutical Principles of Saint Augustine in *Teaching Christianity*," in *Teaching Christianity: De Doctrina Christiana. The Works of Saint Augustine: A Translation for the 21'st Century, Part I, vol. 11*. [Hyde Park, NY: New City, 1996], 86).

exegetical approach which builds extensively upon these two thinkers, but I may part company with Childs and Augustine at points.

3.1 The Hermeneutic of De doctrina Christiana

In Book I of *De doctrina*, Augustine establishes the goal of interpretation as the identification of the things to which signs, such as words, refer. Augustine then undertakes a discussion of the "things" to which the signs of Scripture point, wherein he summarizes "the content of Christian doctrine,"[140] which includes the believer's participation in the truths of that doctrine.[141] Augustine goes on to assert that the apprehension of the "thing" (reality) that lies behind the signs of Scripture produces "love."[142] Thus, a proper understanding of the Scriptures will bring about love—love of God and of neighbor—as a result. This is not to say that every passage simply means "love God and love your neighbor." "Love" for Augustine is "the motion of the soul toward the enjoyment of God for his own sake, and the enjoyment of one's self and one's neighbor for the sake of God."[143] Thus, the reader's ultimate goal is not a mere cognitive apprehension of data, but a transformation by and participation in faith, resulting in a life of self-giving love.[144]

Augustine later describes how, when the tools available through common human knowledge are insufficient for the interpretation of Scripture, the interpreter of Scripture is to proceed.[145] When a passage's interpretation is uncertain, Augustine says, the reader "should refer it to the rule of faith, which you have received from the plainer passages of scripture and from the authority of the Church."[146] Thus, the relationship between the rule of faith, Scripture,

---

[140] O'Donnell, "*Doctrina Christiana, De*," 279.

[141] Lewis Ayres points out that Book I is not simply a static description of abstract doctrine, but also a statement of the Christian's participation in the Truth of that doctrine. "If Book I of *De doctrina* sets out the rule of faith," he writes," then the journey of the affections that constitutes Christian life in Christ is itself at the heart of the rule ("Augustine on the Rule of Faith," 38).

[142] "So what all that has been said amounts to, while we have been dealing with things, is that 'the fulfillment and the end of the law' and all the divine scriptures 'is love' (Rom 13:8; I Tm 1:5); love of the thing which is to be enjoyed, and the thing which is able to enjoy that thing together with us" (*Doc Chris.*, Book I).

[143] Donnelly, *Rhetorical Faith*.

[144] See, for example, Tarmo Toom, who argues that Augustine's hermeneutic is Christological (*Thought Clothed With Sound: Augustine's Christological Hermeneutics in De Doctrina Christiana* [New York: Peter Lang, 2002]).

[145] *Doc Chris.*, Book III.

[146] *Doc Chris.*, Book III: 2. Book I addresses the "things" to which Scripture bears witness. Special care is necessary at this point to understand what Augustine means by "the rule of faith." The reader might be tempted to assume that the early church shared one uniform conception of the definition of the term "rule of faith," and fail to understand Augustine on his own terms. As Lewis Ayres demonstrates, however, it would be a mistake to identify Augustine's use of the phrase "the rule of faith" with earlier writers

and the teaching of the Church is mutually reciprocal, and Augustine's hermeneutic is a mutually interpretive circle. The goal of scriptural exegesis is to move from the sign to the "thing," or reality, which is the faith in which the believer participates for the sake of love. When, due to difficulties in the exegetical task, the believer is unsure what, exactly, is the "thing" to which a given "sign" refers, she is to consult the rule of faith, which is itself a summation of the Scriptures' *res*.

Thus, some have seen Augustine's hermeneutic as "une interprétation finaliste"[147] that exhibits a circularity such that "Augustine knows what scripture will say before he begins to read it."[148] Yet, in the first place, God, not Augustine, is the author of the hermeneutical process at every point, and the interpreter seeks out and anticipates the transformation of the self.[149] One might respond that Augustine has, in fact constructed the divine author within his own hermeneutical thought in a way that ultimately results in self-fulfilling circularity. Such an account of Augustine is problematic on two levels: 1) It rejects any hermeneutic wherein God is involved in the process, taking a stance that eliminates the possibility of any approach to the text that seeks to encounter the divine. 2) It misconstrues the aim of Augustine's hermeneutic. As Donnelly notes, one must be careful to avoid "imposing upon [Augustine's] terms the rationalist categories of a mastering subject and a sub-personal object."[150] The goal of Augustine's hermeneutic is an encounter with the divine resulting in a life of love, not the mere apprehension of data.

To summarize, then, while God stands outside of the hermeneutical circle, the human interpreter stands within the circle, and the process of interpretation is not a mere cognitive act, but a participation in the ascent of the soul to God.[151]

---

such as Origen, or even contemporaries such as Ambrose. One must look to Augustine himself to understand what Augustine means by "the rule of faith."

[147] Tzvetan Todorov, *Symbolisme et Interprétation* (Paris: Seuil, 1978), 91-124. According to Todorov, patristic exegesis, exemplified in *De doctrina Christiana*, was merely a means of artificially manipulating the text so that the sense of the text could be forced into an identification with the teaching of the Church. For a brief survey of Todorov's approach that insightfully highlights the problems inherent in Todorov's view, see Isabelle Bochet, "Le cercle herméneutique dans le *De doctrina christiana* d'Augustin," *Studia Patristica* 33 (1997), 16-18.

[148] O'Donnel, 281.

[149] Augustine is clear that God alone stands outside the circle as the author of the hermeneutical circle, of the interpretive process, and of the text itself (*De doctrina Christiana*, Book II: 6, Book III: 27). God alone is the author of the task, the "thing" (*res*) which alone is to be enjoyed, the content of the Christian faith, and the "thing" to which the "signs" in Scripture refer (Book I: 22).

[150] Donnelly, *Rhetorical Faith*, 96.

[151] Lewis Ayres's treatment of Augustine's use of the rule of faith in light of his structure of Book I is instructive at this point: Book I contains two sections: pars. 5-19, and pars. 22-40. The first section, which addresses the "thing," has a creedal structure, and addresses specifically "the journey that must be made to see that which is to be enjoyed." That journey is made possible through Christ's descent in the incarnation and his ascent which "forms hope: the Church his body is trained for life with Him." The second

The "rule of faith," then, is not merely a static set of data. It is the believer's participation in redemption through Christ, an ascent of the soul wherein she moves towards the enjoyment of "the Thing" which alone is to be enjoyed above all else: the triune God. This distinctive aim of interpretation results in a hermeneutical circle that is neither vicious nor solipsistic. Having thus adumbrated the hermeneutic of *De doctrina Christiana*, we may now attend to bringing Augustine's hermeneutic to bear upon a canon-exegetical approach.

3.2 De Doctrina Christiana *and Canonical Exegesis*

How, then, is *De doctrina Christiana* relevant for ongoing attempts to forge a successful canon-exegetical program? In the first place, the focus of the first three books is the articulation of a theoretical and theological basis for exegesis.[152] As a result, *De doctrina Christiana* provides a point from which to address the allegation of critics such as Barr that, despite a superficial "sense of religious satisfaction," the canonical approach is methodologically and theologically flimsy.[153] Significantly, *De doctrina Christiana* provides a valuable starting point for articulating how one might evade attempts to force the canonical approach into one side or the other of the totalizing/relativizing binary. *De doctrina Christiana* does so by 1) acknowledging the situatedness of the interpreter without relativizing all knowledge, 2) conceiving of the ultimate goal of exegesis as an encounter with the divine, not the cognitive apprehension of data or mastery of the world, while 3) seeing the acquisition of knowledge from the text as an important part of the exegetical process.

Barr might respond that, like the canonical approach, *De doctrina*'s hermeneutic is actually "in tune with . . . 'cultural relativism'"[154] since the interpreter knows "what scripture will say before he begins to read it."[155] Yet it bears repeating that one must be careful to avoid "imposing upon [Augustine's] terms the rationalist categories of a mastering subject and a sub-personal

---

section, which addresses the "use" of things (and of "The Thing," the triune God) culminates by returning to Christ as "both way and goal through the divine condescension." From this, Ayres concludes that "if Book I of *De doctrina* sets out the rule of faith, then the journey of the affections that constitutes Christian life in Christ is itself at the heart of the rule." Ayres, 37-38. See also, *doc Chr.* Book I: 8, and 34.

[152] As Christoph Schäublin points out, *De doctrina Christiana* is neither an exegetical handbook nor a treatise on the Christian usage of the liberal arts; too many questions of exegetical practice are left unanswered and the liberal arts are not in the foreground. Schäublin, Rather, Books I-III of *De doctrina Christiana* are concerned with articulating a theological framework for scriptural hermeneutics. "[W]e might say," writes Schäublin, "that Augustine . . . on a theoretical level, embraces in *De doctrina christiana* the question of how such a science [of *praecepta* of biblical interpretation] should ideally be presented and carried out" ("*De doctrina christiana*" 53-55).

[153] Barr, *Holy Scripture,* 104.

[154] Barr, *Holy Scripture,* 65.

[155] O'Donnel, "*Doctrina Christiana, De,*" 281.

object."[156] For Augustine, the interpreter is not merely looking for knowledge, but is looking for a transformative encounter with the divine.[157] Thus, the interpreter does not know in advance what that encounter will entail. Furthermore, Augustine's interpreter is not free to find any meaning she wishes; rather, she is constrained both by the mutually interpretive elements of Augustine's hermeneutical circle and by the divine author. Insofar as Augustine's hermeneutic is predicated upon the belief in a divine author who is the ground of all "mind-independent reality,"[158] it cannot be said to be "in tune with" Barr's description of "cultural relativism."[159]

Escaping the totalizing/relativizing binary in this way provides a framework which can deal with some of the tensions inherent in the implementation of the canonical approach. The theology of *De doctrina Christiana* enables Augustine to hold in balance, on the one hand, a) an understanding of the text as having an intentionality that supplies the normative context within which legitimate interpretation must operate and, on the other hand, b) an understanding of the text as having a multivalence. According to Augustine,

> When from the same words of scripture not just one, but two or more meanings may be extracted, even if you cannot tell which of them the writer intended, there is no risk if they can all be shown from other places of the holy scriptures to correspond with the truth . . . [C]ertainly the Spirit of God who produced these texts through him foresaw without a shadow of doubt that [a meaning not intended by the human author] would occur to some reader or listener; or rather he actually provided that it should occur to them, because it is upheld by the truth [that is, it does not violate the rest of Scripture or Church teaching].[160]

Thus, by identifying God as both the author and the object of the hermeneutical task, Augustine is able to maintain a fruitful tension between intentionality and multivalence. Maintaining this tension is especially important for a canon-exegetical approach which seeks to relate a text's historical function with its canonical function and to relate both to the life of the contemporary believer.

---

[156] Donnelly, *Rhetorical Faith*, 96.

[157] Augustine's view, then, is markedly different from that of Barr. Barr claims that "theology begins when we pass by the sense of religious satisfaction and begin to pose the question of truth" (*Holy Scripture*, 104), implying that "truth" is reducible to abstract propositional facts. For Augustine, by contrast, the *res* which is the object of exegesis (and theology) is the personal, trinitarian God (c.f. Donnelly, *Rhetorical Faith*, 73).

[158] In contrast, Donnelly, describing Stanley Fish's attempt to embrace anti-formalism over and against formalism, argues that Fish "never admits even the consideration of mind-independent reality" (Donnelly, *Rhetorical Faith*, 73). Fish, no doubt, would see Barr as a "proud formalist." Augustine's approach differs, then, from both Fish and Barr. As Kevin Vanhoozer points out, while the belief in reality beyond the text (or even beyond the interpreter) is an act of faith, so, also, is the belief that there is no such reality (*Is There A Meaning in This Text*, 455-457).

[159] Barr, *Holy Scripture*, 65.

[160] *Doc Chr.*, Book III: 27.

Furthermore, bringing Augustine's hermeneutic into dialogue with the canonical approach provides a context for addressing adequately some of the more difficult issues involved in the implementation of canonical exegesis. Four such issues demand special attention: 1) the question of the interpretive relationship between the final form of the text and the shape of the broader canon within which the final form of the text appears; 2) the question of the interpretive relationship between the final form of the text and hypothetical pre-canonical forms of the text; 3) the question of determining appropriate boundaries for legitimate interpretation; and 4) the question of which Old Testament canon ought to serve as the basis for canonical interpretation—the Septuagint, the Masoretic Text, or something else. I will take each issue in turn.

1) Augustine's hermeneutic provides a starting point for understanding the relationship between the hermeneutical roles of the final canonical form of the text and the location of a given text within the broader canonical context by maintaining the tension between the intention of the divine author and the multivalence of the text. The Scriptures and the tradents of the Scriptures, for Augustine, both have an interpretive function. Thus, if it can be shown that the ordering of various books within the canon reflects the way in which the later collectors of those books have understood them to relate to one another, the situation of a text within the ordering of the broader canon is hermeneutically informative.[161] So, in the case of Psalm 8, a canonical exegesis ought to attend to signs of intentional placement in connection with the location of the psalm in the Psalter, and the location of the Psalter within the Ketuvim, Tanakh, and Christian Bible.

The question remains, however, as to how the interpreter ought to negotiate the interplay between Scripture and tradition. Bringing *De doctrina* into dialogue with canonical exegesis provides an opportunity to delineate more precisely the mutually interpretive relationship between the two. On the one hand, the canonical approach acknowledges a canonical authoritative status only for the final form of the Christian Scriptures. On the other hand, Augustine's hermeneutic places church teaching, the rule (*kanon*) of faith, and the canon of Scripture all within the interpretive circle; one might therefore conclude that all of the elements of Augustine's hermeneutical circle are equally authoritative.[162] To proceed clearly and consistently, a canonical approach must begin by affirming that, while a canonical exegesis gives a significant interpretive role to church teaching and the tradition (especially in the case of the reception and shaping of the canon), it gives pride of place to the role of the Scriptures themselves. Richard Hays' description of the relationship between the Scrip-

---

[161] I do not here mean to imply that this mutually interpretive relationship led Augustine to draw any conclusions concerning the ordering of canonical texts.

[162] So, for example, concerning the question of what constitutes "the canon of the scriptures," Augustine says that "for the canonical scriptures, they should follow the authority of the majority of the Catholic Churches, among which, of course, are those that have the privilege of being apostolic sees and having received letters from the apostles," *Doc Chr.*, Book II, 12.

tures and tradition aptly summarizes the view presupposed by the canon-exegetical approach of this book:

> The classic formula remains serviceable: Scripture is *norma normans* ("the norming norm"), while tradition is *norma normata* ("the normed norm"). Still, tradition gives us a place to start in our interpretation . . . Only where there is an appropriate concern for the witness of tradition in the church will we find it possible to sustain what Hauerwas calls a "conversation with one another and God . . . across generations."[163]

Canonical exegesis, then, takes seriously the hermeneutical tradition's role, but distinguishes that role from the authority of the Scriptures themselves. In this way, it is possible to use the hermeneutical circle derived from *De doctrina Christiana* as a heuristic summary of the theological hermeneutic underlying the canonical approach, with the qualification that the other elements of the circle are derivative, and that the canonical form of the text is the basis for exegesis.

Naturally, difficult questions will arise as one addresses material that lies on the border, as it were, between tradition and Scripture, where it is unclear whether something belongs to the *norma normans* of Scripture or the *norma normata* of tradition. For example, one might ask of Psalm 8 whether the superscript is part of Scripture or tradition, whether the location of Psalm 8 in the Psalter is part of Scripture or tradition, whether the Psalter's location within the Ketuvim is part of Scripture or tradition, etc. This book will give a full treatment of such situations throughout the course of the study, recognizing that a canon-exegetical approach can adequately deal with these "border-line" scenarios only if one is clear about the normative hermeneutical role that the canonical Scriptures play as the *norma normans*.

2) What, then, of the relationship between the canonical form of the text and hypothetical pre-canonical forms of the text? What ought a canon-exegetical approach to do with pre-canonical forms of a text, such as M. Smith's proposed textual emendation of Psalm 8 that results in a poem that speaks of violent children of the deity El devouring and threatening creation?[164] The canonical form of Psalm 8 speaks instead of pacific babies and sucklings that stand against the foes of YHWH; should Smith's reading establish the parameters for legitimate interpretation of a text within a canonical approach? Given the theology of exegesis articulated thus far, neither the pre-canonical form nor a hypothetical process transforming the pre-canonical form into the final form ought to have the same interpretive importance as either the canonical final form

---

[163] Richard B. Hays, *The Moral Vision of the New Testamet: Community, Cross, New Creation: A Contemporary Introduction to New Testament Ethics* (San Francisco: Harper, 1996) 210. Hays quotes the words "conversation with one another and God . . . across generations" from Stanley Hauerwas, *A Community of Character: Toward a Constructive Christian Social Ethic* (Notre Dame, IN: University of Notre Dame Press, 1981), 64.

[164] Mark S. Smith, "Psalm 8 2b-3: New Proposals for an Old Problem" *CBQ* 59 (1997): 637-641.

or later Church tradition.¹⁶⁵ Thus, as Childs says in his *Exodus* commentary, "the study of the prehistory [of the text] has its proper function within exegesis only in illuminating the final text."¹⁶⁶

3) Turning to the question of establishing reasonable parameters for legitimate exegesis, one might object that the hermeneutic briefly adumbrated here is problematic in that, while it insists that there are parameters within which normative interpretation must take place, it does not articulate with sufficient clarity what the parameters should be. If a text can have multiple meanings, as long as "they can all be shown from other places of the holy scriptures to correspond with the truth," ¹⁶⁷ it follows logically that "other places of the holy scriptures" can also have multiple meanings. How, then, is one to judge the legitimacy of an interpretation of a passage?

In addressing this question, one must bear in mind that Augustine first instructs his reader to "make every effort to arrive at the intention of the author through whom the Holy Spirit produced that portion of scripture."¹⁶⁸ Only after attempting to discover the inspired author's intention does Augustine give his reader interpretive freedom.¹⁶⁹ As Mazzeo notes, "[t]he first and most important thing to say about St. Augustine's conception of allegory and his techniques of biblical exegesis is that he considered them, in the last analysis, relatively unimportant. All of the teaching on faith and morals necessary to salvation is quite plain in Scripture."¹⁷⁰ Childs argues that, in setting "apart apostolic witness (text) from later church tradition," the Church "assigned a unique role to the text's plain or literal sense. Implicit thereby was the concern to maintain some form of authorial intent."¹⁷¹ So Childs and Augustine are unanimous: the first interpretive task for exegesis is to determine the plain sense of the passage, and then from there to determine the legitimacy of any other sense.

Yet, talk of the intention of the human author and the "plain" or "literal" sense of the text introduces a whole host of questions. In the first place, a canonical exegesis presupposes a multivalence of meaning that transcends any single human author. Furthermore, the question of defining and discovering the text's "plain" or "literal" sense is contentious. Moreover, an understanding of "the plain sense" that gives pride of place to the intention of a human author as

---

[165] Childs, I would argue, does not clarify his views on this point and, as a result, conflates those who preserve, pass on, and interpret the final form of the text with the final form of the text itself. This confusion leads Childs to conflate Scripture with tradition in a confusing and ambiguous way, saying that "the text is the tradent of authority" (Brevard S. Childs, "Retrospective Reading of the Old Testament Prophets," *ZAW* 108 [1996], 375).

[166] Childs, *Exodus*, xiv. Again, when Childs deviated from this commitment to the final form of the text, he undermined his own attempts to forge a set of working canon-exegetical principles.

[167] *Doc Chr.*, Book III: 27.

[168] *Doc Chr.*, Book III: 27

[169] Augustine, *Doc Chris.*, Book III: 27.

[170] Cited in Donnelly, *Rhetorical Faith*.

[171] Childs, "Critique of Recent Intertextual Canonical Interpretation," 177.

understood by Barr's "modern biblical research," which seeks to reconstruct a putative historical reality behind the text, is inconsistent with the claim that the normative interpretation lies in the final form of the text.

Childs, building upon Hans Frei's *The Eclipse of Biblical Narrative*,[172] has addressed the question of the "literal sense" of the text in a way that points forward.[173] According to Childs, post-reformation critical approaches to the text resulted in an altered understanding of the meaning of the phrase "*sensus literalis*," as follows:

> The historical sense of the text was construed as being the *original* meaning of the text as it emerged in its pristine situation. Therefore, the aim of the interpreter was to reconstruct the original occasion of the historical reference on the basis of which the truth of the biblical text could be determined.[174]

This marked a shift from Calvin, who defined the literal sense against the allegorical sense, but did not see any need to get behind the text to find a historically pristine original sense.[175] Childs does not endorse a complete return to Calvin's conception, but argues that interpretation within a canonical context is the way to recover the reformers' emphasis upon the text itself, over and against an emphasis upon something behind the text.[176] Interpretation within a canonical context leaves the door open to figural interpretation in the spirit of the reformers.[177]

According to Childs, "[t]he role of canon as scripture of the church . . . is to provide an opening and a check to continually new figurative applications of its apostolic content as it extends the original meaning to the changing circumstances of the community of faith."[178] For example, the canonical context of Gen 1-3 provides a literary context that extends beyond its original *Sitz im Leben*, so that it becomes part of the Bible's story of redemption. Thus, in the canonical context, it is legitimate to speak of Adam as a figure of Christ (Romans 5). The canon opens the possibility of such interpretation, but also provides the context and the limits for such interpretation. In short, the canon itself establishes the boundaries for legitimate interpretation.

Yet, Childs's work on the *sensus literalis* leaves some difficulties unresolved,[179] so I will attempt to clarify the interpretive parameters of canonical

---

[172] Hans W. Frei. *The Eclipse of Biblical Narrative: A Study in Eighteenth and Nineteenth Century Hermeneutics* (New Haven: Yale University Press, 1974).

[173] Brevard S. Childs, "The *Sensus Literalis* of Scripture: An Ancient and Modern Problem," in *Beiträge zur Alttetestamentlichen Theologie: Festschrift für W. Zimmerli*. (Ed. Herbert Donner; Göttingen: Vandenhoeck und Ruprecht, 1977): 80-93.

[174] Childs, "Sensus Literalis" 89.

[175] Childs, "Sensus Literalis" 84. Also see Childs, *Biblical Theology of the Old and New Testaments*, 724, and Noble, *The Canonical Approach*, 307-312.

[176] Childs, "Sensus Literalis," 92-93.

[177] See Frei, *Eclipse*, 2, and Noble, *The Canonical Approach*, 309.

[178] Childs, *Biblical Theology of the Old and New Testaments*, 724.

[179] See Noble, *The Canonical Appraoch*, 312.

exegesis throughout this book in two ways. First, I will apply Augustine's hermeneutical circle, asking how an understanding of my own situation within the circle clarifies my interpretation. Secondly, I will distinguish between various levels of meanings, as follows: Level One: The first level of meanings occurs at the level of the final form of the text as a unit, where the final form itself clearly demarcates a beginning and an end of that unit—*not* where form or source criticism postulates a pre-canonical beginning or end of the unit.[180] Polyvalence is possible within this level (indeed, within all levels), especially in the case of poetry, which lends itself to ambiguity and adaptability. Level Two: The second level of meanings extends beyond the boundary of the text itself, to consider the meaning of the text within the canonical context. At this level a reader may find figural meanings. Thus, figural level two meanings emerge when the human in Psalm 8 is read in light of Adam of Genesis 2 or in light of the Second Adam of 1 Corinthians 15. It is here that, in the words of Waltke, "the "text's intention became deeper and clearer as the parameters of the canon were expanded."[181] Level Three: The third level goes beyond the plain sense of the passage on any level and includes allegorical meanings which do not violate the teachings of Scripture. Since the first two levels are determinative, a canonical exegesis must pay most attention to the meanings found at levels one and two.

4) Finally, the question must be raised: Which collection of sacred writings will the following study use as the starting point for Old Testament exegesis, a Greek canon like the one Augustine used, or the Hebrew Masoretic Text, as per Seitz, Childs, Jerome, Calvin, and others? The present work takes as its starting point the MT for several compelling reasons which can here be only briefly adumbrated. While it is true that the New Testament authors seem to cite and interpret Greek forms of the Old Testament, concluding from this that the Church then ought to take as its exegetical starting point a Greek text finalized and canonized by the Church is problematic.[182] In the first place, it raises a host of questions concerning which Greek text ought to be used.[183] Furthermore, this book proceeds from the presupposition that Scripture is to be understood as the *norma normans* that stands above tradition, and they do not derive their authority from the tradition or from the Church, the *norma normata* that stands under Scripture's authority.

Moreover, a move towards the Greek and away from the MT as a starting point attenuates the bond that connects the Church of today with God's revelatory work in the Scriptures and history of Israel. Providing a brief gloss of Jerome's rationale for preserving the Hebrew text, Childs writes

---

[180] While many biblical books lack clearly demarcated internal breaks (for example, Genesis, Job, Matthew) the Psalter introduces several possible levels of "level one" meanings by integrating each psalm into the rest of the Psalter, while maintaining a level of independence for each individual psalm.

[181] Waltke, "Canonical," 7.

[182] Childs, *Biblical Theology* 65.

[183] See Seitz, "Canonical Approach," 92-93.

[Jerome] argued that the word of God to Israel had been best preserved in the Hebrew Scriptures on which the various translations had been dependent and from which they had often strayed. Equally important was the theological argument that the Jews had been given the "covenant, . . . the law, the worship, and the promises" (Rom. 1.4) and were the proper tradents of this tradition. Moreover, Paul had also made the argument of the solidarity between Christ and the patriarchs . . . (Rom. 9.5).[184]

Whether or not Childs was motivated by a desire to see a rapprochement between the synagogue and the Church, the central issue here is one of Christian theology, not inter-faith dialogue—namely, the issue of preserving within the Church the theological continuity between Christ and the apostles on the one hand and God's revelation to Israel through the Law, Prophets, and Writings on the other. As Seitz notes, "what is at stake is the canonical authority of the Hebrew Scriptures as foundational and antecedent to Christian claims, claims that have to do with accordance and fulfillment and not with first-time establishment."[185] In sum, then, the present work takes as its starting point for Old Testament exegesis the Masoretic Text of the Hebrew Bible for several reasons; chief among these is the desire to maintain clearly the link between God's word to the community of faith today and God's word to the community of ancient Israel in the Hebrew Scriptures.

This brief treatment of the difficulties facing the canon-exegetical approach is not intended to address every question exhaustively. The thornier issues can only be adequately addressed in the context of the practical implementation of the approach, not in extended discussions of prolegomena. Therefore, this book is not primarily a work of theory but of exegetical practice, and the foregoing discussion is meant merely to set some guidelines within which the rest of the study will proceed, emphasizing that the foundational convictions necessary for establishing methodological controls are: 1) that the canon itself sets the parameters for understanding the plain meaning of the text; and 2) that the interpreter stands within and is constrained by the hermeneutical circle.

Thus, this study deploys the canonical approach to the Bible to accomplish three interrelated goals: 1) To put into practice an exegesis that preserves Childs's emphases while at the same time addressing some questions concerning both the theoretical basis and the implementation of the approach. To this end, the preceding dialogue with *De doctrina Christiana* has yielded at least three major theological affirmations undergirding the present study: a) that the ultimate goal of exegesis is an encounter with the divine; b) that the interpreter engages in exegesis in the context of the hermeneutical circle that includes Church teaching and the Scriptures; and c) that the Scriptures themselves are ultimately authoritative and set the parameters for exegesis.

2) To apply the canonical approach to Psalm 8. By so doing, this study will demonstrate the benefits of the approach by presenting a canonical exegesis of a single passage that is especially well suited to serve as a test case for canonical

---

[184] Childs, *Biblical Theology*, 64-65.
[185] Seitz, "Canonical Approach," 94.

exegesis. Perhaps more importantly, however, this book will contribute to the attempts by Christian scholars to understand the Eighth Psalm as Christian Scripture. Psalm 8 intersects with various passages of Scripture in both testaments and touches upon profound theological questions that run across the canon. How does God relate to and maintain his created order? What is the proper role of humanity *vis-à-vis* the rest of creation? What is one to do with the juxtaposition of royal terminology and "democratizing" imagery in Psalm 8? How does this psalm about YHWH's reign through corporate humanity speak of Christ, as the New Testament seems to believe it does (Matt 21:16; Heb 2:6-8)?

A careful and consistent application of the canonical approach that interprets Psalm 8 in light of the broad sweep of the biblical corpus can go a long way towards clarifying the psalm's theological significance. I turn, therefore, to survey the state of scholarship on Psalm 8. The following will highlight both the ways in which Psalm 8 is an appropriate test case for the canonical approach and the ways in which a canonical exegesis is especially well suited for elucidating the theological significance of Psalm 8. The chapter will then conclude by outlining how the rest of the book will apply the canon-exegetical approach to Psalm 8.

4. Current Scholarship on Psalm 8

Throughout the history of interpretation of Psalm 8, Christian individuals and communities of faith have unanimously acknowledged its status as inspired Scripture and have striven to understand how to apply its theological message to their own context. From the quotation of the psalm by Jesus in Matt 21:16 to its use in monastic prayer and Puritan worship to the various exegeses of it offered by Augustine, Luther, and others,[186] Psalm 8 has had an important role as God's word of canonical Scripture; it has served as part of the *norma normans*, the rule which sets the standard for Christian faith and practice. What issues, then, face us as we attempt to hear its message afresh and apply it to the life and belief of today's Church?

In considering Psalm 8 as a discrete unit, scholars have posited divergent views about the original setting of Psalm 8, ranging from the 12th to the 5th Centuries BCE.[187] Scholars have come to equally varied conclusions about the

---

[186] See Gillingham, "Through the Looking Glass" and Margaret Kim Peterson, *Psalm 8: A Theological and Historical Analysis of its Interpretation* (Ph.D. diss., Duke University, 1998).

[187] Dates range from "the early years of the Jewish settlement" (Wenceslaus M. Urassa, *Psalm 8 and its Christological Re-Interpretations in the New Testament Context: An Inter-Contextual Study in Biblical Hermeneutics* [EUS 23:577; New York: Peter Lang, 1998], 241), to the time of David (Felix Asensio, "El Protagonismo del 'Hombre-Hijo del Hombre' del Salmo 8," *Estudios Biblicos* 41 [1983]: 18-19), to the Persian era (Raymond J. Tournay, "Le Psaume VIII et la Doctrine Biblique du nom," *RB* 78 [1971]: 18-30), with Oswald Loretz positing a detailed account of the development of Psalm 8 over several stages, culminating in the Persian era ("Die Psalmen 8 und 67, Psalmstudien V," *UF* 8 [1976]: 117-122).

related question of the proper cultural/ideological context for understanding Psalm 8, ranging from Egypt to Mesopotamia, often emending the text of Psalm 8 based in part on what one might expect to find in that ideological context.[188] Scholars less concerned with questions of the origins and pre-history of the text have attended to the final canonical form of Psalm 8, arguing that the MT 150 edition of Psalm 8 constitutes a satisfactory syntactical unity without emendation or recourse to a hypothetical pre-canonical form.[189] Thus, diverse interests and methodologies have given rise to contradictory interpretations of the Psalm.[190] This state of affairs poses some special problems for a canon-exegetical approach, which must convincingly address the relationship between the final canonical form of the text with potential pre-canonical forms. Thus, Psalm 8 serves as a good basis for testing a proposed canon-exegetical method.

Turning to the relationship between Psalm 8 and the rest of the Psalter, much has been written in recent years about the canonical shape of the Psalter, often hinting at Psalm 8's special role within that shape.[191] Yet no study has given exclusive attention to Psalm 8's role within the shape of the Psalter. As a result, a canonical exegesis of Psalm 8 will have a three-fold significance. By applying the yields of the burgeoning literature about the editorial shaping of the Psalter to a canon-exegetical approach, the study will contribute 1) to the study of the shaping of the Psalter, 2) to ongoing attempts to develop a viable canon-exegetical program, and 3) to attempts to interpret Palm 8 as Christian Scripture.

---

[188] Scholars have situated Psalm 8 in the context of Egyptian royal ideology (Manfred Görg, "Königliche Eulogie. Erwägungen zur Bildsprache in Ps 8,2," *BN* 37 [1987]: 38-47), Assyrian astral worship (so, tentatively, Jeffrey H. Tigay, "What is Man that You Have Been Mindful of Him?" in *Love and Death in the Ancient Near East: Essays in honor of Marvin H. Pope* [ed. John H. Marks and R. M. Good; Guilford, CT: Four Quarters Publishing Co., 1987], 169-171), and Ugaritic mythology (Alberto J. Soggin, "Textcritische Untersuchung von Ps 8:2-3 und 6" *VT* 21 [1971]: 565-571; Mark S. Smith, "Psalm 8 2b-3: New Proposals for an Old Problem" *CBQ* 59 [1997]: 637-641).

[189] Øystein Lund, "From the Mouths of Babes and Infants You have Established Strength," *SJOT* 11 (1997): 78-99; Pierre Auffret, "Qu'est-ce que l'Homme que tu t'en Souviennes? Étude structurelle du Psaume 8," *SeE* 54 (2002): 25-35.

[190] Smith, whose concern is interpreting Psalm 8 in light of Ugaritic mythology after correcting the corrupted MT 150 version through emendation, argues that the ינקים and עוללים of Ps 8:3[2] are chaos monsters militating against YHWH ("Psalm 8 2b-3," 638-639). Auffret and Lund, whose concern is the text as it now stands and interpreting Psalm 8 in light of biblical parallels, see the ינקים and עוללים as beings that have been granted strength by YHWH to militate against his enemies (Lund "From the Mouths of Babes," 79-83, and Auffret, "Qu'est-ce que l'Homme," 25-26).

[191] Gerald H. Wilson sees Psalm 8 as part of "a thematic unity" in Pss 7-10 (*Psalms I* [NIVAC; Grand Rapids: Zondervan, 2002], 237). Matthias Millard sees Psalm 8 as the central *Orakel* in the *Mittelstück* of the *Kompositionsböge* containing Pss 1-10, (*Die Komposition des Psalters, Ein formgeschichtlicher Ansatz* [FzAT 9; Tübingen: J. C. B. Mohr, 1994]). Rolf Rendtorff sees Psalm 8 as connecting Ps 9 with Ps 7 in such a way that Psalms 8 and 9 together serve to provide "a strong, thankful conclusion" to the grouping of Pss 3-9, "David in the Psalms," in *The Book of Psalms: Composition and Reception* (VTSup 49:4; ed. Craig A. Evans and Peter W. Flint; Boston: Brill, 2005), 56.

Concerning the relationship between Psalm 8 and the broader Old Testament context, several scholars have seen fit to interpret Psalm 8 in light of the same Old Testament passages that Childs referred to in his "Psalm 8" article (Gen 1; Job 7; Ps 144).[192] While other scholars with diverse interests have seen it worthwhile to discuss the relationship between Psalm 8, Genesis 1, and other creation passages, their works do not attempt a canonical exegesis, and no one has attempted to clarify how or why a canonical exegesis should read Psalm 8 in light of the passages that Childs selected in his seminal article.[193] On the other hand, these studies have made observations that could contribute much to a canon-exegetical reading of Psalm 8. Thus, the state of scholarship on Ps 8's relationship with the rest of the Old Testament canon makes Psalm 8 well suited to serve as a test case for a canon-exegetical approach.

Finally, scholars have written much about the use of Psalm 8 by New Testament authors, but this literature has the New Testament text, not Psalm 8, as its primary focus.[194] Urassa's monograph stands out as one exception.[195] Urassa traces the tradition history of Psalm 8 from its hypothetical origins to its Christological interpretation in the New Testament. Urassa's work is helpful in that he explores how an understanding of early Jewish interpretations of Psalm 8 may help to make sense of the New Testament citations of Psalm 8 that speak of Jesus as the "new Adam" and the "Son of Man." Yet, as Urassa admits, his work is "only a humble beginning." There is ample room for more research to be done that examines the New Testament authors' interpretation of Psalm 8 alongside an exploration of the psalm's role in its Old Testament canonical

---

[192] Jerome F. D. Creach, *Psalms* (IBS; Louisville: Geneva, 1998), 74-75, James L. Mays, *Psalms* (Interpretation; Louisville: John Knox, 1994), 68, Peter C. Craigie, *Psalms 1-50* (WBC 19; Waco, TX: Word, 1983), 106.

[193] To name a few examples: Thomas F. Dailey, "Creation and Ecology—the 'Dominion' of Biblical Anthropology," *ITQ* 58 (1992), 1-13; James L. Mays, "The Self in the Psalms and the Image of God," in *God and Human Dignity* (ed. Kendall Soulen and Linda Woodhead; Grand Rapids: Eerdmans 2006), 27-43; Ute Neumann-Gorsolke, *Herrschen in den Grenzen der Schöpfung: Ein Beitrag zur Alttestamentlichen Anthropologie am Beispiel von Psalm 8, Genesis 1 und verwandten Texten* (WMANT 101; Göttingen: Universität Göttingen, 2004); and Manfred Görg, "'Alles hast Du Gelegt under seine Füsse,' Beobachtungen zu Ps 8,7b im Vergleich mit Gen 1,28," in *Freude an der Weisung ders Herrn: Beiträge zur Theologie der Psalmen* (ed. E. Haag and F. L. Hossfeld; Stuttgart: Katholisches Bibelwerk, 1986), 125-148.

[194] To name a few representative examples: Francis J. Moloney, "The Targum on Psalm 8 and the New Testament," *Salesianum* 37 (1975), 326-336; idem, "The Reinterpretation of Psalm 8 and the Son of Man Debate," *NTS* 27 (1981), 656-672; Wilhelmus J. C. Weren, "Jesus' Entry into Jerusalem: Mt 21, 1-17 in Light of the Hebrew Bible and the Septuagint," in *The Scriptures in the Gospels* (ed. C. M. Tucket; Louvain: Leuven Universty Press, 1997), 116-141; George H. Guthrie, "A Discourse Analysis of the Use of Psalm 8:4-6 in Hebrews 2:5-9," *JETS* 49 (2006), 235-246; and Roy A. Harrisville, "Paul and the Psalms," *Word and World* 5 (1985): 168, 174, 178-179.

[195] Urassa, *Psalm 8 and its Christological Re-Interpretations*. Another exception is Felix Asensio "El Protagonismo del 'Hombre-Hijo del Hombre' del Salmo 8." *Estudios Biblicos* 41 (1983): 17-51.

context with a view towards forging a canonical exegesis of Psalm 8 itself.[196] Again, this state of affairs poses intriguing questions that make Psalm 8 well suited as a test case for a canonical exegesis.

In the rest of this book, therefore, I will use Psalm 8 as a concrete test case within which to conduct a canonical exegesis in order to demonstrate the viability of my proposal, to address questions that scholars have about Psalm 8, and to set forth a Christian theological interpretation of Psalm 8. Chapter two will analyze the final canonical edition of Psalm 8 and then address the possibility of earlier versions. In this section I will argue that the canonical edition has theological priority for a canonical exegesis, but the pre-canonical history of the text, to the extent that it can be recovered, can illuminate the significance of the final received form. Chapters three and four will address the relationship between Psalm 8 and the rest of the Old Testament. Chapter three will address the shape of the Psalter and the role of Psalm 8 in that shape. Chapter four will consider some other Old Testament passages that resonate strongly with Psalm 8 (Genesis 1-2; Job 7:17-21; Psalm 144). Using Childs's article on Psalm 8 as a starting point, I will argue that these passages are especially well suited as entry points into the rest of the Old Testament canon for the purpose of building a canonical exegesis of Psalm 8. In this chapter I will draw upon Noble's "new typology"[197] as well as Childs's distinctive intertextual approach developed in his *Isaiah* and *Exodus* commentaries. Chapter five will attend to the New Testament, considering passages that allude to or cite Psalm 8 (Matt 21:16; 1 Cor 15:27; Eph 1:22; Heb 2:6-8). I will argue that, within my proposed canonical-exegetical approach, it will not suffice simply to describe the way in which the New Testament authors use Psalm 8. Rather, a canonical exegesis must read these passages alongside Psalm 8 as constituent parts of the Christian canon, allowing them to inform and to be informed by Psalm 8. Each chapter will attend briefly to the role of Augustinian *caritas* in the process, asking how the exegesis engenders love of God and love of one's neighbor. The sixth and final chapter will summarize the findings of the preceding chapters and argue for a canonical exegesis of Psalm 8. I will distill, from the foregoing chapters, an exegesis of Psalm 8 that preserves the emphases of Childs in a theologically informed and intellectually rigorous manner.

---

[196] Urassa, *Psalm 8 and its Christological Re-Interpretations*, 248-249.
[197] Noble, *The Canonical Approach*, 314-322.

2

READING PSALM EIGHT AS A DISCRETE UNIT

This chapter will examine the Eighth Psalm as follows: The bulk of the chapter will contain an extended analysis of Psalm 8 from a canon-exegetical perspective, presenting a close reading and interpretation of the psalm. Then, the chapter will conclude by setting the agenda for the rest of the book, first by highlighting key theological motifs and issues arising from those motifs that will inform the way that the rest of the book is to proceed, and then by proposing ways of discerning canonical "points of entry," or parts of Scripture that can serve as contact points to illuminate and be illuminated by Psalm 8.

1. Reading the Eighth Psalm[1]

In order to arrive at an adequate understanding of Psalm 8 in its discrete context, following a presentation of a translation of Psalm 8, this section will begin with a brief treatment of some of the more difficult text-critical problems facing the interpreter of Psalm 8. After briefly attending to the date and setting of the psalm, I will survey various themes that scholars have recognized as central to its message. Next, I will present a close reading of the thematic development of the psalm that will show how Psalm 8's themes are intertwined and work together to drive the internal movement of the psalm through several key reversals. This reading will lead to an interpretation of Psalm 8, highlighting some salient themes that will set the agenda for the rest of the study.

1.1 Translation

1 (Title) For the leader of music, on the gittith, a song of David.
2 (1) YHWH, our ruler, how majestic is your name in all the earth!
    You who have set your splendor above the heavens!
    [*alternatively*, Therefore, set your splendor above the heavens!] [2]

---

[1] A revised version of material in this section also appears in my article, "YHWH's Subversive Order: Reconsidering the Structure and Thematic Development of the Eighth Psalm," *PRSt* 40 (2013): 321–35.

[2] The first reading of this line follows the interpreters, ancient and modern, who interpret the text as reflecting a grammatically acceptable form of the verb נתן, either by emending the text to yield a perfective form נתתה (John Goldingay, *Psalms Volume 1: Psalms 1-41* BCOT [Grand Rapids, MI: Baker, 2006], 153; Samuel Terrien, *The Psalms: Strophic*

3 (2) From³ the mouths of babies and sucklings you have founded strength⁴
    because of your adversaries to silence the enemy and the avenger.
4 (3) When I consider your heavens, the work of your fingers,
    The moon and the stars which you have established,
5 (4) What is humankind⁵ that you are mindful of it,
    The child of humanity,⁶ that you care for her/him?
6 (5) Yet you have made him/her only a little less than divine,⁷

Structure and Theological Commentary ECC [Grand Rapids, MI: Eerdmans, 2003], 124, 128) or by reading the MT as containing a rare, but not unattested form of the infinitive functioning as a finite verb (Nahum M. Sarna, *Songs of the Heart: An Introduction to the Book of Psalms* [New York: Schocken, 1993], 228 n. 37). The alternative in brackets understands the MT to contain an imperative form of נתן following אשר functioning as a conjunction, "Therefore, oh, set." Others repoint the text to read "I will worship" (אשרתנה, Mitchell Dahood, *Psalms I, 1-50* [AB 16; Garden City: Doubleday, 1965], 48-49; Peter C. Craigie, *Psalms 1-50* (WBC, 19; Waco, TX: Word Books, 1983), 104) or "is chanted" (pual תנה, Claus Schedl, "Psalm 8 in ugaritischer Sicht," *FuF* 38 (1964): 183-185). For a full yet brief presentation of these and other proposals, see Alberto J. Soggin, "Textcritische Untersuchung von Ps 8:2-3 und 6" *VT* 21 (1971): 565-571; Mark S. Smith, "Psalm 8 2b-3: New Proposals for an Old Problem." *Catholic Biblical Quarterly* 59 (1997): 638-639.

³ H. Kruse's proposal that the מן here is functioning comparatively ("Two Hidden Comparatives," *JSS* 5 (1960): 345) is unlikely. It is more common to take the מן as a preposition meaning "out of/from," such that the פ (mouth) is the source either of the acclamation of YHWH's splendor in verse 2b (Alberto J. Soggin, "Textcritische Untersuchung von Ps. viii vv. 2-3 und 6," 565-571; Goldingay, *Psalms* vol. 1, 153; NRSV) or the source of the עז (strength/stronghold) of verse 3 (Øystein Lund, "From the Mouths of Babes and Infants You have Established Strength," *SJOT* 11 [1997]: 78-99; Samuel Terrien, *Psalms*, 124; NIV).

⁴ Rather than rendering עז as "a stronghold" (see BDB, 739; NRSV; RSV), it is preferable to preserve poetic multivalence by using "the more general" term "strength," (Craigie, *Psalms 1-50,* 105). This enables a Level One interpretation that is not unnecessarily over-specific, so that the Level Two canonical interpretation may consider several possibile ways of understanding the "strength" described here. The more general translation of "strength," moreover, makes sense in light of Lund's argument that YHWH is seen to use mouths to establish strength (generally defined) throughout the OT (Lund, "From the Mouths," *SJOT* 11 [1997]: 78-99).

⁵ While, as Victor P. Hamilton states, "there are probably no major differences in meaning or nuance between" אנוש and אדם, ("אנוש," *NIDOTTE* 1: 453), I have tried to use "humankind" and "humanity" to differentiate the two. See BDB, 60.

⁶ Though it is legitimate to regard the phrase בן אדם as "simply a poetic synonym of 'man' in v. 5a," (Craigie, *Psalms 1-50*, 108), I am rendering this phrase more literally as "child of humanity" to preserve other possibilities of interpretation this phrase may have evoked for both the ancient and modern reader, such as evoking the "sonship" model of the Davidic Kingship (see also James Luther Mays, *Psalms*, (Interpetation, Louisville: John Knox, 1989), 67), and by extension, evoking messianic associations.

⁷ The rendering of the LXX and the NT of אלהים as ἀγγέλους, the mixed opinion of early translations, and the apparent meaning of the word in context make a literal translation of אלהים difficult. While I have taken it to carry the literal meaning of "God" rather than that

and you have crowned him/her with glory and honor.
7 (6) You have made her/him to rule over the works of your hands.
You have put all things under his/her feet.⁸
8 (7) All sheep and oxen, and also the beasts of the field,
9 (8) The birds of the sky, and the fish of the sea,
whatever swims along⁹ the paths of the seas.
10 (9) YHWH, our ruler, how majestic is your name in all the earth!

1.2 Some Text-Critical and Translational Concerns

While most of the MT version of the text of Psalm 8 is grammatically intelligible as it stands,¹⁰ the opening words of verse 2b in the MT, אשר תנה, are notoriously difficult to translate, leading some to conclude that the phrase "defies translation."¹¹ The relative pronoun אשר seems to be grammatically out of place. Furthermore, the verb תנה, as the Masoretes have pointed it, is most likely in the imperative form, and it is difficult to see how an imperative ought to fit in this context, although it is possible to read the MT's תנה as a rare infinitive form of נתן, which is also somewhat awkward in context.¹²

Thus, many emendations have been proposed.¹³ Two somewhat similar proposals are compelling in that they do no violence to the consonantal text: 1) combining the consonants of both words, resulting in the single word, אשרתנה, to form a piel imperfect form of שרת, meaning "I will adore your majesty;"¹⁴ and 2) repointing the verb to read תֻנָּה, the Pual perfect of תנה, meaning "is sung, is

---

of "heavenly beings" (so ASV), I have gone with a more dynamic rendering as "divine" to indicate its purpose in this verse (cf NJPS, JPS). The point is not so much the nature of the אלהים, but that humanity has been exalted to an unfathomably high place in the created order, next to God (see Craigie, *Psalms 1-50*, 108).

⁸ I have translated all of the verbs in vv. 5 and 6 in the past perfect. For difficulties in translating the tenses of these verbs, see Craigie *Psalms 1-50*, 112-113.

⁹ A more literal rendering could read "wanders/passes through" (compare with NASB; NJPS; see BDB, 72). "Swims along" certainly fits within the semantic range of the word and is a much more natural (dynamic) English rendering (compare with the NIV).

¹⁰ See, however, Claus Schedl, "Psalm 8," 183-185. Schedl proposes several changes in verses 2, 3, 4, and 9. Many of these changes, such as the deletion of אדוניו (verse 2), שמיך (verse 5), and ים (verse 9) as later additions are unnecessary, and few contemporary commentators follow his suggestions.

¹¹ Willem VanGemeren, *Psalms* (EBC 5; Grand Rapids: Zondervan), 139, n. 1b.

¹² Ibn Ezra and Kimhi read this "as a feminine infinitive like *redah* in Gen. 46:3," (Sarna, *Songs of the Heart*, 228 n. 37). Moses Buttenwieser similarly sees the MT text "as a correct text" to be read, "with Sym., Hier., and Syr., as an infinitive, formed like that of the *primae Yod* verbs," *The Psalms: Chronologically Treated with a New Translation* (Chicago: The University of Chicago Press, 1938), 180. See Smith, "Psalm 8:2b-3," 638.

¹³ See note 4 above and Franz Delitzsch, *Biblical Commentary on the Psalms* (FBL; London: Hodder and Stoughton, 1908), 191-193, Soggin, "Textcritische Untersuchung," 565-571, and Smith, "Psalm 8:2b-3," 638-639.

¹⁴ Dahood, *Psalms I, 1-50*, 49, and Craigie *Psalms 1-50*, 104.

chanted."[15] The former, while not impossible, is problematic in that "it has to assume a meaning for *šrt* which is not attested elsewhere."[16] Taking their cue from some ancient translations, the editors of the BHS have proposed emending the text to read נתחה (the second person perfect of נתן) or some other form of the verb נתן.[17] While Soggin dismisses these ancient attempts to retain נתן as "Verlegenheitslösungen," not as "wirkliche Übersetzungen,"[18] others have adopted the emendation to נתחה with BHS.[19]

How ought a canon-exegetical approach to adjudicate between such competing interpretations? Insofar as the reader is dependent upon the tradents—either of the Church or the academy—to define and preserve the final form of the text, the interplay between the *norma normans* and the *norma normata* is incredibly tight at this point. While textual emendation may be necessary, it should always be done with great care. The reader ought first to ask whether the final form of the text as the Masoretes have preserved it can provide any meaningful interpretation, and then carefully consider later tradents, including the ancient translations, before positing changes to the text.

Can the MT rendering stand? Taken separately, there is no problem with אשר or תנה.[20] Taken together, however, "such a use of the *imper.* after אֲשֶׁר is unheard of."[21] Nevertheless, one could read אשר, which "as a rule" functions as "a mere connecting link,"[22] as a grammatically awkward but poetic and ejaculative use of the relative conjunction,[23] rendering the phrase in English as "Therefore, set your glory above the heavens!"[24] The psalmist's grammatically

---

[15] So Schedl "Psalm 8," 183, see also RSV and Goldingay, *Psalms I*, 153 n. a.
[16] Helmer Ringgren, "Some Observations on the Text of the Psalms," 308.
[17] Of the translations that BHS cites, the Syriac and Targum (*djhbt*), Symmachus (ὅς ἔταξας) and the *Psalterium juxta Hebraeos*, seem almost certainly to presuppose a form of נתן. Only the LXX's rendering, ἐπήρθη, "is raised," may reflect another verb—although, even the LXX may reflect the translation of a form of נתן. In addition to the feminine perfect form, BHS also proposes emending the text to read נתן and נְתַנָּה, BHS 1091.
[18] Soggin, "Textcritische Untersuchung von Ps. viii vv. 2-3 und 6," 566.
[19] Terrien, *Psalms* 124, 128; VanGemeren, *Psalms*, 138-139; NIV; NRSV.
[20] If one makes modifications to the following verb, the MT rendering of the word אשר may function as a causative conjunction, or as a relative pronoun (see GKC 444-446, 492). The slight awkwardness of the location of אשר does not render the word unintelligible, and may even enhance its poetic role, especially if the second of the above three options is the case. Similarly, if one accepts that תנה is an imperative form with a paragogic תנה and omits the word אשר, the phrase תנה הודך על־השמים is not so problematic, meaning simply "Oh, set (imperative) your splendor upon the heavens!"
[21] Delitzsch, *Psalms* 191.
[22] BDB, 81.
[23] On אשר used to connect consecutive clauses, sometimes combining with the imperfect to create a jussive force, see GKC 505 (paragraph 166b).
[24] Some older translators interpret these words as containing an imperative form of נתן, such as Charles Augustus Briggs and Emilie Grace Briggs, *Psalms* (2 vols; ICC; New York: Scribners, 1906), I: 61, who translated the phrase to read "O set Thy splendour

awkward opening reveals that the psalmist, who "can only babble like an infant," identifies with YHWH's humble infantile instruments described in the following verse.²⁵ Furthermore, the use of the verb נתן fits in well in this psalm, which describes YHWH's actions with concrete verbs of building in verses 3 (יסד) and 4 (כנן). So, it is possible to read the text as it stands in the MT in a poetically meaningful manner, although the occurrence of אשר poses a problem in this context.

Turning to later tradents, namely the ancient translations, the verbs used in the Targum, Syriac, Symacchus, and Jerome all point strongly toward some from of the verb נתן in the *Vorlagen* underlying these translations, yet none of these forms is imperative.²⁶ Similarly, some medieval Jewish interpreters followed the MT pointing, yet understood it to reflect an infinitive form of נתן functioning as a finite verb,²⁷ a view shared by Calvin's commentary on the Psalms and the Hebrew Old Testament Text Project.²⁸ The translations of the LXX (ἐπήρθη) and Vulgate (*elevata*), "lifted up/elevated," have some semantic overlap with the Hebrew נתן, but the correlation is not direct.²⁹ If, however, Soggin is correct that all of these ancient renderings are "Verlegenheitslösungen,"³⁰ then it seems that the ancient translators were as confused by the original text as modern commentators have been.³¹ Thus, it could be that the *Vorlage* of the LXX was the same as the text preserved by the MT, with its exclamatory (mis)use of the relative pronoun, forcing the ancient translators to make some alteration in an attempt to provide a smooth paraphrase. In any event, the early translations point strongly in the direction of some form of the verb נתן.

---

above the heavens!" Similarly, Delitzsch cites Gesenius as translating Ps 8:2b to read "quam tuam magnificentiam pone in coelis," *Psalms* 191.

²⁵ Dahood, *Psalms 1-50*, 49. Note, however, the difference with Dahood who connects מפי grammatically with what has gone before. *Contra* Dahood, the psalmist is not one and the same with the babies and infants. Rather, he poetically identifies with them in their humility.

²⁶ BHS 1091.

²⁷ See Sarna, 227-228, n. 37.

²⁸ John Calvin, *Commentary on the Book of Psalms I*, James Anderson, trans. (Grand Rapids: Eerdmans, 1949), 93, n. 1, 94-95; HOTTP cited in Robert G. Bratcher and William D. Reyburn, *A Translator's Handbook on the Book of Psalms* (HTS; New York, NY: United Bible Societies), 78.

²⁹ They could be seen as having some semantic overlap with other verbs such as Schedl's passive form of תנה, "chanted" or Dahood's imperfect form of שרת, "I will worship."Reformation era translations vary, with the Geneva Bible, KJV (both "hast set"), and Reina Valera ("has puesto") clearly reading the verb as a form of נתן, Louis Segund following the Vulgate ("s'élève"), and the Luther Bibel rendering the phrase "da man dir danket in Himmel."

³⁰ Soggin, "Textcritische Untersuchung von Ps. viii vv. 2-3 und 6," 566.

³¹ But see Terrien, who believes that "the LXX appears to have read . . . different vocalic sounds," 128.

Augustine's advice is relevant here: "When, on paying closer attention you still see that it is uncertain how something is to be phrased, or how to be pronounced, you should refer it to the rule of faith, which you have received from the plainer passages of scripture and from the authority of the Church."[32] Therefore, I propose a cautious course of action. While it is preferable to read the text as reflecting some form of the verb נתן, it is less clear whether this reflects a) the consonants of the MT functioning either as an imperative or an infinitive functioning as a perfect, or b) a corrupted form of a now lost perfect form of the verb נתן. Therefore, in my translation above I have offered two possible renderings: "You who have set" and "Therefore, set," both of which will be considered throughout the course of the interpretation of the psalm.

One more translational question demands special attention. The noun עז in verse three is translated variously either as "praise" (NIV), as "a stronghold" (see RSV and NRSV), or, in the case of some of the more stringently literal translations, as "strength" (ASV, NASB, ESV).[33] The translation of the noun as "praise" reflects the LXX translation of עז as αἶνον rather than reflecting the Hebrew itself, and such a translation is unnecessary in context.[34] Translating עז as "a stronghold," which fits well within the semantic range of the word, seems initially to make good sense in context; YHWH here establishes עז in order to stop the enemies. Yet, as Lund has shown, the metaphor of YHWH establishing strength through the mouths of the humble is quite common in the rest of the Old Testament, even if the phrase "to found strength" is strange to 21st century ears.[35] Thus, I have chosen, with Craigie, to retain the broader semantic range of עז by translating it with "the more general" term "strength" in order to preserve the polyvalent potential of the poetic text before looking more closely at its meaning in context.[36]

---

[32] *Doc. Chr.* Book III: 2. Similarly, Brevard Childs recommends deferring decisions about vv. 2b-3 until after a consideration of the clearer parts of Psalm 8, in "Psalm 8 in the Context of the Christian Canon," *Interpretation* 23 (1969), 23.
[33] BDB, 739.
[34] Moreover, rendering עז as "praise" is as much an act of interpretation as translation insofar is it represents an attempt to understand and interpret what may initially seem to be a perplexing poetic image of YHWH using babies' mouths to build עז.
[35] Øystein Lund, "From the Mouths of Babes," 78-99.
[36] Craigie, *Psalms 1-50,* 105. Preserving the poetic polyvalent potential of the text in this way is especially important for a canonical exegesis, which seeks to allow the canonical context to shine light on more ambiguous words and phrases. Moreover, translating עז with the narrower lexeme "stronghold" prejudices the discussion of whether or not verses 2-3 relate a primeval mythical battle at the outset by portraying YHWH as building a military fortification when the word itself need not be read so narrowly.

1.3 Date and Setting

Scholars have posited dates for the origin of the composition of Psalm 8 ranging from the 12th to the 5th Centuries BC, and possibly beyond.[37] Scholarly answers to the related question of the proper cultural and ideological setting for understanding Psalm 8 have been equally diverse, positing Ugarit, Egypt, Mesopotamia, and the synagogue as the proper context,[38] at times emending the text of the psalm based in part on what one might expect to find in that ideological context.[39] Given the emphasis that the canonical approach places upon the final form of the text, this book will be less concerned with discovering a now lost *Sitz im Leben*.[40] Moreover, the poetic nature of Psalm 8 results in a

---

[37] Dates range from "the early years of the Jewish settlement" (so Urassa, *Psalm 8*, 241), to the time of David (so Asensio, "El Protagonismo," 18-19), to the Persian era (so Raymond J. Tournay, "Le Psaume VIII et la Doctrine Biblique du nom," *Revue Biblique* 78 (1971), 18-30), and the era of the synagogue (so Erhard S. Gerstenberger, *Psalms, Part 1, with an Introduction to Cultic Poetry*, [FOTL 15; Grand Rapids, MI: Eerdmans, 1988], 67-68), and Thorne Wittstruck cites Oswald Loretz as positing a detailed account of the development of Ps 8 over several stages, culminating in the Persian era (Oswald Loretz *Die Gottebenbildlichkeit des Menschen. Mit einem Beitrag von Erik Hornung: Der Mensch als "Bild Gottes" in Ägypten*, [SDIWP; Munich: Kösel-Verlag, 1967], "Die Psalmen 8 und 67, Psalmstudien V," *Ugarit-Forschungen* 8 [1976], 117-122, and "Psalmstudien III. Poetischer Aufbau von Psalm 8," *UF* 3[1971], 104-112, as cited in Thorne Wittstruck, *The Book of Psalms: An Annotated Bibliograpy, vol. II* [BoB 5; New York: Garland, 1994], 518).

[38] For Ugarit, see Soggin, "Textcritische Untersuchung," 565-571; Mark S. Smith, "Psalm 8 2b-3," 637-641; Schedl, "Psalm 8," 183-185; Helmer Ringgern, "Some Observations on the Text of the Psalms," 307-308. For Egypt, see Manfred Görg, who interprets Psalm 8 in light of Egyptian royal ideology in "Königliche Eulogie. Erwägungen zur Bildsprache in Ps 8,2," *Biblishe Notizen* 37 (1987), 38-47. For Mesopotamia, see Jeffrey H. Tigay, who tentatively connects Psalm 8 with Assyrian astral worship in "What is Man that You Have Been Mindful of Him?" in *Love and Death in the Ancient Near East: Essays in honor of Marvin H. Pope* (ed. John H. Marks and R. M. Good; Guilford, CT: Four Quarters Publishing Co., 1987), 169-171. For the synagogue, see Gerstenberger, *Psalms, Part 1*, 68.

[39] See, for example, the many emendations and deletions proposed by Schedl, "Psalm 8," 183-185.

[40] Herman Gunkel identifies Psalm 8 as a hymn of early date (22, 27), possibly intended to be sung at night in conjunction with a festival at a large sanctuary (45), and meant for antiphonal performance with a choir in the cult (312), *Introduction to Psalms: The Genres of the Religious Lyric of Israel*, James D. Nogalski, trans. (MLBS; Macon, GA: Mercer University Press, 1998). Sigmund Mowinckel saw Psalm 8 also as an early hymn, albeit stylistically unique (I: 97), which was connected with YHWH's enthronement festival, and associated with a mythic presentation of creation at the festival (I: 85, 167), *The Psalms in Israel's Worship*, D. R. Ap-Thomas, Trans. (2 vols.; Nashville, TN: Abingdon, 1979). Similary, A. A. Anderson associates Psalm 8 with the feast of Tabernacles, *Psalms 1-72* (NCBC; London, UK: Marshall, Morgan, and Scott, 1981), 100.

song that is adaptable to many contexts, so that to limit the psalm's meaning to one historical setting is to miss the multivalent beauty of the poetry.

Nevertheless, one can draw some limited conclusions concerning the background of the psalm. First of all, the psalm has many affinities with Genesis 1, making it almost certain that the two passages are somehow related, as will be demonstrated below.[41] Although this conclusion may not indicate a post-exilic date, a proper exegesis of Psalm 8 must understand that Psalm 8 is a song of creation that parallels the tradition preserved in Genesis 1. Secondly, while it is appropriate to understand Psalm 8 as a hymn of praise,[42] the psalm also "has an originality and distinctiveness which defy" categorization, so that some see an "apparent mixture of forms" within it.[43] Finally, while it is unclear how Psalm 8 originally functioned cultically,[44] the psalm is "certainly most appropriate for use in the cult's mode of worship."[45]

1.4 Themes and Motifs

Interpreters have recognized several prominent motifs running throughout Psalm 8. As already mentioned, virtually all modern scholars identify the psalm as a hymn reflecting on creation.[46] Craigie, however, argues that "nature," which he identifies elsewhere with "the created world," "is not the central theme of the psalm;"[47] taking his clue from the inclusio bracketing the Psalm (verses

---

[41] According to Childs, "Psalm 8 makes use of the priestly creation tradition, but whether in its literary or oral form is unclear," *Biblical Theology of the Old and New Testaments: Theological Reflection on the Christian Bible* (Minneapolis MN: Fortress, 1993), 113. Craigie, however, is less confident, concluding that the "similarities [between Genesis 1 and Psalm 8] do not permit either precise dating or even a firm judgment as to historical sequence," *Psalms 1-50*, 110. This study will defer a full examination of the relationship between Psalm 8 and the creation tradition until chapter four.

[42] Gunkel, *Introduction to the Psalms*, 22; Mowinckel, *The Psalms in Israel's Worship*, 97.

[43] Craigie, *Psalms 1-50*, 106. See, for example, Walter Beyerlin, "Psalm 8: Chancen der Überlieferungskritik," *ZTK* 73 (1976): 1-22. Odil H. Steck avers that "Nahe liegt die Vermutung, in v. 2b-9 einen weisheitlichen Text zu sehen, der mittels der Rahmenverse 2a, 10 zur hymnischen Verwendung durch die Kultgemeinde bestimmt wird.," "Beobachtungen zu Psalm 8," *BN* 14 (1981): 64.

[44] To find clues to the psalm's original function, scholars have looked both to reconstructed festivals (Mowinckel [*The Psalms in Israel's Worship*, 97]; Anderson [*Psalms 1-72*, 100]), and to the psalm's references to evening heavenly bodies (וכוכבים ירח), (Briggs and Briggs, *Psalms*, I: 61; Anderson *Psalms 1-72*, 100; VanGemeren, *Psalms*, 137; all conclude that the psalm may have been connected with an evening cultic ceremony).

[45] Craigie, *Psalms 1-50*, 106.

[46] Delitzsch, *Psalms*, 188; A. A. Anderson, *Psalms (1-72)*, 100; Hans-Joachim Kraus, *Theology of the Psalms*, Keith Crim, trans. (Minneapolis: Augsburg, 1986), 62-64; Walter Brueggemann, *The Message of the Psalms: A Theological Commentary* (AOTS; Minneapolis, MN: Augsburg, 1984), 28-38.

[47] Craigie, *Psalms 1-50*, 109.

2a, 10), Craigie identifies "the majesty of the divine name" as the central theme.[48] Within Psalm 8's reflection on the created order, the psalmist's reflection on the specific place of humanity within that order takes up over half of the psalm, and so commends itself as a major theme, so that Asensio describes it as having a "cáracter teocéntrico-antropocéntrico."[49]

While some scholars would prefer to give pride of place to one of these three themes over another, none of these themes is particularly controversial; one could summarize Psalm 8 as a contemplation and celebration of 1) YHWH's glorious name, 2) YHWH's created order and 3) the place of humanity within that created order. Such a summary, however, is inadequate for a theological exegesis which seeks to identify the distinct theological contribution of Psalm 8 to the canon. This summary fails to explain adequately 1) how these themes relate to one another in Psalm 8,[50] and 2) the nature of the intricate relationship between the major themes and other minor themes in the psalm, including the problematic children and sucklings of verse 3. Therefore, in order to clarify how the various themes of Psalm 8 cohere together, it will be important to consider the progression of the thought of Psalm 8.

1.5 A Close Reading of Psalm 8

How does the flow of thought in Psalm 8 progress? In order to address this question, this section proceeds in three parts: The first part outlines an initial skeletal framework for understanding the flow of the psalm by examining how the psalmist presents each of the major topics addressed by Psalm 8. The second part attends to a particularly problematic passage (v. 3) to assess how it fits into the psalm. The third part presents a summary of the psalm to make clear the central flow of the psalm that drives the psalm along from topic to topic and unifies its various themes.

1.5.1 An initial skeletal framework: Analyzing the topical presentation. How does the psalm present, develop, and connect the various topics which it addresses? The psalm "is framed in verse 1a and verse 9 by an envelope of praise to the regal Creator."[51] The inclusio and the body of the psalm are reciprocally interpretive. On the one hand, the refrain frames the psalm within "an inclusio of great power" proclaiming the psalm's "central message of

---

[48] Craigie, *Psalms 1-50*, 107.
[49] Felix Asensio, "El protogonismo del 'Hombre-Hijo del Hombre' del Salmo 8," 17.
[50] Is the psalmist reflecting on "special revelation," whereby YHWH reveals himself to be the creator, so that her reflection on YHWH's creation is derived from an a-priori theology (so Craigie, 109, and Kraus, *Theology of the Psalms*, 36)? Or is she instead reflecting on "general revelation," as YHWH makes his attributes known through creation in a way that is manifest to all? Is the human a main theme of the Psalm, or a secondary theme illustrating YHWH's glory in creation (So James L. Mays, *Psalms*, 67)?
[51] Brueggemann, *The Message of the Psalms*, 36.

wondrous awe"[52] from the outset. On the other hand, the reader cannot fully appreciate the refrain's import until after considering the thematic development of the body of the psalm, and then returning to the refrain where the "perfect circle is closed."[53]

In the body of the psalm, the psalmist moves from one topic to another, addressing the following primary topics (i.e., topics that occupy the direct attention of the psalmist at one point or another): YHWH's majesty (v. 2), babies and sucklings vs. enemies (v. 3), the evening heavenly bodies (v. 4) and humanity (vv. 5-9). The psalmist does not move haphazardly from one topic to the next, with little or no logical connection. Rather, the poet treats each topic in a similar programmatic way and interweaves the topics together artfully, creating, in the words of Alter, "a single panorama with multiple elements held nicely together."[54] One element of the psalmist's programmatic presentation is the way in which he consistently defines the topic under consideration by comparing it with another secondary topic. The result is a series of juxtapositional pairings of primary topics with secondary topics. The last of these juxtapositional pairings, which places humanity in juxtaposition with the rest of the created order, makes up roughly half of the Psalm, delineating at length both the primary topic (humanity) and the secondary topic (the rest of creation). So, the presentation of topics in Psalm 8 is as follows:

[Framing context: majesty of YHWH's name in all the earth (v. 2a)]
(A) YHWH's splendor *vis à vis* the heavens (v. 2b)
(B) The babies and sucklings *vis à vis* the adversaries/enemy and avenger (v. 3)
(C) The heavens/heavenly bodies *vis à vis* the human (vv. 4-5)
(D) Humanity *vis à vis* the rest of the created order (vv. 6-9)
- Humanity's exaltation (vv. 6-7)
- The creatures subjected to humanity (vv. 8-9)[55]

[Framing context: majesty of YHWH's name in all the earth (v.10)]

In each case, the primary topic is somehow superior to the secondary topic: (A) YHWH's splendor is "above the heavens," (B) the babies and sucklings are able "to silence the enemy and the avenger," (C) a contemplation of the majestic heavenly bodies (v. 4) leads to a contemplation of humanity's "finitude and fallibility,"[56] and (D) a discussion of humanity's royal role in creation leads to a

---

[52] Gerald H. Wilson, *Psalms I* (NIVAC; Grand Rapids: Zondervan, 2002), 199.
[53] Robert Alter, *The Art of Biblical Poetry* (New York: Basic Books, 1985), 118-119.
[54] Alter, *The Art of Biblical Poetry*, 118.
[55] While verses 8-9 define the "all things" at length ("all sheep and oxen . . . whatever swims along the paths of the seas"), this list serves the purpose of describing the extent of the dominion of the human, and therefore never develops into a primary topic in its own right. For a careful assessment of the ordering of vv. 8-9, see Richard Whitekettle, "The Taming of the Shrew, Shrike, and Shrimp: The Form and Function of Zoological Function in Psalm 8," *JBL* 125 (2006), 749-765.
[56] Mays, *Psalms*, 67-68.

description of the rest of creation as "under [humanity's] feet."[57] Thus the psalmist portrays each primary topic as occupying a relatively exalted position in reference to the created order, and each secondary topic as occupying a relatively insignificant position within that order.

In addition to the relationship between the primary and secondary topics within each individual topical pairing, each pairing relates somehow with the pairing that precedes it and follows it in the psalm, with one purposeful exception. The relationship between pairing (A) and what follows may not be clear at the outset, because there is no readily evident point of contact between (A) and (B). To quote Alter, however, "the heavens" in v. 2 "lead directly to the assertion of [verse] 4 about the awe-inspiring sign of heaven and moon and stars."[58] Thus pairing (C) is logically connected with pairing (A). Verse two speaks of setting (or worshipping or chanting) YHWH's splendor above the heavens (A), and that leads to a contemplation of the impressive night sky, which evokes immediate feelings of insignificance resulting in a contemplation of the role of the "puny man"[59] (C). Thus, verse four presents the heavenly bodies as simultaneously awesome (compared with humanity) and puny (compared with God). Craigie puts it beautifully:

> The vastness of the universe is subtly magnified, for the heavens are the work of God's "fingers!" . . . The poet makes a striking point. In contrast to God, the heavens are tiny, pushed and prodded into shape by the divine digits; but in contrast to the heavens, which seem so vast in the human perception, it is mankind that is tiny.[60]

So, the heavens are the hinge between pairing (A) and pairing (C).

Yet, where, then, does pairing (B) fit in? Along with the problematic phrase אשר תנה of the preceding verse, the material about babies and sucklings, enemy and avenger, is particularly problematic.[61] In his article on Psalm 8, Childs says of verses 2b-3 "it is a sound principle to work from the clearer portions and later attempt to place these more difficult verses in the larger

---

[57] The final primary topic, humanity is presented in a slightly more nuanced manner, as it is juxtaposed against two secondary topics: "אלהים" and "all things," the first element (אלהים) actually being *higher* than/superior to humanity, and the second ("all things") is lower than//inferior to humanity. The intent of the phrase "מעט מאלהים" seems to be to communicate that humanity occupies the absolute highest place in the created order possible (hence my idiomatic rendering, "less than divine"). As a result, I am treating this entire complex of ideas as a juxtapositional comparison between humanity and the rest of the created order.
[58] Alter, *The Art of Biblical Poetry*, 119.
[59] Delitzsch, *Psalms*, 187.
[60] Craigie, *Psalms 1-50*, 108.
[61] As Lund observes, "[a]t first sight, Ps 8,3 seems to be composed of metaphors that perhaps can make sense separately, but it seems impossible to combine them" ("Mouths," 78). For a list of works contributing to the ongoing debate about how these various metaphors are to be understood, see ibid., 78, n. 2.

context which emerges."[62] Thus, for now, it suffices to recognize that pairing (A) and pairing (C) find a link in their mutually shared references to the heavens, and to defer a full consideration of the role of pairing (B) until after treating the thematic development of the clearer parts of the rest of the psalm.

Just as pairings (A) and (C) connect thematically, so too pairings (C) and (D) relate to one another. The topics considered in vv. 4-9 follow upon one another in logical succession. A contemplation of the majestic heavenly bodies leads the psalmist to a contemplation of the relatively frail human (vv. 4-5, pairing C). This, in turn, leads to a consideration of the status of the human, which culminates in a recitation of the various creatures that the human has dominion over (vv. 7-9, pairing D). The human is a hinge that links together juxtapositional pairing (C) with juxtapositional pairing (D) in a way that subverts the reader's expectations. The language of pairing (C) emphasizes the insignificance of the human, and pairing (D) immediately reverses this insignificance by declaring that YHWH has exalted the "puny man"[63] to be among the most significant beings on the hierarchy of creation. In the words of Gerald Wilson,

> The psalmist lays out two ways Yahweh's creation of humans counters their seeming powerless insignificance. Having created them as weak and powerless creatures, with one foot firmly planted in the creaturely world . . . God goes on to plant the other human foot squarely and uniquely in the divine realm, both by the unique gift of the divine image and by the role of responsibility and authority given only to humans.[64]

So, temporarily setting aside pairing (B) as per the advice of Childs,[65] each topical pairing is connected to the preceding pairing and the following pairing in such a way as to move the psalm along through a series of descending comparisons. This reading can be mapped out to represent the flow of thought of the body of the psalm graphically:

[Framing context: majesty of YHWH's name in all the earth]
(A) YHWH's splendor
    above→the heavens (v. 2)
        [(B) sucklings and enemies]
    (C) The heavens (v. 4)
        demonstrating the insignificance of→humanity (v. 5)
        (D) Humanity (vv. 6-7) given dominion over→
            the rest of the created order (vv. 8-9)
[Framing context: majesty of YHWH's name in all the earth]

---

[62] Childs, "Psalm 8," 23. These words are reminiscent of Augustine's advice, quoted earlier, to consult the "plainer passages of Scripture" to elucidate more problematic passages, *Doc. Chr.* Book III: 2.
[63] Delitzsch, *Psalms*, 187.
[64] Wilson, *Psalms I*, 206.
[65] Childs, "Psalm 8," 23.

The effect of this descending chain of juxtapositional pairings is that two pivotal primary topics (the heavens and the human) are *first* presented as relatively inferior, and then presented as occupying an exalted place in the created order. In this way, the psalmist manages to effect a series of reversals that "turn the tables" on the reader. She does so by describing something in insignificant terms before proclaiming how YHWH has taken that insignificant thing and put it in an exalted place within the created order. These two reversals drive along the progression of the psalm, and the first reversal (heavens) sets the stage for the second reversal (human) which is the central moment in the psalm wherein readers see how YHWH makes his name majestic in all the earth.[66]

The second reversal (pairing D) has special significance for several reasons. As noted above, it constitutes about half of Psalm 8, dedicating two verses to the exaltation of the human and two verses to the subordination of the rest of the created order.[67] Thus, in the case of the human, the psalm emphasizes the role reversal, as it describes at length what God has done to take the human from a place of evident insignificance and put the human in a place of royal significance (vv. 6-7). In the case of the rest of the created order, however, there is no role reversal (vv. 8-9). To the contrary, these verses list the creatures that are in submission to the human in an order that reverses the order of the Genesis 1 creation account, listing land, air, and sea animals, respectively.[68] This "top down" listing is consistent with the movement of the rest of Psalm 8 (God→heavenly bodies→humanity→the rest of creation) and in no way reverses the reader's expectations. Rather, it serves rhetorically to convince the reader of the veracity of verse 7's claim of human dominion,[69] and rounds out the body of the Psalm in a way that leads into the worshipful reiteration of the refrain in verse 10. To quote Wilson,

---

[66] The contemplation of the heavens occupies just over one verse, but the contemplation of the humans occupies over half of the Psalm. Also, the repetition of the key words מה and כל in connection with YHWH in the inclusio ("how (מה) majestic . . . in all (כל) the earth") and with the human toward the center of the Psalm ("What (מה) is humanity . . . yet you have put all (כל) things under his feet") further serves to highlight the centrality of humanity in the psalm. See J. Clinton McCann, Jr., "Psalms," in *The New Interpreter's Bible* (12 vols.; Nashville, TN: Abingdon, 1994-2004), 4:712; Lund, "From the Mouths of Babes and Infants," 96-97.

[67] Beyerlin, "Psalm 8: Chancen der Überlieferungskritik," 3-4; Frank-Lothar Hossfeld and Erich Zenger, *Die Psalmen I* (NEB; Würzburg: Echter Verlag, 1993), 78-80; Gesrstenberger, *Psalms, Part 1*, 67-70. All three divide the body of Psalm 8 into two uneven sections: Ps 8:2b(or c)-3, and Ps 8:4-9.

[68] For a thorough treatment of the way in which the psalmist has ordered the animals of verses 8-9, see Whitekettle, "The Taming of the Shrew, Shrike, and Shrimp," 749-765. For an assessment of the structure of vv. 8-9 and their role in the overarching structure of the psalm, see Pierre Auffrett, "Qu'est-ce Que L'homme, Que Tu T'en Souviennes? Étude structurelle du Psaume 8," *SeE* 54 (2002), 28-33.

[69] Whitekettle, "Taming of the Shrew, Shrike, and Shrimp," 763-765.

Subtly our understanding of the ground for praising Yahweh has shifted from the first verse to the last. At the beginning our praise began by affirming the magnificence of the creator. At the end, we stand in awe at the unexpected grace that has elevated his human works to unimaginable heights of glory, honor, and responsibility.[70]

1.5.2 Babies and sucklings/enemy and avenger. Having adumbrated the thrust and thematic development of the clearer portions of Psalm 8, we are now in a position to turn to the more ambiguous material in verse 3. This verse is problematic for at least three reasons: 1) The ambiguities arising from the letters אשרתנה in verse 2 result in undertainty as to the grammatical relationship between verses 2 and 3.[71] 2) If a strong connection binds together the references to the heavenly bodies in verses 2 and 4, it remains to be seen how verse three fits between them. 3) Commentators and translators (including the LXX) have struggled with understanding the poetic imagery of this verse, asking, "How can God 'found a bulwark [עז]' 'by the mouths of babes'" against his foes?[72] This last difficulty is of special importance, since arriving at a clear understanding of the meaning of the poetic imagery of this verse will go far to solving the other two difficulties.

Since the discovery of the Ugaritic texts at Rash Shamra, several scholars have looked to Canaanite mythology to find new answers.[73] So, Claus Schedl identifies the ינקים with the beings that the Rash Shamra texts describe as "gracious gods . . . who suck the nipple of the Athiaratu."[74] Concerning the עוללים he avers that "[i]m Zusammenhang des Psalmes geht es aber nicht um Kinder auf Erden, sondern um . . . die 'Göttersöhnne,'" or בני אלהים.[75] Thus, he translates both words together as "mächtigen Wesen," from whose mouth the majesty of YHWH is sung about in heaven (verse 2b).[76] Smith follows Schedl in identifying the עוללים וינקים with Canaanite beings, but argues that the children of El in *CTA* 23 rebel against El and are expelled.[77] Thus, he regards the phrases עוללים וינקים and אויב ומתנפם "as examples of hendiadys," rendering verse three to

---

[70] Wilson, *Psalms I*, 209. Thus, VanGemeren's peremptory treatment of verse 10, "[s]ee comments at v. 1," does not do justice to the second iteration of the refrain.
[71] For a summary treatment of some of the ways in which scholars have struggled to understand Ps 8:3a and its relationship with Psalm 8:2b, see Soggin, "Textkritische Untersuchung," 566-568.
[72] Gerstenberger, *Psalms Part 1*, 68.
[73] Soggin, "Textcritische Untersuchung," 565-571; Schedl, "Psalm 8;" Smith, "Psalm 8:2b-3;" 637-641; Ringgern, "Some Observations on the Text of the Psalms," 307-308.
[74] Schedl, "Psalm 8," 180-181. English translation taken from KTU 1.23 in Johannes C. De Moor, *An Anthology of Religious Texts from Ugarit,* Religious Texts Translation Series NISABA, 16 (New York: Brill, 1987), 122.
[75] Schedl, "Psalm 8," 183.
[76] Schedl, "Psalm 8," 183. Schedl points the verb in Ps 8:2b as תִנָּה, translating it as "besugen."
[77] Smith, "Psalm 8:2b-3," 637-641.

read: "From [that is, against] the mouths of suckling babes you established a strong place, for your stronghold you indeed ended the avenging enemy."[78]

There is good reason to question whether decades of recourse to Ugaritic literature has really resulted in any satisfying solution to the alleged problem of the poetic imagery of Ps 8:3. The use of עולל to refer to בני אלהים is unattested elsewhere in the Old Testament.[79] Furthermore, scholars who read Psalm 8 in light of Ugaritic mythology have failed to arrive at a consensus.[80] Also, while the Canaanite context is the most often appealed to, other scholars propose competing extra-biblical contexts as the proper place for understanding the origins of Ps 8, such as Egyptian royal ideology[81] and Assyrian astral worship.[82] When one turns to assess proposals positing several putative stages for the gradual development of the psalm,[83] the options become bewildering. Moreover, all such proposals rest upon an accumulation of probabilistic inferences, which run the risk of falling into what Alvin Plantinga refers to as "the fallacy of creeping certitude."[84]

Even if one were to find the Ugaritic parallels compelling, one would have to acknowledge that the psalm's final form had a different meaning, at least for the compilers of the Psalter. As Schedl himself admits, his proposal entails "archaische, mythologische Spuren" that "später . . . umgedeutet werden,"[85] and that the text survived intact only after the mythological worldview had been lost.[86] Furthermore, in the context of the Old Testament, the Hebrew terms עוללים ("babies") and ינקים ("sucklings") almost certainly refer to earthly beings

---

[78] Smith, "Psalm 8:2b-3," 638-639.

[79] The term עולל refers to human infants 1) killed or captured in conquest (I Sam 15:3; 22:19, II Ki 8:12, Ps 137:9, Isa 13:16, Jer 6:11; 9:21; 44:7, Lam 1:5, Hos 13:6, Mic 2:9, Nah 3:10), 2) starving under siege (Lam 2:11, 19-20; 4:4), 3) who inherit from human parents (Ps 17: 14), or 3) as part of the congregation of human Israelites (Joel 2:16). See Goldingay, *Psalms 1-41*, 156.

[80] In addition to the disagreement between Smith and Schedl concerning the nature of the עוללים וינקים, scholars who read Psalm 8 in light of Ras Shamra disagree about how to interpret other parts of Psalm 8, as well. For example, Schedl posited many textual alterations to the MT version of Ps 8, from the beginning (repointing אשר and attaching it to the first clause in Ps 8:2a to read "Wie Herrlich ist, Jahwäh, deine Name, gerümt in der ganzen Weld") to the end (deleting the second occurrence of יה in Ps 8:9 and inserting the now repointed letters אשר into Ps 8:10) of the psalm, but neither Smith nor Soggin have followed suit. Moreover, disagreement persists concerning the proper solutions to the text-critical question of understanding the letters אשרתנה the question of how the preposition מן of מפי in v. 3a ought to be understood, the very problems which they purport an investigation into the Ugaritic texts will solve.

[81] Görg, "Königliche Eulogie," 299-308.

[82] Tigay, "What is Man that You Have Been Mindful of Him?" 169-171.

[83] Loretz, as cited in Wittstruck, *The Book of Psalms*, 518.

[84] Alvin Plantinga, *Warranted Christian Belief* (New York: Oxford University Press, 2000), 402.

[85] Claus Schedl, "Ps 8 in Ugaritischer Sicht," 183.

[86] Claus Schedl, "Ps 8 in Ugaritischer Sicht," 184.

and evoke weakness and vulnerability,[87] especially when they appear together.[88] This usage contrasts sharply with the depiction of the children of El in the Ugaritic Myth and Ritual text. So, while Schedl's and Smith's proposed recovery of an archaic interpretation of the psalm may have historical importance, a canonical exegesis ought not to grant canonical status to this archaic interpretation; in Schedl's own estimation, it was not the interpretation of the tradents of the text, nor does it fit in with the "weltbildes" of the broader Hebrew canon.

Recently, other scholars attending directly to the Old Testament rather than Ugaritic, Egyptian, or Mesopotamian literature for interpretive insight have done work better suited for a canon-exegetical approach to the text. Øystein Lund has turned to other OT material to illuminate the poetic imagery of verse three.[89] In the estimation of Auffret,

> Lund a montré comment Ps 8,3 comme unite syntaxique prenait un sens pleinement satisfaisant pour peu qu'on comprenne, à partir d'une conception biblique parfaitement fondée, que la bouche des enfants et des rejetons reçoit bel et bien une *force* (*'wz*) qui leur permet de lutter efficacement contre tous les ennemis qui, dans le cosmos même, s'opposent à cette vie qu'ils ont reçue de créatur.[90]

As Lund aptly demonstrates, the OT frequently describes "the mouth as an instrument for the display of power," even, at times, wielding weapons.[91] Thus, in Ps 8:3, "God provides the babes and infants with strength, and establishes this strength in a place where it is natural to locate it—*in the mouth*."[92] It is also natural that this strength, in turn, is able to "silence" (השבית) YHWH's enemies, as "a goal in the struggle against [enemies] is to neutralize the mouth, and silence then becomes the utmost symbol of this."[93]

---

[87] See, for example, the עוללים in Lam 4:4 who are helpless to get food or drink for themselves, or the various references where helpless עוללים are killed in holy war (I Sam 15:3, Ps 137:9), see BDB 760. For ינקים see Num 11:12, I Sam 15:3, and Isaiah 66:11, BDB 413.

[88] So, too, I Sam 15:3; 22:19, and Lam 2:11; 4:4, and Joel 2:16. See Lund, "Mouths," *SJOT* 11 (1997): 85-86; Walter Beyerlin, "Psalm 8: Chancen der Überlieferungskritik," *ZfTuK* 73 (1976): 15-17.

[89] Lund, "Mouths," 78-99.

[90] Pierre Auffret, "Qu'est-ce que L'Homme," 25.

[91] Lund, "Mouths," 79-83. Lund finds poetic descriptions of the mouth as a source of power in Isa 9:12; 11:4; and 48:2, Ps 18:9; 22:14; 57:5; 59:7; and 107:15, and II Sam 22:9, and other passsages.

[92] Lund, "Mouths," 83.

[93] Lund, "Mouths," 82-83. Lund cites examples where shutting the mouth of something or silencing it amounts to neutralizing its power, especially Job 5:16 and Ps 107:42. See also R. E. Watts, "The Meaning of 'ĀLĀW YIQPESÛ MELĀKÎM PÎHEM in Isaiah LII 15," *VT* 40 (1990), 327-335, who argues that the phrase "shutting of the mouth" in Isa 52:15 is "a metonymy of effect signifying the subjugation of the arrogant kings to the servant," 335.

Furthermore, it is not altogether out of place to see YHWH as using the mouths of the יונקים and עוללים as a source of strength. The expectation of and/or request for God's intervention on behalf of the "lowly-poor-needy" over and against the "strong-arrogant-ruthless"[94] is a common theme in the Psalter. Such an action on the part of YHWH fits in perfectly in the immediate context of Psalm 8, which, as I have shown above, depicts God as reversing the readers' expectations. Furthermore, one other passage containing the word pair יונק and עולל describes how the helpless Israelites gather to pray (presumably with their mouths) for God to intervene for them against strong, oppressive enemies (Joel 2:16);[95] there, God's strength is manifest by his answering the prayers of the weak and helpless against the oppressors. Therefore, when one looks to the canon of the OT to clarify the poetic language in Ps 8:3, it makes the most sense to read the prepositional phrase מפי עוללים ויונקים as grammatically connected with what follows. Returning briefly to the question of the translation of אשרתנה, this reading fits better if, with the majority tradition, one reads תנה as reflecting a form of the verb נתן.[96] Nevertheless, such a reading is not entirely incompatible with other proposals.[97]

Who, then, are the יונקים and עוללים? In addition to the mythological interpretation of Schedl and Smith, scholars have identified them with: 1) the children of "Tochter Zion,"[98] 2) Israelite children—a democratization of an idea formerly connected with the son of the Pharaoh,[99] 3) children in general,[100] 4) the psalmist himself,[101] or a poetic representation of either 5) all human beings,[102] or 6) weak and humble human beings.[103] The last of these interpreta-

---

[94] James L. Mays, *Psalms*, 23. Here Mays describes the prayers in the individual lament psalms.
[95] See Lund, "Mouths," 86.
[96] So Auffret, "Que'est-ce que l'homme," 25-26.
[97] So, for example, while Dahood translates Ps 8:2b-3 to read "I will adore your majesty above the heavens, with the lips of striplings and sucklings" (*Psalms*, 48), one could accept his pointing of the verb אשרתנה yet accept Lund's reading of verse three, rendering the verses to read "I will adore your majesty above the heavens. Out of the mouths of striplings and sucklings you have established strength . . ." So, too, while the RSV renders vv. 2b-3a as a syntactical unity, one could conceivably agree with the RSV's rendering in following the pointing that results in a pual form of the verb תנה, and yet render vv. 2b and 3a as syntactically separate to read "your glory is chanted above the heavens. Out of the mouths of babes and infants you have established strength/a stronghold . . ."
[98] Beyerlin, "Psalm 8," 15-17.
[99] Manfrend Görg, "Der Mensch als königliches Kind nach Ps 8.3," *BN* 3 (1977), 7-13.
[100] Lund, "Mouths," 86.
[101] Dahood, *Psalms*, 49-50.
[102] Steck sees Ps 8:3 and Ps 8:5-9 as reiterating the same theme twice: that of "Schöpferwirken auf Erden am Menschen zur Bändigung von Feinden" (v. 3) or "Schöpferwirken auf Erden am Menschen zur Bändigung der Tiere" (vv. 5-9) ("Beobachtungen zu Psalm 8," 57).
[103] Craigie, *Psalms 1-50*, 107.

tions is the most compelling, and it is better to understand Ps 8:3 as a malleable poetic scene of YHWH's triumph over his foes than to posit a specific historical or mythological referent for the ינקים, עוללים, עז, צורר, אויב, or מתנקם.

The alternation between the perfect (שתה, כוננתה, יסדת) and the imperfect (תמשילהו, תעטרהו, ותחסרהו, תפקדנו, תזכרנו, אראה) verb tenses give the psalm a timeless quality, making a single historical referent unlikely.[104] The result is a picture of, on the one hand, a creation that has been established at some point in the past, and, on the other, the psalmist's experience of and contemplation of the resulting created order. While one could read the perfect verbs, especially יסדת in verse 3, as alluding to a past mythical event, elsewhere the word pair יונק and עולל refers to earthy humans, not mythic creatures.[105] Also, the status of a human as vicegerent in the cosmos implies the ongoing necessity to maintain the created order, making it difficult to see the אויב, צורר, or מתנקם of verse 3 as past enemies that have now been "sabbatized" or caused to cease (השׁבית). Rather, the enemy, foe, and avenger may represent together anyone (or anything) opposing God's created order and therefore posing a threat to the manifestation of the majestic name of YHWH in all the earth.

So, VanGemeren is correct when he describes the creation theology of Psalm 8 as "phenomenal (i.e., it focuses on effects rather than causes)."[106] The emphasis is upon the created order as it is (or ought to be) rather than the way that the created order came to be.[107] Understood this way, the MT's choice to point תנה as an imperative form of נתן makes some sense. The psalmist begins his contemplation of the created order with a terse prayer: "Oh [YHWH]! Set your glory above the heavens!" Or, "Continually intervene over and against those who would upset your intended order and thus defame your glory!" However one points these contested radicals, it is not necessary to posit here "a foreign particle of pagan mythology" reflecting the text's "long history of the struggle to overcome the myth" resulting in the remnant of some "mutilated and half-digested particle" of alien legend (as Childs describes Gen 6:1-4 in its

---

[104] Concerning the tenses of the verbs in Psalm 8, see Craigie, *Psalms 1-50*, 105 n. 7.a., 110-113.

[105] So, too, I Sam 15:3; 22:19, and Lam 2:11; 4:4, and Joel 2:16. See Lund, "Mouths," 85-86; Beyerlin, "Psalm 8: Chancen der Überlieferungskritik," 15-17.

[106] VanGemeren, *Psalms*, 137. Readers must take care to avoid confusing the use of the word "phenomenal" here with discussions about the phenomenological definition of myth as found in Childs, *Myth and Reality in the Old Testament* (SBT 27; London: SCM, 1960), 13-16. Here, I (following VanGemeren) speak of the focus of the creation account upon effects and reality rather than causes and origins. Childs, however, is concerned with providing a definition of myth focused upon its phenomenon, rather than superimposing a "historico-philosophical definition" upon myth (*Myth*, 14). The terms phenomenal and phenomenological take on very different foci and meaning in each distinct context.

[107] Contra, Alberto J. Soggin, for example, who argues that "in diesem Fall ist das von Jahwe erbaute Bollwark," so that the עז ("strength"="Bollwark") of v. 3, is "mit der רקיע von. Gen. i 6 identisch," in "Textcritische Untersuchung," 569-570.

context).¹⁰⁸ Nor do we find a clear allusion to foreign mythology adapted only for its "illustrative value as an extended figure of speech" (as Childs describes the mythic metaphor of Isa 14:12-21).¹⁰⁹ Rather, Psalm 8 reflects "the Old Testament's concept of reality" which is distinct from the mythical categories of Ugarit.¹¹⁰ As a piece it is a poem that is not time-bound; the psalm's phenomenal focus on the created order results in a poetic dynamism that is able to encompass simultaneously the reality of creation past, present, and future. Even if "old fashioned creation mythology" wherein "creation is not a peaceful affair but a war against chthonic powers"¹¹¹ may have formed part of the cultural background shared by the original readers of the psalm, the message of these poetic verses is not reducible to the recounting of a creation story.¹¹²

In the light of the foregoing analysis of the thematic development of Psalm 8, verse 3 makes the most sense as a programmatic, idealized summary of the rest of the psalm. Towards the beginning of the hymn, it gives one poetic scene which embodies in sum the thrust and theme of the rest of the psalm and is not time-bound. So far I have argued that the flow of thought of the body of Psalm 8 is driven by two parallel reversals. In each case the reader is first introduced to a relatively inferior thing (heavens/humans), and then lead into a contemplation of the exalted position that the inferior thing has in the created order. We find all of these elements in brief in the juxtaposition of the babies/sucklings and the enemy/avenger.¹¹³ Thus, Ps 8:3 serves as a brief excursus which deviates slightly and intentionally from the main thrust of the psalm. Verse 3 speaks to the way in which YHWH maintains the created order, as he continues to take relatively insignificant things and exalt them over and against stronger enemies. The point of this verse, then, is to illustrate the thrust of the rest of the Psalm by relating how, in the words of Bellinger, God "create[s] strength even out of weakness."¹¹⁴

1.5.3 Tying it all together. Having surveyed the thrust of thought throughout the body of the psalm, I will now summarize how the thematic development of Psalm 8 ties the various themes of the psalm together. The body of the Psalm consists of two unequal parts, as follows:

---

¹⁰⁸ Childs, *Myth and Reality*, 56-58.
¹⁰⁹ Childs, *Myth and Reality*, 72.
¹¹⁰ Childs, *Myth and Reality*, 73. Childs does not speak of Psalm 8 here.
¹¹¹ Gerstenberger, *Psalms 1*, 69.
¹¹² It is not insignificant that Childs does not include Psalm 8 in his discussion of mythic texts incorporated into the OT in *Myth and Reality*, nor does he give much consideration to possible mythic elements in Psalm 8 in his article "Psalm 8."
¹¹³ By YHWH's action, the mouths of the humble and weak ינקים and עוללים are used to thwart (השבית) the foes of YHWH (צורריך, אויב, and מתנקם) with their God given strength (עז).
¹¹⁴ W. H. Bellinger, *Psalms: Reading and Studying the Book of Praises* (Peabody, MA: Hendrickson, 1990), 86.

Inclusio: "how[מה] excellent your name in all [כל] the earth" (v. 2a)
    A. Reversals One and Two (vv. 2b-4):
        1. Insignificant heavenly bodies (vv. 2b, 4)
        2. Imbedded paradigmatic reversal: babes and infants/
           enemy and avenger (v. 3)
        1'. Majestic heavenly bodies (v. 4).
    B. Reversal Three (vv. 5-9):
        1. Insignificant human: "what [מה] is the human?" (v. 5)
        2. Majestic human: "you have placed all things [כל] under his feet" (vv. 6-7)
        3. *Denouement*:
           a. Animals from creation day six (v. 8)
           b. Animals from creation day five (v. 9)
Inclusio: "how[מה] excellent your name in all [כל] the earth" (v. 10)[115]

The first iteration of the inclusio turns the reader's attention to YHWH's majestic name in verse one. This flows into the first line of the first part of the body (Part A) that begins with a terse prayer for YHWH to glorify himself above the relatively insignificant heavens in verse two.[116] Employing three concrete verbs of creation (נתן, יסד, and כנן), Part A demonstrates YHWH's majestic splendor in the created order through two intertwined reversals: 1) a timeless, paradigmatic scene in which YHWH takes the evidently weak babies and infants and uses them to neutralize (השבית) his enemies (verse 3), and 2) a celebration of the way that God takes things that are but "finger toys" to him (the heavenly bodies) and imbues them with awesome majesty (verses 2b, 4). The second section (Part B) begins with the third reversal. Here, YHWH takes the even less significant human, makes him "a little less than divine," and puts him over "all things." The thematic development of the psalm, the place and length of Part B in the Psalm, and the use of the key words מה and כל, which frame the psalm in the inclusio, all serve to highlight verses 5-7 as the central moment in the body of the psalm. This leads into verses 8-9, the *dénouement* of

---

[115] For the strategic positioning of the words כל and מה see McCann, "Psalms," 712, and Lund, "From the Mouths of Babes and Infants, Strength," 96-97. For two different but insightful and harmonious treatments of the structure of Psalm 8, see Auffret "Qu'est-ce que l'Homme que tu t'en Souviennes?" 25-35, and Terrien, *The Psalms*, 124-126.

[116] The initial iteration of the inclusio and the first line of v. 3 are in parallel with one another (YHWH's majestic name (v. 2) // YHWH's splendor (v. 3), and "in all the earth" (v. 2) // "above the heavens," heavens and earth being a common hendyadis for the entire created order, as in Gen. 1:1). Thus, Verse 2a begins the body of the psalm by restating the framing context. See Alter, 118. That verse 1 can serve a double function, standing in parallel with verse 2 while at the same time anticipating the reiteration of the refrain in verse 10, should not surprise anyone who is familiar with the Psalter. For example, Ps 103:1a forms an inclusio with Ps 103:22c, and Ps 103:1a also stands in parallel with Ps 103:1b.

part B, describing the domain of the human ruler in top-down fashion, completing the panoramic portrait of creation.

The psalm then returns to reiterate in the refrain the majesty of YHWH's name. In its second iteration the refrain takes on the "sense accrued through the intervening eight lines of what concretely it means for His name to be majestic throughout the earth."[117] The reader of Psalm 8 now understands that YHWH makes his name excellent in all the earth by establishing and maintaining the created order through the exaltation of things that seem otherwise to be insignificant. Thus, YHWH simultaneously subverts human expectations and all attempts to thwart his order. In what follows I will use the label "reversal motif" to refer to the resulting complex of theological ideas woven together in Psalm 8—namely, the way in which YHWH makes his name excellent in the cosmos by maintaining the created order through the exaltation of weak and humble things over and against proud and self-strong things.

1.5.4 Encountering the res *and engendering* caritas. The informed reader of this book is not likely to have any difficulty understanding how the reading of Psalm 8 presented here fits in with the sort of canonical exegesis practiced by Waltke, Childs, Seitz, and others. What may seem less obvious, however, is the linkage between the reading proffered here and Augustinian hermeneutics. Indeed, in contrast with the level one reading presented here, Augustine's own exposition on Psalm 8 seems almost exclusively concerned with an allegorical (level 3) interpretation—the "wine-presses" of the title in the LXX version are the Church or martyrs; the heavens are the law; the moon and the stars are churches; etc.[118] Certainly the canonical approach practiced here, as elsewhere,[119] does not attempt to repristinate the allegorizing aspect of Augustine's technique.

Yet the reading proffered here is Augustinian in that it understands the psalm as the setting for an encounter with the divine *res* that produces love for God and neighbor. In the first place, the believer who reads Psalm 8 as Scripture does not envision herself as standing outside of the text and examining it as one inspects an ancient artifact of purely antiquarian interest. Rather, she envisions herself as a part of the larger community entering into the recitation of a worshipful hymn of praise; such a reader (including this book's author and readers) will be moved to contemplate the majesty of YHWH and the splendor of his created order. The ebb and flow of the poem, as outlined above, is a vehicle for the "ascent of the soul" to an encounter with the LORD whose name is majestic in all the earth.

---

[117] Alter, *The Art of Biblical Poetry*, 119.

[118] Saint Augustine, *Enerrat. Ps.* 8 (*Expositions of the Psalms: 1-32. The Works of Saint Augustine: A Translation for the 21'st Century, Part III, vol. 15*, Maria Boulding, trans. [Hyde Park, NY: New City, 2000], 129-138).

[119] On Childs and Augustine, see Daniel R. Driver, *Brevard Childs, Biblical Theologian: For the Church's One Bible* (Grand Rapids, MI: Baker Academic, 2012), 265-278.

Contemplating the cascading series of reversals which demonstrate how YHWH maintains the created order to manifest the glory of his name naturally moves the reader to love both God and his creation. The specific application of the *caritas* engendered by Psalm 8 will depend upon the reading community's own context, as it finds ways to identify the weak and the humble in its own time and space with the weak and the humble things described in the psalm. The Church of today will have no trouble finding such points of contact: the innocent victims of heinous crimes such as those perpetrated by Dr. Kermit Gosnell; oppressed ethnic minorities the world over such as the Karen of Southeast Asia who have been persecuted by the government of Myanmar for over half a century; the orphans, fatherless, and widows all over the world that have been forgotten by society and often by the Church itself.

The specific identification and resulting application will differ in various corporate and individual contexts, but the principles encapsulated in the reversal motif of Psalm 8 remain the same. Psalm 8 encourages its readers to envision the weak and humble of their own context as YHWH's tools for maintaining order and manifesting his glory. Such a vision will shape the ethical praxis of the Church in various contexts. The way in which Psalm 8 facilitates an encounter with God that engenders love will become clearer as the rest of the book considers the psalm's level two canonical meaning by bringing it into dialogue with the rest of Scripture.

2. Tracing Trajectories for Canonical Exegesis

How, then, ought one to bring Psalm 8 into dialogue with the rest of the canon? In order to address this question, it will be helpful to distill some key theological motifs and questions from the foregoing analysis of the hymn, paying special attention to the way in which interpreters, both ancient and modern, have interacted with its theological message. Then, looking to Childs's early article on Psalm 8 for guidance,[120] this section will propose several ways of discerning "points of entry," or parts of Scripture which have special affinities with Psalm 8 and can, therefore, serve as contact points to illuminate the Eighth Psalm and to be illuminated by it, concluding the chapter and setting the trajectory for the rest of the book.

From the above analysis, four motifs emerge as deserving special attention throughout the rest of this book: 1) YHWH's majestic name, 2) the created order, 3) the role of humanity, and 4) the reversal motif—whereby YHWH makes evident his majestic name and maintains the created order by taking seemingly insignificant things, most notably, humans, and imbuing them with strength. The following will highlight how each of these themes, individually and in concert with each other, gives rise to issues and questions that will be illuminated by bringing Psalm 8 into dialogue with the rest of the canon.

---

[120] Childs, "Psalm 8," 20-31.

2.1 YHWH's Majestic Name

This theme will inform the following chapters in two ways: 1) A distinct question arises from the declaration of the LORD's majestic name "in all the earth:" Are humans, according to Psalm 8, able to know God or something about God by means of the created order?[121] Or is the emphasis rather upon the need for special revelation?[122] Psalm 8 alone is not sufficient to settle the question of if (and how) God reveals himself by means of the creation to finite humans, and an exhaustive treatment of this complex question is beyond the scope of this study; such a question is not the central preoccupation of the psalm itself and may very well not have been considered by ancient Israelites reading or singing the psalm. Nevertheless, the following chapters may shine some light on the question by bringing Psalm 8 into dialogue with the rest of the canon.

2) More central to our purposes is the hymnic tenor and worshipful stance of the psalm. In bringing Psalm 8 into dialogue with the rest of the canon, I will consider some passages that share the psalm's worshipful tone (i.e., Eph 1:20-23), and others that reflect a more pessimistic outlook (i.e., Job 7). The distinct focus of Psalm 8 upon the majestic name of YHWH will play a role in informing our understanding of a) the distinct theological contribution of Psalm 8 to the rest of the canon, and b) the way in which the rest of the canon can inform our understanding of the hymn that is Psalm 8.

---

[121] John Calvin says of verses 8-9, that "[t]here is no man of a mind so dull and stupid but may see, if he will be at the trouble to open his eyes, that it is by the wonderful providence of God that horses and oxen yield their service to men" (*Commentary on the Book of Psalms I*, 107). So, too, Mays: "The LORD who is sovereign over the congregation that sings the hymn possesses a cosmic majesty evident in all the earth" (*Psalms*, 63), Terrien: "The revelation of the name allows humans to raise slightly the veil of transcendental mystery" (*Psalms*, 128), and Goldingay: There is "something splendid about creation that makes people wonder at God's glory" (*Psalms*, vol. 1, 154).

[122] Craigie insists that "[n]ature . . . does not contain in this context any inherent qualities of revelation" (Craigie, *Psalms 1-50*, 109). Similarly, in a section entitled "The Knowability of God," Karl Barth undertakes an excursive exegesis of Psalm 8, asking whether one can "understand Ps. 8 in the sense that an appeal is made to man in the cosmos in himself and as such as a witness of God," so that Ps 8 argues for a "natural theology." He concludes that one cannot understand Psalm 8 in this way, which can only properly be understood as pointing one to the special revelation which is to be found in "the man," who is Jesus (*Church Dogmatics*, G. W. Bromiley, O. Bussey, J. W. Edwards, J. L. M. Hare, W. B. Johnston, Henry Kennedy, Harold Knight, A. T. MacKay, John Marks, T. H. L. Parker, G. T. Thomson, and T. F. Torrance, trans.; 4 vols.; [New York: Charles Scribners, 1949-1962], 3/2, 112-113). Hans Kraus seems to agree: "How can mankind . . . know this [that YHWH has created everything]? In the type of statements about creation to which we turn first, the name of Yahweh (Ps. 8:1) is the key to the secret of creation . . . The statement that Yahweh created the world is not something obvious, but it is a confession of faith, based on the self-communication of Yahweh's name" (*Theology of the Psalms*, 36).

2.2 The Created Order

According to Susan Gillingham's survey of the history of interpretation of Psalm 8, the psalm's expositors have chosen to focus either upon salvation or upon creation in their interpretation.[123] According to the reading of Psalm 8 proposed above, Psalm 8 itself emphasizes the created order as it ought to be, as YHWH intends to maintain it, yet it also hints at the need for salvation by mentioning the existence of enemies in the paradigmatic scene in verse three, indicating that the maintenance of the created order currently entails a struggle necessitating divine intervention.

Summarizing pre-modern Christian interpretations of Psalm 8, Peterson states, "[c]rea-tion is not as it should be . . . However, at the resurrection of the dead, there will be a new creation."[124] Bringing Psalm 8 into contact with other passages will enable this seminal tension between the way that things ought to be and the way that things are to germinate into a robust theology of the already and the not yet. Thus, both creation and the need for redemption will be in the fore of the discussion as this study turns to other passages that emphasize disorder in creation (such as Job 7) and others that speak of salvation (such as Hebrews 2).

2.3 The Role of Humanity

When Christian interpreters have considered Psalm 8 in connection with salvation, they have often also used Psalm 8 to speak of the savior. In her dissertation surveying 10 pre-modern interpreters, including Augustine, Aquinas, and Calvin, Margaret Kim Peterson finds that they all "without exception interpret the Psalm christologically, although they do so in somewhat different ways."[125] The precedent for this is found in the quotation of Psalm 8 in the New Testament.[126] Some interpreters in our own era have seen images of Christ in Psalm 8, either in ways that differ substantially from pre-modern exegesis,[127] or by looking to the pre-modern tradition as an aid in understanding the psalm and its New Testament appropriations.[128] How is a Christian to

---

[123] Gillingham cites the LXX translation, the NT authors, various other patristic writers (including Theodore of Mopuestia and Ambrose of Milan), and Thomas Aquinas as examples of salvation/redemption-oriented readings ("Psalm 8," 169-170, 176-180). Augustine sees salvation/redemption throughout the psalm. For example, "the man" in verse 5a as referring to fallen, unregenerate humans, and the "son of man" in verse 5b as referring to both Christ and spiritual humans, indicating a movement from fall to redemption that is accomplished in Christ, *Enerrat. Ps.* 8:10-11.

[124] Peterson, "Psalm 8," 234.

[125] See also Peterson's helpful, if somewhat simplistic in its harmonization, summary of the pre-modern interpreters' understanding of Christ in Psalm 8 ("Psalm 8," 236-241).

[126] Gillingham "Psalm 8, Through the Looking Glass," 176-177.

[127] For example, Creach, *Psalms*, 74-76, Mays, *Psalms*, 70.

[128] Asensio, "El Protagonismo del 'Hombre-Hijo del Hombre' del Salmo 8," 17-51.

understand Psalm 8 as bearing witness to Christ without unintentionally overriding the psalm's level one meaning? This study, by seeking to read Psalm 8 on its own terms while at the same time bringing it into contact with other passages of Scripture, will grapple directly with this question.

Another salient theological issue that arises when one considers the message of Psalm 8 concerning the role of humanity in the cosmos is that of how humans ought to govern the rest of the created order. In recent years, Psalm 8 has become something of a *locus classicus* for biblical scholars and theologians concerned with issues related to the just human rule of creation, especially ecological issues.[129] At issue is the question of whether the corporate human monarch has license to exploit the rest of nature for its own ends, or if the human, as vice-gerent and steward, is to attend benevolently to the rest of creation. An entire book could be dedicated to investigating Psalm 8 alone in order to address this question.[130] The present work, however, will defer a full treatment of this question for the following chapters, when a fuller answer will emerge as Psalm 8 comes into interaction with the rest of Scripture.

A related question pertains to how humans ought to relate to and govern one another. Some contemporary scholars have seen egalitarian overtones in Psalm 8, describing it as "democratizing."[131] Is this correct? On the one hand, it is correct that the portrayal of corporate humanity in Psalm 8 as ruling the created order together contrasts with Egyptian[132] and Mesopotamian[133] royal ideology, resulting in an increased sense of dignity for the common human. On the other hand, Psalm 8 does not say anything explicitly about the form that human government ought to take. Moreover, one must ask why, if Psalm 8 is anti-royal, the tradents associated Psalm 8 with David in the title; to speak of Psalm 8 as "democratic" goes beyond the evidence of the psalm itself. Once again, bringing Psalm 8 into dialogue with other passages will elucidate the issue of proper human government from a canonical perspective.

---

[129] Focusing on Genesis 1, James Barr argues that "the biblical foundations of" the doctrine of creation "tend . . . away from a license to exploit and towards a duty to respect and to protect," "Man and Nature: The Ecological Controversy and the Old Testament," *BJRL* 55 (1972): 30. More recently, scholars have given increasing attention to Psalm 8, often alongside Genesis 1 (see Ute Neumann-Gorsolke, *Herrschen in den Grenzen der Schöpfung: Ein Beitrag zur alttestamentlichen Anthropologie am Beispiel von Psalm 8, Genesis 1 und verwandten Texten* [WMANT 101; Germany: Neukirchener, 2004]; Marvin E. Tate "An Exposition of Psalm 8," *PRS* 28 (2001): 356-359).

[130] Neumann-Gorsolke, *Herrschen in den Grenzener Schöpfung*, does not treat Psalm 8 exclusively, but she dedicates over 100 pages to her exegesis of Psalm 8 alone (20-135), and focuses heavily on Psalm 8 throughout the course of the rest of the 350 page book.

[131] Eckart Otto, "Myth and Hebrew Ethics in the Psalms," in *Psalms and Mythology*, Dirk J. Human, ed. (LHB/OTS 462; New York: T&T Clark, 2007), 29, 35, Manfred Görg, "Der Mensch als königliches Kind nach Ps 8.3," 13. See Terrence E. Fretheim, *God and World in the Old Testament: A Relational Theology of Creation* (Nashville: Abingdon, 2005), 47.

[132] So Görg, "Der Mensch als königliches Kind," 7-13.

[133] So Otto, "Myth and Hebrew Ethics in the Psalms," 29, 35.

2.4 The Reversal Motif

Since this motif permeates and interweaves each of the other three motifs and is part of the distinct theological contribution of Psalm 8, it will inform much of the discussion that follows in the book. When we consider how other passages relate to the interpretation of Psalm 8, questions emerging from the other three motifs may influence the understanding of the reversal motif. When the trajectory runs in the other direction, with Psalm 8 elucidating the other passages under consideration, the question becomes "how does the distinct theological contribution of Psalm 8, summarized in the reversal motif, inform the present text?"

3. Selecting Passages for Canonical Exegesis

The study that follows will look to texts that are especially well suited to bring Psalm 8 into dialogue with the rest of Scripture. How, then, ought this book to select texts to engage with? In Childs's seminal article, he considered Psalm 8 alongside several other texts throughout the canon, and the way in which he selected these texts can prove helpful for the present study.[134] While Childs did not explicitly delineate the criteria that he used for choosing the other passages that he brought into dialogue with Psalm 8, a careful reading of his article reveals three types of passages that Childs turns to: 1) passages that have strong thematic parallels with Psalm 8, indicating either direct dependence or indirect dependence;[135] 2) passages that aid in dealing with an exegetical problem growing out of Psalm 8 and that exhibit some thematic parallels and/or semantic similarities;[136] 3) passages that cite Psalm 8.[137] To these three categories I will add a fourth category that Childs's article does not address: 4) The immediate literary context of Psalm 8; one must attend to the Psalter and to the burgeoning literature on the shape and shaping of the Psalter to develop a fully informed canonical exegesis of Psalm 8. I will also modify category 2 slightly, focusing only upon passages which overlap semantically with Psalm 8 in order to reign in the number of passages considered.

In what follows, then, the study will consider passages that fit into one or another of these four categories, and I will utilize these passages as "entry points" through which Psalm 8 may enter into dialogue with the rest of the canon. It should be pointed out, however, that the fundamental question underlying the selection of texts and contexts in the following chapters will not be whether or not a given text fits into one of the four categories mentioned above. Rather, the driving question is: "Which texts are best suited to serve as

---

[134] Childs, "Psalm 8 in the Context of the Christian Canon," *Interpretation* 23 [1969], 20-31.
[135] Genesis 1 (Childs, "Psalm 8," 21-22).
[136] Job 7 (with reference to Psalm 144); Ecclesiastes 3 (Childs, "Psalm 8," 28-30).
[137] Heb 2:6-9 (with reference to Matt 21:16; 1 Cor 15:27; Eph 1:22; Childs, "Psalm 8," 24-26).

representative entry points through which Psalm 8 can engage the rest of the canon?" These four categories are simply meant to serve as heuristic tools to assist in locating texts that are well suited to serve as "entry points." In structuring the study, Psalm 8 will be the interpretive center. The chapters that follow will first consider the material nearest "the center" in the canon (the Psalter, chapter three), then move on to the more remote material in the Old Testament (chapter four) and then finally the New Testament (chapter five). The hope is to allow Psalm 8 and the other passages to be mutually interpretive. Interpretive influence runs two ways: centripetally, so that Psalm 8 informs the passage under consideration, and centrifugally, so that the rest of the canon in turn informs a canonical understanding of Psalm 8. In this way, each passage will be able to speak on its own terms, without being overwhelmed by the message of another passage.

3

PSALM EIGHT IN THE CONTEXT OF THE PSALTER

Turning to the canonical literature most immediately connected with Psalm 8, the Psalter, of the four types of texts described in chapter two that will serve as entry points for a canonical exegesis, this chapter will focus exclusively upon the fourth type—that of the immediate literary context of the passage.[1] Thus, this chapter focuses exclusively upon the shape of the final form of the Psalter and the hermeneutical implications that this has for a canonical exegesis of Psalm 8; the primary focus will be the text itself, not the community that gave it that shape.[2] Moving from the more immediate to the more distant contexts, this chapter will examine Psalm 8 in the context of Pss 7-10, Pss 1-14, Book I of the Psalter, and finally the entire Psalter (MT). Throughout, I will trace the mutually interpretive influences of Psalm 8 and the rest of the Psalter, paying special attention to the way in which the shape of the Psalter points the reader "to the substance (*res*) of its witness, to the content of its message, namely to the ways of God in the world."[3] The chapter will conclude by summarizing the thematic development of the Psalter, emphasizing the role that Psalm 8 plays in that development.

---

[1] The Psalter contains Psalms that fit into category two—passages that aid in dealing with an exegetical problem growing out of Psalm 8 and that exhibit some thematic parallels and/or semantic similarities—e.g., the other creation psalms (Walter Brueggemann, *The Message of the Psalms: A Theological Commentary* [AOTS; Minneapolis MN: Augsburg, 1984], 28-38), and Psalm 144 (see Jerome F. D. Creach, *Psalms* [IBS; Louisville: Geneva, 1998], 74-75; James L. Mays, *Psalms* [Interpretation; Louisville: John Knox, 1994], 68). I will defer a full treatment of such passages until chapter four, where I can consider them in connection with the rest of the Old Testament.
[2] Like William H. Bellinger, "I am interested in the shape of the Psalter . . . rather than the shaping of the Psalter" ("Reading from the Beginning (Again): The Shape of Book I of the Psalter," in *Diachronic and Synchronic: Reading the Psalms in Real Time: Proceedings of the Baylor symposium on the Book of Psalms* [LHB/OTS 488; ed. Joel S. Burnett, William H. Bellinger, and W. Dennis Tucker; New York: T & T Clark, 2007], 115).
[3] Brevard S. Chids, *Isaiah: A Commentary* (OTL; Philadelphia: Westminster, 2001), 4.

1. Psalm 8 in the Context of Psalms 7-9/10

Psalm 8 sits between two individual lament/complaint psalms, Psalm 7 and Pss 9-10[4]—the latter of which, when read together, form a unified acrostic poem.[5] Thus, to use Brueggemann's terminology, Psalm 8 is a psalm of orientation immediately surrounded by psalms of disorientation.[6] Furthermore, as the following analysis will demonstrate, several verbal links create a strong connection between Pss 7, 8, and 9, indicating that the decision to place Psalm 8 in its "current position is an editorial one."[7] The linkage is strong enough to justify reading Pss 7-10 as a miniature cluster.[8] Therefore, the following will analyze Pss 7, 8, and 9-10, paying special attention to the way in which the three

---

[4] The identification of the genre of Psalm 7, which follows nicely the pattern of the typical lament of the individual (see Herman Gunkel, *Introduction to Psalms: The Genres of the Religious Lyric of Israel*, James D. Nogalski, trans. [MLBS; Macon, GA: Mercer University Press, 1998], 121-221], is uncontroversial. Gunkel, however, saw a mix of forms in Pss 9-10 (*Introduction to the Psalms*, 309), and some recent commentators have identified this poem as a thanksgiving of the individual (Ernest C. Lucas, *Exploring the Old Testament, Volume Three: A Guide to the Psalms and Wisdom Literature* [Downer's Grove, IL: Zondervan, 2002], 11; Susan E. Gillingham, *The Poems and Psalms of the Hebrew Bible* [OBS; New York: Oxford University Press, 1994], 231). While thanksgiving elements are present in the poem, Mitchell Dahood (*Psalms I, 1-50* [AB 16; Garden City: Doubleday, 1965], 54-55) and William H. Bellinger (*Psalms: Reading and studying the Book of Praises* [Peabody, MA: Hendrickson, 1990], 45) are correct to identify Pss 9-10 as a lament of the individual.

[5] For a brief recounting of the evidence for the unity of Pss 9-10, well recognized by now, see Hans J. Kraus, *Psalms 1-59*, Hilton C. Oswald, trans. (ACC; Minneapolis, MN: Fortress, 1993), 191.

[6] Brueggemann, *The Message of the Psalms*. I do not here unqualifiedly endorse Brueggemann's entire proposal nor do I engage directly with any of the work's psychological assertions or presuppositions. Rather, I simply find Brueggemann's terminology helpful as a "heuristic proposal" (Patrick D. Miller, *Interpreting the Psalms* [Philadelphia, PA: Fortress, 1986], 12). I find the terms "orientation" and "disorientation" to be helpful headings under which to organize psalms such as hymns (orientation) on the one hand and the laments of the Psalter (disorientation) on the other.

[7] Patrick D. Miller, "The Beginning of the Psalter," in *The Shape and Shaping of the Psalter* (JSOTSup 159; ed. J. Clinton McCann; Sheffield: JSOT Press, 1993), 89. See also Joseph P. Brennan, "Psalms 1-8: Some Hidden Harmonies," *BTB* 10 (1980): 28-29. While Brennan regarded Psalm 8 as a later insertion between Pss 7 and 9, there is no way to know for sure when or how Pss 7-10 came together into their current final form.

[8] The strong connections led Max Löhr to argue that "Ps 7 9 und 10 haben ursprünglich ungetrennt neben einander gestanden" ("Psalm 7 9 10," *ZAW* 36[1916]: 225-226), though he would also contend that "Ps 8 is erst später zwischen 7 und 9 eingefügt worden" (226). While Kraus is correct to reject Löhr's view on the grounds that "[r]elated themes and motifs do not provide a right to reconstruct literary complexes," there are enough "related themes and motifs" in Pss 7-10 to create a strong literary bond between them (*Psalms 1-59*, 168).

psalms relate to one another, and then move on to consider what hermeneutical implications arise from reading Pss 7-10 in connection with one another.

Psalm 7, the first psalm in this mini-cluster, contains two roughly equal halves, the first part being a prayer to God for deliverance from unjust persecutors (vv. 2-9a), and the second part being a description of the expected deliverance by YHWH (vv. 9b-18).[9] In the first half of Psalm 7, verses 5-7 anticipate Ps 8:3 by speaking, in chiastic arrangement, of צוררי "my foe" (Ps 7:5, 7 // צורריך in Ps 8:3) and איב, "the enemy" (Ps 7:6, // אויב in Ps 8:3). The second half of Psalm 7 anticipates the hymn of Psalm 8 in a somewhat different way.[10] Verses 16-17 anticipate the reversal motif of Psalm 8 by describing a divine reversal wherein the wicked attempt to ensnare the innocent, but are instead caught by their own traps.[11] The motif of the wicked falling into their own trap, common in the psalms (Ps 9:15; 35:7-8; 57:6), occurs for the first time in the Psalter here in Ps 7:16-17.[12] This reversal of the plans of the wicked is followed by Psalm 7's concluding postlude: "I will sing praise to the name of YHWH, the Most High" (v. 18).

From there, Psalm 8, "vollzieht dieses Lob" of the name of YHWH that the conclusion of Psalm 7 calls for.[13] Then, as the first part of Psalm 7 prayed for YHWH to thwart the psalmist's צורר and איב, the body of Psalm 8 begins by describing a reversal wherein YHWH has thwarted his own צורר and איב in verse 3. Whereas the description of the expected reversal in Ps 7:15-17 left off with imperfective verbs (ירד, ישוב, יפל), Ps 8:3 describes a reversal with a perfect verb

---

[9] Terrien discerns a chiastic structure in Psalm 7, with the words אלהים צדיק, "God the righteous (so NJPS)" in verse 9b at the center (Samuel Terrien, *The Psalms: Strophic Structure and Theological Commentary* [ECC; Grand Rapids, MI: Eerdmans, 2003], 118), outlining Ps 7 as follows:

>Prelude (vv. 2-3)
>I. The Enemies (vv. 4-6)
>II. Request for Trial (vv. 7-9a)
>III. (Core): Just God! (vv. 9b-11)
>IV. retribution (vv. 12-14)
>V. The Enemies (vv. 15-17)
>Postlude (v. 18)

[10] The second half of the Psalm, despite Terrien's misleading heading for verses 15-17, drops the language of enmity, emphasizing instead the moral depravity of the רשעים, "the wicked" (verse 10).

[11] Kraus quotes the expositions of the reformers to capture aptly the image of divine reversal described in these verses: "Luther declares: 'This is the incomprehensible manner of divine judgment, that God does not catch the wicked except properly in their own scheme and leads them to the ruin they have themselves devised' (WA 5; 246, 26 f.). In Calvin we find the statements: '. . . By the wondrous providence of God things have been turned to the opposite goal'" (Kraus, *Psalms 1-59*, 174).

[12] But see Ps 5:11, which prays "let them [enemies] fall by their own counsels."

[13] Franz Lothar Hossfeld and Erich Zenger, *Die Psalmen I, 1-50* (DNEB 29; Würzburg: Echter Verlag, 1993), 82. See Bellinger, "Reading from the Beginning," 120; Brennan, "Psalms 1-8," 28-29.

(יסדת). When read in connection with Psalm 7, the choice of a perfect verb form connotes a shift in emphasis from a hope that God will restore order in Ps 7:15-17 to a celebration of the fact that God has, does, and will maintain the created order in Ps 8:3.[14] From there, the hymnic praise of the name of YHWH develops thematically, as I have shown in chapter two, around two more reversals—that of the heavens and that of the human, both of which are first shown to be relatively insignificant, but then shown to hold exalted positions within YHWH's created order (Ps 8:4-7). The latter reversal's focus upon humanity at the center of Psalm 8 (בן־אדם/אנוש, verse 5), points backward and forward to the focus upon humanity that one finds in Pss 7 and 9, as well. The balance of the body of Psalm 8 describes the rule of the human over the created order (verses 6-9), and the psalm concludes by repeating the opening declaration of the majesty of YHWH's name in the created order (Ps 8:10).

Psalm 8 "leads quite directly to" the first stanza of Psalm 9, which praises YHWH and echoes the final words of Psalm 7: "I will sing praise to your name, Oh Most High!" (v. 3).[15] Miller notes that the slight variation of wording between the almost identical phrasing in Ps 7:18b (ואזמרה שמ־יהוה עליון, "and I will sing praise to the *name of YHWH* the Most High") and 9:3b (אזמרה שמך עליון, "I will sing praise to *your name*, oh Most High") serves to link together Pss 7, 8, and 9 editorially; by substituting שמך for שמ־יהוה, Ps 9:3b echoes the שמך found in the inclusio of Ps 8:2, 10.[16] Psalm 9's second stanza then carries forward the note of praise in a way that "introduces another prayer for help"[17] in the verses that follow.

At this point, it is important to recognize that the Masoretic form of the Psalter probably preserves two alternate traditions concerning the relationship between Pss 9 and 10: one where each of the two psalms was read as its own distinct poem, and one where the two psalms were read as a single unit.[18] Thus, for our purposes, it is worth considering both traditions. Following the former tradition, Pss 7, 8, and 9 parallel one another in several interesting respects, such that, when read together, Pss 7-9 form a coherent, balanced psalms grouping. Paralleling the discussion of enemies in the earlier parts of Pss 7 and 8, Psalm 9 only speaks of the enemies (אויב) in the beginning praise section (Ps 9:4, 7;

---

[14] Although, as noted in chapter two, the scene depicted in Ps 8:3 serves a paradigmatic function, and the use of a perfect verb here ought not to be interpreted narrowly as referring to a specific, past event.

[15] Miller, "The Beginning of the Psalter," 90; compare with Brennan, "Psalms 1-8," 28.

[16] Miller, "The Beginning of the Psalter," 90.

[17] Bellinger, "Reading from the Beginning," 120.

[18] On the one hand, Pss 9 and 10 are divided into two separate units, perhaps preserving a tradition that considered each psalm to be a discreet poem in its own right. On the other hand, read together, the two psalms form a somewhat imperfect acrostic, and Psalm 10 lacks a superscription—an anomalous situation in Pss 3-41, indicating that the two psalms together form one poem. See Gerald H. Wilson,*The Editing of the Hebrew Psalter*, (SBLDS 76; Chico, CA: Scholars, 1985), 135, 173-174.

Psalm 10 does not speak of the psalmist's enemies).[19] Furthermore, the description of YHWH's thwarting of the enemy in Ps 9:6-7 parallels that of Ps 8:3, although the fate of the wicked is more devastating in Psalm 9 than it is in Psalm 8:

להשבית אויב	האויב תמו
To silence the enemy	The enemy came to an end
Ps 8:3	Ps 9:7

Later in Ps 9:13—just before the psalmist turns to voice his petition—the concept of God's remembrance of and attention to humanity, which lies at the structural heart of Ps 8,[20] comes into view once again: Just as Ps 8:5 wonders at the fact that YHWH "remembers" (זכר) and "attends to" (פקד) the בן־אדם/אנוש, Ps 9:13 reassures the reader that YHWH will "remember" (זכר) and "not forget" (לא שכח) the plight of the afflicted. Furthermore, the description of hoped for deliverance in the latter part of Psalm 9 echoes that of Psalm 7.[21] Significantly, both psalms describe a divine reversal, wherein "the wicked is snared by his own devices" (Ps 9:17 // Ps 7:15-17). Once again, this reversal motif occurs for the first time in the Psalter in Pss 7 and 9.[22] Thus, just as Psalm 7 transitions from lament to praise in ways that anticipate the themes of Psalm 8, Psalm 9 transitions back from praise to lament in ways that recall the themes of both Psalm 7 and Psalm 8.

When one reads Pss 9 and 10 as a unit, the return to the lament theme of Psalm 7 is emphasized even more emphatically than it is in reading Pss 7-9 without Psalm 10. The close of Psalm 10 returns briefly to praise, with the affirmation that יהוה מלך, "YHWH is king/rules" (v. 16).[23] Thus, after an extensive outpouring of prayer for divine intervention in the midst of chaos, Psalm 10 assures the reader that YHWH will hear the prayers of Pss 7 and 9-10

---

[19] Ps 10:5 uses the word צורר, but there the word describes the foes of the wicked.
[20] In addition to the treatment of the thematic development of Psalm 8 in chapter two above, see J. Clinton McCann, *A Theological Introduction to the Book of Psalms: The Psalms as Torah* (Nashville, TN: Abingdon, 1993), 57-58, idem, "Psalms," in *The New Interpreter's Bible* (12 vols.; Nashville, TN: Abingdon, 1994-2004), 4:712, and Lund, "From the Mouths of Babes and Infants," 96-97.
[21] For a treatment of the various verbal and thematic connections between Psalm 7 and Pss 9-10, see Hossfeldt and Zenger, *Die Psalmen 1-50*, 82-83.
[22] These intertextual connections and thematic parallels make it likely that the tradition which considered Psalm 9 a poem in its own right was the starting point for the editorial linkage binding together Pss 7-9. However, the focus of this chapter is not the editorial process leading to the final form of the text, but the final form of the text itself.
[23] As will be discussed fully below, the declaration that יהוה מלך is common throughout the Psalter, but it is especially emphasized in Books IV-V. See Gerald H. Wilson, *Editing*, 214-228; Nancy DeClaissé-Walford, *Reading from the Beginning: The Shaping of the Hebrew Psalter* (Macon, GA: Mercer University Press, 1997), 73-91.

in order to maintain the created order of Psalm 8 by thwarting the enemies, because YHWH is king.

In sum, whichever tradition one follows, when one reads Pss 7-9 or Pss 7-10 together, one is able to discern a degree of thematic development that goes beyond the mere editorial juxtaposition of psalms that happen to share similar vocabulary. Read together, Pss 7-9/7-10 form a poetic triptych that moves from lament (Psalm 7) to hymn (Psalm 8) back to lament again (Psalm 9/ Pss 9-10).[24] Psalm 7 transitions from lament to praise in a way that anticipates Psalm 8's intertwined hymnic themes, and then Psalm 9/Pss 9-10 transitions from praise to petition in a way that echoes the themes already put forward in Pss 7 and 8. Two types of reversals run throughout, one at the center (the glorification of the seemingly insignificant, Ps 8:3, 5), and the other in the triptych's exterior panels (the demise of the wicked by their own devices, Pss 7:15-17; 9:17).

This reading yields some implications for the reciprocally interpretive influence between Psalm 8 and its immediate context. As the center of the triptych of Pss 7-9/10, Psalm 8 reminds the reader why she can expect God to intervene on her behalf: Because YHWH shows his name to be majestic in all the earth by maintaining the created order. Brennan summarizes the role that Psalm 8 plays in this context as follows:

> Psalm 8 can thus be interpreted as a brief outburst of jubilation . . . its reminiscences of the priestly account of creation make it clear to the reader that the struggle in which we are invited to participate [in the surrounding laments] is not one with limited national and geographical implications. Its goal is nothing less than the restoration of that cosmic order for which humanity was given responsibility by its creator.[25]

Furthermore, Psalm 8 reminds the reader that YHWH accomplishes the maintenance of the created order in a surprising way—he takes relatively insignificant human beings and uses them to thwart his enemies (v. 3b) and govern as God's vice-gerent over the rest of YHWH's subjects (vv. 7-9). Thus, when read in connection with Psalm 8, the reversals described in Pss 7:15-17 and 9:17 make sense as part of God's programmatic way of maintaining the created order—through a reversal that exalts the seemingly insignificant over and against the self-strong enemies of God.[26]

Conversely, Pss 7 and 9-10 inform how a reader encounters Psalm 8. Psalm 7:18b (ואזמרה שם־יהוה עליון) and Ps 9:3b (אזמרה שמך עליון) make clear to the reader that the ultimate focal point of YHWH's activity in Psalm 8 is the glorification of his name, not the glorification of the human for the human's sake. Moreover,

---

[24] For a full treatment of the semantic and thematic connections that Pss 9-10 share with the preceding psalms (esp. Pss 5, 7, and 8) and the following psalms, see Hossfeld and Zenger, *Die Psalmen I, 1-50*, 82-83.
[25] Brennan, "Psalms 1-8," 28.
[26] For a discussion of the "enemies" of Ps 8:3 as those who seek to claim strength in their own power while denying the name of YHWH, see Peter C. Craigie, *Psalms 1-50* (WBC 19; Waco, TX: Word Books, 1983), 107.

Pss 9 and 10 pick up the term אנוש (Ps 8:5),[27] but they use it to describe the enemies that YHWH militates against; thus, the reader of Psalm 8 is reminded that the glorified humans of Ps 8:5-9 can become the enemies of Ps 8:3 if they oppose king YHWH's rule (Ps 10:16-18). As Craigie says, the "position of strength" given to the human in Ps 8:5-9 "is not a natural human right (persons who think that it is are enemies), but something God-given."[28] Furthermore, reading Psalm 8 in the context of Pss 7:16-17 and 9:16-17 produces a level two canonical meaning for the scene described in Ps 8:3. In the context of Psalm 8, verse three declares *that* God effects a power reversal by using the mouths of infants to thwart his foes, but it does not describe *how* God does this. Pss 7 and 9 lead the reader to enact figurally such a reversal. First, the reader of Pss 7-9 prays to YHWH for deliverance (using her mouth; Pss 7:2-10 and 9:14-15). Then, the psalmist declares (and the reader affirms) that YHWH will hear the reader's prayer to effect a divine reversal by using the weapons of the wicked against the wicked themselves (Psalms 7:16-17 and 9:16-17). Thus, the insignificant (עוללים וינקים) pray with their mouths (מפי), and YHWH then neutralizes (השבית) the enemies (אויב ומתנקם) with their own weapons.[29]

Finally, a tension runs throughout the triptych which permeates the whole of the Psalter and, therefore, deserves special attention: the tension between the king and the common individual, between the royal "I" and the "I" of the reader. As Miller notes, Pss 7 and 9 imply a royal orientation by identifying the "enemies" as the עמים, "peoples" (Ps 7:9) and גוים, "nations" (Ps 9:17, 20).[30] On the other hand, as Miller says elsewhere of the Psalter as a whole: "The Psalms are by their *history* [and] . . . *content* not time bound,"[31] so that the common reader of Pss 7-10 may—indeed, ought to—pray these psalms as her own prayers, rather than to read them as the prayers of a king.[32] Furthermore, Ps 10:12 introduces another dynamic into the question of kingship by affirming that "YHWH is King!" Mays aptly describes the resulting dilemma for the interpretation of Psalm 8 in its context in the Psalter:

> The epithets of royalty (splendor, glory, honor) are used in the psalms for God, king, and humanity to indicate royal identity. The Davidic king is

---

[27] Löhr, "Psalm 7 9 10," 226.

[28] Craigie, *Psalms 1-50*, 107.

[29] For a discussion of the description of mouths as weapons and sources of strength in the OT, see Øystein Lund, "From the Mouths of Babes and Infants you have Established Strength," 78-99.

[30] Miller, "The Beginning of the Psalter," 90. The Davidic association in the superscriptions of Pss 7-10 is strengthened by the now obscure reference to an event in the life of David in Ps 7:1. Furthermore, while the meaning of the term עלמות לבן in Ps 9:1 is disputed, some translate this phrase to read "upon the death of a son," possibly implying an intended historical reference point from the life of David for Pss 9-10, as well (so NIV). See Willem A. VanGemeren, *Psalms* (EBC 5; Grand Rapids: Zondervan), 144-145.

[31] Miller, *Interpreting the Psalms*, 22-23, emphasis original.

[32] See Brennan, "Psalms 1-8," 28-29.

given dominion over the nations; humankind, over living creatures . . . The two are side by side in the Psalter. How is their relation to be understood? The theory of "democratization" suggests that the office was transferred to all people when there was no longer a king in Israel. That does not do justice to the prominence of the anointed king in the Psalter.[33]

Psalm 8, rather than favoring one of these three royal identities (YHWH, humanity, or Davidic king), uses language that could be amenable to all three. Psalm 8 makes it clear that YHWH maintains his created order by effecting a divine reversal by means of human agents, and describes these human agents in royal terms, allowing for one to affirm both that "YHWH is king" and that "humanity is king." Furthermore, as I have already pointed out in Chapter Two, Psalm 8 says nothing about human-to-human relationships and politics.[34] To appreciate fully the way in which Psalm 8 and the Psalter deals with the tension implied by speaking of three different types of royalty, we must consider Psalm 8's role within the context of the rest of the Psalter.

2. Psalm 8 in the Context of Psalms 1-14

Turning to the broader context surrounding Pss 7-10, the shape of the Psalter contains several clues indicating that Psalm 8 has a special role. Psalms 7 and 9-10 each conclude and introduce, respectively, a series of laments of the individual (Pss 3-7 and 9-14).[35] So, on the one hand, the surrounding songs of lament ground the idealized imagery of Psalm 8 in the chaotic reality of a beleaguered world, "suggest[ing] a crucial interpretive question . . . : What is the coherence between a weak, needy, suffering humankind and a humanity 'crowned . . . with glory and honor' (Psalm 8:5)?"[36] On the other hand, Psalm 8 offers hope to the one who prays through the otherwise lament-dominated collection of Pss 3-14. As the reader asks God to intervene in a disordered world, she encounters in Psalm 8 a beacon of hope and order in the midst of threatening chaos.[37]

Preceding Pss 3-14, Pss 1 (a wisdom psalm) and 2 (a royal psalm) together serve an introductory function, both for Book I, and for the entire Psalter.[38]

---

[33] Mays, *Psalms*, 67.
[34] Psalm 8 does, however, situate king YHWH's human vice-gerents in a hierarchical context, leaving open the possibility that, within human-to-human political relations, God might choose to govern in a hierarchical fashion, utilizing an individual human to rule other humans as king.
[35] See Bellinger, "Reading from the Beginning," 120.
[36] McCann, *Great Psalms of the Bible* (Louisville, KY: Westminster/John Knox, 2009), 18.
[37] See Miller, "The Beginning of the Psalter," 89.
[38] Wilson (*Editing*, 204-209) and Brevard S. Childs (*Introduction to the Old Testament as Scripture* [Philadelphia, PA: Fortress, 1979], 513-514) both regarded Psalm 1 alone as the introduction to the Psalter and Psalm 2 as the introduction to Book I of the Psalter. Recent commentators, however, have largely regarded Pss 1 and 2 as together

Thus, as Bellinger notes, when one reads the Psalter "from the beginning," there is a "primacy effect" wherein Pss 1 and 2 together set the framework for the way in which the reader is to understand all that follows.³⁹ When Psalm 8 is read in connection with both Pss 1 and 2 and the prayers of petition that surround it in Pss 2-7 and 9-14, the עוללים/יונקים and בן־אדם/אנוש of Psalm 8 become part of the same story as the various other characters of Pss 1-14. The insignificant ones glorified by YHWH and used by him to thwart his enemies (Ps 8:3, 5) identify to a certain extent with others who delight in the Torah and seek godly counsel (Psalm 1), submit to king YHWH and "kiss" his anointed (Psalm 2), and look to YHWH to act on their behalf in the midst of tribulation (Pss 3-7, 9-14).⁴⁰

Yet it would be unwise simply to conflate all of these several characters in Pss 1-14, without recognizing the diverse identities involved. The introductory nature of Pss 1 and 2 combined with the strategic place of Psalm 8 increases the tension between the royal "I" and the "I" of the common reader already present in Pss 7-9. To quote Miller,

> Psalm 8 . . . contribut[es] to the need to read the two subjects of Psalms 1 and 2 in lively tension with each other to the extent that they identify the voices and subjects of the psalms that follow them. For in Psalm 8, we encounter one of the clearest collections of royal motifs outside the explicitly royal psalms. But there, the royal figure is not a specific king or ruler . . . The *'îš* of Psalm 1 is as much a ruler as the ruler of Psalm 2 is an *'îš*.⁴¹

Looking at the canonical shape of the Psalter from a slightly different point of view, Matthias Millard's careful work offers further insight into the role that Psalm 8 plays in the beginning section of the Psalter.⁴² Building upon the work of Claus Westermann, who identified a movement from lament to praise across the entirety of the Psalter,⁴³ Millard divided the Psalter into smaller *Komposi-*

---

introducing the Psalter (Bellinger, "Reading from the Beginning," 119; Miller, "The Beginning of the Psalter," 84-85; Jerome F. D. Creach, *The Destiny of the Righteous in the Psalms* [St. Louis, MO: Chalice, 2008], 55-59). For a helpful summary of the views regarding the historical and literary relationship between Pss 1 and 2 and their role in introducing the psalms that follow, see deClaissé-Walford, *Reading from the Beginning*, 38-41.

³⁹ Bellinger, "Reading from the Beginning," 115, 119-120. Bellinger's title, which enjoins us to "read" the Psalter "from the beginning," is taken from DeClaissé-Walford, *Reading from the Beginning*.

⁴⁰ Jerome F. D. Creach first brought this reading to my attention by personal correspondence.

⁴¹ Patrick Miller, "The Beginning of the Psalter," in *The Shape and Shaping of the Psalter*, 92.

⁴² Matthias Millard, *Die Komposition des Psalters* (*FAT* 9; Tübingen: Mohr Siebeck, 1994).

⁴³ Claus Westermann, *Praise and Lament in the Psalms*, Keith R. Crim and Richard N. Soulen, trans. (Atlanta GA: John Knox, 1981), 250-258.

tionsbögen, identifying Pss 1-10 as the first *Kompositionsbogen*.[44] According to Millard, each *Kompositionsbogen* moves through several stages, as follows: an introduction (containing a wisdom psalm, a royal psalm and sometimes a song of thanksgiving), *Kern* I (containing lament psalms), the centerpiece (containing an oracle and/or a wisdom psalm), *Kern* II (containing a hymn and sometimes a song of thanksgiving), and a conclusion (containing royal, lament, and wisdom psalms).[45] Within the *Kompositionsbogen* of Pss 1-10, Millard identifies Psalm 8 as the centerpiece, perhaps functioning as an oracle.[46]

While Millard's work is not without its problems,[47] several insights about the shape of the Psalter emerge from his and Westermann's work that elucidate the interpretive implications arising from Psalm 8's position within the first section of the Psalter: 1) A discernible movement from lament to praise runs across the entire Psalter.[48] 2) A movement from lament to praise also seems to take place within smaller groupings of psalms, so that those who pray the words of the psalmists "journey" from lament to praise. 3) As the first hymn of praise following the first series of lament psalms, Psalm 8 represents the first instance where the reader's lamentation turns to praise.

Thus, if one reads the entire Psalter, "from the beginning," as deClaissé-Walford and Bellinger have enjoined,[49] Psalm 8's place within the first part of the Psalter gives it a special relevance for the entire Psalter. As "the first hymn of praise in the Psalter,"[50] Psalm 8 shapes how one reads both Pss 1-14 and the rest of the Psalter. When the reader, with the psalmists, once again expresses

---

[44] Millard, *Die Komposition des Psalters*, 127-135.
[45] Ibid. 162-168.
[46] Millard, *Die Komposition des Psalters*, 127-135, 162-163, 168.
[47] Millard's claim that Pss 1-10 functioned as a post-exilic liturgy is not impossible, but it is far from certain, and an over-emphasis on a theoretically reconstructed historical context such as the one that Millard posits could lead one away from a consideration of the text itself, which is the focus of a canonical exegesis. Furthermore, the way in which Millard envisions the structure of the *Kompositionsbogen* of Pss 1-10 is problematic, particularly in his treatment of Pss 9 and 10. He draws on both of them to serve several functions within his schema, with 9 functioning as a thanksgiving psalm, a wisdom psalm (together with 10) and a lament psalm, while 10 functions as a wisdom psalm (with psalm 9) and a concluding lament. This confusion gives the reader the impression that his decision to demarcate the end of the first *Kompositionsbogen* after Psalm 10 is forced and arbitrary, determined as much by a presupposed schematic form as by a close reading of the text itself. See Millard, *Die Komposition des Psalters*, 26, 127-135, 162-163. For a balanced critique of the problems inherent in Millard's approach, see Patrick Miller, review of Matthias Millard *Die Komposition des Psalters: Ein Formgeschichtlicher Ansatz*, *JBL* 116 (1997), 539-541.
[48] Westermann, *Praise and Lament in the Psalms*, 257-258. For further evidence of this movement from lament to praise, see J. Clinton McCann, "Books I-III and the Editorial Purpose of the Hebrew Psalter," in *The Shape and Shaping of the Psalter*, 96-98.
[49] DeClaissé-Walford, *Reading from the Beginning*, and Bellinger, "Reading from the Beginning."
[50] Mays, *Psalms*, 65.

her anguish and suffering and asks for divine intervention in the individual laments of Pss 9-14, she will remember Psalm 8's depiction of creation, and in this she will have hope. This initial journey in Pss 1-14 and Psalm 8's role in that journey will, in turn, strongly influence the way in which the reader understands both the rest of Book I and the whole of the Psalter.

It is possible to outline the contents of Pss 1-14, then, as follows: Psalms 1, 2, and 8, as psalms of orientation, offer a framework of hope, while Pss 3-7 and 9-14 lead the reader through an honest articulation of anguish in a world "characterized by violent opposition."[51] Various characters and themes appear throughout: the wise person (Psalm 1), the king (Psalm 2), the afflicted and needy (Pss 3-7; 9-14), the עוללים/יונקים and the אנוש/בן־אדם (Psalm 8:3, 5, both exalted through a divine reversal), and the sundry enemies. All of these characters become part of the same drama, yet tension emerges from the close association of various royal figures and the juxtaposition of psalms of orientation and psalms of disorientation. As the reader prays through Pss 1-14, she journeys with the various characters, from the introductory orienting framework of Pss 1-2, through lament (Pss 3-7), to praise (Psalm 8), and back to lament (Pss 9-14), feeling all of the tension. This initial journey, with Psalm 8 occupying a key role, will shape the reader's understanding as he continues his journey through the rest of the Psalter. Therefore, I now turn to consider Psalm 8 in the context of Book I.

3. Psalm 8 in the Context of Book One of the Psalter

Book I of the Psalter contains many indicators of structure and development, and a good deal of literature has already been written on the subject.[52] In what follows, I will attempt to outline Book I's structure by surveying three structural markers: 1) the Psalms at the "seams"—or at the beginning and end of Book I, 2) the major psalms groupings in Book I, and 3) the location of acrostic poems in Book I. After surveying the data, I will proffer an outline of Book I of the Psalter for heuristic purposes, and then I will summarize the internal movement of Book I and Psalm 8's place within that movement.

Concerning the psalms at the seams of Book I, I have already briefly discussed the introductory nature of Pss 1 and 2. At the end of Book I, G. H.

---

[51] McCann, *Great Psalms of the Bible*, 18.
[52] For a brief survey of recent research on the shape of Book I of the Psalter, see Bellinger, "Reading from the Beginning," 116-119. Also, see Peter Enns, *Poetry and Wisdom* (IBRB 3; Grand Rapids, MI: Baker, 1997), 135-138 for a brief bibliography of works on the macro-structure of the Psalter. Also, see deClaissé-Walford, *Reading from the Beginning*, 1-14 for a summary of two of the major approaches (the canonical approach of Childs and the canon-critical approach of Sanders) to discerning the Psalter's shape.

Wilson and others consider Psalm 41 to have a special function.⁵³ Wilson recognizes that, while the king is not explicitly identified in the psalm, Psalm 41 echoes the kingly concerns of Psalm 2 and has strong affinities with Psalm 72, the explicitly royal psalm that concludes Book II.⁵⁴ As Creach notes, Psalm 41 describes as "blessed" one who carries out traditionally royal duties, and "Psalm 41 is . . . like the psalms at the beginning of the Psalter in that it seems to identify the king as the model of righteousness."⁵⁵ Thus, "Book 1 ends just as the Psalter began."⁵⁶ It is fitting, then, to see Psalm 41—which begins with the key word that brackets Pss 1 and 2 (אשרי, Ps 1:1; 2:11)⁵⁷—as forming an envelope with Pss 1-2 around Book I.⁵⁸ By looking back to Pss 1 and 2, Psalm 41 does two things: 1) It brings the reader back to the twin themes of torah wisdom and God's provision for his anointed, highlighting these themes as important to an understanding of Book I. 2) As a transitional psalm that leads into Book II, it sets the tone for what follows, highlighting the themes that introduced the Psalter in Pss 1 and 2 as important for understanding Pss 43-150.

Between the "seams," W. H. Bellinger helpfully identifies four groupings of psalms in the body of Book I, as follows: 1) Psalms 3-14, discussed above.⁵⁹ 2) Pss 15-24, which, like the rest of Book I, contains many prayers of petition, yet constitutes a "distinct part of the first book" in that, as several scholars acknowledge, it is arranged chiastically with "a creation psalm of praise centered upon torah" at the climax.⁶⁰ 3) Psalms 25-34, a psalms grouping that is characterized by a "hopeful" and "positive tone."⁶¹ 4) Psalms 35-41, where "prayer again dominates, and enemies are ever-present," yet "God's protecting

---

⁵³ Wilson, *Editing*, 209-211; Miller, "The Beginning of the Psalter," 88; McCann, "Books I-III and the Editorial Purpose of the Hebrew Psalter," 94; Creach, *Destiny of the Righteous*, 61-63.
⁵⁴ Wilson, *Editing,* 209-210. Although, see idem, "The Use of Royal Psalms at the 'Seams' of the Hebrew Psalter," *JSOT* 35 [1986]: 87-88, where Wilson modifies his view, claiming that Psalm 41 ought not to be understood in royal terms.
⁵⁵ Creach, *Destiny of the Righteous*, 61.
⁵⁶ Ibid.
⁵⁷ DeClaisse-Walford, *Reading from the Beginning*, 55.
⁵⁸ Some readers may object to this reading, believing that this violates the majority view that sees Pss 1-2 as together introducing the Psatler, not Book I. I, however, contend that Pss 1-2 serve a dual introductory function: introducing Book I and the Psalter. Introductions frequently function in this way, so that, for example, Genesis 1 serves an introductory role for the primeval history of Gen 1-11, the whole of Genesis, and the whole of the Torah. Or, again, the first stanza of Sir Walter Scott's *The Lady of the Lake*, which bears affinities with Pss 1-2 in that its lack of enumeration sets it off from the Canto First (just as Pss 1 and 2 have no superscription), though Scott includes it as part of Canto First, so that it introduces both the first canto and the entire poem.
⁵⁹ Bellinger, "Reading from the Beginning," 120.
⁶⁰ Bellinger, "Reading from the Beginning," 120-121. Compare with Millard, *Die Komposition des Psalters*, 25; Miller, "the Beginning of the Psalter," 86.
⁶¹ Bellinger, "Reading from the Beginning," 122.

presence," is ever-present as well.⁶² The only modification that I would offer to Bellinger's survey is to treat Psalm 41 as the conclusion of Book I.⁶³

The meaningful arrangement of Book I becomes more evident when one considers these four major psalms groupings in connection with the location of the acrostic poems in Book I. Building on the work of David N. Freedman,⁶⁴ Les Maloney argues that the four acrostic psalms in Book I have certain affinities indicating that their placement in the Psalter is significant.⁶⁵ The acrostic Pss 25 and 34 exhibit stylistic and metrical similarities that set them apart as "a distinctive, in fact unique, pair."⁶⁶ These two psalms introduce and conclude Book I's third psalm grouping, Pss 25-34. Psalms 9-10 and 37 also exhibit stylistic similarities, such that "Ps 9/10 and Ps 37 serve as bookend songs to the . . . alphabetic acrostics" in Book I.⁶⁷ These two psalms are situated towards the middle of the first and final psalms groupings that Bellinger identifies. Some readers, however, might not find these observations compelling enough to warrant identifying Book I's acrostic psalms as structural markers, legitimately asking whether or not these affinities are actually due to intentional editorial activity. Nevertheless, taking note of the location of the acrostic psalms within Book I can serve as a helpful tool for the present purposes; the purpose of this structural survey is to adumbrate heuristically Book I's thematic development, not to draw conclusions about the intention of the editor(s) of the Psalter.

By way of synthesis, then, the psalms at the seams, the psalms groupings, and the acrostic poems can be brought together to adumbrate an outline of Book I as follows:

---

⁶² Ibid.

⁶³ Even this slight alteration is of less consequence than it might appear at first blush. In the first place, just as Pss 1 and 2 serve a dual introductory function, Psalm 41 concludes *both* the preceding collection of Pss 35-41 and Book I. In the second place, as I say below, the purpose of this survey of formal indicators of the structure of Book I is to adumbrate heuristically the thematic development of Book I of the Psalter, not to draw dogmatic conclusions about the intention of the editor(s) of the Psalter.

⁶⁴ David N. Freedman with Jeffrey C. Geoghegan and Andrew Welch, *Psalm 119: The Exaltation of Torah* (BJS 6; Winona Lake, IN: Eisenbrauns, 1999), 1-23.

⁶⁵ Les D. Maloney, "Intertextual Links: Part of the Poetic Artistry within the Book I Acrostic Psalms," *RQ* 49 (2007): 11-21; idem *A Word Fitly Spoken: Poetic Artistry in the First Four Acrostics of the Hebrew Psalter* (Ph.D. diss., Baylor University, 2007).

⁶⁶ Freedman, *Psalm 119*, 9. Freedman points out, for example, that "Psalms 25 and 34 have single line units [and] . . . a bicolon for each [acrostic] letter" (2), and that Pss 25 and 34 share some "deliberate deviations" from established acrostic patterns, in that "[b]oth psalms omit the *waw* line or bicolon, and both psalms add a second *peh* line after the *taw* line that normally would end the poem" (9). See also Maloney, "Intertextual Links," 11-12 n. 3 and 18 n. 24.

⁶⁷ Maloney, "Intertextual Links," 21, c.f. Freedman, *Psalm 119*, 13-19, wherein Freedman delineates remarkable structural similarities between Ps 9/10 and 37.

Introduction/Seam: Psalms 1-2: The way of wisdom and the anointed king.
   A. Psalms 3-14: Lament dominates.
       Acrostic A (Pss 9-10) embedded.
   B. Psalms 15-24: Framed by temple liturgy (Pss 15, 24) and
       centered on Torah (Ps 19).
   B'. Psalms 25-34: Framed by wisdom acrostics B and B' (Psalms
       25, 34). Hopeful tone.
   A'. Psalms 35-40: Lament dominates.
       Acrostic A' (Psalm 37) embedded.
Conclusion/Seam: Psalm 41: The wise way of the anointed king.[68]

Thus, Book I of the Psalter, begins and ends with the twin themes of the way of wisdom and the wise anointed king, with the sovereign LORD overseeing both. The body of the book, although dominated by lament songs,[69] oscillates between praise and lament, orientation and disorientation, assurance and agony, so that hope undergirds the afflicted and gives them strength to voice their complaints to God. The oscillation continues throughout, but there is a general movement as follows: The book begins dominated by lament, with Psalm 8 serving as an isolated island of hope (A), but the theme of lament begins to lessen via a temple pilgrimage and meditation on Torah (B). Then, joy and praise briefly come to the fore (B'), until the distressing realities of life once again dominate the rest of the body of the book (A').

What role does Psalm 8, the first hymn of praise in this lament dominated book, play? The way in which Psalm 37 thematically and structurally recalls Pss 9-10 is instructive here. Psalm 37, a didactic poem contrasting the fate of the wicked with the fate of the righteous,[70] is the last orientation psalm in Book I and is followed by prayers of petition. Thus, the location of Psalm 37 at the end of Book I mirrors the location of Psalm 8 at the beginning of Book I. Furthermore, Maloney points out several intertextual resonances between Psalm 37 and its fellow "bookend" acrostic poem, Pss 9-10.[71] Among these, Ps 37:14-15's recapitulation of the "theme of ironic divine reversal" (// Ps 9:16-17) is noteworthy.[72] As Maloney points out, aside from one brief, suggestive prayer in Ps 5:11, Ps 37:14-15 contains the only appearance of the motif of the demise of the

---

[68] The reader should bear in mind that these groupings outlined above are not discrete units, each block in isolation from what precedes and follows.
[69] See Westermann, *Praise and Lament in the Psalms*, 257, and Bellinger, *Psalms: Reading and Studying the Book of Praises*, 45. Bellinger identifies 22 individual and two communal lament songs in Book I of the Psalter.
[70] See Hans-Joachim Kraus, *Psalms 1-59*, 404.
[71] Maloney, "Intertextual Links," 14-17.
[72] Maloney, "Intertextual Links," 16. In Ps 37:14, the wicked draw (lit. "open") their swords (חרב פתחו), but in Ps 37:15, they are stabbed by those very same swords (תבוא בלם חרבם).

wicked by means of their own instruments in Book I of the Psalter outside of Psalm 7 and Psalm 9.[73]

Thus, one who reads "from the beginning," upon coming to Ps 37:15 may recall the reversals in Pss 7-10. There, the prayers of the afflicted, represented by the mouths of the infants, are answered; God brings the weapons of the wicked down upon the wicked themselves, effecting a reversal that sustains the created order. Psalm 8 promises just such a reversal, providing the central moment of hope in Pss 7-10. The other points of intertextual resonance and structural similarity shared by Pss 9-10 and 37 that Maloney and Freedman identify[74] increase the likelihood that a careful reader of Ps 37:14-15 would recall the complex of reversals in Pss 7-10. Thus, the hope stated in Pss 7-10 (especially in Psalm 8) is part of the orienting hope sustaining the petitioner as she prays the prayers of disorientation that Psalm 37 introduces (Pss 37-40). Finally, Psalm 41, which does not fully abandon the tone of lament, reminds the reader of the hope for the righteous (Ps 41:11-12//Ps 1) and of the royal figure "who considers the poor" (Ps 41:1//Ps 2), providing hope that God will hear and reinstate the order that Psalm 8 describes.[75]

I do not suggest here that every informed reader of Pss 37-41 would immediately think of Pss 7-10 in a conscious fashion. Yet, the opportunity for an attentive reader to hear the resonance is there, and it is one of many points throughout the Psalter which create the possibility of the recollection of Psalm 8. Within the canonical exegesis that this book proposes, such resonances would not only shape the way in which a reader reads the text, but they would also influence the prayers of the reader, leading the reader into an encounter with the divine *res* to whom the Scriptures point, the triune God whom Christians confess. Thus the primacy effect ensures that Psalm 8, as the first hymn of the Psalter, casts a long shadow across Book I; even towards the end of the book, Psalm 8's promise that YHWH will maintain the created order by acting on behalf of the seemingly insignificant is shaping the reader and her encounter with the rest of the Psalter.

One more element of the theology of Book I demands acknowledgement before moving on to consider the Psalter as a whole. Across Book I, the tension between the royal "I" and the "I" of the common reader persists. On the one hand, quoting Wilson,

> If Book One is viewed as an independent unit bounded by Pss 2 [or, in the view of this author, Pss 1*and* 2] and 41, the resulting effect is a very Davidic group of pss in which the proclamation of YHWH's special covenant with his king in Ps 2 is matched by David's assurance of God's continued preservation in the presence of YHWH.[76]

---

[73] Ibid.
[74] Maloney, "Intertextual Links," 14-18; Freedman, *Psalm 119*, 13-19.
[75] See also Creach, *The Destiny of the Righteous*, 61-62.
[76] Wilson, *Editing,* 210. For an alternative view, see Bellinger, who concludes that "I do not find the royal dimension so structurally important in Book I" ("Reading from the Beginning," 124).

On the other hand, each individual psalm in this book that is dominated by prayers of the individual is "by [its] content not time bound,"⁷⁷ and is intentionally adaptable to the situation of any individual. Further, the plight of the poor (עני, as in Ps 10:2) and weak (דל, as in Ps 9:18) is very much central to Book I. Such language may be implicitly associated with a young anointed David on the lam, or a king outnumbered by his foes, but the most obvious referent to whom the "poor" and "needy" point is the common afflicted person, to the extent that she is, or, at least, ought to be, "righteous."⁷⁸ Once again, this tension has special significance for Psalm 8, which applies royal language to the human race. Rather than proposing a trite harmonization at this point, the next section will move on to consider Psalm 8 within the context of the entire Psalter, paying special attention to the way in which the entire Psalter handles the tension between the various types of royalty, namely the divine king, the corporate king, and the Davidic king.

4. Psalm 8 in the Context of the Entire Psalter

4.1 An Overview of the Shape of the Psalter

Before proceeding to look specifically at Psalm 8 within the context of the Psalter, it is necessary to adumbrate the shape and themes of the Psalter, first by identifying the formal indicators of shape running across the Psalter already recognized by scholars in recent years, and then by utilizing the canon-exegetical principles put forth in this study to interpret those indicators of shape. In his seminal work *The Editing of the Hebrew Psalter*, G. H. Wilson identifies several indicators of shape in the Psalter.⁷⁹ Following Childs and taking his cues from some Qumran manuscripts, Wilson identifies Psalm 1 as an introduction to the Psalter as a whole.⁸⁰ Noting significant differences between Books I-III and

---

⁷⁷ Miller, *Interpreting the Psalms*, 22-23.
⁷⁸ Bellinger correctly notes that "ritual prayers are spoken out loud or 'sung' in public; therefore, people accused in the prayers are often present, able to overhear them or at least to hear about them" ("Reading from the Beginning," 123). Even the "enemies" who hear the prayer, however, are enjoined to repent and become "righteous" and, thus, identify with the "poor" and "needy" whom they are oppressing.
⁷⁹ Wilson, *Editing*. DeClaissé-Walford (*Reading from the Beginning*), McCann (*A Theological Introduction to the Book of Psalms*), and Miller ("The Beginning of the Psalter") largely accept Wilson's view. Wilson's detractors include Norman Whybray (*Reading the Psalms as a Book* [JSOTSup 222; Sheffield UK: Sheffield Academic, 1996]), and M. A. Vincent ("The Shape of the Psalter: An Eschatological Dimension?" in *New Heaven and New Earth: Prophecy and the New Millenium, Essays in Honour of Anthony Gelston* [P. J. Harland and C. T. R. Hayward, eds.; VTSup 77; Leiden: Brill, 1999], 61-82).
⁸⁰ Wilson, *Editing*, 204-207. See also Childs, *Introduction to the Old Testament*, 513-514.

Books IV-V,[81] he argues that the former emphasizes the Davidic king, and the latter emphasizes the kingship of YHWH.[82] In subsequent works, Wilson elaborates by demonstrating that royal psalms and wisdom psalms had been placed strategically throughout the Psalter.[83] Many scholars accept Wilson's identification of the various indicators of the Psalter's structure as correct,[84] with the only significant modification being that most scholars now see Pss 1 and 2 both as introductory, whereas Wilson sees Psalm 1 alone as the Psalter's introduction.[85] Nevertheless, there is not a universally accepted scholarly consensus concerning how these markers ought to be interpreted.[86]

For his part, Wilson concludes from the data that Psalm 1 places the Psalter's emphasis upon "meditation rather than cultic performance," and the importance of Torah obedience rather than hope in the Davidic king.[87] Books I-III, with the strategic placing of Ps 89, describe "a [Davidic] covenant remembered, but a covenant *failed*."[88] Books IV-V, then, replace hope in the Davidic king with Torah obedience and trust in king YHWH.[89] According to Wilson, the juxtaposition of the wisdom Psalm 1 with the royal Psalm 2, combined with the strategic placement of other wisdom psalms at the seams and alongside royal psalms, serves to integrate editorially Books I-III and IV-V into a single volume. In its final form, then, the "Psalter counters continuing concern for the restoration of the Davidic dynasty and kingdom with the wise counsel to seek refuge in a kingdom 'not of this world'—the eternal kingdom in which YHWH alone is king."[90] A shift from a focus on the individual and lament to a focus on the community and praise accompanies the movement from an emphasis upon king David to an emphasis upon king YHWH.[91] Thus, says Wilson, the final form of the Psalter responds to the crisis of exile and the failure of the monarchy.[92]

---

[81] Wilson, *Editing*, 207-208; idem "The Shape of the Book of Psalms" *Int* 46 [1992]: 129-142.
[82] Wilson, *Editing*, 209-228.
[83] Gerald H. Wilson, "Royal Psalms," 85-94; idem, "The Shape of the Book of Psalms," 133-134; idem, "Shaping the Psalter: a Consideration of Editorial Linkage in the Book of Psalms," in *The Shape and Shaping of the Psalter*," 72-82.
[84] Most of the works that Enns lists in his bibliography on the Psalter's macrostructure (*Poetry and Wisdom*, 135-138), accept the bulk of the data as put forth by Wilson, even if they do not agree with Wilson's interpretation of the data. For a critical survey of the secondary literature on the Psalter's structure, see Whybray, *Reading the Psalms*, 15-35.
[85] See deClaissé-Walford, *Reading from the Beginning*, 37-47.
[86] Whybray, *Reading the Psalms*, 31-35, highlights some of the major differences of opinion among scholars concerning the significance of the final form of the Psalter.
[87] Wilson, *Editing*, 204-207.
[88] Wilson, *Editing*, 213.
[89] Wilson, *Editing*, 214-228.
[90] Wilson, "Shaping the Psalter," 81.
[91] Wilson, "The Shape of the Book of Psalms," 138-139.
[92] Wilson, "The Shape of the Book of Psalms," 139; see also McCann, "Books I-III and the Editorial Purpose of the Hebrew Psalter," 98-99; deClaissé-Walford, *Reading from the Beginning*, 21-31.

DeClaissé-Walford, McCann, and others largely agree with Wilson's interpretation of the Psalter's structure.[93]

Other scholars, however, call for some modifications to Wilson's view.[94] Most significantly, several scholars convincingly and correctly argue "that the Psalter does not, in the end, speak of the 'failure' and 'rejection' of the Davidic Covenant."[95] First of all, Wilson's initial assessment was influenced largely by his conclusion that Psalm 1, a wisdom psalm, introduced the Psalter, and Psalm 2, a royal psalm, introduced Book I—resulting in a Wisdom frame for the entire Psalter that muted the Davidic frame around Book I. Since it is more likely that Pss 1-2 form a dual introduction to the entire book,[96] Psalm 2's positive assessment of the Davidic hope presents itself as an integral part of the overall message of the entire Psalter, not just of Book I.[97] Thus, as Howard points out,

> [t]he juxtaposition of wisdom and royal psalms noted by Wilson (e.g., Psalms 1 and 2, 72 and 73, 89 and 90, 144 and 145) can just as easily be seen as the Psalter's *affirmation* of both traditions, rather than the subordination or negation of one of them.[98]

---

[93] See, deClaissé-Walford, *Reading from the Beginning,* McCann, *A Theological Introduction to the Book of Psalms: The Psalms as Torah.* As already noted, however, both deClaissé-Walford and McCann see Pss 1 and 2 together, not just Psalm 1, as introducing the Psalter.

[94] Whybray notes six "disputed matters" among scholars seeking to discern the editorial message of the final form of the Psalter (*Reading the Psalms,* 31-32). Many of those areas of disagreement, however, are not of pressing concern for a canonical exegesis. So, persisting disagreement and/or uncertainty concerning whether the Psalter was intended for personal or corporate use (Whybray's "disputed matters" number 1 and number 2), or concerning the "identify of the final compilers of the Psalter" ("disputed matter" 3) are of some interest to a canonical exegesis, but they are not the most pressing concerns. This is because a canonical exegesis focuses primarily upon the final form of the text and its divine author, not the editors responsible for the final form or the original community's use of the final form.

[95] David M. Howard, Jr., *The Structure of Psalms 93-100* (BJS 5; Winona Lake, IN: Eisenbrauns, 1997), 201-207. Others express concerns about Wilson's overstatement of the demise of the Davidic covenant in the final form of the Psalter, including Jamie A. Grant ("The Psalms and the King," in *Interpreting the Psalms: Issues and Approaches,* David Firth and Philip S. Johnston, eds. [Downer's Grove, IL: IVP Academic, 2005], 108-109; *The King as Exemplar: The Function of Deuteronomy's Kingship Law in the Shaping of the Book of Psalms* [AB 17; Atlanta, GA: SBL, 2004]) and David C. Mitchell (*The Message of the Psalter: An Eschatological Programme in the Book of Psalms* [JSOTSup 267; Sheffield, UK: Sheffield Academic, 1997], 243-271). Vincent allows for the possibility of seeing a general trend that indicates a failure of the Davidic monarchy, but expresses some concern about seeing this as the final editorial word on the matter ("The Shape of the Psalter" 61-82).

[96] As already noted, most scholars today agree that Pss 1 and 2 are better understood as together forming the introduction to the Psalter. See DeClaissé-Walford, *Reading from the Beginning,* 38-41.

[97] Howard, *The Structure of Psalms 93-100,* 202-205.

[98] Howard, *The Structure of Psalms 93-100,* 203, emphasis original.

Moreover, while YHWH's kingship does come to the fore in the latter part of the Psalter, focus on the Davidic covenant "does not completely disappear, (see, for example, Psalms 132, 144)"[99] and "Royalist/Zion" motifs are evident in Book IV of the Psalter.[100] As Grant points out, Wilson's contention that "David no longer reigns—Yahweh does! . . . does not seem to give full voice to the royal emphases which are found in Books IV and V."[101]

At this point, the present study must address two salient questions: 1) If the formal indicators of structure do not signal a complete rejection of the Davidic covenant, how ought a canonical exegesis to go about interpreting them? 2) What implications do these structural markers have for a canonical exegesis of Psalm 8? Concerning the first question, a canonical approach seeks to read the constituent parts of the Bible as reciprocally interpretive. While Psalm 8 may elucidate other psalms and passages of Scripture, and vice-versa, each passage of Scripture must retain its own distinct voice; one part of the canon cannot negate or override another part of the canon. When reading different voices within the canon in light of one another, as Childs says in another context, "the Christian interpreter [ought], first of all, [to] commit himself only to hearing both witnesses as clearly as possible, but then in relation to one another."[102]

Applying this to the Psalter, in contrast with other biblical books (such as Isaiah, for example), the final form of the MT 150 text preserves the 150 Psalms of the Psalter as distinct units, and a canonical exegesis ought to attempt to respect the integrity of each unit. So, for example, the juxtaposition of Pss 1 and 2 ought not to lead one to conclude that either psalm overrides the other. Thus, a canonical exegesis ought not to minimize the role of the משיח in Psalm 2 by insisting that he is not really a royal figure, but merely an exemplar of Psalm 1's wisdom piety, so that "wisdom has had the last word."[103] Neither ought a canonical exegesis to reverse the priority, with Psalm 2 overriding Psalm 1, such that "[t]he principal focus of Psalm 1 when read in concert with Psalm 2 is not Torah nor wisdom, but rather [Psalm 2's] individual of kingly and military trappings."[104] Thus, the various wisdom-royal pairings throughout the book ought to be read in concert and, perhaps, tension, without allowing one tradition to negate the other. Similarly, a canonical exegesis ought to respect the integrity of both orientation psalms and disorientation psalms,[105] even if they seem to contradict one another.

Even within individual psalms or poems, an oscillation between lament and praise is common. The psalmist's claim in Ps 10:1-2 that YHWH "stands far away" and "the wicked hotly pursue the poor" stands in tension with, but does

---

[99] Howard, *The Structure of Psalms 93-100*, 205.
[100] Howard, *The Structure of Psalms 93-100*, 205-207.
[101] Grant, "The Psalms and the King," 108.
[102] Brevard S. Childs, *Biblical Theology in Crisis* (Philadelphia: Westminster, 1974), 159.
[103] Wilson, "The Shaping of the Psalter," 81.
[104] Robert Cole, "An Integrated Reading of Psalms 1 and 2," *JSOT* 98 (2002): 75.
[105] Brueggemann, *The Message of the Psalms*. Once again, I do not here unqualifiedly endorse Brueggemann's schema for understanding various types of psalms.

not negate, the claim in Ps 9:6-7 that "the enemy came to an end" and "YHWH sits enthroned forever." The psalmists' ability to voice despair and then, soon thereafter, confess hope within a single psalm has implications for the various tensions found in the Psalter. For example, Psalm 89 reminds YHWH of his promise towards David that "I will establish his offspring forever and his throne as the days of the heavens" (v. 29) and then contends with YHWH that "now you have cast off and rejected . . . you have defiled [David's] crown in the earth" (vv. 38-39). The two claims remain in tension, and the latter admission of disillusionment does not negate the former reminder of YHWH's promise.

Moreover, tension between any two themes in the final form of the Psalter exists precisely because the final form of the Psalter preserves both of those themes.[106] Thus, a canonical exegesis ought not to insist on false alternatives, forcing the interpreter to choose between wisdom and royal motifs, or between King YHWH, King David, and King אדם. On the one hand, insofar as the king of the royal psalms is the royal exemplar of wisdom, royal psalms and wisdom psalms can be read as complementing one another. On the other hand, the entire role of the figure of the Davidic king in the Psalter cannot be reduced simply to his function as a wise exemplar; royal and wisdom psalms must each retain their integrity and distinctiveness within the collection. Similarly, on the one hand it is true that Books IV-V shift the reader's primary focus towards king YHWH. Yet, on the other hand, the preservation of the royal psalms leaves the possibility open that "since God is king his promises will yet be fulfilled,"[107] and the Davidic monarch might yet be restored to function as YHWH's vice-gerent to assist in YHWH's rule.

4.2 Psalm 8 and the Shape of the Psalter

What, then, is the mutually reciprocal influence between Psalm 8 and the rest of the Psalter, in light of the above survey of the Psalter's themes and shape? To address this question, the following will utilize some psalms in Book V of the Psalter as entry points through which Psalm 8 may come into dialogue with the latter part of the Psalter. Psalm 144 exhibits certain affinities with Psalm 8 that are worth noting. While Psalm 8 is the first hymn of the Psalter, Psalm 144 is the last lament of the Psalter. Also, whereas Psalm 8 introduces the concept of the corporate royalty of humanity for the first time in the Psalter, Psalm 144 is the last royal psalm of the Psalter and contains the last reference to the Davidic covenant in the Psalter. Psalm 144 also uses language similar to that found in Psalm 8 in several places,[108] most prominently when the psalmist

---

[106] Those who maintain that the editors of the Psalter wished to portray the Davidic Covenant as an abject failure must explain why those editors did not expurgate the positive Davidic elements that are still so prominent in Books I-III.
[107] Vincent, "The Shape of the Psalter," 77.
[108] Other points of resonance include a shared concern about enemies (Ps 144:7-8, 10-11//Ps 8:3), descriptions of the enemies using their "mouth" as weapons (Ps 144:11//Ps 8:3), and claims that YHWH subdues people "under me" (Ps 144:2//Ps 8:5).

asks: "Oh YHWH, what is the human, that you take knowledge of him? Or the child of humanity, that you think of him?" (Ps 144:3).[109] All of these factors, together, make Psalm 144 a suitable entry-point through which to consider how the continuing resonance of Psalm 8 would influence a reader's understanding of the latter part of the Psalter.

Another commonality shared by Pss 8 and 144 is the fact that they both introduce acrostic psalms, Pss 9-10 and 145, respectively. Les Maloney argues that these two acrostic poems, as the first and last acrostic psalms in the Psalter, seem to serve a "bookending" function.[110] Thus, Pss 9-10 and 145 form the first ("א") and the last ("ת") of the Psalter's acrostic poems which sum up "the memory and praise of YHWH as sovereign from א to ת."[111] Interestingly, the Psalter contains eight acrostic poems all together: four in Book I and four in Book V. Thus, Psalm 145's function as the last of four acrostic psalms placed throughout Book V mirrors Pss 9-10's function as the first of four acrostic psalms placed throughout Book I.[112] Furthermore, the acrostic genre is a genre associated with wisdom, making Pss 9-10 and 145 worth considering as places where the tension between wisdom and royalty might be addressed.

Once again, the present survey need not demonstrate that Maloney's observations prove intentional editorial activity in the placement of the acrostic psalms, nor does it need to demonstrate that the editor(s) of the Psalter intentionally placed Psalm 144 at the end of the Psalter to serve as a mirror for Psalm 8 at the beginning; the goal here is not to uncover the aims of the human editor who compiled the text. Rather, the present study asks how a canonically informed reader might read Psalm 8 in light of the rest of the Psalter. Independent of the question of editorial intention, the final form of the Psalter contains affinities between Pss 8 and 144 and affinities between Pss 9-10 and 145. These affinities, combined with the respective locations of Pss 8-10 and 144-145 within the Psalter, make Pss 8-10 and Pss 144-145 convenient points for considering the thematic shape of the Psalter, and bringing Pss 144-145 into dialogue with Pss 8-10 should yield insight into how one might read Psalm 8 in light of the rest of the Psalter and vice versa.

Briefly, then, one must first hear the discrete witness of Pss 144-145 "as clearly as possible,"[113] before fruitful dialogue with Pss 8-10 is possible. Psalm 144 is a prayer for David and for the community that asks for God to deliver the king (Ps 144:3-11) and then to bless the community (Ps 144:12-15).[114] Psalm

---

[109] Mays, *Psalms* 68; Childs, "Psalm 8 in the Context of the Christian Canon," *Int* 23 [1969]: 29.
[110] Maloney also contends that the two Psalms share "two juxtaposed roots," הלל and ברך, though he does not explain how these roots are "juxtaposed" in these two psalms ("Intertextual Links," 16).
[111] DeClaissé-Walford, *Reading from the Beginning*, 99.
[112] Maloney, "Intertextual Links."
[113] Brevard S. Childs, *Biblical Theology in Crisis* (Philadelphia: Westminster, 1974), 159.
[114] The two sections of Psalm 144, vv. 1-11 and vv. 12-15, are so markedly distinct as to lead Leslie C. Allen to conclude that "vv 12-15 [are] puzzling . . . in relation to vv 1-

145 is a hymn that then turns to praise YHWH. Intertwined with promises that the individual (Ps 145:1-2, 21), the community (Ps 145:4-7), and creation (Ps 145:10-12) will praise YHWH are declarations of the greatness of YHWH (Ps 145:3, 8-9, 13-20). "The LORD's kingship" and "the LORD's covenant fidelity" are of special interest to Psalm 145.[115]

In their immediate context, the preceding psalms (Pss 138-143) are part of the last Davidic collection in the Psalter, which Pss 144 and 145 conclude. This Davidic collection moves from thanksgiving (Psalm 138) and wisdom (Psalm 139), to individual lamentation (Pss 140-143). Then come Pss 144-145, which, as the last two Davidic psalms, are of special import for an understanding of the overall message of the Psalter concerning the Davidic Covenant. The *hallel* psalms that follow constitute the conclusion of the Psalter (Pss 146-150). Thus, Psalm 145 serves the dual function of concluding the preceding collection of Davidic psalms while at the same time serving, as a hymn, as a transition into the series of hymns that follows (Pss 146-150).

Thus, Pss 144-145 round out the body of the Psalter and introduce the concluding hymns of praise. Psalm 144 picks up the Psalter's meditations on the beleaguered Davidic line by using language strikingly similar to that of Psalm 18 in a way that "chang[es] the perspective from a royal thanksgiving [Psalm 18] to a royal lament [Psalm 144],"[116] while still affirming that God "gives victory to kings" and "rescues David his servant from the cruel sword"(Ps 144:10). This affirmation leads to a prayer for the king's deliverance (verse 11) and the concluding prayer for the blessing of the nation (verses 12-15). Ps 144:12-15's benediction gives way to an outpouring of praise (Psalm 145) that in turn paves the way for the Psalter's conclusion (Pss 146-150).[117]

We can now turn to "hearing both witnesses" of Pss 8-10 and of Pss 144-145 "in relation to one another."[118] First of all, the function of Pss 8-10 is somewhat symmetrical with that of Pss 144-145. The former finds its place just after the beginning of the Psalter, and the latter just before the ending. While Pss 8 and 9-10 connect king אדם with the acrostic genre "used by wisdom writers," Pss 144 and 145—the last two Davidic Psalms—connect king David with the acrostic genre.[119] As a hymnic meditation on YHWH's glorification by means of all humans, Psalm 8 foreshadows the emphasis in Books IV-V upon praise and the community. Symmetrically, Psalm 144 recalls the emphases of Books I-III by carrying forward a tone of lament while at the same time

---

11," *Psalms 101-150* (WBC 21; Nashville: Thomas Nelson, 2002), 361. Yet, once brought together into a single poem, "the canonical unity reveals the need for God to act (a royal lament vv. 1-11) and the resultant blessings of his actions (a psalm of blessing, vv. 12-15), VanGemeren, *Psalms*, 982.
[115] VanGemeren *Psalms*, 987.
[116] Allen, *Psalms 101-150*, 361.
[117] For the function of Pss 146-150 as together concluding the Psalter, see Wilson, *Editing*, 193-194, 226-228 and deClaissé-Walford, *Reading from the Beginning*, 99-103.
[118] Brevard S. Childs, *Biblical Theology in Crisis* (Philadelphia: Westminster, 1974), 159.
[119] DeClaissé-Walford, *Reading from the Beginning,* 99.

reaffirming YHWH's commitment to "David his servant" (v. 10). Psalms 9-10 transition from the hymnic praise of Psalm 8 back to the tone of lament that dominates Book I, while still anticipating Books IV-V by stating in its conclusion that יהוה מלך עולם ועד ("YHWH is king forever and ever," Ps 10:16). Conversely, Psalm 145 transitions from the royal lamentation of Psalm 144 to hymnic praise, while implicitly recalling the prayers of lamentation that have preceded in the Psalter by reassuring the reader that YHWH hears and will act on behalf of "all who are falling" (Ps 145:14).

Thus, the positioning of Pss 8 and 9-10 *vis à vis* Pss 144 and 145 create the strong possibility that one who "reads the Psalter from the beginning" will read the latter psalms in light of the former. As noted above, the reader's initial encounter with Psalm 8 as an isolated beacon of hope and as "the first hymn of praise in the Psalter"[120] gives the reader reason to look for hope and the restoration of order through divine reversal, even in the midst of chaos, as she prays through the rest of the book of Psalms. A reader of Psalm 144 so influenced by reading Psalm 8 may hope and expect that, even though the human king and the community are beset by enemies, YHWH will act on behalf of his king and nation. Psalm 8 would also temper the resulting Davidic hope that Ps 144:10 evokes by reminding the reader that YHWH uses corporate humanity (Ps 8:5), not just the Davidic king, to effect reversals and bring about order. The fact that Pss 8 and 144 each directly precede acrostic poems with wisdom motifs could reinforce this tempering of the Davidic hope by reminding the reader of Pss 144-145 that, just as the ideal Davidic king is to function as YHWH's vice-gerent through wisdom and Torah piety, so also is corporate humanity to function as YHWH's vice-gerent through wisdom and Torah piety.[121]

Furthermore, all human hope, be it in Ps 144's king David or Ps 8's corporate humanity, is tempered by the fact that Ps 8:5 and Ps 144:3 both ask, in similar terms "what is the human child," that YHWH should give it this royal status? King YHWH, not any human, is the one deserving of attention. Finally, the symmetrical positioning of Pss 8 and 144 reminds the reader to hold all of the themes that run throughout the Psalter in constant tension, in the Psalter as in life. Even in the midst of chaos, Psalm 8 promises hope, and, even as the Psalter

---

[120] Mays, *Psalms*, 65.

[121] One may ask, then, why I prefer not to describe this tempering as "democratizing" (*contra*, for example, Grant, *The King as Exemplar*, 280-289). I prefer to avoid this terminology for two reasons: 1) I agree with Mays that this language "does not do justice to the prominence of the anointed king in the Psalter" (Mays, *Psalms*, 67). As I have insisted throughout, the Davidic King is not rejected by the final form of the Psalter. 2) On a related note, the term "democratizing" has a political meaning (though, often, those who apply it to Psalm 8 do not seem to have that meaning primarily in mind), which I believe Psalm 8 does not support, as I have argued above.

is moving towards its exultant conclusion of overflowing praise, Psalm 144 confesses that chaos still exists (esp. Ps 144:4, 7-8).[122]

In summary, then, using Psalm 144 as a point of entry through which to consider the hermeneutical influence of Psalm 8 upon the Psalter provides us with a window through which to examine how Psalm 8 might shape a reader's understanding of other parts of the Psalter, and vice-versa. Yet, Psalm 144 is just one psalm. Therefore, the following section will conclude this chapter by briefly summarizing the thematic development of the entire Psalter as surveyed above, focusing on how this thematic development informs a canonical exegesis of Psalm 8.

5. Summary

As noted above, the Psalter begins with a dual introduction focusing the reader's attention upon meditation and Torah observance (Psalm 1), the Davidic king (Psalm 2), the contrast between the fate of the righteous and the fate of the wicked, and the sovereignty of YHWH (Pss 1 and 2) all as central themes of the Psalter. These psalms exert a primacy effect as the reader prays through the individual laments that follow in the next cluster of Psalms (Pss 3-14) and later throughout the Psalter. Thus, when the reader comes to Psalm 8, the insignificant babies and human ruler of the psalm cohere with the righteous characters of Pss 1-7, 9-14, and the enemy and avenger in Ps 8:3 is parallel with the wicked who will perish (Pss 1 and 2) and the enemies who oppress (Pss 3-7, 9-14). As the first hymn in the Psalter, Psalm 8 itself exerts an influence upon the way in which one reads the laments of the rest of the Psalter, most of which are to be found in the first three books. Thus, as the Psalter oscillates between lament and praise, with the latter increasing and the former fading into the background, the reader's constant expectation is that YHWH will intervene into a disordered world to take insignificant humans and use them to neutralize his enemies.

In addition to the shift from lament to praise, there is another shift, from an emphasis on the Davidic king in Books I-III to an emphasis on king YHWH in Books IV-V. The decisive break comes at Psalm 89:38 where the psalmist cries out "But now you have cast off and rejected; you are full of wrath against your anointed!" Nevertheless, the human king does not completely disappear, and, in fact, reappears in Psalm 144 at a pivotal point in the Psalter. Furthermore, reading Psalm 144 and other royal Psalms in light of Psalm 8 tempers, but does not negate Davidic hope. Read in light of Psalm 8, the Davidic covenant is another opportunity for YHWH to intervene on behalf of the insignificant to effect a reversal over and against his enemies and maintain the created order. It is, therefore, overstating the shift to describe the Davidic covenant as "failed" and "rejected." Moreover, from the perspective of a post-exilic reader living

---

[122] Once again, I do not intend to imply that all readers of Psalm 144 would consciously think of Psalm 8 in this way. Nevertheless, it is possible to read Psalm 8 and Psalm 144 in light of one another, and in so doing to generate some level 2 canonical meanings.

under the boot of Greek and then Roman rule,[123] what more surprising, and yet longed for, reversal could there be than for YHWH to somehow once again intervene on behalf of David and reestablish a Davidic reign? Psalm 8 reminds the reader that it is his responsibility not to seek to use human strength to bring about a new Davidic regime, but rather to identify with the weak and humble, the "babies and sucklings," and to allow YHWH to somehow establish strength from their weak, prayerful mouths.

Yet, there is a shift in emphasis from Books I-III to IV-V, reminding the reader of Psalm 8 and the Psalter that, in the final analysis, it is the reign of king YHWH which the Psalter puts at the center of an ordered cosmos, and all other rule within that hierarchy is subject to his rule. To say "YHWH reigns" is to affirm that: 1) YHWH rules, with or without a Davidic king on the throne, and 2) YHWH is capable of acting on behalf of the Davidic covenant when and how he sees fit. This shift is accompanied by another shift from lament to praise, which points the reader to expect God to effect divine reversal and maintain the created order, as described in Psalm 8, and, indeed, even to look for ways in which God is now already maintaining order.

6. Encountering the res and engendering caritas.

This brief adumbration of the flow of the Psalter and the place of Psalm 8 within that flow is not intended to be merely an abstract investigation into the life and beliefs of an ancient and far off religious sect. I proffer here a canonical reading for today's Church in Augustinian fashion, as one situated within the hermeneutical circle who seeks an encounter with God that produces love. In this light, the shape of the Psalter becomes a tool for shaping the belief and worship of today's Church. As those in the community of faith today apprentice themselves individually and corporately to the model of worship and prayer presented in the Psalter, an encounter with the divine can occur. Those praying the psalms move away from lamenting, with the psalmists, the brokenness of their own context and towards praising YHWH and celebrating his deliverance; they experience a shift from a focus upon earthly polity (represented by King David) to a focus upon the divine rule of King YHWH. Through both shifts, honest expressions of pain that are rooted in the inescapable realities of life become the first step on a journey towards praise and hope. Psalm 8 and its reversal motif plays a prominent role in the process, as today's readers see in the hymn's reversal motif both a) reason for lament, as they see how far their world falls short of the ideal created order, and b) reason for praise and hope, as they remember that God continues to maintain that order through the exaltation of the humble.

---

[123] For a brief, helpful survey of the historical situation of Second Temple Judaism in which the final form of the Psalter took shape, see deClassé-Walford, *Reading from the Beginning*, 106-112.

The many ways in which reading the Psalter in this way engenders love for God and neighbor in today's believing community are beyond the scope of this brief study. As today's Church finds points of contact and identification between the various situations and people (both protagonistic and antagonistic) described across the Psalter, and as those identifications are further enriched and informed by Psalm 8 and its reversal motif, love will result. Significantly, the Christian reader will find many points of identification between Jesus the Messiah and the ideal figures of the Psalter (including the ideal wise person in Psalm 1, the ideal anointed person in Psalm 2, and the ideal human ruler in Psalm 8), engendering love for Christ and his Church.

Yet a full exploration of these points of identification and other implications for reading Psalm 8 and the Psalter in the believing community today must be taken up later in the study. Indeed, the Psalter does not provide neat and tidy resolutions to the many tensions that permeate the book of Psalms and permeate life. YHWH is effecting order, yet there is still chaos. YHWH reigns, yet he uses human rulers. Thus, with James L. Mays, one may ask of the themes that give rise to these tensions "[h]ow is their relation to be understood? . . . Is the question only taken up in the New Testament?" [124] In order to address Mays's question, I now turn to consider Psalm 8 in light of the entire Christian canon, beginning with other Old Testament passages that might serve to elucidate a canonical exegesis of Psalm 8.

---

[124] Mays, *Psalms*, 67. Mays is speaking specifically here of the relationship between the various royal figures in the Psalter.

4

PSALM 8 AND THE OLD TESTAMENT

This chapter will move beyond the immediate literary context of Psalm 8 (the Psalter) to consider the canonical relationship between Psalm 8 and other Old Testament passages. If the present study is to yield a reading that is canonical, insightful, and relevant, it must seek to bring Psalm 8 into meaningful dialogue with the voluminous material that constitutes the Old Testament canon.[1] Due to the massive amount of material available for consideration, this chapter must exercise special care in selecting texts to serve as such entry points. Thus, this chapter will focus upon texts that are especially well suited to bring Psalm 8 into dialogue with the rest of the Tanakh by examining the relationship between three texts that exhibit a high degree of semantic and thematic affinity with Psalm 8: Gen 1:1-2:3, Job 7:17-18, and Ps 144:3-4; I will argue below that all three of these texts either allude to Psalm 8 (Job 7 and Psalm 144) or underlie Psalm 8 (Genesis 1).[2] Taken together, these texts are uniquely qualified to serve as entry points by which Psalm 8 can come into dialogue with the broad sweep of Old Testament literature in two significant ways:

1) Insofar as the various texts exhibit awareness of Psalm 8 (or vice versa) they represent an inner-biblical dialogue concerning the central themes of Psalm 8—God's glory, the created order, and humanity's place within that created order. Some of these points of contact seem to represent clear instances of inner-biblical exegesis as defined by Michael Fishbane running in one direction or the other; that is, the text under consideration reflects upon Psalm 8 (or vice versa) in such a way as to constitute a part of "the canonical corpus['s] . . . vast range of annotations, adaptations, and comments on earlier traditions."[3]

---

[1] The reader should bear in mind, however, that the canonical approach does not amount to a scientific method that dictates which passages are to be considered. Thus, there is not only one legitimate method that one might employ to bring any given text into dialogue with the rest of the canon.

[2] For connections between Genesis 1 and Psalm 8, see Franz Lothar Hossfeld and Erich Zenger, *Die Psalmen I, 1-50* (DNEB 29; Würzburg: Echter Verlag, 1993), 77, 80, and Peter C. Craigie, *Psalms 1-50* (WBC 19; Waco, TX: Word Books, 1983), 106. See also Ute Neumann-Gorsolke, *Herrschen in den Grenzen der Schöpfung: Ein Beitrag zur Alttestamentlichen Anthropologie am Beispiel von Psalm 8, Genesis 1 und verwandten Texten* (WMANT 101; Göttingen: Universität Göttingen, 2004).

[3] Michael Fishbane, "Inner-Biblical Exegesis," in *Hebrew Bible/Old Testament: The History of its Interpretation I/1: Antiquity* (ed. Magna Sæbø, Göttingen: Vandenhoek und

Yet, even if some readers do not find the arguments for the historical dependence between Psalm 8 and these other texts compelling, the semantic and thematic affinities between the texts are strong enough to open up a venue where the canonically minded reader can find level two canonical meanings by bringing the various texts into dialogue with each other; they allow the reader to consider how different canonical texts utilize language that overlaps with Psalm 8 to reconsider themes taken up in Psalm 8 in new contexts and in new ways.[4]

2) Each of these three texts provides a bridge between Psalm 8 and other sections of the Tanakh. Genesis 1 serves as a point of contact linking Psalm 8 with the Torah and with a creation theology that runs throughout the Tanakh. By asking the same question posed in Ps 8:5 in a new context, Job 7 and Psalm 144 bring the idealized view of the world reflected in Genesis 1 and Psalm 8 into dialogue with a more disordered and chaotic view of the world. Furthermore, Job 7 serves as an entry point between Psalm 8 and other wisdom literature and the rest of the Writings. Similarly, Psalm 144 bridges the gap between the Psalter and the Nevi'im by addressing the Davidic covenant and YHWH's promise to maintain it, which is a theme that runs throughout much of the Former Prophets and the Latter Prophets.

The following will examine each of these texts in three stages: 1) In order to hear the distinct voice of each witness "as clearly as possible,"[5] the first stage will summarize the level one message of each passage by reading the passage "in itself."[6] 2) Next, the question of the nature of the literary dependence between the text under consideration and Psalm 8 will be addressed. 3) Finally, the various witnesses will be considered "in relation to one another," focusing upon the level two question of how Psalm 8 might be read in light of the other passages.[7] This chapter will conclude by synthesizing the findings to articulate a canonical exegesis of Psalm 8 that reads the psalm in light of the entire OT

Ruprecht, 1996), 35. See also *idem, Biblical Interpretation in Ancient Israel* (Oxford: Clarendon, 1985). On points of contact and divergence between Childs and Fishbane, see Daniel R. Driver, *Brevard Childs, Biblical Theologian: For the Church's One Bible* (Grand Rapids, MI: Baker Academic, 2012), 182-184.
[4] Put another way, I will argue that Genesis 1, Job 7, and Psalm 144 all belong to the first category of entry points discussed in chapter two (texts exhibiting affinities resulting from direct or indirect dependence). Nevertheless, even if these texts did not exhibit direct dependence, they would still be of interest as entry points for a canonical exegesis because all three passages certainly belong to the second category listed in chapter two (passages that aid in dealing with an exegetical problem growing out of Psalm 8 and have semantic similarities with Psalm 8).
[5] Brevard S. Childs, *Biblical Theology in Crisis* (Philadelphia: Westminster, 1974), 159.
[6] Here I am following the example of R. W. L. Moberly, a practitioner of canonical exegesis, in first reading a text "in itself" before bringing it into dialogue with other interpretive contexts, and, like Moberly, am putting the phrase "in itself" in "scare quotes . . . to indicate that the notion of reading a text 'in itself' is less straightforward than it sounds." R. W. L. Moberly, *The Theology of the Book of Genesis* (OTT; New York: Cambridge University Press, 2009), 43 n. 2.
[7] Childs, *Biblical Theology in Crisis*, 159.

canon. The next section begins, then, by considering Psalm 8 in light of the first creation account in Gen 1:1-2:3 (or simply, "Genesis 1").[8]

1. The First Creation Account and Psalm 8

1.1 Reading Genesis 1:1-2:3 "In Itself"

"Genesis 1," writes Bill T. Arnold, "has been studied, debated, and expounded as much as any text in world history."[9] The following treatment, therefore, will only lightly touch on the issues pertaining to a level one reading of Genesis 1. After briefly addressing the state of the field regarding the historical origins of the first creation account, I will adumbrate the literary structure of Gen 1:1-2:3.[10] Concerning the current state of scholarship on the first creation account, there is something of a critical consensus in Pentateuchal scholarship which views the first creation account as representing a literary unit that, unlike the second creation account (Gen 2:4[b]-24), originates from a "Priestly" writer or source (P).[11] Yet, it would be misleading to characterize the question of the origins of Genesis 1 as a settled matter. Wellhausen's Documentary Hypothesis has fallen into disfavor, and no universally accepted model

---

[8] Although the first creation account technically runs from Gen 1:1-2:3 (or 2:4a, depending upon whether one connects Gen 2:4a with what precedes it or with what follows it), throughout this chapter the following terms are used interchangeably: Genesis 1, Genesis 1:1-2:3, the first creation account, and (acknowledging the traditional nomenclature, without positing any judgment as to the validity of the nomenclature) the priestly creation account.
[9] *Genesis* (NCBC; New York: Cambridge, 2009), 29.
[10] Many commentators, on the basis of the identification of the תולדות formula as part of P, read Gen 2:4a in connection with the first creation account, so that the entire account runs from Gen 1:1 to Gen 2:4a (Claus Westermann, *Genesis 1-11, A Commentary* [John J. Scullion, trans.; Minneapolis: Augsburg, 1984], 12,14, 76-78 and E. A. Speiser, *Genesis* [AB C1; New York: Doubleday, 1963], 3-13, and John E. Hartley, *Genesis* [NIBC 1; Grand Rapids: Hendrickson, 2000], 51, 55). Victor Hamilton, however, notes that Gen 2:4a makes more sense as an introduction to Gen 2:4-25 for the following reasons. 1) All of the other occurrences of the תולדות formula introduce what follows. 2) The ancient translations construe Gen 2:4a as part of the following verses, rather than the preceding verses. 3) The "X תולדות" formula introduces a recitation of the progeny of X, not an account of the origin of X; while the first creation account recounts the origin of the "heavens and the earth," the second creation account speaks of the things which the heavens and the earth produce (*The Book of Genesis Chapters 1-17* [NICOT 1; Grand Rapids: Eerdmans, 1990], 4-5). Thus, I agree with Childs that Gen 2:4 "serves as a superscription to the account which follows" while at the same time serving to "connect the creation of the world [Gen 1:1-2:3] with the history which follows" (*Introduction to the Old Testament as Scripture* [Philadelphia: Fortress, 1979]; see also *idem, The New Testament as Canon: An Introduction* (Philadelphia: Fortress, 1984], 145-146).
[11] For a summary of the state of the field in the early 1990's, see Joseph Blenkinsopp, *The Pentateuch: An Introduction to the First Five Books of the Bible* (ABRL; New York: Doubleday, 1992), 26.

has replaced it.¹² Instead, there is now broad disagreement concerning the nature and origin of "P,"¹³ and the other sources of the Pentateuch have been called into question.¹⁴ Furthermore, some conservative scholars continue to argue that Moses is primarily responsible for the shape and contents of the book of Genesis.¹⁵ Finally, an increasing number of scholars are treating Genesis as a literary unity and attending to the question of the role that Genesis 1 plays in the final form of the book of Genesis, without placing their primary focus upon the question of the historical origins of the passage, and at times using "canonical" language similar to the canonical exegesis employed here.¹⁶

The present book fits most comfortably with this last type of scholarship for several reasons. First, if one turns to the final form of the text itself to find some explicit explanation of the origins of the text, one is bound for disappointment; there is no more mention of Mosaic authorship within the text itself than there is of authorship by an anonymous Priestly writer. More significantly, as many recent works have recognized, when one reads Genesis and the Torah as a whole, one discovers a high degree of artistry working towards a satisfying unity.¹⁷ This artistry and unity is of most interest to a hermeneutic that takes as its starting point the canonical form of the text.

---

¹² For a thorough critique of the documentary hypothesis, see Roger N. Whybray, *The Making of the Pentateuch: A Methodological Study* (Sheffield, UK: JSOT Press, 1987). For a helpful treatment of recent trends in Pentateuchal scholarship outlining the demise of the documentary hypothesis and attempts to forge a new model for the origins of the Torah, see Gordon J. Wenham, "Pondering the Pentateuch: The Search for a New Paradigm" in *The Face of Old Testament Studies: A Survey of Contemporary Approaches* (ed. David W. Baker and Bill T. Arnold; Grand Rapids MI: Baker, 2004), 116-144.

¹³ While several scholars argue for a later date for P than the exilic date posited by the documentary hypothesis (John Van Seters, *Abraham in History and Tradition* [New Haven, CT: Yale University Press, 1975; idem, *Prologue to History: The Yahwist as Historian in Genesis* [Louisville, KY: Westminster/John Knox, 1992]), other scholars have argued that P is earlier than the documentary hypothesis had claimed (Gordon J. Wenham, *Genesis 1-15* (WBC 1; Waco, TX: Word, 1982; idem "Pondering the Pentateuch," 142-144).

¹⁴ Already in 1991, Blenkinsopp notes that, among the four sources originally posited by the documentary hypothesis, only P has "stood up . . . to scrutiny" (*Pentateuch*, 26). See also Wenham, "Pondering the Pentateuch."

¹⁵ Duane Garrett, *Rethinking Genesis* (Grand Rapids: Baker, 1991), John H. Sailhammer, *The Meaning of the Pentateuch: Revelation, Composition, and Interpretation* (Downers Grove, IL: IVP Academic, 2009).

¹⁶ David J. A. Clines, *Theme of the Pentateuch* (JSOTSup 10; Sheffield UK: Sheffield Academic Press, 1997), Moberly, *The Theology of the Book of Genesis*, Walter Brueggemann, *Genesis: A Bible Commentary for Teaching and Preaching* (Interpretation; Atlanta, GA: John Knox, 1982), and Thomas W. Mann, *The Book of the Torah: The Narrative Integrity of the Pentateuch* (Atlanta, GA: John Knox, 1988).

¹⁷ In addition to the readings of Genesis as a whole presented by Clines (*Theme of the Pentateuch*) and Mann (*The Book of the Torah*) see Gordon J. Wenham's "The Coherence of the Flood Narrative," (*VT* 28[1978]: 336-348) for one example of a reading

A related question that is relevant to our study of Psalm 8 pertains to how this creation account relates to other ancient Near Eastern stories of creation. Scholars have often been concerned with investigating the nature of the relationship between Genesis 1 and Babylonian and Egyptian mythology.[18] In a monograph written before launching his canon-exegetical program, Childs examined the relationship between myth and what he called "the Old Testament's categories of reality" wherein Genesis 1 received special attention (especially verses 1 and 2).[19] While the following treatment will pay attention to the ancient Near Eastern context as it may have been understood by the readers of Genesis 1 (and Psalm 8), it will not posit a genealogical relationship between the account of Genesis and similar ancient Near Eastern creation myths for several good reasons.

While the view that Gen 1:1-2:4 was dependent upon the Babylonian *Enuma Elish* once held hegemony,[20] this consensus has been erased in light of a) differences between the two stories; b) the awareness that *Enuma Elish* is just one of several Babylonian creation accounts; c) affinities between Genesis 1 and Egyptian creation accounts; and other factors, and a new consensus is not forthcoming.[21] As Westermann concludes, "Gen 1 must be seen in the context of a number of creation stories."[22] Furthermore, as Wenham rightly notes, "Gen 1 is a deliberate statement of [the] Hebrew view of creation over against rival views. It is not merely a demythologization of oriental creation myths, whether Babylonian or Egyptian; rather it is a polemical repudiation of such myths."[23] Paying attention to the final form of Genesis 1 as it is now, then, enables the reader to perceive with clarity the distinctive theology of the Hebrew Bible.

Turning to the literary structure, Gen 1:1-2:3 exhibit a formalized surface structure organized around the seven days of creation organized into a "three days plus three days plus one day" arrangement; days one through three and days four through six each form two parallel panels, with Gen 1:1-2 serving as a brief introduction, and day seven rounding off the passage.[24] This surface structure drives the passage's narrative development; God forms the תהו ("formless," verse 2) world, on days 1-3, fills the בהו ("void," verse 2) world on

---

of a text as a unity that is arguably more compelling than the fragmentary readings posited by the Documentary Hypothesis.

[18] See, for example, Speiser, *Genesis*, 9-10; Westermann, *Genesis 1-11*, 127; Brevard S. Childs, *Myth and Reality in the Old Testament* (SBT 27; London: SCM, 1960), 31-43.
[19] Childs, *Myth and Reality*, 31-43.
[20] This view is argued for by Speiser, *Genesis*, 9-10.
[21] See Wenham, *Genesis 1-15*, 8-9, Westermann, *Genesis 1-11*, 80-81.
[22] Westermann, *Genesis 1-11*, 81.
[23] Wenham, *Genesis 1-15*, 9.
[24] David W. Cotter, *Genesis* (Berit Olam; Collegeville MN: Liturgical, 2003) 11; Westermann, *Genesis 1-11*, 88-90. For a thorough examination of the structure of MT Genesis 1 in comparison with the structure of the LXX Genesis 1, see William P. Brown, *Structure, Role, and Ideology in the Hebrew and Greek Texts of Genesis 1:1-2:3* (SBLDS 132; Atlanta, GA: Scholars, 1993).

days 4-6 (though the filling actually begins on day 3b), and rests on day 7.[25] Yet the contents of the two main units (days 1-3 and 4-6) do not parallel each other perfectly;[26] as Wenham points out, days one, two, and four focus on one pole, the "heavens" (אור "light," Gen 1:3, רקיע "expanse," Gen 1:6, and בריקע מארת "lights in the expanse," Gen 1:14), while days three, five, and six deal with the "earth" (plants, Gen 1:11, sea and air creatures, Gen 1:20, and land creatures, Gen 1:24).[27] Also, the plants of day three have clear affinities with the חיה/חיים נפש ("living things/living creatures") of days 5-6, all of which are to reproduce and פרה ("produce fruit").

Neumann-Gorsolke has set forth an alternative two-paneled schema, grouping days 1-4 together as describing the "Grundgegebenheiten der Welt" and days 5-6 together as describing the "Bevölkerung der Weltbereiche."[28] Yet, Neumann-Gorsolke's new arrangement creates as many problems as it solves; her schema still leaves many organizational questions unresolved, and it ignores the parallelism evident between days one and four, two and five, and three and six. It is better, therefore, to understand the apparent aberrations as a result of themes interweaving between the two main units of the passage. Thus, rather than destroying the two panels, these interweaving themes strengthen the integrity of the section as a unit by tying them together like a lace woven through two pieces of material. Read in this way, the first panel anticipates the second, while the second panel recalls the first. The thematic overlap between the panels is the strongest between days three and four, at the point of transition from panel one to panel two.[29] In summary, then, the complex surface structure of Gen 1:1-2:3 is as shown in figure 1.[30]

---

[25] See Wenham, *Gensis 1-15*, 7; Bruce K. Waltke with Kathi J. Fredricks, *Genesis: A Commentary* (Grand Rapids MI: Zondervan, 2001), 57.
[26] Brown points out that the two part triadic structure is more clearly developed in the LXX version of Gen 1:1-2:3 than in the MT Hebrew edition. Nevertheless, Brown overstates the case severely when he concludes that "the MT of Gen 1:1-2:3 exhibits both an inconsistent formal structure and an unclear thematic organization" (*Structure*, 31).
[27] Wenham, *Genesis 1-15*, 7.
[28] Neumann-Gorsolke, *Herrschen*, 154.
[29] Furthermore, day three actually inaugurates the "filling" that pertains to days four through six, as the earth תדשא ("brings forth") and the vegetation flourishes. So also the "forming" of days 1-3 is incomplete until the sun, moon, and stars make concrete the demarcation of day and night in day 4.
[30] For a brief explanation of the ways in which the seventh creation day in Gen 2:2-3 is distinct from the first six creation days, see Westermann, *Genesis 1-11*, 167-169. For the way in which Gen 2:2-3 parallels Gen 1:1 and forms a fitting conclusion to the entire passage, see Wenham, *Genesis 1-15*, 7, 34-35.

	Introduction (1:1, 2)		
Day 1 (1:3-5)	Light (Inorganic/Heavenly)	Day 4 (1:4-19)	Heavenly Bodies/Lights (*Inorganic/Heavenly*)
Day 2 (1:6-8)	Expanse(Inorganic/Heavenly) Sky (Inorganic/Heavenly) Seas (Inorganic/*Earthly*)	Day 5 (1:20-23)	Birds and Fish (Organic/Earthly)
Day 3 (1:9-13)	Dry Land (Inorganic/*Earthly*) Vegetation (*Organic/Earthly*) (filling begins)	Day 6 (1:24-31)	Land Animals/ Human Beings (Organic/Earthly) (filling ends)
	Day 7 (2:2, 3) God Rests		

Figure 1. The structure of Genesis 1:1-2:3

1.2 Genesis 1 and Psalm 8

How, then, does Genesis 1 relate to Psalm 8? As a beautiful hymn of creation praise,[31] Psalm 8 picks up the same themes found in Genesis 1 and instructs its readers about the world as it should be—as it was at the creation. How might a reader attempting a canonical exegesis understand the relationship between these two passages? Once again, the canonical approach this study undertakes is not a scientific method which is intended to be applied consistently and methodically in order to produce assured scientific results; rather, it is an approach to the text that aims at an encounter with the divine for the believer today. Therefore, the following does not pretend to set forth a single, scientifically assured reading of the two texts, but sets forth a possible way of reading the two texts in tandem.

To this end, the following treatment will read Psalm 8 in light of Genesis 1 in two stages: First, the question of literary dependence and priority will be addressed; I will argue that Psalm 8 is drawing either upon Genesis 1 or, perhaps more likely, upon another version of the creation tradition that is strikingly similar to Genesis 1. From there, the study will explore the ways in which Psalm 8 recasts material from the seven day creation tradition; this section will attempt to "discern the influence of one text on another, the meaning effects generated when a later text alludes to and absorbs an earlier text, thus activating it and bringing it into interaction with a new context."[32] There the question of the historical relationship between the two texts will only be of secondary importance; the primary focus will be the literary relationship between the two

---

[31] A. A. Anderson, *Psalms (1-72)*, (NCBC; London, UK: Marshall, Morgan, & Scott, 1981), 100.

[32] Andrew C. Brunson, *Psalm 118 in the Gospel of John: An Intertextual Study on the New Exodus Patten in the Theology of John* (Hemsbach: Mohr Siebeck, 2003), 10.

texts within the canon. The argument will not, therefore, depend upon an establishment of a historical relationship between the texts, because it proceeds from the acknowledgment that the two texts now constitute the Church's canon, and, within the community of faith, can and should be read in light of one another.

1.2.1 Literary dependence. How do the two passages under consideration relate? The secondary literature widely recognizes that "there are certain affinities with [Psalm 8] and Genesis 1" indicating some sort of direct or indirect compositional relationship.[33] Most scholars see these affinities as a result of Psalm 8 drawing either on Genesis 1 or on a creation account related to Genesis 1.[34] While it is impossible to establish the historical relationship with certainty, the evidence seems to support this scholarly consensus. As already noted in chapter two, Psalm 8 gives a "top down" description of creation that looks very much like the ordering of creation described in Genesis 1, if selectively described, rearranged and, at times, in reverse order. If one were to ascribe priority to Psalm 8, this would mean that Genesis 1 (or some other intermediate creation tradition derived from Psalm 8 and giving rise to Genesis 1) has, for some reason, rearranged and expanded upon the creation order described in Psalm 8; while this relationship is possible, it is hard to imagine what would give rise to the new arrangement and expansion.

Yet, if Psalm 8 is drawing upon Genesis 1 or a related creation account, there are good explanations for why the psalmist has chosen to focus on certain elements of that creation account and rearranged those elements; as the analysis of Psalm 8 in light of Genesis 1 below will show, Psalm 8 offers a contemplation upon the heavenly rulers (the moon and stars) and the earthly rulers (the human) in order to make its point. Psalm 8 also seems to assume that the singer/reader is familiar with some version of the account of creation. For example, in verse 5(4), the psalmist asks a rhetorical question about the nature of humanity, and then, in verses 6-9, she answers her own question by recounting the created order of Genesis 1 in reverse order, as though this created order were common knowledge.[35] Additionally, the intertextual comparison of the two texts below will show that Psalm 8 seems to select material from Genesis 1

---

[33] Craigie, *Psalms 1-50*, 106. See also James L. Mays, *Psalms* (Interpretation; Louisville, KY: John Knox, 1989), 67.

[34] Briggs and Briggs, conclude that verse 4 and 5 of Psalm 8 are drawing on a compacted version of the creation account derived from Genesis 1 some time after Ezra (Charles Augustus Briggs and Emilie Grace Briggs, *Psalms, vol I*, ICC [New York: Scribners, 1906], 62). Craigie agrees that Psalm 8 derives from the first creation account, but is less certain about the date (Craigie, *Psalms 1-50*, 106). Similarly, Childs avers that the psalmist "was dependent on the tradition of the priestly writer which is reflected in Genesis 1" ("Psalm 8 in the Context of the Christian Canon," *Interpretation*, 23 [1969]: 22). Elsewhere, however, he expresses uncertainty regarding whether this is an oral or a literary version of the tradition (*Biblical Theology of the Old and New Testaments* [London: SCM, 1992], 113).

[35] See Craigie, *Psalms 1-50*, 108.

at strategic points (namely, days four and six), possibly betraying an awareness of the broader context of the creation tradition preserved in Genesis 1, rather than a mere awareness of the parts selected.

The question remains, however, whether the psalmist is utilizing Genesis 1 as we have it, or some other version of the first creation account. As the following intertextual comparison will show, while the two passages share strong thematic and structural parallels, the vocabulary is, at points quite different.[36] In light of these divergences, it seems reasonable to conclude that Psalm 8 reflects another version of the creation account that is similar in substance to, yet distinct in vocabulary from Genesis 1. Nevertheless, this question cannot be answered conclusively. Furthermore, attempts to account for the precise nature and provenance of the creation account underlying Psalm 8 are problematic; hypotheses positing that the psalm draws upon either a later, condensed version of Genesis 1[37] or an earlier oral version of it[38] are interesting, but inconclusive.

What, then, is the present canonical exegesis to make of the relationship between the two texts? On the one hand, it bears repeating that the focus of the present chapter is canonical, asking how a reader today may understand the two scriptural texts in tandem. Historical questions, therefore, are not the primary focus. What follows, then, is a theological reading of the texts, not a case for the dependence of Psalm 8 upon Genesis 1. Yet, on the other hand, an awareness of their historical relationship has some relevance for such a canonical reading. First of all, in considering the level one meaning of the text, an awareness of the fact that Genesis 1 (or something conceptually similar to it, to be more precise) lies in the background of Psalm 8 ought to inform how one reads Psalm 8 "in itself;" indeed, such an awareness has already informed the exegesis of Psalm 8 proffered in chapter two. Secondly, this awareness strengthens the level two canonical connection of the two passages, encouraging the reader to consider the two texts in tandem. Of course, the canonical exegesis argued for in this book does not insist that there be any sort of historical relationship between any two texts before they are read in light of one another; the mere fact that any two texts are part of the community's received canon means that members within the

---

[36] Psalm 8 uses vocabulary distinct from that of Genesis 1 to express concepts similar to those found in Genesis 1 at the following points: The framing context of Psalm 8 is God's glory בכל הארץ ("in all the earth," Ps 8:1, 10), while Genesis 1 describes the creation of [את] השמים ו[את] הארץ ("the heavens and the earth," Gen 1:1, 2:3). Ps 8:4 meditates upon the creation of the evening heavenly bodies, calling them ירח וכוכבים ("the moon and the stars"), whereas Gen 1: refers to the same heavenly bodies as המאור קטן ("the lesser light") and הכוכבים ("the stars"). Finally, while Genesis 1 and Psalm 8 both list animals that humans are to rule over (Gen 1:26, 28 // Ps 8:8-9) the two lists differ; Genesis 1 mentions עוף ("birds"), and רמש ("creeping things"), which are not found in Psalm 8, and Psalm 8 mentions עוף ("birds"), צנה ("sheep") and אלפים ("goats"), and עבר ארחות ימים ("things passing through the paths of the sea"), which are not mentioned in Gen 1:26, 28.
[37] Briggs and Briggs, *Psalms, vol I*, 62.
[38] Childs, *Biblical Theology of the Old and New Testaments*, 113.

community can and should read these texts in light of one another. Yet, in looking for texts to bring into interaction with Psalm 8, it is reasonable to look for texts that a) Psalm 8 itself gestures towards and b) many others within the community of faith will find beneficial for illuminating Psalm 8.[39]

1.2.2 Reading Psalm 8 in light of Genesis 1. We now turn, therefore, to reading Psalm 8 in light of Genesis 1. Since it is probable that Psalm 8 draws upon material from some version of the first creation account and, whether one looks to the Jewish, Orthodox, Catholic, or Protestant tradition, Genesis 1 always precedes Psalm 8 in the arrangement of the canon, it is worth exploring how Psalm 8 has responded to Genesis 1. Therefore, I will first survey the points of contact between Psalm 8 and Genesis 1, and then explore simultaneously the way in which Psalm 8 has reconfigured the themes of Genesis 1 and the way in which a knowledge of the first creation account shapes the reader's understanding of Psalm 8.

What, then, are the points of verbal and semantic overlap between Psalm 8 and Genesis 1? The first and last indication that Psalm 8 is drawing upon some version of the first creation account is found in the inclusio's extolling of the manifestation of God's glorious name בכל הארץ ("in all the earth," Ps 8:2, 10); Genesis 1 sets God's creative activity in the context of הארץ ("the earth"), using the word 21 times. Thus, the phrase בכל הארץ in Ps 8:2 functions in a similar way to the phrase [את] השמים ו[את] הארץ ("the heavens and the earth") that brackets the first creation account in Gen 1:1 and 2:1; both phrases indicate the universe in its totality.[40] Moreover, when the first iteration of the inclusio is read in conjunction with the first line of the body so that הארץ and השמים stand in parallel,[41] the language in Psalm 8 is even closer to that of the first creation account; the inclusio and the first line of the body of Psalm 8 use the same vocabulary that Genesis 1 uses to refer to the totality of creation by hendiadys; if a reader comes to Psalm 8 with Genesis 1 in mind, he will see a connection between the all encompassing glory of YHWH in Psalm 8 and the universal creation of YHWH in Genesis 1.

---

[39] Furthermore, the reader must remember that a) the canonical approach does not posit a static formula for determining which two texts ought to be read in light of one another, and b) the canonical approach recognizes that the reader's own context informs the way in which the reader will choose to read the canon. Therefore, it is fully expected that another reader from another context could very well choose different texts to consider along side of Psalm 8. For example, if a reader's concern is to hear the biblical witness concerning the way in which God uses children, that reader might begin with Psalm 8, and then read Psalm 8 in tandem with other texts speaking about children (e.g., Deut 6:7, Ps 127:3, Eph 6:1, etc.), texts which will not be examined in this study.

[40] See Westermann's treatment of את השמים ואת הארץ, *Genesis 1-11*, 101. Westermann is correct that this phrase does not reflect an opposite duality, as in Egyptian thought. There is no substantial nuance of difference in meaning from את השמים ואת הארץ in Gen 1:1 and בכל הארץ in Ps 8:2, 10.

[41] Robert Alter, *The Art of Biblical Poetry* (New York: Basic Books, 1985), 119.

Turning to the body of the psalm, I have argued in chapter two that Ps 8:2b serves a dual function both as a parallel line joined to the inclusio and as the first line of the body of the psalm. Likewise, Ps 8:2b seems to serve as a transition from the inclusio's contemplation of the totality of the created order (// Gen 1:1-2:3) to a more focused contemplation on one part of the created order: God's creative work "upon the heavens." In Genesis 1, God does creative work in the heavenly realm on days two (Gen 1:8) and four (Gen 1:14). Of these two creation days, the language of Ps 8:2b points most strongly to day four. Just as Ps 8:2b speaks of God setting (from נתן) his "glory upon the heavens," so also Gen 1:14-19 describes how God יתן ("set") lights השמים ברקיע ("in the expanse of the heavens"); by contrast, Gen 1:6-8 describes the creation of the heavens themselves, not of something upon or in the heavens, and there is no use of the verb נתן or any other similarly concrete verb in the creation account of day two.[42] More imagery reminiscent of creation day four appears in Ps 8:4(3). There, the psalmist again contemplates "the heavens" (השמים) turning to the ירח וכוכבים ("the moon and the stars"), which parallels the creation of המאור קטן ("the lesser light") and הכוכבים ("the stars") in Gen 1:16. Once again, the psalmist uses the verb נתן, this time describing the way in which God created the ירח וכוכבים, exactly paralleling the use of the same verb in Gen 1:17.

What, then, ought one to do with Ps 8:3, which does not speak of creation day four? First of all, there are no clear semantic parallels between verse three and the first creation account, and past attempts to connect the "babes and sucklings" with a newly created Adam and Eve are unconvincing.[43] Since the psalmist is meditating on the created order, not giving a homily on Genesis 1, it is more judicious to avoid forcing every part of Psalm 8 to correspond to the Genesis 1 account. Secondly, chapter 2 argues that verse three is a programmatic excursus within Psalm 8 that describes God's *modus operandi* in ordering creation by exalting weak and humble things. Recognizing language in verses two and four that points towards creation day four, therefore, reinforces this view. So, when reading Psalm 8 in light of Genesis 1, one finds in Ps 8:2-4 language reminiscent of Gen 1:16 (Ps 8:3, 4) woven around the "babes and sucklings" excursus.[44]

Thus, reading Psalm 8:2b-4 with Genesis 1 in mind strengthens the connection between the two references to השמים in verses 2 and 4 and connects both with day four of creation. Read in this way, Ps 8:2b and 4 tell and then re-tell of God's establishment of the luminaries (=creation day four) through a chiasm:

---

[42] John H. Walton is correct to point out, however, that the thrust of Gen 1:14-19 puts the emphasis upon God's creative activity through speaking, not through such concrete activity as manufacturing (*Genesis* [NIVAC; Grand Rapids, MI: Zondervan, 2001] 124-126). My point here is to note that the language of Psalm 8 more closely resembles the description of God's creative activity on day four than it does the description of day two, not to claim that the process of creation on day four is somehow more concrete than the process of creation on day two.

[43] *Contra* Briggs and Briggs, *Psalms Vol. I*, 63.

[44] See Alter, *The Art of Biblical Poetry*, 119.

A.   You who have set
B.   your glory
C.   upon the heavens
(babes and sucklings excursus)
C'.   When I consider the heavens
B'.   the moon and stars,
A'.   which you have set in place

Turning, then, to Ps 8:5-7, the preceding contemplation of the heavenly bodies (Ps 8:4//day four) has lead the psalmist to consider the created glory of humans, paralleling day six of Gen 1. While אדם and אלהים are the only direct verbal parallels to Gen 1:26-31 found in Ps 8:5, 6 (both occur twice in Gen 1:26 and 27), there are other clear conceptual parallels.[45] The psalm's declaration that God has "made (the human) a little less than divine" (תחסרהו מעט מאלהים, Ps 8:5) parallels the declaration of Gen 1:26 that God has made humans בצלמנו ("in our [God's] image") and כדמותנו ("according to our [God's] likeness").[46] Similarly, Ps 8:6 declares that God has "crowned" the human "with glory and honor" and "caused (the human) to rule" (תמשילהו) over the works of God's hands; this parallels God's decision to "let (the human) have dominion" (וירדו) over other animals and God's command that humans are to "subdue (the earth) and have dominion over" (וכבשה ורדו) other animals in Gen 1:26, 28. Finally, both Gen 1:26, 28 and Ps 8:8-9 elaborate on what, exactly, the human will rule with lists of animals that are similar, but not identical.[47]

Within this framework, then, we can return to address the question of the role of the "babes and sucklings excursus" within this reading; what are we to make of the fact that Ps 8:3 does not seem to reflect directly the language or concepts of the first creation account while the rest of the psalm does? On the one hand, as I have already argued, it is wise to avoid forcing verse three to fit into the creation motif reflected in the rest of the psalm by making it say more than it does—for example, by understanding the "babes and sucklings" to be either monsters of chaos vanquished at creation or an infantile Adam and Eve.[48] On the other hand, reading Psalm 8 as a meditation upon creation days four and

---

[45] See Neumann-Gorsolke, *Herrschen* and James L. Mays, "The Self in the Psalms and the Image of God," in *God and Human Dignity* (ed. R. Kendall Soulen and Linda Woodhead; Grand Rapids, MI: Eerdman's 2006).

[46] In Willem VanGemeren's words: "human beings are not divine; they are in 'the image and likeness of God' (Gen 1:26-27). In this exalted status, he may be said to be 'less than God'" (*Psalms* [EBC 5; Grand Rapids: Zondervan], 141).

[47] Genesis 1 rehearses the formulaic litany of דגה ("fish"), עוף ("bird"), בהמה ("beast/cattle"), and רמש ("creeping things"). the list in Psalm 8 includes בהמה and דגה, but replaces עוף with צפור, omits רמש, and adds צנה ("sheep") and אלפים ("goats"), and (perhaps in description of the "fish") עבר ארחות ימים ("things passing through the paths of the sea").

[48] Contra Mark S. Smith, "Psalm 8 2b-3: New Proposals for an Old Problem." *CBQ* 59 (1997): 638-639 and Briggs and Briggs, *Psalms Vol. I*, 63.

six may still yield insight for the role of verse 3 within that meditation. While the second half of the chiasm bracketing Ps 8:3 (Ps 8:4) leads the psalmist to meditate upon the role of the human, the first half of the chiasm (Ps 8:2) similarly leads towards a preliminary meditation upon the nature of humanity in the "suckling and babies" excursus. In Ps 8:2b-3, a contemplation of YHWH setting his majesty "above the heavens" leads to a meditation upon the insignificant "sucklings and babies" that wonders at how God uses them to continually maintain creation; in Ps 8:4-5, a contemplation of the heavenly night time luminaries leads to a meditation upon the comparatively insignificant Human/Child of Humanity that wonders at how God exalts the human.[49] Thus, it is possible to read Ps 8:3 as anticipating Ps 8:5-9 by briefly painting a picture of divine reversal through human agents that parallels the psalm's central moment of reversal in Ps 8:5-6.

Having surveyed the points of contact between the two passages, we are now in a position to consider the way in which Psalm 8 recasts the material from the first creation account. At this point, it is important to bear in mind that I am not making a case about the historical development of Psalm 8 or the creation tradition, nor am I attempting to divine the intentions of the original historical author of Psalm 8. Rather, I am exploring ways in which the two texts may be read inter-textually; by approaching the text as a canonical reader who approaches Psalm 8 with Genesis 1 as part of my "cave of resonant signification,"[50] I am undertaking to investigate how themes in Genesis 1 are addressed later in the canon in Psalm 8.

Significantly, while the inclusio points the reader to consider the entire created order, the body of the psalm then goes on to focus its attention only on two parts of that created order: the evening heavenly luminaries of day four and the human of day six. What is significant about the Psalm's focus upon these two points of the creation account? Within the structure of Gen1:1-2:3 (fig. 1), the heavenly bodies occupy a place that looks forward to the rest of the second panel (days four through six), while, as inorganic and heavenly creations, looking back towards the first panel. Furthermore, though day four belongs to the second panel, it is at the middle of the seven day week.[51] Similarly, the

---

[49] For a discussion of the way in which the contemplation of the heavenly bodies in Ps 8:4 relates to the declaration of the exaltation of the humans in Ps 8:5, see Jeffrey H. Tigay, "What is Man that You Have Been Mindful of Him?" in *Love and Death in the Ancient Near East: Essays in Honor of Marvin H. Pope* (ed. John H. Marks and R. M. Good; Guilford, CT: Four Quarters Publishing, 1987), 169-171. See also Craigie, *Psalms 1-50*, 108.

[50] John Hollander, *The Firgure of Echo: A Mode of Allusion in Milton and After* (Berkeley: University of California Press, 1981), 65; compare with Brunson, *Psalm 118*, 9-10.

[51] See Wenham, *Genesis 1-15*, 7, 21-22.

creation of humanity is the point of culmination of God's creative activity,[52] and, when humans are given dominion of the rest of creation (Gen 1:28-30//Ps 8:7-9), the account of day six recalls the creation of the cosmos that has led up to day six. So, when the reader of Psalm 8 meditates upon the creation of the luminaries and of the human, this meditation points the reader to consider the totality of the created order as described in Genesis 1. Thus, when one reads Psalm 8 with Genesis 1 in mind, the scope of the meditation is wider than merely a meditation upon humans and the evening luminaries; these are merely two examples of the way in which YHWH makes his name great בכל הארץ.

Furthermore, similarities between the creation of the luminaries on day four and the creation of the humans on day six stand out. Both the evening heavenly bodies and the human represent a point of filling culmination in the creation process. The luminaries are at the pinnacle of the inorganic/heavenly creations, and the humans are at the pinnacle of the organic/earthly creations. Furthermore, while Psalm 8 makes reference only to the governing function of the human vice-gerent, Genesis 1 describes the luminaries and the humans both as reigning over (משל) their respective domains. Thus, the psalmist alludes to two parts of creation that have similar privileged status and corresponding responsibility. In "acting as God's representative(s),"[53] they maintain order in the universe that God has ordered. Throughout chapters two and three, I have shown that Psalm 8 reflects upon the way in which God maintains his created order. The observation that Psalm 8 focuses its attention upon the tools that God uses to govern the cosmos reinforces this reading. When read in light of Genesis 1, then, Psalm 8 speaks to God's concern that the entire created order be governed properly, and highlights his method of ensuring that order and governance.

The evening heavenly bodies and the human beings, however, are not exactly on the same plane in the first creation account. The account of the sixth day of creation is longer than that of any other day (7 verses), and the creation of humans dominates this section. Also, as Brueggemann notes, "the special clustering of the word 'create' [ברא] in [Genesis chapter one] verse 27 suggests that the text wishes to *focus on the creation of humankind*."[54] Furthermore, after day six "the identification formula is . . . modified . . . to emphasize the perfection of the final work."[55] Wherever one locates the culmination of the passage, day six occupies a place that is more significant than day four and the ruling function of the humans is articulated more extensively than is the ruling function of the heavenly luminaries.[56] When Psalm 8 recasts the creation

---

[52] See Brueggemann, *Genesis*, 30-32. For a careful look at the structure of Gen 1:1-2:4a with an eye to the role that the creation of humanity plays in that structure, see Neumann-Gorsolke, *Herrschen*, 154-167.
[53] Wenham, *Genesis 1-15*, 33.
[54] Brueggemann, *Genesis*, 31.
[55] Wenham, *Genesis 1-15*, 34.
[56] While the heavenly luminaries are said to משל ("rule") their domain, the humans, are told to משל, כבש ("subdue") and רדה ("have dominion over") their domain. Furthermore, Westermann identifies a "gradual ascent—toward the creation of human beings" (*Genesis*

material, the focus upon humanity is even more emphatic, with the human figure dominating the psalm, and the heavenly bodies taking a secondary role.[57] Thus, the two uneven meditations serve to clarify the place of the human in creation by contrasting the human with the heavenly bodies. The psalmist's failure to mention the moon's governing function, the disproportionate emphasis upon the human ruler, and the counterintuitive observation that the human, not the moon, has "all things under his feet" all serve to humble the human reader. When the reader of Ps 8:2b, 4 is aware of the special governing role that the moon plays in Genesis 1, this heightens the feeling of reversal evoked by Psalm 8.

Comparing the description of the heavenly bodies in these two biblical creation texts with the treatment of heavenly bodies in Mesopotamian religion is instructive at this point. Westermann speaks of Genesis 1 as demythologizing ancient Near Eastern conceptions of creation by stripping the heavenly luminaries of any divinity.[58] While I agree with Westermann's general point, I agree with Wenham that it is better to decribe the contrast between Genesis 1 and ancient Near Eastern mythology as a "polemical repudiation" of the latter rather than "merely a demythologization."[59] In a similar vein, Childs argues that the function assigned to the heavenly luminaries of marking and perpetuating time speaks to a concept of time that "stands in striking opposition to that of the Babylonians."[60] Significantly for our purposes, Childs emphasizes how the function of the heavenly lights as markers of time is a "witness to the perpetuity of the creation," which is unlike the Babylonian view of the movement of the stars as revelatory omens caught up in a cyclical pattern of time.[61]

Similarly, Tigay argues that, when read in light of ancient Assyrian astral worship, Psalm 8 subverts the reader's expectation by making the human, and not the moon and stars, the royal representative of the divine.[62] Regardless of what one thinks of Westermann's view of the origins of Genesis 1 or Tigay's more tentative suggestions about a possible Assyrian setting of Psalm 8, reading Psalm 8 in light of Genesis 1 generates a trajectory that simultaneously minimizes the heavenly royalty (the luminaries) and magnifies the earthly royalty (humanity); this trajectory is perceived all the more forcefully when one bears in mind the differences between these two canonical texts on the one hand and Mesopotamian views on the other. Genesis 1 has already put the heavenly

---

1-11, 177), though Brueggemann identifies the culmination of the text as Gen 2:1-4a (*Genesis,* 35).
[57] The body of Psalm 8 has two unequal parts (Ps 8:2b-4, 5-9) which are parallel in content but unequal in weight. As already noted in chapter two, the meditation on the role of humanity in creation is introduced at the crux of the psalm (Ps 8:5-7), occupies the psalmists attention for over half of the poem (Ps 8:5-9), and is already anticipated in Ps 8:3, at the crux of the chiasm that makes up Ps 8:2b-4.
[58] Westermann, *Genesis 1-11,* 127.
[59] Wenham, *Genesis 1-15,* 9.
[60] Childs, *Myth,* 40.
[61] Ibid.
[62] Tigay, "What is Man," 169-171.

luminaries "in their place" in relation to YHWH by describing them as objects that he has set in place to serve his purposes.[63] Psalm 8 goes further, first by omitting the governing language that Genesis 1 had applied to the luminaries, and then by utilizing the luminaries to introduce the real ruler of creation: the human.[64] These glorious lamps of the night are not astral deities, forming the creation with their hands; rather, they are the works of God's hands (Ps 8:3a). Yet, according to Genesis 1, they rule the night sky, not as lesser divine beings, but as the instruments of YHWH, put there to establish order by marking time (Gen 1:14). In so doing, they are reminders that YHWH will continue to perpetuate the created order so that his name (and not the moon or the stars) will be shown to be majestic in all the earth (Ps 8:2).

To summarize, then, when one reads Psalm 8 in light of Genesis 1, the body of Psalm 8 becomes two meditations upon the way in which YHWH establishes his ruling agents within the cosmos, as follows:

YHWH's majestic name is displayed in the creation:	
Ps 8:2b, 4 YHWH's majesty in the creation of the moon and the stars (// creation day four)	Ps 8:(3) 5-9 YHWH's majesty in the creation of humanity (// creation day six)
A reflection upon the relatively insignificant heavenly bodies.	A reflection upon the relatively insignificant humans.
The heavenly bodies set in their exalted place by God.	The human ruler installed in its exalted place by God.
Reader's response: awe, humility.	Reader's response: awe, praise.

In the first meditation, the reader marvels at the way in which God has created lights that are but play things from the divine perspective, but unfathomably majestic rulers of the night sky, from the human perspective. In the second meditation, the marvel and wonderment is even greater, as the reader contemplates how YHWH has taken the human creature, which seems even less significant than the night sky, and made that creature his agent of order and governance. More than that, even within the human race, the most insignificant "sucklings and babies" are the agents through which YHWH chooses to continue to maintain his created governance.

Reading Psalm 8 in this way impacts upon many theological issues germane both to the interpretation of Psalm 8 and to the situation of the 21st century Church. Specifically, I have already noted that both passages highlight the human and the human's place in the created order as deserving of special attention; the question posed in Ps 8:5, "What is the human?" is as relevant and

---

[63] Westermann, *Genesis 1-11*, 127.
[64] Tigay, "What is Man," 169-171.

pressing today as it has ever been.⁶⁵ Thus, this question deserves special attention for a canonical exegesis of Psalm 8. My assessment of this question must be limited at this point for three very important reasons: 1) The literature addressing this question in light of these two passages is already copious;⁶⁶ a full assessment of all of the literature and issues involved would require more space than the limits of the present project will allow. 2) Among the literature addressing the question, some of the more fruitful work has approached the question not simply by thoroughly examining these two passages in isolation or in relation to one another, but by examining these two passages canonically in light of the broader context of Scripture, including both the Old and New Testaments.⁶⁷ 3) I have already noted that Genesis 1 and Psalm 8 both describe the world in fairly idealized terms, speaking of the world as it ought to be, while other parts of the Bible speak to the world as it is now, in far less idealized language. Thus, attempting to draw ethical conclusions about who the human is in the present chaotic world and how the human ought to act by reading Genesis 1 and Psalm 8 in isolation from the rest of Scripture could be misleading. As a result, the present study will not attempt to cull some propositional truths from Genesis 1 and Psalm 8 that one might then apply to 21st century ethical dilemmas. Rather, the study will trace a trajectory through biblical texts addressing the place of humanity in the cosmos, asking how the various answers that the Old Testament gives to the question "what is the human?" relate to one another.

Nevertheless, if such a trajectory is to be traced, it will be necessary to make at least some limited observations about the idealized view of humanity that emerges when one reads Psalm 8 in light of Genesis 1. Where does the ideal human fit in relation to the human's creator and in relation to the rest of creation? In relation to the creator, Brueggemann highlights three aspects of the human's status from Gen 1:26-31, all of which are echoed in Ps 8:5-9: 1) The humans are unique in that, in Genesis 1, they are the only creatures to whom God speaks.⁶⁸ Similarly, Ps 8:5 wonders why YHWH is mindful of (פקד) and cares for (זכר) humans, and both verbs carry a subtle communicative element. 2) The description of humans as bearers of "the image of God (vv. 26-27) must be understood in juxtaposition to Israel's resistance to any image of God."⁶⁹ Only humans, not idols, can bear God's image on earth. Furthermore, the "demythol-

---

⁶⁵ Neumann-Gorsolke, *Herrschen*, 1.
⁶⁶ Studies focusing on this question and paying special attention to Genesis 1 and Psalm 8 in order to cull answers to the question include: Neumann-Gorsolke, *Herrschen*; James Barr, "Man and Nature: The Ecological Controversy and the Old Testament," *BJRL* 55 (1972), 9-32; Marvin E. Tate, "An Exposition of Psalm 8," *PRS* 28 (2001): 356-359; Mays, "Self;" Marsha M. Wilfong, "Human Creation in Canonical Context: Genesis 1:26-31 and Beyond," in *God Who Creates: Essays in Honor of W. Sibley Towner* (Ed. William P. Brown and S. Dean McBride Jr.; Grand Rapids, MI: Eerdmans, 2000), 42-52. For a brief list of other literature on the issue, see Tate, "Psalm 8," 357 n. 64.
⁶⁷ Mays, "Self;" Wilfong, "Human Creation;" Childs, "Psalm 8."
⁶⁸ Brueggemann, *Genesis*, 31.
⁶⁹ Ibid.

ogized" status of the celestial lights in Genesis 1 and Psalm 8 emphasizes not only YHWH's exclusive right to claim divine status, but also the exalted status of the human in the cosmology of these two texts; when compared with other ancient Near Eastern belief systems, Gen 1 and Ps 8 are exceptional in that no entities are closer to the supreme Deity (in rank or in relationship) than the human is. 3) "It is now generally agreed that the image of God reflected in human persons is after the manner of a king who establishes statues of himself to assert his sovereign rule where the king himself cannot be present . . . The image of God in the human person is a mandate of power and responsibility."[70] In this role, as Marsha Wilfong says, "humankind is, in fact, the lynchpin that holds creation together."[71]

The human's function as "lynchpin" brings us to the question of the relationship between humanity and the other creatures. Quoting Wilfong again, "humankind . . . enables God's purpose for creation to be fulfilled, keeping chaos at bay by faithfully carrying out the task of dominion in God's image."[72] In light of the authority that YHWH gives to the human "lynchpin," Lynne White argues that Genesis 1 lies at the "historical roots of our ecological crisis."[73] Genesis 1, says White, gives humans license to exploit nature for humanity's benefit.[74] Some scholars have defended the biblical depiction of the human ruler against charges such as White's by arguing that the ruling language of Genesis 1 (משל, כבש, and רדה) describes not militant subjugation, but rather beneficent administration.[75] How ought one to adjudicate between these two opposing viewpoints? On the one hand, Tate is correct to point out that "it is hard to escape elements of severity in the use of the verbs [משל, כבש, and רדה] in the OT."[76] On the other hand, in the context of Genesis 1 and Psalm 8, the subjects of the human ruler seem to be the benefactors of that rule; the militant actions implied by the verbs משל, כבש, and רדה would be felt only by those who would seek to do harm to God's "good/טוב" creation. Moreover, White severely mischaracterizes the creation account when he alleges that "God planned all of [creation] explicitly for man's benefit."[77] To the contrary, the idealized description of creation in Psalm 8 depicts the human as ruling for the benefit of the created order in order to show the excellence of YHWH's name in the earth.

---

[70] Brueggemann, *Genesis*, 32.
[71] Wilfong, "Human Creation," 46.
[72] Ibid.
[73] Lynne White, "The Historical Roots of Our Ecological Crisis," *Science* 155 (1967):1203-1207.
[74] According to White, "God planned all of this [creation] explicitly for man's benefit and rule: no item in the physical creation had any purpose save to serve man's purposes . . . Especially in its Western form, Christianity is the most anthropocentric religion the world has seen" ("Historical Roots," 1205).
[75] See Tate, "Psalm 8," 356-358, for a brief survey of this argument.
[76] Tate, "Psalm 8," 358.
[77] White, "The Historical Roots of Our Ecological Crisis," 1205.

The works of Othmar Keel and Ute Neumann-Gorsolke reading Ps 8:7 in light of ancient Near Eastern iconography are insightful at this point.[78] The iconography most closely resembling Ps 8:7 is found on Neo-Assyrian seals depicting a (sometimes royal) human standing with his foot on a docile animal (caprid?) and protecting the animal against a predator.[79] Whether or not this iconography points to a Neo-Assyrian provenance for Psalm 8, these images illustrate well the nature of the relationship between the human ruler and the rest of creation; to the good creation, the human is a protector, but to the parts of creation that threaten the created order, the human is a militant threat. Is the human ruler then free to trample creation and exploit it? One must bear in mind that Genesis 1 and Psalm 8 speak of the world in idealized terms; as the following discussion will show, in the less-than-ideal world, humans are often the threat to the created order, not its protectors. The rest of Scripture makes clear what is already implicit in Psalm 8: When humans exalt themselves rather than humbly praising YHWH as the babes and sucklings do, such humans become God's enemies (Ps 8:3). I turn, then, to consider Psalm 8 in light of two other passages of Scripture that deal with a less-than-ideal world.

2. Reading Psalm 8 in Light of Job 7

Job 7:17-18, and Ps 144:4 both explore the question "what is the human?" in ways that echo Ps 8:5. Both passages have the following elements in common with each other and with Psalm 8: 1) The speaker in the text is addressing YHWH. 2) The passage's main clause poses the question "what is the human?" introduced by the interrogative מה ("what"). 3) The main clause is followed by a subordinate clause, introduced with the word כי ("that"), which speaks of the way in which YHWH attends to the human. 4) All three passages reflect upon the nature of the human-divine relationship.[80] According to the pattern already outlined above, the following will read Psalm 8 in light of these two passages in two stages. First, I will examine Job 7:17-18 and Ps 144:4 each

---

[78] Othmar Keel, *The Symbolism of the Biblical World: Ancient Near Eastern Iconography and the Book of Psalms* (Timothy J. Hallett, trans.; New York, NY: Seabury, 1978), 58; Neumann-Gorsolke, *Herrschen*, 112-121.
[79] Keel, *Symbolism*, 58, figures 60-61; Neumann-Gorsolke, *Herrschen*, 112, figure 1.
[80] George W. Coats treats the similar formula utilized by these three texts form critically ("Self-Abasement and Insult Formulas," *JBL* 89 [1970]: 24-26). While Coats includes Job 15:14 in his discussion, This chapter does not focus upon Job 15:14, which is a less promising canon exegetical "entry point" for elucidating Psalm 8. Of the four commonalities shared by Ps 8:5, Job 7:17, and Ps 144:3, Job 15:14 only shares two; in Job 15:14, the speaker does not address YHWH, and Job 15:14 is not primarily concerned with the divine-human relationship, but with the possibility of the human being just. Furthermore, while Job 7:17 and Psalm 144:3 may very well be quoting Psalm 8:5, Job 15:14 is most likely an inner-Joban echo of Job 7:17 (so Michael Fishbane, "The Book of Job and Inner-Biblical Discourse," in *The Voice from the Whirlwind* [ed. Leo G. Perdue and W. Clark Gilpin; Nashville, TN: Abingdon, 1992], 93-95).

in their respective contexts, paying attention to historical questions, and reading the discrete witness of each passage. Then, I will bring each passage in turn into dialogue with Psalm 8, examining the nature of the relationship between each passage with Psalm 8 and asking how an understanding of Job 7:17-18 (and, by extension, the book of Job) and Ps 144:4 together can inform a canonical reading of Psalm 8.

2.1 Job 7:17-18

2.1.1 Reading Job 7:17-18 "in itself." Turning first to the question of the origins of the book of Job, as Pope concludes, "[t]he fact that the dates proposed by authorities, ancient and modern, span more than a millennium, is eloquent testimony that the evidence is equivocal and inconclusive."[81] Furthermore, while much of 20th century scholarship tended to focus upon reconstructing the sources and development of the book of Job,[82] Recent scholarship has given more attention to reading the book as a unity in its final form and to the dialogic nature of the material preserved within that final form.[83] Once again, the canonical approach of this study is in keeping with this recent trend in that it attends to the final form of the book of Job.

Job 7:17-18 asks of YHWH: "What is humanity, that you make so much of it, and that you set your heart upon it, visit it every morning and test it every moment?" To understand this text in its literary context, I will examine Job's question first in its broader contexts of Job 4-7 and of the entire book of Job, and then its more immediate context of Job's speech in Job 6-7 and the final portion of that speech in Job 7:17-21.

2.1.2 The broader literary contexts (Job 4-7 and the book of Job). Job asks this question in the context of the latter part of Job's second speech (Job 6-7) in the book, which he speaks in reply to the accusatory speech of Eliphaz (Job 4-5).[84] Under the inspiration of a night-time vision (Job 4:12-15), Eliphaz has

---

[81] Marvin H. Pope, *Job* (AB C15; New York: Doubleday, 1965), xl. More recently, Douglas G. Lawrie has surveyed historical critical approaches to the book of Job. Lawrie concludes that historical critical investigations of the book of Job have failed to produce any consensus and have largely failed to curb the subjectivity of the practitioners of historical critical approaches ("How Critical is it to be Historically Critical? The Case of the Composition of the Book of Job," *JNSL* 27[2001]:121-146).
[82] For a survey of scholarship on the book of Job through 1993, see Carol Newsom, "Considering Job," *CR* 1 (1993):87-118.
[83] For a survey of scholarship on Job from 1993 to 2007, see Carol Newsom, "Re-Considering Job," *CBR* 5 (2007):155-182. Newsom notes a distinct shift during this time period from scholarship focused upon historical questions to scholarship focused upon literary and theological questions.
[84] For an assessment of the discourse between Eliphaz's speech in Job 4-5 and Job's speeches in Job 3 and Job 6-7, see William A. Beuken, "Job's Imprecation as the Cradle of a New Religious Discourse: The Perplexing Impact of the Semantic Correspondences

concluded that Job's calamity (recounted in Job 1-3) is divine discipline, and that Job ought not "despise the discipline of the almighty" (Job 5:17). Job then defends himself by pleading his own innocence (Job 6-7). How, then, ought the reader to understand this interchange between Job and Eliphaz in light of the final form of the book of Job? On the one hand, as Parsons notes, the book of Job "seems to defy more than a superficial analysis;"[85] reading Job in its final form does not provide a simplistic hermeneutical solution either to understanding the book of Job or to the problematic philosophical question of theodicy. On the other hand, the final form of the book does seem to give the reader some guidance in how to adjudicate between the claims of Job and claims of his friends. The debate between Job and his friends centers around the interrelated questions of the source of Job's suffering and whether or not God reserves suffering for the wicked, and Job consistently requests an audience before God to settle these questions.[86] Thus, God's speeches at the end of the book (Job 38-41) occupy "a climactic position in the book" and play special hermeneutical importance for understanding the debate between Job and Eliphaz.[87]

Yet, "[d]eciding how to characterize this divine appearance is a difficult matter that has occupied interpreters of the book since the beginning."[88] On the one hand, YHWH's climactic response to Job in chapters 38-41 has a chastening tenor, and Job responds as one humbled, saying "I am of small account" (Job 40:4) and "I despise myself, and repent in dust and ashes" (Job 42:6). On the other hand, as Wilson astutely observes, "[i]t should be clear from the outset that the fact [that] God . . . appears in response to Job's plea for a meeting immediately puts the lie to any claims to the contrary that" Job's "friends have made. God *does* appear in response to Job. His very appearance proves Eliphaz's earlier claim false—that God will not respond to Job because he has already spoken his final word of judgment in Job's suffering."[89] Moreover, when God adjudicates between Job and his friends in Job 42:7-8, YHWH declares to Eliphaz, "you have not spoken of me (or "to me")[90] what is right, as my servant Job has," singling Eliphaz out while at the same time indicting Eliphaz's

---

Between Job 3, Job 4-5, and Job 6-7" in *The Book of Job* (ed. William A. M. Beuken; Louvain: Leuven University Press/Peters, 1994), 41-78.

[85] Gregory W. Parsons, "The Structure and Purpose of the Book of Job," *BibSac* 138 (1981): 139.

[86] Job 9:32-35; 13:20-28; 14:13-17; 23:1-9; and 31:35-37. See Kathryn Schifferdecker, *Out of the Whirlwind: Creation Theology in the Book of Job* (HTS 61; Cambridge: MA: Harvard University Press, 2008), 121-122.

[87] Schifferdecker, *Out of the Whirlwind*, 122.

[88] Gerald H. Wilson, *Job* (NIBC 10; Peabody MA: Hendrickson, 2007), 420.

[89] Wilson, *Job*, 420. While Wilson speaks here specifically of Elihu's claim that God will not respond to Job, his point is also valid for Eliphaz's speech. For example, Eliphaz derides Job, saying "Call now; is there anyone who will answer you? To which of the holy ones will you turn?" (Job 5:1, ESV).

[90] See Elaine A. Phillips, "Speaking Truthfully: Job's Friends and Job," *BBR* 18 (2008): 39-40.

companions. In the final analysis of the book, then, Job has won the exchange with Eliphaz, because God has declared Job to be in the right.

How, then, ought one to understand Job's rather brazen question posed in 7:17-18 in light of the broader context of the book of Job and the speeches of YHWH at the end of the book? [91] If one were to read Job 7 as a stand-alone poem, one might conceive of God as a petty tyrant, like the "bully" that David Hester describes:

> Job's God is . . . mean spirited, like a cosmic bully constantly picking on weaker kids, heckling, hitting, and making someone else's life miserable, until, in the end, the victim finally disappears. Then the game is no fun any longer, since watching the victim suffer was part of its attraction.[92]

Yet such a view of the God of Job 7 fails to take into account the broader context of the book of Job and the fact that YHWH has made his own voice heard in the book.[93] In light of YHWH's harsh rebuke of Eliphaz (Job 42:7-8), the reader of the book of Job knows, even if Job does not, that Eliphaz's description of God, to which Job is responding, is not "right" (נכונה). Furthermore, the reader of the entire book of Job has insight into the ways of God that neither Job nor Eliphaz has, having been privy to the activity in the divine council in the opening scenes (Job 1), and having knowledge of the way in which YHWH will ultimately answer Job (Job 38-42). Therefore, while some consider plausible a reading of the passage that sees God as a cosmic bully, it is at least equally as plausible, in light of the context of the entire book, to read the passage as reflecting both Job's anguish and his limited knowledge of the elusive divine, so that the Joban God is mysterious, but he is no bully.

In any case, Job's words express an honest and human anguish, and God imputes no sin to Job for asking "what is the human?" so boldly. Yet, God's majestic reply to Job in chapters 38-41 and Job's humbled response (Job 40:3-5; 42:1-6)[94] together make the point that Job's brazen question does not baffle YHWH; rather, YHWH's response to Job's questions will silence and humble Job. At the risk of oversimplifying a very complex book, then, one can trace a

---

[91] David Robertson finds Job's stance in Job 7:17-21 to be so bold that he believes "it is likely that most readers tend to go too far in their identification with" Job. He even describes Job's questions as an "attack on God [that] is truly virulent" (*The Old Testament and the Literary Critic* [OTS; Philadelphia, PA: Fortress, 1977], 40).

[92] David C. Hester, *Job* (IBS; Louisville, KY: Westminster John Knox, 2005), 36.

[93] For an intriguing reading of the book of Job that takes seriously the literary unity of the poetic body of the book of Job and its narrative framework, see Phillips, "Speaking Truthfully," 31-43.

[94] "Job's response in ch. 42," writes William P. Brown, "presents a major crux for interpreting his transformed character" (*Character in Crisis: A Fresh Approach to the Wisdom Literature of the Old Testament* [Grand Rapids, MI: Eerdmans, 1996], 108).

narrative movement within the book wherein Job matures,[95] and the reader is invited to mature with him, all the while recognizing that honestly expressing one's anguish and bewilderment before God is a necessary part of that process. To quote Clines, as far as the question of suffering goes,

> [t]he argument of the Book of Job is: By all means let Job the patient be your model so long as that is possible for you; but when equanimity fails, let the grief and anger of Job the impatient direct itself and yourself toward God, for only in encounter with him will be [*sic*.] the tension and suffering be resolved.[96]

2.1.3 The Nearer Literary Contexts (Job 6-7 and Job 7:17-21). Job's response to Eliphaz in Job 6-7 consists of two sections.[97] In the first section (Job 6), Job addresses his friends, first defending his right to lament (verses 1-13),[98] and then accusing his friends of treachery (verses 14-21).[99] In the second section (Job 7), Job addresses a lament to God, first bemoaning his woeful fate (verses 1-10),[100] and then bringing a complaint against God "in the style of [one] cross examining the plaintiff" (verses 11-21).[101] Job presents his question "what are mortals" towards the end of this lament.

Job's question introduces a final flourish of rhetoric in the climactic strophe of Job 6-7,[102] wherein Job makes his case to God that God ought to leave him alone. In verses 17-21, Job presents a plea that ironically contrasts with the pleas of the psalms of lament. First Job presents a "bitter parody of Psalm 8" that portrays God's attention as a curse, not a blessing (Job 7:17-18).[103] Pope frames the contrast starkly:

---

[95] See Brown's chapter "The Reformation of Character: Job 32-42" (*Character in Crisis*, 83-119).
[96] Clines, *Job 1-20*, xxxix. Not all commentators would agree with Clines' summation. Newsom, for example, implies that Clines oversimplifies the message of Job ("Considering Job," 90-91).
[97] See John E. Hartley, *The Book of Job* (NICOT; Grand Rapids, MI: Eerdmans, 1988), 130. For a full treatment of the rhetorical development and structure of Job 6 and 7, see Pieter Van der Lugt, *Rhetorical Criticism and the Poetry of the Book of Job* (OS xxxii; New York: Brill, 1995), 80-101.
[98] Hartley, *Job*, 130-135.
[99] Hartley, *Job*, 136-141. For an alternative way for dividing Job 6, see Van der Lugt, *Rhetorical Criticism*, 80-85.
[100] Hartley, *Job*, 142-147.
[101] Hartley, *Job*, 147-153. Van der Lugt counts three strophes: verses 1-8, 9-16, and 17-21.
[102] For Job 7:17-21 as the climactic strophe of Job 6-7, see Van der Lugt, *Rhetorical Criticism*, 101.
[103] Clines, *Job 1-20* (WBC 17; Dallas TX: Word, 1982), 192; see also Paul E. Dion, "Formulaic Language in the Book of Job: International Background and Ironical Distortions" *SR* 16 (1987): 190-191.

What in happier circumstances would be regarded as providential care (cf. Pss viii, csliv 3) is here ironically presented as overbearing inquisitiveness and unrelenting surveillance. If what he has received is divine providence, Job would prefer to be spared such.[104]

Then, Job "tak[es] the opposite attitude to that of the sufferers who speak in the Psalms" by asking that God "look away" from him where the psalms ask for God to "'consider' . . . or not' hide [his] face' . . . from them" (Job 7:19).[105] Then, again, Job ironically reconfigures the conventional language of the lament psalms by using the verb נצר ("to watch over"), which usually connotes God's protection, to describe God instead as a "spy or scrutineer of humans" (Job 7:20).[106] Job's ironic travesty of a lament then concludes with an aggrieved plea asking that God תעביר (literally "cross/pass over," often "take away" [so NRSV, ESV], but possibly "overlook") Job's sin—if there could possibly be some unnoticed sin causing Job's suffering ("[if] I have sinned")[107]—lest Job die (Job 7:20-21).[108] Having thus surveyed the discrete "level one" witness of Job 7:17-18, the next section considers Job 7:17-18 in its relationship with Psalm 8.

2.2 Job 7:17-18 and Psalm 8

2.2.1 Literary dependence. Turning, then, to the question of the historical relationship between Job 7:17-18 and Psalm 8:5, a strong scholarly consensus recognizes Job 7:17-18 as an intentional parody of Psalm 8:5,[109] although this consensus has not gone unchallenged.[110] By placing Job 7:17-18 and Ps 8:5 side by side and underlining the points where they both use the same lexemes, the strong points of connection between the passages become visible:[111]

---

[104] Pope, *Job*, 75.
[105] Clines, *Job 1-20*, 193.
[106] Clines, *Job 1-20*, 194.
[107] Norman C. Habel regards Job's confession of sin here as "a mock plea for absolution" (*The Book of Job: A Commentary* [OTL; Philadelphia, PA: Westminster, 1985]).
[108] For a balanced and insightful treatment of the question of why Job speaks of his sin at this point, when he has thus far pleaded his innocence, see Clines, *Job 1-20*, 194-195.
[109] So Pope, *Job*, 75, Clines, *Job 1-20*, 192, Wilson, *Job*, 72, Dion, "Formulaic Language," 190-192, Fishbane, "The Book of Job and Inner-Biblical Discourse," 87-89, and Hartley, *Job*, 151.
[110] Raymond C. Van Leeuwen, "Psalm 8.5 and Job 7:17-18: A Mistaken Scholarly Commonplace?" in *The World of the Aramaeans I: Biblical Studies in Honour of Paul-Eugène Dion* (JSOTSup 324; ed. P. M. Michèle Daviau, John W. Wevers and Michael Weigl; Sheffield, UK: Sheffield Press, 2001), 205-215; and Coats, "Self-Abasement and Insult Formulas," 14-26.
[111] See also Fishbane, "The Book of Job," 87; idem, *Biblical Interpretation*, 285-286.

Job 7:17-18	Psalm 8:5
מָה־אֱנוֹשׁ כִּי תְגַדְּלֶנּוּ What is humankind that you magnify it,	מָה־אֱנוֹשׁ כִּי־תִזְכְּרֶנּוּ What is humankind that you are mindful of it,
וְכִי־תָשִׁית אֵלָיו לִבֶּךָ׃ And that you are concerned about (literally, "set your heart upon") it,	וּבֶן־אָדָם כִּי תִפְקְדֶנּוּ׃ And the child of humanity, That you care for (or "visit") her/him?
וַתִּפְקְדֶנּוּ לִבְקָרִים לִרְגָעִים תִּבְחָנֶנּוּ׃ And you examine (or "visit") him/her every morning and try him/her every moment?	

Note that these semantic parallels reflect more than a mere use of common vocabulary, as the structure of each passage is identical; in each case, the speaker asks "what is man?" (מה אנוש, so RSV) and then continues to describe how YHWH deals with humankind in two parallel clauses introduced by כי followed by a second person imperfective verb form. In addition to these direct semantic parallels, Fishbane notes two more points of possible overlap. 1) Both Job 7:15 and Ps 8:7 use the verb שית (תשית, "you set" [Job 7:15], and, שתה "you have set," [Ps 8:7]). 2) While Job 7:15 speaks of God making the human great (תגדלנו, piel of גדל), Ps 8:6 says the opposite, that God has "made him/her less (ותחסרהו, piel of חסר) than divine."[112] In light of the strong semantic and thematic connections that they share, it is highly probable that one of these texts is alluding to the other.[113]

---

[112] Fishbane, "The Book of Job," 87. Concerning this second parallel, חסר is not completely equivalent to an antonym for גדל. While the piel of גדל speaks of causing to grow, making great or powerful, and magnifying (see BDB 152), the piel of חסר only occurs in Ps 8:6 and Eccl 4:8, meaning "to cause to lack" or "to deprive oneself" (see BDB 341). Nevertheless, given the other semantic parallels, the use of the piel in both verb forms, and Job's penchant for ironically subverting the language of the Psalms, it is not unreasonable to see Job's use of גדל as a deliberate mockery of the psalmist's use of חסר.

[113] Van Leeuwen's argument that "[s]uch shared lexemes are better explained as literary adaptations still standing close to a living, oral formula" is unconvincing ("Psalm 8.5 and Job 7.17-18," 210). While it is true that the "what/who is A that B" formula occurs elsewhere in the ancient Near East, both inside of and outside of the Hebrew Bible (see Coats, "Self-Abasement and Insult Formulas," 14-26), such a formula does not sufficiently explain the high level of semantic overlap between these two passages. Moreover, none of the other occurrences of the formula cited by Coats, with the possible exception of Ps 144:3, a) have the degree of semantic overlap that Job 7:17-18 has with Ps 8:5, or b) speak specifically of the question of God's attention to humanity. See Fishbane, *Biblical Interpretation*, 285-286.

Furthermore, several factors argue for the probability that Job 7 is taking up the language of Psalm 8 in a satirical fashion. While, it is difficult to see why, in the midst of a hymnic celebration of the created order, Psalm 8 would borrow language from the book of Job, Job's decision to allude to Psalm 8 makes sense in context; Job's ironic reversal of the message of Psalm 8 is a most fitting introduction to the strophe (verses 17-21), and it fits in perfectly with the pattern of allusion that follows. In Job 7:17-18, Job subverts the message of Psalm 8 to make the point that, as far as Job is concerned, God's attention is a plague. Then, as already noted above, in 7:19-21, Job subverts the language and pattern of the lament psalms by pleading for God to leave Job alone.[114] Furthermore, the book of Job frequently uses irony to communicate its message, and allusions to both earlier parts of the book of Job and other biblical texts frequently serve as the source of the irony.[115] Thus, an ironic parody of Ps 8:5 fits naturally within both the broader context of Job 7 and the entire program of the book of Job.

To summarize, then, in Job 7:17-18, Job has taken the words of the psalmist and turned them on their head. Whereas the psalmist describes YHWH as exalting the human to an almost divine status (Ps 8:6), Job complains that YHWH "make[s] so much of him" (Job 7:17, ESV). Whereas the psalmist uses the verb פקד to describe "divine visitation for the good of humans," Job employs the same verb to speak of "divine acts of punishment" that seem to be "unwarranted harassment."[116] For the one who seeks to read Psalm 8 in light of its canonical context, then, Job 7 presents a counter-point to Psalm 8 that the reader must take seriously. How, then, ought Job's challenge to the psalmist inform a canonical reading of Psalm 8? Because a proper understanding of Job 7:17-18 is caught up with understanding the entire book of Job, the following will attend to reading Psalm 8 in light of Job 17:17-18 and the broader context of the book of Job.

2.2.2 Reading Psalm 8 in light of Job 7:17-18 and the book of Job. Reading Job 7 (or the entire book of Job, for that matter) reminds the reader of Psalm 8 that the world is not now as it ought to be. Bringing Psalm 8 and Job 7 into contact brings to the fore "the problem between man as a creation of God and man living life as it actually is."[117] Faced with this problem, the reader of Psalm 8 is reminded by Job to avoid reading Psalm 8 in a simplistic, Eliphazesque, fashion. In the first place, Job's ardent complaint emphasizes that the chaotic threat represented by the "enemy and avenger" (Ps 8:3) is very real. Read in

---

[114] Clines, *Job 1-20*, 193-195.
[115] Fishbane, "The Book of Job and Inner-biblical Discourse," 86-98 and Dion "Formulaic Language," 187-193. In a similar vein, see David Robertson, *The Old Testament and the Literary Critic*, 33-54. Robertson argues that irony is found even at the macro-level, where the unity of the book of Job preserves ironic diversity, such that "irony pervades the entire book and provides the decisive key to understanding its complicated theme" (34).
[116] Habel, *The Book of Job*, 165.
[117] Childs, "Psalm 8 in the Context of the Christian Canon," *Interpretation* 23 (1969), 28.

isolation, Psalm 8 might seem to imply that any disorder in the cosmos is relatively minor, serving only as a plot device whereby YHWH demonstrates his glory by immediately disposing of any threat to his order. When one reads Psalm 8 in light of Job 7 and the entire book of Job, however, she remembers that chaos is often instantiated in the real world in horrific and devastating ways. Furthermore, the frankness of Job's challenge coupled with YHWH's affirmation that Job has "spoken properly about me" (so *Stone Edition Tanach*, אלי נכונה [דבר]תם, Job 42:8)[118] reminds the reader of Psalm 8 that an expression of grief and profound confusion is not inappropriate when faced with chaos and pain. Read in isolation, Psalm 8 might seem to indicate that the only proper response to threatening chaos is to humbly and unquestioningly "take the *name* of God on [one's] lips" and, in so doing, obtain "a strength greater than that of God's enemies."[119] Thus, a simplistic reading of Psalm 8 might lead the reader to expect the enemies and chaos to be vanquished in short order, so long as the reader takes an unquestioning and praiseful stance. Yet, such a simplified understanding of the ways of God in the world is consonant with the views of Eliphaz and his friends, which view YHWH condemns.

The most shocking challenge, however, that Job 7 poses to Psalm 8 lies not in the mere fact that chaos poses a constant and real threat; this much is already evident in the Psalter's lament songs. Job's challenge to God goes one step further than the laments by seeing God, instead of the "enemy and avenger" (Ps 8:3), as the source of Job's pain. How does a canonical exegesis deal with such evident dissonance? In the first place, it is important to resist the temptation to overstate the nature of the dissonance, as a reading of Job 7 in the broader context of the book of Job already plays a mitigating role. As already noted above, Job's challenge is as much a challenge to Eliphaz's mistaken conception of YHWH as it is a challenge to YHWH himself, and the introduction (Job 1-2) describes how YHWH, while complicit in Job's pain, is not the immediate cause of Job's trouble. Indeed, the immediate cause of Job's grief is "השטן" ("the Satan" or "the adversary," Job 1:12; 2:7-8), a figure not unlike the איוב mentioned in Ps 8:3.[120]

Even so, though, YHWH does not deny any role in Job's suffering, but rather affirms it (Job 2:4, "you incited me against him"). Furthermore, Job's challenge to YHWH in Job 7 brings to the fore the problem of theodicy in a shocking and visceral way, whereas the question of theodicy is latent, at best, in

---

[118] One might argue that, even if one reads Job holistically, YHWH's statement that Job's friends, unlike Job "have not spoken properly about me" does not amount to a *carte blanche* approbation of everything that Job has said. Even so, it is significant that the book of Job does not portray YHWH as imputing sin to Job for his challenge.
[119] Craigie, *Psalms 1-50*, 107.
[120] Indeed, some interpreters, seizing upon the similarity in spelling between the word אויב/enemy and the name איוב/Job have argued that the entire role of the character Job in the book of Job is that of God's enemy (see Wilson, *Job*, 18).

Psalm 8.[121] Even if YHWH's role in Job's demise is mediate, why does YHWH grant the requests of השטן, in Job 1-2, and why does he allow the איוב ומתנקם of Ps 8:3 to exist at all? The closest one gets to finding an answer to these questions is in the divine speeches (Job 38-41) which are so difficult to interpret that Newsom describes them as being full of "irreducible ambiguities."[122]

How, then, does Job's complex exploration of theodicy inform a reading of Psalm 8? The fact that YHWH defends his justice in the divine speeches by speaking directly to his maintenance of the created order ought to produce humility in the reader of Psalm 8. YHWH begins his speeches by pointing to "his 'design' of the cosmos" to instill in Job a sense of the mysteriousness of God's ways.[123] When reading Psalm 8 in light of Job 38-39, then, the reader is more aware that, despite the human's role as vice-gerent, ultimately YHWH, not humanity, has the prerogative to administer order. The divine speech concludes (Job 40:15-41:34) with YHWH making the point that YHWH alone, not Job, can control the Behemoth and Leviathan (בהמות and לויתן). Insofar as these two beasts parallel the בהמות שדי and ארחות ימים of Ps 8:8, 9, Job 40-41 counterbalances the seemingly pacific and symbiotic relationship between the human vice gerent and his creaturely subjects in Ps 8:8-9; the reader of Psalm 8 must bear in mind, then, that YHWH maintains the created order, and YHWH has the right to do so in mysterious ways. The human rules only in the role of a servant of YHWH. Thus, as Jerome Creach writes: "Hubris . . . misleads many to believe that they are independent caregivers of creation. What has been given to human charge, though, is much less—only a sublease."[124] Furthermore, insofar as the לויתן of Job 41 brings to mind mythical creatures of chaos,[125] Job 41 reminds the reader of Psalm 8:7-9 that chaos is ever present, even within the creaturely realm that the human has been charged by YHWH to govern; there are other creatures that the human, in fact, cannot control, but YHWH can.

In short, the book of Job as a whole reminds the reader of Psalm 8 that God's ways are mysterious and life is unpredictable, sometimes to the point of seeming pernicious. Therefore, the psalm's description of YHWH's program of maintaining the created order through the exultation of the relatively insignificant over and against the self-strong does not amount to an algebraic formula whereby one can predict what YHWH will do by supplying the correct varia-

---

[121] To quote Samuel E. Balentine, "In the broken world of Job . . . innocent suffering calls every faith assertion into question" ("'What are the Humans that You Make so Much of Them?' Divine Disclosure from the Whirlwind: 'Look at Behemoth,'" in *God in the Fray: A Tribute to Walter Brueggemann* [ed. Tod Linafelt and Timothy K. Beal; Minneapolis, MN: Augsburg, Fortress, 1998], 264).

[122] Carole A. Newsom, "Job," in *The New Interpreter's Bible*, vol. 4 (Nashville TN: Abingdon, 1994), 595.

[123] Habel, *Job*, 530.

[124] Jerome F. D. Creach, *Psalms* (IBS; Louisville, KY: Geneva, 1998), 75.

[125] Pope, *Job*, 339. I do not intend to imply here that, as Pope seems to assume, Ugaritic mythology, rather than the OT canon, is the proper context for the interpretation of Job 41.

bles. Nor is it correct to interpret the character-consequence nexus articulated in Hebrew wisdom literature (as in Prov 10-15, for example) as a formula for guaranteeing personal wealth and prosperity.[126] In this context, Job's challenge of YHWH's complicity in allowing chaos within his created order in Job 7 shows that it is legitimate for the human to express angst before God in light of God's mysteriousness and life's unpredictability. As Walter Brueggemann writes, "God does not want to be an unchallenged structure, but one who can be frontally addressed."[127]

Yet, if our intention is to hear the voice of both passages in order to forge a canonically informed understanding of the theological themes of Psalm 8, one more question of vast import remains: What, then *is* the human? A beleaguered creature who is mere הבל who would be better off without God's attention, as per Job? A relatively insignificant creature who has been endowed with imaginable honor, as per the psalmist? Or something else altogether? In response to this question, the reader must bear in mind that Job 7:17-18 reflects Job's human perspective, a perspective that is skewed by the influence of Eliphaz's bad theology, and the perspective of the implied author mitigates Job's description; Psalm 8, on the other hand, as a reflection upon the creation account, speaks to God's activity in the world, and, as such, reflects what God has done from God's perspective.[128] Yet, this does not negate the tension that arises when considering Job's reflection upon the human within the chaotic world as it is in tandem with the psalmist's reflection upon the ordered world as it ought to be. Thus, it is possible to trace a trajectory from the world as it was at creation (Genesis 1) and ought now to be (Psalm 8) to the world as it is, often in chaos (Job 7). To further develop the trajectory and bring clarity to the question "what is the human?" the next section will consider another passage. Having already considered Pss 8 and 144 in connection with the role of Psalm 8 in the shape of the Psalter in chapter three, I now take up Psalm 144 again.

3. Reading Psalm 8 in Light of Psalm 144

3.1 Reading Psalm 144:3-4 "in itself"

The date of Psalm 144 is so uncertain that, in one single breath, Terrien posits that it could be either a pre-exilic "royal canticle composed for a king of the Davidic dynasty," or a Persian era eschatological meditation upon "the story

---

[126] See Raymond Van Leeuwen, "Wealth and Poverty: System and Contradiction in Proverbs" *HS* 33 (1992): 25-36, Craig G. Bartholomew and Ryan P. O'Dowd, *Old Testament Wisdom Literature: A Theological Introduction* (Downers Grove, IL: IVP Academic), 270-275.

[127] Walter Brueggemann, "A Shape for Old Testament Theology, II: Embrace of Pain," *CBQ* 47 (1985): 401.

[128] Or, at the very least, from the perspective of the implied narrator of Genesis 1, which, as both canonical literature and the introduction to the canon, reflects the divine perspective.

of David from Bethlehem."¹²⁹ The difficulty involved in assigning a date to the psalm is related to the apparent diversity of material within the psalm, with verses 1-11 expressing a prayer for the Davidic king, and verses 12-15 expressing a prayer for the nation.¹³⁰ While it is not unreasonable to conclude that Ps 144:1-11 represents an early, pre-exilic royal psalm that has been augmented by the communal prayer in verses 12-15,¹³¹ this study focuses upon reading the final form as a unity. Therefore, it is important to note that, in light of the use of late vocabulary in Ps 144:12-15 (for example, זן, "kind," in verse 13 and the relative prefix -שׁ in verse 15),¹³² it is most likely that the psalm as we now have it derives from the post-exilic era. While our focus here is not upon the psalm's precise historical origins, noting that the final form of this psalm has such a late provenance (for a royal Psalm) is important in one regard: the final form of Psalm 144 most likely reflects an eschatological meditation upon "the story of David from Bethlehem."¹³³

Turning, then, to reading the psalm as a unity, Terrien's strophic analysis demonstrates that, despite the possibility that Ps 144:1-11 has been augmented by Ps 144:12-15, "a remarkable symmetry characterizes the entire poem."¹³⁴ Thus, while Psalm 144 contains elements commonly found in various genres, including possible wisdom elements (Ps 144:3-4), royal elements (Ps 144:1-11), and thanksgiving elements (Ps 144:12-15),¹³⁵ these diverse elements cohere together as a unified royal prayer. Together, the two major sections of the psalm address "the need for God to act (a royal lament, vv. 1-11) and the resultant blessings of his actions (a psalm of blessing, vv. 12-15)."¹³⁶

In the broader context of Psalm 144, verses 3-4 pose the question "מה־אדם /what is the human?" after the psalm's opening praise (Ps 144:1-2) and before the psalm's petition for YHWH to intervene on behalf of the Davidic king (Ps 144:5-11). The martial and royal imagery of verses 1-2 and 5-11 suggest a king's prayer to "God before a decisive combat."¹³⁷ Embedded in the prayer for help of verses 5-11 is a promise of praise to YHWH for the anticipated deliver-

---

[129] Samuel Terrien, *The Psalms: Strophic Structure and Theological Commentary* (ECC; Grand Rapids, MI: Eerdmans, 2003), 901.

[130] Thus, Herman Gunkel concludes that Ps 144:1-11 and Ps 144:12-15 are two different poems (*Introduction to Psalms: The Genres of the Religious Lyric of Israel*, James D. Nogalski, trans. [MLBS; Macon, GA: Mercer University Press, 1998], 99, 230, 246), and Franz Delitzsch takes the same view in the 19th century (*Commentary on the Psalms, Volume III* [Edinburgh, UK: T & T Clark, 1871], 379, 382-383). Others, however, such as Terrien (*Psalms*, 901) and Hans-Joachim Kraus (*Psalms 60-150*, Hilton C. Oswald, trans. [ACC; Minneapolis, MN: Fortress, 1993], 541) regard Psalm 144 as a unity.

[131] Leslie C. Allen, *Psalms 100-150* (WBC 21; Waco, TX: Word Books, 1982), 290.

[132] See Allen, *Psalms 100-150*, 290.

[133] Terrien, *Psalms*, 901.

[134] Terrien, *Psalms*, 898.

[135] See Allen, *Psalms 100-150*, 289-291, Terrien, *Psalms*, 898.

[136] Van Gemeren, *Psalms*, 982. See also Kraus, who regards the petition of Ps 144:12-15 as "a resumption of the petition from vv. 7 ff." (*Psalms 60-150*, 541).

[137] Delitzsch, *Psalms III*, 378.

ance (verses 9-10), and a prayer for divine blessing upon the entire nation rounds out the psalm (verses 12-15). How, then, does the brief meditation upon "the transitoriness of the human being"[138] in Ps 144:3-4 fit in with the internal development of the thought of the psalm?[139] While I will explore this question more fully below, a brief answer is in order at the outset: When Psalm 144 is read as a unity, Ps 144:3-4 serves to transition from the praise that precedes to the petition that follows in two ways: 1) These verses demonstrate that the royal petitioner is humble, not self-strong, and, therefore, worthy of the divine intervention that he is about to ask for; 2) These verses remind YHWH that YHWH does, indeed, "regard" the human and "think of" the child of humanity, in order to motivate YHWH to take the following petition seriously, despite the transient nature of the human (verse 4).[140] Thus, while Ps 144:3-4 does not present a view of the human's role in creation that is quite as optimistic as that of Psalm 8, [141] one should not conclude that Psalm 144 gives a completely negative answer to the question "what is the human?" After all, the psalm proclaims of YHWH that "you regard" (תדעהו) and "think of" (תחשבהו) the human, and the psalmist hopes and expects YHWH to protect (verses 1-2), rescue (verses 10-11) and bless (verses 12-15) humans.

3.2 Psalm 144:3-4 and Psalm 8

3.2.1 Literary dependence. How, then, does Ps 144:3-4 relate to Psalm 8? While commentators do not tend to make much of the semantic overlap between Ps 144:3-4 and Ps 8:5,[142] Coats believes that "Ps 144:3 looks more like a conscious imitation of Ps 8:5 than does Job 7:17."[143] Once again, placing Ps 144:3 and Ps 8:5 side by side and underlining the points where their vocabulary overlaps illustrates the strong connection between the two passages:[144]

---

[138] Kraus, *Psalms 60-150*, 542.

[139] "The questions of the fragility of human life" in this context, writes Terrien, "seem at first to constitute a *non-sequitor*" (*Psalms*, 898).

[140] The royal speaker's realization of his frailty in verses 3-4 stands "[i]n significant contrast to v. 2," on the one hand, and introduces the petitions that follow, on the other (*Psalms 60-150*, 542).

[141] Creach, *Psalms*, 74.

[142] Kraus (*Psalm 60-150*, 542), Terrien (*Psalms*, 899), and Van Gemeren (*Psalms*, 984) all restrict themselves to a brief "c.f. Ps 8:5." In Thorne Wittstruck's extensive bibliography on the book of Psalms, he does not include a single entry addressing the relationship between Pss 8 and 144 (*The Book of Psalms, an Annotated Bibliography* [2 vols.; New York, NY: Garland Publishing, 1994]).

[143] Coats, "Self Abasement and Insult Formulas," 26.

[144] See also Fishbane, "The Book of Job," 87.

Psalm 144:3	Psalm 8:5
יְהוָה מָה־אָדָם וַתֵּדָעֵהוּ O LORD, what is humanity that you regard it,	מָה־אֱנוֹשׁ כִּי־תִזְכְּרֶנּוּ What is humankind that you are mindful of it,
בֶּן־אֱנוֹשׁ וַתְּחַשְּׁבֵהוּ׃ or the child of humankind that you think of him?	וּבֶן־אָדָם כִּי תִפְקְדֶנּוּ׃ And the child of humanity, That you care for (or "visit") her/him?

At first glance, one might question whether Coats overestimates the connections between the two psalms; the כי element, common to both Ps 8:5 and Job 7:17, is missing in Ps 144:3, and Ps 144:3 and Ps 8:5 do not use the same verbs. Yet, Ps 144:3 contains six striking similarities with Ps 8:5: 1) Both psalms ask "what is the human" and "child of the human," twice in two parallel lines. 2) Both psalms introduce the question with the interrogative מה. 3) Though Ps 144:3 reverses the order of אדם and אנוש, both psalms use the same three lexemes to describe the human (בן, אדם, and אנוש). 4) Both psalms modify the two parallel questions about humanity with two parallel dependent clauses describing YHWH's attention to humanity. 5) These dependent clauses contain second person singular imperfective verb forms, which 6) are augmented with a third person singular suffix.[145]

Yet, one might argue that these points of overlap alone are not enough to establish an allusion between the two passages.[146] Nevertheless, there are other signs beyond these lexical and semantic parallels which may indicate that Psalm 144 is reworking material from Psalm 8. First of all, Psalm 144, as is widely recognized, reworks the material of Psalm 18 (which is, itself, very similar to David's song in II Samuel 22).[147] The psalmist's willingness to utilize material from at least one other psalm makes it more likely that the overlap between Ps 8:5 and Ps 144:3 is also the result of an intentional reworking of older material gleaned from Psalm 8. Furthermore, the strongest points of semantic overlap between Pss 144 and 18 are found in verses 1-2 and 5-8 of Psalm 144. The psalmist, then, briefly departs from his meditation upon Psalm 18 precisely at the point where his language overlaps with the language of Psalm 8. Also, while questions of dating are particularly problematic and are not the primary focus of this book, Psalm 144, in its final form, contains post-exilic vocabulary,[148] but

---

[145] See Coats, "Self Abasement and Insult Formulas," 26.
[146] Van Leeuwen argues that the similarities of vocabulary in Psalm 8, Job 7, and Psalm 144, arise from the common use of the same form, not from any form of literary dependence, "Psalm 8.5 and Job 7:17-18."
[147] See Kraus, *Psalms 60-150*, 541. The following verses contain varying degrees of semantic overlap: Ps 144:1// Ps 18:32, 35; Ps 144:2//Ps 18:3, 48; Ps 144:5//Ps 18:10; Ps 144:6//Ps 18:15; Ps 144:7//Ps 18:17, 45-46; Ps 144:10//Ps 18:51.
[148] Allen, *Psalms 100-150*, 290.

Psalm 8 contains vocabulary that some scholars believe parallels Ugaritic usage.[149] Thus it could very well be that Psalm 8 is of greater antiquity than Psalm 144. If so, then the odds that Psalm 144 is drawing upon Psalm 8 (or at least some pre-canonical form of Psalm 8) increase.[150]

Finally, the broader context of Psalm 144 contains two other indicators that Ps 144:3-4 is a meditation upon Ps 8:5-9: 1) more subtle instances of semantic overlap between other parts of Psalm 144 and Psalm 8, and 2) a sense of "satisfaction," wherein reading Ps 144:3-4 as an allusion to Ps 8:5-9 makes good exegetical sense in light of the rest of Psalm 144.[151] I will highlight both the instances of overlap and the sense of satisfaction by briefly proffering a reading of Psalm 144 in light of Psalm 8. While not all readers will be equally convinced of an intentional allusion here, it is helpful to bear in mind that the ultimate goal of the present volume is to read the text canonically; so, reading Psalm 144 in light of Psalm 8 is justified canonically, given the position of the two psalms in the Psalter, even if the author of Psalm 144 did not intend to allude to Psalm 8.

I begin, then, by investigating the way in which the psalmist has woven allusions to Psalm 18/II Samuel 22 around this allusion to Psalm 8. If the questions posed in Ps 144:3-4 do not allude to Ps 8:5, they "seem at first to constitute a *non-sequitur*,"[152] deviating from both the psalmist's topic of prayer before battle and the psalmist's meditation upon Psalm 18. Yet, read as a reflection upon Psalm 8, verses 3-4 make sense in context in that they point the reader to consider YHWH's promise to intervene against the enemy and avenger (Ps 8:3) to maintain the created order. Furthermore, it makes sense that Psalm 144, when focusing upon the individual king, quotes from Psalm 18 (a royal psalm associated very strongly with David himself both through the historical superscription [Ps 18:1] and the close relationship between Psalm 18 and II Samuel 22), and then when focusing upon humanity in general, quotes from Psalm 8. Thus, when the allusions to Psalm 8 and Psalm 18 are brought together, they explore the relationship between corporate humanity and the Davidic monarch. On the one hand, Ps 144:3-4 reminds the reader that the king himself is a "mere mortal" who must humble himself before God. Yet, an allusion to Psalm 8 here, spoken thus by the ideal/eschatological Davidic king, does not indicate a democratizing triumph of king Adam over king David. The

---

[149] Wenceslaus M. Urassa, *Psalm 8 and its Christological Re-Interpretations in the NewTestament Context: An Inter-Contextual Study in Biblical Hermeneutics* (EUS 23:577; New York: Peter Lang, 1998), 32.

[150] Richard Hays lists "availability" as one of his seven criteria for establishing an allusion in *Echoes of Scripture in the Letters of Paul* (New Haven: Yale University Press, 1989).

[151] Hays, *Echoes of Scripture*, 31. "Satisfaction" is the seventh of Hays' seven criteria for an allusion. While "satisfaction" as a stand-alone criterion is quite subjective and cannot establish an echo, taken in connection with the other six criteria, it can provide a helpful check for determining whether an allusion is real or imagined.

[152] Terrien, *Psalms*, 898.

allusion to Psalm 8 in verses 3-4 follows directly upon the king's proclamation that YHWH "subdues peoples [or "my people"] [153] under me (תחתי)" (Ps 144:2; cf. Ps 18:48//II Sam 22:48) echoing the declaration that God "has placed all things under (תחת)" the human's feet (Ps 8:7). On the other hand, these verses, when read as an allusion to Psalm 8, point out that God's king is YHWH's tool for establishing order among humans in order to establish order in creation. If humans play a "lynchpin" role in relation to the rest of creation, the idealized king has a "lynchpin" role to play in relation to the rest of humanity.[154]

There are three other instances of semantic overlap between Pss 8 and 144 which are so subtle that they do not constitute a clear allusion, yet may inform how one reads Psalm 144 in light of Psalm 8 and, taken together, increase the probability that Psalm 144:3 is an echo of Psalm 8:5. First, in Ps 144:11 the king prays to be rescued from his enemies "whose mouths (פיהם) speak lies." Read in light of Ps 8:3, this serves to heighten the contrast between the enemies of the Davidic king, who misuse their mouths, and the humble children and infants who stop the enemy through the proper use of their mouths. Read in light of Ps 8:3, then, Psalm 144 evokes the image of an ideal Davidic figure and thus creates anticipation for a messianic royal individual, one who will simultaneously a) humbly identify with the babies and sucklings and b) militantly decimate the enemies of YHWH.

The final two instances of semantic overlap come in verses 13-14, where the psalmist prays for YHWH's blessing upon Israel's sheep (צאוננו) and cattle (אלופינו), both of which appear in the list of animals in Ps 8:8. Thus, whether or not there is an intentional allusion here, there are two semantic connections between the *dénouement* of Psalm 8 and the *dénouement* of Psalm 144. When reading Psalm 144 in light of Psalm 8, the Davidic lynchpin of Psalm 144 parallels the corporate Adamic lynchpin of Psalm 8. Within the internal movement of Psalm 144, the Davidic monarch prays first for his own triumph over his enemies (verses 1-11), then for divine blessing within his kingdom (verses 12-15); a king whose rule is secure can then attend to domestic prosperity and order. This mirrors the movement of Psalm 8, which moves towards a contemplation of the installation of the divine vice-gerent, king אדם (Ps 8:5-6) and then resolves in a description of the order of king Adam's reign. Thus, while Psalm 144:12-15, read by itself, asks for God to bless the king's human subjects (who are to benefit from the full granaries and bountiful livestock), when one reads Psalm 144 in light of Psalm 8, the prayer that humans might be blessed becomes a prayer that the entire created order might flourish. In sum, then, when one reads Psalm 144 in light of Psalm 8, the Davidic king becomes God's instrument for ordering corporate humanity, so that corporate humanity might then become God's tool for ordering the rest of the created order.

---

[153] Whether one reads עמים (Dead Sea Scrolls, Jerome, Syriac, and Aquila), or עמי (MT) is of little consequence here. See Allen, *Psalms 101-150*, 287, note 2c.
[154] Wilfong, "Human Creation," 46.

3.2.2 Reading Psalm 8 in Light of Psalm 144. Since the preceding reading has already examined in depth the points of contact between Pss 8 and 144, this section will only briefly touch on one key question pertaining to the hermeneutical influence that Psalm 144 plays upon a canonical reading of Psalm 8: How does the answer that Psalm 144 presents for the question "what is the human?" stand in tension and in continuity with the way in which Psalm 8 approaches that same question, and how do these points of tension and continuity inform one's reading of Psalm 8? First of all, as I have already noted, Psalm 144 presents a less optimistic answer than that of Psalm 8, and, as a result, poses a subtle challenge to Psalm 8. The distinct emphases of Psalm 144 remind the reader of Psalm 8 that the human's place in the created order is less than ideal.[155] Rather, not only does chaos threaten through the militant activity of Israel's enemies (Ps 144:7-8, 11), but also the human is faced with a fleeting frailty (Ps 144:3-4) and desperately needs to call out to YHWH for help (Ps 144:5-11). Furthermore, insofar as Psalm 144, a meditation upon the Davidic king written in the Persian Era and situated in the Psalter after Psalm 89, implicitly recalls the downfall of the Davidic line, the reader of Psalm 144 remembers that the Davidic monarch is also ephemeral.

Yet, one must be careful not to overstate the contrast between the two passages.[156] In many ways, Ps 144:3-11 has a thrust that runs parallel to Ps 8:5-6. In Ps 144:5-11, the psalmist is hoping for a reversal not unlike the reversal of Ps 8:5. When the speaker of Psalm 144 acknowledges that humanity is "like a breath," the king (or the psalmist on the king's behalf) acknowledges his relative insignificance, placing himself in a position to experience the exaltation of YHWH over and against his enemies, a subversive reestablishment of order on the part of YHWH. In this way, when one reads Psalm 8 in light of Psalm 144, she is reminded that God responds to humble human prayers in order to "establish strength because of his foes" (Ps 8:3), even if the human must engage in the prolonged struggle of battle and the unseemly study of war (Ps 144:1) to see that strength established. Furthermore, as a meditation upon God's activity on behalf of David, the positive thrust of Psalm 144 does not ultimately leave the reader in a state of despair, as does Psalm 89. Rather, it encourages the reader to hope that YHWH may yet act on behalf of the Davidic line to restore the "shoot from the stump of Jesse" (Isa 11:1, RSV).

In short, of the three passages that ask "what is the human," Psalm 144 stands between the two poles of the idealized world of Psalm 8 and the tortured world of Job in Job 7. How, then, do these passages relate with the rest of the Tanakh, including the creation account of Gen 1:1-2:3? What does this all mean for a biblical concept of anthropology? And how, if at all, does this anthropology relate to the New Testament's willingness to identify Jesus as the "Son of Man"? In order to tie together these various passages in an integrative way that

---

[155] Jerome F. D. Creach, *Psalms* [IBS; Louisville: Geneva, 1998], 74-75.
[156] Creach's conclusion that Psalm 144 stands "in stark contrast to the more positive view of humanity in Psalm 8" is a bit of an overstatement (*Psalms*, 74).

gives a canonical exegesis of Psalm 8 in its Old Testament context, this chapter will conclude by briefly reversing the interpretive influence and considering the rest of the Tanakh in light of Psalm 8. Throughout, I will emphasize how the exegesis proffered here intends, in Augustinian fashion, to bring the reader into an encounter with the divine that produces love for God and neighbor.

4. Reversing the Dialectic: Reading the Old Testament in Light of Psalm 8[157]
Encountering the res *and engendering* caritas

We return, now, to the very beginning to look once again, at Genesis 1. As noted above, Psalm 8 and Genesis 1 occupy a similar space conceptually, insofar as Genesis 1 speaks of an ideal original human state at creation, and Psalm 8 presents the continuing maintenance of creation in a way that almost idealizes the role of the human. Yet, when one turns to read Genesis 1 in light of Psalm 8, several subtle shifts already qualify the ideal image of humanity in Genesis one. In addition to the mention of the (evidently human) enemies in verse three, Psalm 8 emphasizes the relative insignificance of humans in a way that Genesis 1 does not; Psalm 8 asks, in humbled awe, "what is the human," and, in asking the question, Ps 8:5 sets אדם in a parallel relationship with the word אנוש, which carries a strong connotation of frailty and often appears in the Psalter in contexts emphasizing human mortality and weakness.[158]

The reminder of frailty in Psalm 8 is consonant with the literary context that follows the first creation account. A shift begins with Gen 2-3 (the "story of the fall" or "Eden narrative," typically identified as "J" or "non-P" material), which contains a second account of creation (Gen 2:4-24) followed by the story of humanity's disobedience and "fall."[159] Together, Genesis 1 and 2 describe a "picture of the world" in its "sublime" created state,[160] while Genesis 3 envisions the disruption of this sublimity as man, woman, and serpent defy God and suffer the consequences of this defiance. Gen 1-3 constitute the first of several cycles that make up the primeval history recounted in Gen 1-11. In each cycle, humanity experiences grace (often accompanied by an act of creation), but then rebels, faces God's judgment, and experiences grace again.[161] Genesis 1-2, read

---

[157] The title of this section is a direct quote from Childs, "Psalm 8," 31. Childs is speaking here of the dialectic between the Old Testament witness and the New Testament witness. Nevertheless, the canonical movement, wherein one part of the canon is read in light of another and vice versa, still applies here.

[158] It is likely that this word is related to the verb אנש ("to be weak, sick"). See BDB, 60 and Claus Westermann, "אדם 'adam person," in *The Theological Lexicon of the Old Testament, vol. 1* (Peabody, MA: Hendrickson, 1997), 33.

[159] For a recent, thorough treatment of the Eden Narrative in light of ancient Near Eastern parallels, see Tryggve N. D. Mettinger, *The Eden Narrative: A Literary and Religio-Historical Study of Genesis 2-3* (Winona Lake, IN: Eisenbrauns, 2007).

[160] Moberly, *The Theology of the Book of Genesis*, 42. Moberly speaks here only of Genesis 1.

[161] See Mann, *The Book of the Torah*, 10-29.

in isolation, only intimate the potential of chaos through the oblique use of the words תהו ובהו in Gen 1:2. In Gen 1-11, however, chaos, not creative order, comes to the fore.[162] Gowan summarizes the canonical thrust of Genesis 1-11 beautifully: "In brief, these chapters depict movement from a world none of us has ever known toward the" world that we now know.[163] "In the world we have *not* known," writes Gowan, "everything is all right, in accord with the will of God. In the real world, some things are all right, but dissension, oppression, violence, and pain also abound."[164]

Read in light of Psalm 8, then, Genesis 1-11 give an account of the origins of the tension felt in Psalm 8 between the exalted human who maintains order and the human enemy who constantly undermines the order. As the biblical drama moves from what was to what is, "the picture of humanity" becomes "that of a fractured and flawed race. The corporate humanity crowned with glory and honor and ordained to dominion over other creatures [Ps 8:5-9] is distorted."[165] Reading the book of Genesis and the Torah with Psalm 8 in this way facilitates an encounter with the divine *res*. When read "from the beginning," Genesis 1 plays an important role in the context of the broader narrative; especially from the point of view of readers within the community of faith, Genesis 1 and 2 together play a role within the book of Genesis and the Pentateuch similar to the role of the orientation psalms of the Psalter. Genesis 1 and 2 inaugurate history itself and remind readers that "the world was not always as it is now."[166] They describe how the world ought to be, even if the rest of the narrative describes the chaotic world as it is.

This description creates a longing in the reader for the lost world of Genesis 1, and every act of grace, of new creation, of deliverance, or of blessing in the following narrative is a gesture toward the recovery of the paradise that has been lost. The longing for restoration propels the reader towards an encounter with the God who created the cosmos, maintains the cosmos in ways that are in keeping with the reversal motif, and is even now bringing about the recovery of paradise. This encounter with the divine in turn engenders love for the divine as well as love for the creation which is, on the one hand, marred and corrupt and yet, on the other hand, in the process of being renewed through divine reversal.

Among the two other entry points surveyed above, Job 7:17-18 has its feet most firmly planted in the realm on this side of Genesis 1-11, describing life as

---

[162] As Childs notes, the words תהו ובהו already introduce "the troubling presence of the chaos" (*Old Testament Theology in a Canonical Context* [Philadelphia: Fortress, 1986], 222-223). Nevertheless, the problem of living "life under threat" is not a prominent part of the narrative until Genesis 3.

[163] Donald E. Gowan, *From Eden to Babel: A Commentary on Genesis 1-11* (ITC; Grand Rapids, MI: Eerdmans, 1988), 3. See also Terence E. Fretheim, *Creation, Fall, and Flood: Studies in Genesis 1-11* (Minneapolis, MN: Augsburg Publishing, 1969).

[164] Ibid.

[165] Mays, "Self," 34. Mays is speaking here of reading Psalm 8 in the context of the petitions of the Psalter.

[166] Walton, *Genesis*, 65.

we know it in its most brutal state. If one is to trace a trajectory through the ways in which the Old Testament Scriptures address the question "what is the human?" Psalm 8 occupies a space that simultaneously overlaps with Genesis 1 and with Job 7. In contrast with Genesis 1, Psalm 8 does not speak exclusively of the world as it was in a lost, idealized, primeval state, but of God's continuing maintenance of the created order. Yet, neither does Psalm 8 speak exclusively of things as they are now (certainly not when they are at their worst, as Job does); as an orientation psalm it speaks of things as they *ought to be* now, and in this way it more closely resembles Genesis 1 than the book of Job.

Thus, for the canonically minded reader informed by Augustine's hermeneutic, Psalm 8 carries forward the hope that the lost world of Genesis 1-2 might be restored in two significant ways: 1) In terms of canonical shape, whether the arrangement is Jewish, Orthodox, Catholic, or Protestant, Psalm 8 places a reflection upon the created order as it was intended to be late in the canon, even after the rise, fall, and exile of God's chosen people has been recounted. 2) More importantly, the psalm's ability to overlap simultaneously with the known world and with the ideal world at creation re-energizes the lost world of Genesis 1-2 in the mind of the reader, even as she reads bleak descriptions of the human condition such as those found in Job 7. Reading Job 7 and similar OT texts in light of Psalm 8 can bring the reader into a worshipful encounter with the divine *res* that creates within the reader a love for God and neighbor.

Following upon the bleak cycle of sin and rebellion in Gen 3-11, a new movement begins in YHWH's covenant with Abraham that is more hopeful and hints at the possibility that the lost world will be restored, and other similar covenants punctuate the Tanakh.[167] Because the purpose of this book is to offer a canonical exegesis of Psalm 8, not to articulate a comprehensive Old Testament theology, I will limit my focus here to the one covenant that has already occupied our attention in this chapter and in chapter three: the Davidic covenant. Having considered a) the discussion concerning the tension between king Adam and king David in the shape of the Psalter and b) the reading of Psalm 144 in light of Psalm 8 above, how does an understanding of Psalm 8 influence the way in which the canonical reader encounters the Davidic covenant? And how does the resulting reading facilitate an encounter with the divine and produce love in the reader?

First of all, when reading the biblical story of the rise and fall of the Davidic Monarchy in the books of Kings and Chronicles in light of Psalm 8, the human (אנוש /בן־אדם) becomes a paradigm for the way in which YHWH desires to use the Davidic kings to maintain order in the cosmos (cf. Ps 2:7-9; II Sam 7:9-16). The Davidic kings are to side with the humble infants of Ps 8:3, and then they will experience divine reversal on their behalf (cf. Ps 7:15-16). Read in this way, then, insofar as the description of the human in Psalm 8 evokes in the mind of the reader the first human in Genesis 2, the pre-lapsarian Adam becomes a

---

[167] Among the most prominent are the Abrahamic (Gen 12; 15), Mosaic (Exodus 19-20), Davidic (II Samuel 7), and New (Jeremiah 11) Covenants.

figure for the ideal David. Yet, the reader of Psalm 8 knows that humans also have the potential to be enemies of YHWH (Ps 8:3). The reader of the Old Testament also knows that Adam (Genesis 3), David (II Samuel 11), and the Davidic line (2 Kings 25, Psalm 89) will all fail and even find themselves acting as enemies of YHWH at times. When read in light of a more pessimistic passage, such as Job 7, this pattern of failure could lead the reader to believe that the human is destined to side with the enemies of YHWH, and to ask with Eliphaz, "what are mortals that they can be clean . . . or that they can be righteous?" (Job 15:14, NRSV).

Yet, read in light of Psalm 8, this pattern of human failure leads not to despair, but rather to hope. This hope thrusts the reader toward an encounter with God, the source of hope. King YHWH ultimately maintains order, despite the threat of chaos and failure. The question becomes, then, how can YHWH maintain order when his appointed ruling agent consistently fails and often becomes an enemy? In this way, David becomes something of a figure for Adam, as the question of how YHWH will deal with the failure of the Davidic line becomes a microcosm of the question of how YHWH will deal with the failure of humanity in general. I have already shown that the shape of the Psalter addresses the former question in a two-fold way, by leaving hope that YHWH will once again reinstate David (Psalm 144) while at the same time shifting its emphasis toward king YHWH and away from human kings (Ps 146:3-5).

At this point, Paul Noble's suggestion that canonical exegesis adopt a "new typology" may be helpful in terms of understanding the diversity of Old Testament literature.[168] Noble urges that readers of the canon look for narrative patterns occurring in one context and reappearing in another in order to understand one canonical narrative in light of another. Here, I submit that perhaps the broadest pattern possible runs across the Hebrew Bible, regardless of the ordering of the books: that of the conflicted and conflicting human. Again and again, humans such as Adam, Moses, and David follow the same pattern. Such individuals have the potential to be YHWH's agent for order, and, at times, even fulfill this ordering and ruling task. Yet, these same characters fail to live up to this potential, and they are banished from paradise (Gen 3:24), denied entry into the Promised Land (Deut 32:48-52), and stricken by the judgment of YHWH (II Sam 12, 24). The type of the conflicted and conflicting human is even visible at the corporate level in the story of the rise and fall of the Davidic line and in the Israelites' inability to keep the Mosaic covenant (Deut 31:14-29, Jer 31:32). Among these depictions of humans and their plight, the depictions of Adam and Eve, David, and the Davidic line all have special significance for Psalm 8 in light of its literary context (the Psalter, which meditates upon the Davidic line), superscription (לדויד), and content (a meditation upon the human/בן־אדם).

Such a canonical reading can both bring the reader into an encounter with the divine author and engender a love for neighbor within the reader. When the

---

[168] Paul R. Noble, *The Canonical Approach: A Critical Reconstruction of the Hermeneutics of Brevard S. Childs* (BIS 16; New York: E. J. Brill, 1995), 314-322.

reader understands that his own story and the story of all humanity fits within the type of the conflicted and conflicting human, such a realization can produce humility and a deeper sense of love and sympathy for one's neighbor. Specific ethical trajectories will emerge from this *caritas* as the reader finds points of identification and contact between the various humans depicted in the Hebrew Bible, herself, and the various other humans that she encounters in her world.

So, to summarize, the location of Psalm 8 in the context of the Old Testament is best understood in light of the intersection of two trajectories in the broader story: 1) The reversal motif, as distinctly presented in Psalm 8, and 2) the ongoing plight of the humans and humanity, as developed throughout the Hebrew Bible. In the reversal motif of Psalm 8, God maintains the created order by taking relatively insignificant things and exalting them in surprising ways. This is especially seen in the exaltation of the אנוש/בן־אדם to the status of vice-gerent. In the context of the Tanakh, the reversal motif intersects the story of the conflicted and conflicting human, who, on the one hand, is YHWH's chosen agent of rule (Gen 1-2, Ps 8:3a, 5-9), but, on the other hand, has rebelled against God from the start (Gen 3), so that he finds himself on the side of YHWH's enemies (Ps 8:3b), often beset by trouble (Job 7:17-21), and acutely aware of his mortality (Ps 144:4).

In its Old Testament context, then, Psalm 8 serves as a perpetual reminder that God will, in the midst of disorder and human failure, reestablish cosmic order by exalting seemingly insignificant things, even if the human finds herself engulfed in chaos or at enmity with YHWH. In this way, reading Psalm 8 and the Old Testament in connection with one another points the canonically minded reader to the *res*, the God who is at work in the world, engendering love in the reader. The resulting hope and expectation points the Christian reader of the Old Testament towards the New Testament. Indeed, the central affirmation of the Christian faith is that God has dealt with human failure in the person and work of Jesus, the Messiah, who sits on the throne and says "behold, I am making all things new" (Rev 21:5). Therefore, having heard the witness of Psalm 8 in the context of the Tanakh, let us turn now to consider the poem in light of the New Testament witness.

5

PSALM 8 AND THE NEW TESTAMENT

Having examined Psalm 8 and its central question "what is the human" in its Old Testament context, the stage has been set for a consideration of Psalm 8 in connection with the witness of the New Testament. This chapter will examine four passages which cite or echo the language of Psalm 8: Matt 21:1-17, 1 Cor 15:20-28, Eph 1:15-22, and Heb 2:5-9. The chapter will proceed in a manner similar to that of the previous one. Each passage will be considered in turn, offering a level one reading of the passage "in itself," first situating the verses under consideration within their literary context, and then exploring the way in which each passage interprets and applies Psalm 8 to arrive at a level one understanding of each passage. Then, I will bring the message of each passage to bear upon a level two canonical understanding of Psalm 8 by asking how one might interpret Psalm 8 in light of each passage. After considering each of these four passages in turn, the chapter will conclude by synthesizing the results of the survey, paying special attention to the way in which a canonical reading points towards the divine *res* and produces *caritas* in the reader.

One question will impose itself upon every section of this chapter: How do the New Testament authors use and interpret the Old Testament? Much literature has already attended to this question, often paying special attention to the way in which the New Testament applies passages from the Old Testament to Jesus.[1] Because this question has a direct bearing upon how one reads each passage "in itself," I will present my own view concerning the way in which each author is appropriating Psalm 8. Yet, the reader must bear in mind that the

---

[1] Richard Hays, *Echoes of Scripture in the Letters of Paul* (New Haven: Yale University Press, 1989); James H. Charlesworth and Walter P. Weaver, editors, *The Old and the New Testaments: Their Relationship and the "Intertestamental" Literature* (FSC; Valley Forge, PA: Trinity Press International, 1993); Craig A. Evans and James A. Sanders, editors, *Early Christian Interpretation of the Scriptures of Israel: Investigations and Proposals* (JSNTSup 148/SSEJC 5; Sheffield, UK: Sheffield Academic, 1997); Steve Moyise and Maarten J. J. Menken, editors, *The Psalms in the New Testament* (New York, NY: T & T Clark, 2004); Gregory K. Beale and Don A. Carson, *Commentary on the New Testament Use of the Old Testament* (Grand Rapids, MI: Baker Academic, 2007); Donald Juel, *Messianic Exegesis: Christological Interpretation of the Old Testament in Early Christianity* (Philadelphia: Fortress, 1988); and Martin Pickup, "New Testament Interpretation of the Old Testament: The Theological Rationale of Midrashic Exegesis," *JETS* 51 (2008): 353-381.

goal of this study is not to argue for a given view on the question of the New Testament's use of the Old Testament, nor is the ultimate end to present a thorough and final answer to every historical and authorial question raised by the text. Rather, this book intends to articulate a canonical exegesis of Psalm 8 by interpreting Psalm 8 in light of other passages of Scripture. It is my hope, therefore, that readers will find the following canonical reading insightful and persuasive even if they do not agree with me on every point concerning the way in which the New Testament authors have appropriated Old Testament texts.

1. Matthew 21:14-17 and Psalm 8

1.1 Reading Matthew 21:14-17 "In Itself"

1.1.1 The broader context: The Gospel of Matthew. The Gospel of "Matthew is the New Testament book closest to Rabbinical Judaism,"[2] and works on the Gospel of Matthew almost unanimously agree that Matthew was written by a Jewish Christian (or, perhaps, a Christian Jew) for a Jewish Christian audience some time in the latter half of the first century CE.[3] Many distinctive aspects of the gospel of Matthew reflect the Jewishness of the book,[4] and Matthew cites the Old Testament more than any of the other gospels.[5] Matthew also develops Christology in a way that is similar to the Christology of the other gospels, yet reflects Matthew's own emphases and high Christology.[6] Carrying forward themes from his sources, Mark and Q, Matthew utilizes a broad repertoire of images and stories to craft his own distinct portrait of Jesus reflecting the Jewish-Christian concerns of the book; Matthew paints a picture of Jesus as the

---

[2] George D. Kilpatrick, *The Origins of the Gospel According to Matthew* (Oxford, UK: Clarendon, 1946), 101.
[3] Kilpatrick, *Origins*, 101-123; J. Andrew Overman, *Matthew's Gospel and Formative Judaism: The Social World of the Matthean Community* (Minneapolis, MN: Fortress, 1990); Anthony J. Saldarini, *Matthew's Christian-Jewish Community* (Chicago, IL: University of Chicago Press, 1994); David C. Sim, *The Gospel of Matthew and Christian Judaism* (Edinburgh, UK: T & T Clark, 1998); Stephenson H. Brooks, *Matthew's Community: The Evidence of His Special Sayings Material* (JSNTSup 16; Sheffield, UK: Sheffield Academic, 1987). For a survey of approaches to the Gospel of Matthew through the early 2000's, see Donald A. Hagner, "Matthew: Christian Judaism or Jewish Christianity?" in *The Face of New Testament Studies: A Survey of Recent Research* (Grand Rapids, MI: Baker Academic, 2004), 263-282.
[4] See Hagner, "Matthew," 263-264.
[5] John Nolland, *The Gospel of Matthew: A Commentary in the Greek Text* (NIGTC; Grand Rapids, MI: Eerdmans/Paternoster, 2005), 29-33; Robert H. Gundry, *The Use of the Old Testament in Saint Matthew's Gospel, with Special Reference to the Messianic Hope* (NTSup 18; Leiden: Brill, 1975); O. L. Cope, *Matthew: A Scribe Trained for the Kingdom of Heaven* (CBQMS 5; Washington, DC: The Catholic Biblical Association of America, 1976).
[6] "[W]e encounter in Matthew," writes Hagner, "one of the highest Christologies of the NT" ("Matthew," 270).

Son of God, Lord, Son of David, Son of Man, a new Moses, Wisdom, a servant, and one who is with his people.[7]

As Bacon and many others have recognized, the body of Matthew's Gospel seems to have a five-fold structure[8] like many Jewish works of antiquity.[9] Matthew alternates between five narrative sections and five discourse sections. Each of the five discourse sections, with slight variation in wording, conclude with the same formula (Matt 7:28; 11:1; 13:53; 19:1; and 26:1): "when Jesus had finished (these words)/ ὅτε ἐτέλεσσεν ὁ'Ιησοῦς (τοὺς λόγους τούτους)."[10] Several alternatives to Bacon's five-fold construal of Matthew's structure have been proposed,[11] and, among these, Kingsbury's schema is insightful for our purposes.[12] Kingsbury sees the chronological development of Matthew's gospel as developing Matthew's Christology across three sections. The sections focus upon "(a) the genesis and significance of the person of Jesus (1:1-4:16), (b) the nature and effect of his proclamation (4:17-16:20), and (c) the reason and finality of his suffering, death, and resurrection (16:21-28:20)."[13]

Taken together, the two structural proposals of Bacon and Kingsbury can serve as heuristic aids through which to locate the pericope under consideration (21:1-17, especially verses 12-17)[14] in the broader context of the book. Matt

---

[7] I draw these Christological descriptors from Christopher M. Tuckett, *Christology and the New Testament: Jesus and His Earliest Followers* (Edinburgh, UK: University Press, 2001), 119-130. See also J. D. Kingsbury, *Matthew: Structure, Christology, Kingdom* (Philadelphia, PA: Fortress, 1977). For Jesus as a new Moses in the gospel of Matthew, see Dale C. Allison, *A New Moses: A Matthean Typology* (Minneapolis, MN: Fortress, 1993). For Matthew's depiction of Jesus as the Son of David, see Lidija Novakovic, *Messiah, the Healer of the Sick: A Study of Jesus as the Son of David in the Gospel of Matthew* (WUNT 2:170; Tübingen: Mohr Siebeck, 2003).

[8] Scholars usually identify Benjamin W. Bacon (*Studies in Matthew* [New York, NY: Holt, 1930]) as the originator of this hypothesis (so W. D. Davies and Dale C. Allison, *A Critical and Exegetical Commentary on The Gospel According to Matthew in Three Volumes* [ICC; Edinburgh, UK: T & T Clark, 1988] 1:59, and Kingsbury, *Matthew*, 2). Craig S. Keener, however, points out that the notion that Jesus's five discourse sections parallel the five books of the Pentateuch is as old as Papias (*Matthew* [IVPNTCS; Downers Grove, IL: InterVarsity, 1997], 30).

[9] Allison lists the following works as evincing a five-fold structure: "the Pentatuech, the Psalter, the Megilloth, Jason of Cyrene's Maccabean history (c.f. 2 Macc. 2:23), *Jubilees, I Enoch*, [and] the early form of *Mishnah 'Abot*," though Allison also includes several Christian works: "Papias' *Exposition of the Oracles of the Lord* . . . Irenaeus' *Adversus Haereses*, and Hippolytus' memoirs" (*The New Moses*, 296).

[10] See Davies and Allison, *Matthew*, I: 58-72 for a relatively brief yet in depth and judicious treatment of the structure of Matthew. See also Bacon, *Studies*, 80-91.

[11] See Davies and Allison, *Matthew* I: 60-61.

[12] Kingsbury, *Matthew*, 25-37.

[13] Ibid., 36.

[14] For Matt 21:1-17 as a unit, see Norbert Lohfink, "Der Messiaskönig und seine Armen kommen zum Zion: Beobachtungen zu Mt 21,1-17," in *Studien zum Matthäusevangelium: Festschrift für Wilhelm Pesch* (SBS; Stuttgart: Kath. Bibelwerk, 1988), 179-200; Sandra Hübenthal, "'Wer ist dieser?' Mt 21,1-17 in intertextueller

21:1-17 recounts the triumphal entry, and is located in the last part of the book in both the three- and five-fold schemas. In leading up to Matt 21:1-17, the narrative has been simultaneously developing its portrait of Christ and moving towards the climactic death and resurrection of Christ. Matt 21:1-17 represents an elevated point within the book's development, whether it is construed as part of the narrative sequence preceding Jesus's passion (as per the five-fold schema) or as a key moment in a longer final episode of the book encompassing all of Jesus's last days (as per the three-fold schema). If Davies and Allison are correct that Matt 21:1-17 intentionally parallels Matt 1-2 and Matt 28:16-20, the importance of our pericope in the role of the narrative and Christological development of Matthew increases.[15] In Matthew 21 Jesus finally arrives in Jerusalem, the place that he has been progressively moving towards where the pivotal event of his crucifixion will take place (Matthew 27).[16] Furthermore, our pericope and the material adjacent to it (Matt 20:29-21:22) refines the portrait of Jesus, recounting "[t]he miraculous deeds and prophetic acts of the messianic Son of David in and near Jerusalem and its temple."[17]

1.1.2 The nearer context: Matt 21:1-17. Matt 21:1-17 contains several connected episodes. In the first and longest scene (Matt 21:1-11) Matthew recounts the triumphal entry, where the Matthean Jesus sends his disciples to procure two donkeys for him (Matt 21:1-6), then Jesus rides the donkeys into Jerusalem, where he is greeted by a jubilant and amazed crowd (Matt 21:7-11). Next, Matt 21:12-13 recounts Jesus's cleansing of the temple, followed by the verses containing the citation of Psalm 8, which are unique to the Gospel of Matthew and have no synoptic parallels (verses 14-16). These verses recount a conflict between Jesus and the priests centering around Jesus's healing of the blind and lame and his acclamation by children who are crying out "Hosanna to the Son of David" (Matt 21:14-16). Within the context of this conflict, the Matthean Jesus

---

Lektüre," in *Der Bibelkanonon in der Bibelauslegung: Methodenreflexionen und Beispielexegesen* (ed. Egbert Ballhorn and Georg Steins; Stuttgart: Verlag W. Kohlhammer, 2007), 260-277.

[15] See Davies and Allison, *Matthew*, III:3; Wenceslaus M. Urassa, *Psalm 8 and its Christological Re-Interpretations in the NewTestament Context: An Inter-Contextual Study in Biblical Hermeneutics.* (EUS 23:577; New York: Peter Lang, 1998), 145.

[16] Although John Nolland follows neither the five-fold schema nor the three-fold schema, his treatment of Matt 21:1-11 as concluding a section organized around Jesus' progression toward Jerusalem and Matt 21:12-17 as beginning a new section dedicated to Jesus's "provocative ministry in Jerusalem" is insightful in terms of demonstrating the function that Matt 21:1-17 plays within the development of the narrative (*The Gospel of Matthew*, 840-841) as a transition from Jesus's movement toward Jerusalem to Jesus's ministry in Jerusalem.

[17] Davies and Allison, *Matthew*, III: 3.

quotes Psalm 8:3 in his self-defense (Matt 21:16). The pericope then concludes by recounting Jesus' departure from Jerusalem (Matt 21:17).[18]

Several of the various Matthean Christological descriptors mentioned above have special prominence in Matt 21:1-17. The most important of these is the title, "Son of David." This title is affirmed explicitly by Jesus' followers (verses 9 and 15), and implicitly both by Jesus, who enacts the messianic prophecy of Zech 9:9 (verses 1-3, 6), and by the narrator who tells the reader that "this took place so that what was spoken through the prophet might be fulfilled (πληρωθῇ)" (verse 4). In a more subtle vein, Davies and Allison identify several indicators that Matthew's description of Jesus here evokes images of Moses, so that "21.1-17 reactivates the Moses typology apparent in 1.1-8.1"[19] Urassa finds at least one other Christological motif worth considering, as he reads Jesus's citation of Ps 8:3 in light of Matthew's depiction of Jesus as the "son of Man" (compare Ps 8:5).[20] Yet, Matthew 21 never describes Jesus as the "son of Man," and the Matthean Jesus does not cite Ps 8:5; therefore, the question of whether or not Matthew is developing his "son of Man" motif by depicting Jesus as applying Ps 8:3 to himself hinges upon the way in which the Gospel of Matthew (or, perhaps more precisely, the Matthean Jesus) interprets and applies Ps 8:3, which will be discussed below.

Concerning the structure of Matt 21:1-17, in light of the fact that Mark and Luke do not juxtapose the triumphal entry (Matt 21:1-9) with the cleansing of the temple (Matt 21:12-17),[21] some see Matt 21:1-11 and Matt 21:12-17 as two distinct, independent sections.[22] Yet, scholars increasingly recognize an artistic

---

[18] For a brief discussion about the various ways that one might understand the judgment upon the temple establishment depicted in verses 12-17, see Craig S. Keener, *A Commentary on the Gospel of Matthew* (Grand Rapids, MI: Eerdmans, 1999), 495-501.

[19] Davies and Allison, *Matthew*, III:144. Davies and Allison note the following connections between the Moses of tradition and the Jesus of Matt 21:1-17: 1) Both are described as "meek."2) Moses' riding upon two donkeys (Exod 4:19, the LXX) underlies Zech 9:9, and Jesus's riding upon two donkeys fulfills Zech 9:9. 3) The children singing at the Red Sea had been applied by tradition to Ps 8:3, just as the children singing about Jesus is applied by Jesus to Ps 8:3.4) Moses, like Jesus, was both a prophet and king. 5) intriguing lexical similarities are to be found between Moses's sending out of the children of Israel in Exod 12:28 (the LXX) and Jesus' sending out of the disciples in Matt 21:6. 6) Intriguing lexical similarities are also to be found between Moses's doing of wonders in Deut 34:12 (the LXX) and Jesus's doing of wonders in Matt 21:15.

[20] Urassa, *Psalm 8*, 139-153.

[21] In between Mark's account of the triumphal entry (Mark 11:1-10) and the cleansing of the temple (11:15-18), Mark interposes a note about Jesus entering and leaving Jerusalem (Mark 11:11; see also Matt 21:10, 17) and the story of Jesus cursing the fig tree (Mark 11:12-14). Similarly, Luke inserts a description of Jesus weeping over Jerusalem (Luke 19:41-44) between the triumphal entry (19:28-40) and the temple cleansing (19:45-47).

[22] Nolland, for example, reckons verses 1-11 and verses 12-17 as belonging to two distinct blocks of material in the Gospel of Matthew (*Matthew*, 830-849).

unity binding together all of Matt 21:1-17.²³ Lohfink, for example, reads Matt 21:1-17 as a unified chiasm, built around five Old Testament citations, as follows:²⁴

A 21,5: Erzähler (?): Reflexionszitat von Jes 62,11 und Sach 9,9
   B 21,9: Akklamation der Scharen nach Ps 118,25f, vgl. Mt 21,15
      C 21,13: Jesus: Begründung der Reinigung des Temples durch Jes 56,7 + Jer 7,11
   B' 21,15: Akklamation der Kinder nach Ps 118,25, vgl. Mt 21,9
A' 21,16: Jesus: Antwort an seine Gegner: Ps 8,3

Similarly, Sandra Hübenthal, reads Matt 21:1-17 as a chiastic unity, though she proposes a somewhat different structure for the passage.²⁵ She places verses 10 and 11 at the center, making the question "Who is this?/τίς ἐστιν οὗτος" the "Kernsatz" of the pericope.²⁶ According to Hübenthal, the *Zentrum* of the passage (verses 10-11) is flanked by two scenes, each built around two Old Testament citations, "Szene I," the entry into the city, and "Szene II," Jesus in the Temple.²⁷ While the proposals of Hübenthal and Lohfink differ signifi-

---

²³ W. Weren lists five points of evidence for the unity of Matt 21:1-17: 1) Unlike the parallel passages in Mark and Luke, Matt 21:1-17 occurs on a single day, and Jesus does not leave Jerusalem until Matt 21:17. 2) The passage mentions everal locations (Matt 21:1, 10, 12, and 17), which work together to trace a trajectory of movement toward, into, in, and then out of Jerusalem. 3) Several verbal repetitions permeate both halves of the text (verses 1-11 and 12-17). 4) The text, via these repetitions, implies that the shouts of "Hosanna" from the first half have continued without interruption into the second half (Matt 21:9, 15). 5) The pattern of a) people shouting "Hosanna," b) a question arising from the shouts, and c) an answer being given to the question occurs twice, once in each half of the pericope (Matt 21:10-11, 15-16; "Jesus' Entry into Jerusalem: Mt 21,1-17 in the Light of the Hebrew Bible and the Septuagint," in *The Scriptures in the Gospels* [ed. C. M. Tuckett; BETL 81; Leuven: Leuven University Press, 1997], 117-118).
²⁴ Lohfink, "Der Messiaskönig," 187. Lohfink's outline in English, according to my translation with minor alterations, is as follows:
A) 21:5: Narrator (?): Reflection upon the citation of Isa 62:11 and Zech 9:9.
   B) 21:9: Acclamation of the crowds (Ps 118.25 and following, see Mt 21.15)
      C) 21:13: Jesus, justification by the cleansing of the Temple (Isa 56:7 + Jer 7:11)
   B') 21:15: acclamation of the children (Ps 118.25, see Matt 21:9)
A') 21.16: Jesus: Answer to his opponents: Ps 8:3.
The "(?)" after Erzähler/Narrator is original to Lohfink. See also Urassa, *Psalm 8*, 120.
²⁵ Sandra Hübenthal, "'Wer ist dieser?' Mt 21,1-17 in intertextueller Lektüre," in *Der Bibelkanon in der Bibelauslegung: Methodenreflexionen und Beispielexegesen* (Ed. Egbert Ballhorn and Georg Steins; Stuttgart, Germany: Verlag W. Kohlhammer, 2007), 264-268.
²⁶ Hübenthal, "'Wer ist dieser?'" 267.
²⁷ Ibid.

cantly,[28] both construals can yield insight into the role that the citation of Psalm 8 plays in Matt 21:1-17. On the one hand, when one looks to the pericope's content, narrative development, and proportions, verses 10-11 and the pivotal question "who is this?" form a natural center, as Hübenthal observes.[29] Read in this way, the crowd's wonderment at Jesus in verses 10-11 simultaneously 1) heightens the development of Matthews' increasingly refined Christology and 2) encourages the readers to ponder, with the crowd, who Jesus is as they read the text's description of his activity.[30]

On the other hand, Lohfink and Urassa provide insight in that they see Jesus's citation of Ps 8:3 as occupying a special place in "the prophetic drama" of Matt 21:1-16.[31] In the narrative leading up to Matt 21:16, Jesus self-consciously arrives in messianic fashion (verses 1-6), and the crowds and children receive him in a similarly messianic fashion (verses 9-11, 15). While the precise relevance of the healing miracles for the messianic claims of Jesus seems ambiguous,[32] here, as elsewhere, Jesus performs acts of healing in

---

[28] *Contra* Lohfink, Hübenthal sees the pericope as structured around four citations, not five, (reckoning the mention of the children chanting "Hosanna" in Matt 21:15 not as a citation of Psalm 118, but rather as a reference to an earlier citation). This discrepancy results in a shift, wherein Hübenthal reckons the combined citation of Isa 56:7 and Jer 7:11 as standing in the second *tiel*, "*Szene II,*" while Lohfink places them at the center. Hübenthal's center becomes verses 10 and 11, which, according to Lohfink, stand before the center (Hübenthal, "Wer ist dieser?" 265-267 and Lohfink, "Der Messiaskönig").
[29] While both Urassa and Hübenthal urge that the Old Testament citations form the framework for the passage's structure, both produce an outline for the passage that is too tidy and mechanical. Furthermore, neither author makes it clear how one ought to determine which citations form the basis for the structure; in addition to the question of whether or not both quotations of Psalm 118 ought to figure into the structural outline, one might ask whether the allusion to II Sam 5:8 in Matt 21:14 has structural significance. When one considers instead the internal development of the passage, verses 10-11 lie roughly at the middle point of the passage and focus upon a central question which permeates the entire episode ("Who is this?"), and Jesus' entry into Jerusalem is the central point in the spatial movement of the narrative. Also, the observations that verses 10-11 are unique to Matthew and that only Matthew combines the two episodes in verses 1-9 and verses 12-16 argue for the centrality of verses 10-11; Matthew reworks two episodes into a single pericope, using verses 10-11 as a transitional hinge (see Davies and Allison, *Matthew* III:126-127).
[30] "Kernsatz bleibt dabei die Frage," writes Hübenthal, "die nicht nur an die mit Jesus in Jerusalem Einziehenden, sondern auch an die Rezipienten gerichtet ist und die Letztere mit ihrem eigene Schrift- und Glaubenswissen beantworten sollen: Wer ist dieser?" ("Wer ist dieser?" 277). Compare with Davies and Allison, *Matthew*, III: 127.
[31] Adopting Hübenthal's proposal that verses 10-11 form the center of the chiasm does not mean that one cannot recognize the citation of Psalm 8 toward the end of the passage as having an important and climactic role in the development of the passage (see Urassa, *Psalm 8*, 121, Lohfink, "Der Messiaskönig," 185-187. See also Hübenthal, "Wer ist dieser?" 275).
[32] See Novakovic, *Messiah*, 91-95.

connection with the claim that he is the Son of David (verse 14).³³ A conflict accompanies the recognition of Jesus as the "Son of David," as Jesus cleanses the temple in a challenge to the temple establishment (verses 12-14), and the chief priests and scribes are aghast at all that is happening (verse 15). When Jesus rebuts the priests and scribes by quoting Ps 8:3, the passage comes to its full development in terms of 1) the passage's movement towards a heightening emphasis upon and affirmation of (by the children and narrator) Jesus's messianic identity, and 2) the increasing conflict between Jesus and the priests. Here, the Matthean Jesus unambiguously affirms those who identify him as the "Son of David," and he also leaves his opponents speechless.

1.1.3 The use of Psalm 8:3 in Matthew 21:16. Having surveyed Matt 21:16 in context, it is possible now to look more closely at the way in which Matthew (or the Jesus of Matthew) appropriates Ps 8:3.³⁴ The Matthean Jesus seems to assume that the psalm is somehow fulfilled by the children's acclamation of him as the "Son of David" in this episode.³⁵ Furthermore, Matthew's use of the Old Testament is often oriented towards demonstrating how Jesus fulfills the words of the text, a pattern which is explicit in the uniquely Matthean formula, "[ἐ]πληρώθη τὸ ῥηθέν/what was spoken was fulfilled" (Matt 2:17; 13:35; 27:9; passim), including one instance where Jesus is said to "fulfill" a psalm (Ps 78:2 in 13:35).³⁶ Also, the Matthean Jesus interprets a psalm messianically elsewhere (Matt 22:43-45), and Matthew's willingness to interpret the psalms prophetically was not aberrational in comparison with other Second Temple Jewish sects.³⁷ Moreover, the thrust of the context of Matt 21:1-17 moves toward a heightened emphasis upon Jesus as the Son of David, especially as the crowds and the children recognize him as such, and this thrust seems to culminate with the citation of Ps 8:3 in verse 16.

Yet, the question remains: How, exactly does the Matthean Jesus see the words of Ps 8:3 as applying to the scene unfolding in Matthew 21? As already

---

³³ The majority of the occurrences of the moniker "Son of David" in Matthew come in connection with healing stories (See Novakovic, *Messiah*, 2).
³⁴ This section continues the focus upon the level one meaning of Matthew 21:16, reading the text "in itself." I will return below to consider level two meanings, reading Psalm 8 in the light of Matt 21:1-17 and the Gospel of Matthew. In preparation for such considerations, however, this section will explore the way in which the Gospel of Matthew takes up the psalm in the context of Jesus's conflict in the temple.
³⁵ Maarten J. J. Menken, "The Psalms in Matthew's Gospel," in *The Psalms in the New Testament* (ed. Steve Moyise and Maarten J. J. Menken; NTSL; New York, NY: T & T Clark, 2004), 70-72, Craig L. Blomberg, "Matthew," in *Commentary on the New Testament Use of the Old Testament* (ed. Gregory K. Beale and Donald A. Carson; Grand Rapids, MI: Baker Academic, 2007), 70, and J. Samuel Subramanian, *The Synoptic Gospels and Psalms as Prophecy* (LNTS 351; New York, NY: T & T Clark, 2007), 107-109.
³⁶ See Menken, "Psalms in Matthew's Gospel," 81, and Subramanian, 91-123.
³⁷ The Qumran literature, for example applies a fulfillment hermeneutic to the book of Psalms and speaks of David as a prophet. See Subramanian, *Synoptic Gospels*, 19-44.

noted, Urassa interprets the appropriation of Jesus's words here in light of Matthew's claim elsewhere that Jesus is the "Son of Man" (Matt 24:30; 26:64; Ps 8:5).[38] Such a connection makes some sense, insofar as the other references to Psalm 8 in the New Testament apply things that the Lord does to the "Son of Man/Child of Humanity" in Ps 8:6-9, to Jesus (1 Cor 15:27; Eph 1:22; Heb 2:5-9).[39] So, it is not unreasonable to suggest that the author and audience of Matthew would have been aware of the messianic interpretation of Psalm 8 reflected in 1 Cor 15:27 and (arguably) Heb 2:5-9 and that they would have understood such a messianic interpretation in light of the messianic "Son of Man" figure. Yet, such an understanding can, at best, only partially account for the citation of the passage here. The Matthean Jesus makes no mention of the "Son of Man" here, nor does he address the part of Psalm 8 that speaks directly of the "child of humanity" (verses 6-9). Also, as Lidija Novakovic has cautioned elsewhere, one must be careful to avoid the exegetical equivalent of an "illegitimate totality transfer" by reading into Matthew's citations material from the passage's broader context that Matthew may not be addressing.[40]

Furthermore, one need not look beyond Ps 8:3 itself to find points of connection between the two passages; the events of Matt 21:1-17 (especially verses 14-17) parallel the scene described in Ps 8:3. The children proclaiming "Hosanna" in Matt 21:14 parallel the νηπίων καὶ θηλαζόντων (babies and sucklings) of Ps 8:3 (LXX) through whose στόματος (mouth) God establishes αἶνον (praise). Furthermore, though not explicitly mentioned by Jesus, the "foes," "enemy," and "avenger" of Ps 8:3 have their counterpart in the chief priests and scribes of Matt 21:14-17;[41] just as YHWH uses children to silence (MT: להשבית, LXX: καταλῦσαι) his foes in Psalm 8, so the chief priests and scribes have no answer to give to Jesus and are effectively silenced by the children of Matt 21:14.[42] Thus, Subramanian aptly summarizes Matthew's use of Psalm 8 in connection with the broader context of Matt 21:1-17 and its emphasis upon Jesus as the Son of David as follows: "By relating Ps 8.3a LXX to the messianic cry of children (cf. Mt 21.15), Matthew seems to read Ps 8.3a LXX as a

---

[38] Urassa, *Psalm 8*, 149-151.
[39] See Menken, "Psalms in Matthew's Gospel," 80.
[40] "Matthew's Atomistic Use of Scripture: Messianic Interpretation of Isaiah 53.4 in Matthew 8.17" in *Biblical Interpretation in Early Christian Gospels Vol. 2: The Gospel of Matthew* (LNTS 310; ed. Thomas R. Hatina; New York, NY: T & T Clark, 2008), 147-162. But see also Gundry, *Use of the Old Testament*, 205-208, who argues that "Dodd's main thesis that New Testament quotations tend to be drawn from Old Testament contexts which are exploited as a whole by various New Testament authors is remarkably confirmed" in the case of Matthew. Check original.
[41] See Hübenthal, "Mt21,1-17," 275. As Hübenthal notes, what is particularly interesting about Jesus's citation of Ps 8:3 is "was er nicht zitiert."
[42] Subramanian, *The Synoptic Gospels*, 109. See also Peter C. Craigie, *Psalms 1-50* (WBC, 19; Waco, TX: Word Books, 1983), 109-110.

prophecy about the praise of children who disclose the messianic identity of Jesus as the Son of David."[43]

Davies and Allison argue for another messianic motif implied by Matthew's use of the verse, noting that rabbinic tradition connected Ps 8:3 with the Song of the Sea (Exodus 15).[44] It is difficult to establish with certainty that the Rabbinic connection of Ps 8:3 with Exod 15:1 represents an understanding of Psalm 8 that underlies the words of the Matthean Jesus here. Nevertheless, Wisd. 10:21 uses language similar to that of Ps 8:3 to describe children singing the Song of the Sea, increasing the likelihood that Ps 8:3 had been hermeneutically connected with Exodus 15 prior to the time of the writing of the Gospel of Matthew.[45] Furthermore, Davies and Allison point out other possible subtle connections between the depiction of Moses elsewhere and the depiction of Jesus in Matt 21:1-17, increasing the probability that the citation of Ps 8:3 contributes to a larger agenda to subtly portray Jesus as a new Moses.[46] If Davies and Allison are correct, Matthew implies here that Jesus's actions in Matt 21:1-17 parallel those of Moses at the Red Sea; just as the deliverance effected under Moses prompted children to sing in Exodus 15, the anticipated deliverance by the Son of David prompts children to sing in Matthew 21. Read in this way, the subtle "New Moses" motif does not undermine or supplant the identification of Jesus with the "Son of David" in the rest of the passage. Rather, the new Moses motif enriches the Son of David motif and, together, they enhance and develop Matthew's christology.

Yet, at least one question remains. Ps 8:3 speaks of infants praising YHWH, but Jesus applies the verse to children crying out "Hosanna *to the Son of David* (τῷ υἱῷ Δαυίδ)." Is Matthew depicting Jesus here as understanding himself to be God? Or does he depict Jesus as, at the very least, likening his role in relation to the children crying out to the role of YHWH in relation to the

---

[43] Subramanian, *The Synoptic Gospels*, 109.
[44] Davies and Allison, *Matthew*, III: 141-142, 144. Davies and Allison point especially to the *Mekilta* on Exodus 15:1. They also note several texts as deriving the belief that children praised God at the Red Sea from the connection between Ps 8:3 and Exod 15:1 via their shared usage of the word עולל (*Tosefta Sota* 6.4; *Jerusalem Talmud Sota* 5.4; *Babylonian Talmud Berakot* 56b; *Babylonian Talmud Sota* 30b; *Targum Yerušalmi* on Exodus 15:2; *Midrash Psalm 8:5*).
[45] This verse says that, after the crossing of the Red Sea, Wisdom "opened the moth of the dumb, and made the tongues of babes speak clearly." Davies and Allison, *Matthew* III: 142.
[46] Davies and Allison note the following other connections between the Moses tradition and the Jesus of Matt 21:1-17: 1) Moses and Jesus are both "meek" (Matt 21:5); 2) "Moses returned to Egypt with at least two asses (LXX Exod 4.19) which event came to be associated with Zech 9.9," and Jesus rode two donkeys in fulfillment of Zech 9:9 (Matt 21:5); 3) Moses and Jesus are both called a prophet and a king; 4) Exod 12:28 describes the Israelites following the commands of the LORD through Moses, and Matt 21:6 describes Jesus' disciples following his commands in very similar language; 5) Just as Deut 34:12 speaks of "the wonders that Moses did," Matt 21:15 speaks of "the wonders that Jesus did" (*Matthew* III:144).

praising infants and nursing babes in Psalm 8, as Weren and Menken believe?[47] Or, is Blomberg closer to the mark when he says that "[t]he children . . . almost certainly were praising Yahweh for what they believed he was doing in Jesus, not praising Jesus as God directly"?[48] Moreover, does the Jesus of Matthew 21 stand in for God, Moses, the "Son of Man," or someone else?[49]

While many interesting explanations to these questions have been proposed, I will suggest that neither Matthew nor the Matthean Jesus directly address such questions; when Jesus cites Ps 8:3a in Matt 21:16, he does not present a clear explanation of every word of the quotation for his audience. Rather, it is part of the rhetorical strategy of Matthew here to push the reader to ponder the question that Hübenthal identifies as the *Kernsatz*: "Who is this?"[50] Therefore, in light of such ambiguities at the level one meaning of the text, the canonical interpreter ought not to force the text to give a refined and systematic answer to every Christological question that the reader might have. Rather, the reader ought to follow Augustine's advice, and turn to the rest of Scripture for clarification on Christological questions.[51] I turn now, therefore, to consider the implications of the interpretation of Ps 8:3 in Matt 21:1-17 for a canonical understanding of Psalm 8.

1.2 Reading Psalm 8 in Light of Matthew 21:1-17

The Christian canonical reader who returns to consider Psalm 8 after reading Matthew 21:14-17 in its broader context of the Gospel of Matthew must, above all else, reckon with Matthew's portrayal of Jesus as the Messiah, Son of David, and Son of Man. I have already argued that the function of Psalm 8 in the context of the Old Testament can be described as representing the intersection of two trajectories in the broader story: 1) The reversal motif, as distinctly presented in Psalm 8, and 2) the status of the human in the broader context of the Old Testament canon. From the point of view of the Christian, both of these trajectories take a new turn in the person of Jesus, whom the Christian affirms as "the author and perfector of our faith" (Heb 12:2, NIV). Jesus violates the type of the conflicted and conflicting human in radical ways, and in so doing becomes the ultimate instantiation of the reversal motif by which God restores order to the cosmos. Indeed, the Christian understands Jesus to be the *res* to which the text points, the divine reality which the canonical interpreter seeks to encounter. As a result, two claims from Matt 21:1-17 and the Gospel of

---

[47] W. Weren, "Jesus' Entry," 138, Menken, "The Psalms in Matthew's Gospel," 72.
[48] Blomberg, "Matthew," 70.
[49] For Jesus as God here, see Weren, "Jesus' Entry," 139. For Jesus as Moses here, see Davies and Allison, *Matthew*, III: 143-144. For Jesus as the "Son of Man" here, see Urassa, *Psalm 8*, 149-151.
[50] Hübenthal, "'Wer ist dieser?'"
[51] *Doc. Chr.* Book III: 2. See also Brevard S. Childs, "Psalm 8 in the Context of the Christian Canon," *Interpretation* 23 (1969), 23.

Matthew impinge upon our reading of Psalm 8: 1) Jesus is the Messiah, and 2) the scene described in Matt 21:14-17 is an enactment of the scene in Ps 8:3.

Concerning the first claim, I have already noted that, of Matthew's several Christological labels, the most prominent in Matt 21:1-17 is that of "Son of David."[52] Thus, the Gospel of Matthew points the reader back to the Old Testament narrative of the rise, fall, and hoped for restoration of the Davidic line, which narrative I have described in chapter four as fitting into the type of the conflicted and conflicting human. Furthermore, the connection of the proclamation that Jesus is the "Son of David" with the festival recitation of the *hallel* hymn, Psalm 118, provides an entry point through which the canonical reader might move from a consideration of the portrayal of the Son of David in Matt 21:1-17 to a consideration of the portrayal of David in the Psalter and the role of Psalm 8 within that portrayal; while, as Wilson points out, the Septuagint Psalter underlying the chanting of the children is more Davidic than the MT Psalter,[53] the MT Psalter still meditates upon the rise, fall, and hoped for return of David. I have argued in chapter three and four that Psalm 8, in the Psalter as in the Old Testament, provides a moment of "orientation" for the reader, wherein the reader learns to hope that God will intervene on behalf of the insignificant to maintain order. This hope then encourages the reader to focus upon king YHWH, yet leaves the possibility open that king YHWH might act on behalf of the fallen Davidic line (Psalm 144). Thus, when one reads Psalm 8 in light of the claim that Jesus is the "Son of David," one begins to understand Jesus as fulfilling that hope. The orienting hope of Psalm 8, founded in the claim that YHWH exalts babies over his enemies (Ps 8:3) and humans over the majestic lights (Ps 8:4-6), now comes to fruition in the restoration of the Davidic line through Jesus.

Furthermore, while Matthew may not necessarily be portraying Jesus as a "Son of Man" figure in chapter 21, the fact that Matthew describes Jesus as the "Son of Man" elsewhere might inform how one understands the words "אדם־בן/child of humanity" in Ps 8:5. On the one hand, the Christological usage of the phrase "the son of man" in Matthew has greater affinities with Dan 7:13 than Ps 8:5.[54] Therefore, a canonical reading of Psalm 8 in light of the Gospel of Matthew does not need to understand Ps 8:5 as a direct foretelling of an event in the life of Jesus. Yet, on the other hand, the way in which Matthew describes Jesus as "ὁ υἱὸς τοῦ ἀνθρώπου" (Matt 8:20; 9:6 20:18) has implications for a canonical understanding of Psalm 8's בן־אדם. As Urassa notes, "for Matthew . . . the 'term'—'Son of Man' signifies . . . the messianic office given to Jesus

---

[52] In addition to the discussion of verses 1-17 above, see also C. Keener, who construes verses 1-11 as communicating several key points to the audience about the nature of Christ as the Davidic King (*A Commentary on the Gospel of Matthew*, 489-495).
[53] Gerald H. Wilson, *The Editing of the Hebrew Psalter*, (SBLDS 76; Chico, CA: Scholars, 1985), 173-180.
[54] See Delbert Burkett, *The Son of Man Debate: A History and Evaluation* (New York, NY: Cambridge University Press, 1999), 97-120 and James G. Crossley, *The Solution to the 'Son of Man' Problem* (LNTS 343; New York, NY: T & T Clark, 2007), 266-273.

by his Father to restore the creation back to its original condition, before the fall of the first Adam."[55] When one reads Psalm 8 in light of such a depiction of Jesus, both the ideal world of Gen 1-2 and the ordered world of Psalm 8 seem tenable once again; the lost world may yet be found. Jesus, the Son of David and Son of Man, will fulfill the office of Davidic ruler, vanquish YHWH's enemies (Ps 8:3), and thus enable humanity to finally fulfill its corporate role of vice-gerent (Ps 8:5-9). In short, Matthew's claim that Jesus is the Messiah informs the way in which a canonical reader understands God's maintenance of the created order described in Psalm 8.

How then does the claim that Matt 21:14-17 describes an enactment of the scene in Ps 8:3 inform a canonical reading of the psalm? In the first place, if Ps 8:5 need not become a prophetic utterance applicable only to Jesus the "Son of Man," neither does Ps 8:3 need to become a prophetic oracle wherein the psalmist envisioned the events of the temple cleansing.[56] Rather, the scene of Ps 8:2 remains a paradigmatic expression of YHWH's method of maintaining the created order, but takes on a fuller meaning in light of Matt 21:14-17. On the canonical level and in light of the reading of Psalm 8 that I have presented, Jesus's words in Matt 21:16 lead the reader to understand the event of the coming of the Messiah as the moment in which the paradigm of Ps 8:3 is perfectly enacted. At that time, insignificant children silence the enemies of God by acknowledging that the Messiah has come.[57] Thus, when one reads Psalm 8 in light of the complex of characters that enact the scene of Ps 8:3 in Matt 21, one has a clearer understanding of what constitutes an agent of YHWH and what constitutes an enemy of YHWH; not only do the humble agents of YHWH "take the *name* of God on their lips,"[58] unlike the self-strong enemies, but they also acknowledge God's Messiah. Quoting Craigie:

> In his rebuke to the authorities, [Jesus] brought out the inherent contrast in the original psalm; the children take the *name* upon their lips (interpreting *Son of David*, from the perspective of the early church, as a messianic title), but the authorities are indignant and complain—in effect, they are the foes and the avengers of the psalm. But, as in the psalm, it is the children who have the truer perception, not the arrogant enemies.[59]

To summarize, then, one need not reduce Psalm 8 to a source for Christological proof-texts in order to understand Psalm 8 in its canonical context. Rather, when read in light of Matthew 21:1-17, the Christian interpreter sees that God's method of maintaining the created order is played out in the life of the Messiah. In order to flesh out the relationship between Psalm 8 and the

---

[55] Urassa, *Psalm 8*, 141.
[56] So Donald A. Carson, "Matthew," in *The Expositor's Bible Commentary*, vol. 8 (ed. Frank E. Gaebelein; Grand Rapids, MI: Zondervan, 1984), 443.
[57] See C. Keener, *Matthew*, 316-317.
[58] Craigie, *Psalms 1-50*, 107. Emphasis Craigie's.
[59] Craigie, *Psalms 1-50*, 109-110.

canonical witness concerning Jesus the Messiah, the following sections will consider the rest of the New Testament passages that cite Psalm 8.

2. 1 Corinthians 15:25-28 and Psalm 8

2.1 Reading 1 Corinthians 15:25-28 "In Itself"

2.1.1 The broader context: 1 Corinthians. It is fairly certain that Paul wrote his first epistle to the Corinthians some time in the early to middle 50's CE in order to address controversies arising within the fledgling Corinthian church and to counter teaching promulgated by opponents of Paul.[60] While various proposals have been set forth concerning the precise identity of Paul's opponents at Corinth,[61] current research tends to view them as variegated;[62] in light of Paul's description of his opponents as divisive schismatic (1 Cor 1:11-17; 3:4-8) and the various theological issues addressed by Paul in 1 and 2 Corinthians, it seems unlikely that Paul's opponents represent a unified, monolithic group. Rather, 1 Corinthians addresses a wide array of misinterpretations of the gospel arising from the ongoing influence of "culturally ingrained habits from [the Corinthians'] pagan past and . . . values instilled by a popularized secular ethics."[63]

Insofar as "Christ crucified, Christ risen, [and] Christ coming again permeates the whole epistle (1:6; 10:3; 12:12; 15:23; 16:22),"[64] 1 Corinthians exhibits a unity of theme and purpose. Yet, Paul seems to focus his attention upon several diverse theological sub-topics throughout the epistle. Thus, it is possible to understand the structure of the epistle as cohering around the letter's several sub-topics, such that, to delineate the structure of the epistle is to survey the

---

[60] For discussions about questions of chronology, dating, etc., see Alan F. Johnson, *1 Corinthians* (IVPNTCS; Downers Grove, IL: InterVarsity, 2004), 20-22, Gordon D. Fee, *The First Epistle to the Corinthians* (NICNT; Grand Rapids, MI: 1987), 4-15, and J. M. Gilchrest, "Paul and the Corinthians: The Sequence of the Letters and Visits," *JSNT* 34 (1988): 47-69.

[61] For a summary of various approaches to identifying various Pauline opponents throughout the Pauline corpus, see Jerry L. Sumney "Studying Paul's Opponents: Advances and Challenges" in *Paul and His Opponents* (PS 2; ed. Stanley E. Porter; Leiden: Brill, 2005), 7-58. For a survey of approaches to identifying the Corinthian opponents in particular, see Albert V. Garcialazo, *The Corinthian Dissenters and the Stoics* (New York, NY: Peter Lang, 2007), 79-125. Garcialazo himself argues for a primarily Stoic influence upon the Corinthian opponents.

[62] See Ben Witherington (*Conflict and Community in Corinth: A Socio-Rhetorical Commentary on 1 and 2 Corithians* [Grand Rapids, MI: Eerdmans, 1995], 72-78, and David E. Garland, *1 Corinthians* (BECNT; Grand Rapids, MI: Baker, 2003), 13-14. As Garland observes, "[o] ne theological misconception . . . is unlikely to explain the sundry problems Paul addresses in the letter . . . It is far more likely that the influences on them were more amorphous."

[63] Garland, *I Corinthians*, 13.

[64] Johnson, *I Corinthians*, 27.

topics addressed within the epistle.⁶⁵ Read in this way, the structure of 1 Corinthians is as follows:⁶⁶

Greetings and Introduction (1:1-9).
I. The Gospel and Wisdom (1:10-4:21); Paul urges the superiority of his gospel over other modes of knowledge that have rhetorical appeal, but no real spiritual power.
II. Matters in the Everyday Life of the Corinthian Church (5-10); Paul addresses ethical misunderstandings, sexual misconduct, and other moral and practical issues arising in the Corinthian church.
III. The Need for Orderly Worship and the Practice of Spiritual Gifts (11-14); Paul instructs the Corinthian church in proper community conduct.
IV. The Truth of the Resurrection of the Dead (15).
Final Issues and Concluding Salutation (16).

While other thoughtful renderings to the structure of the epistle have been proposed,⁶⁷ the above construal is helpful for the present purposes in that it a) presents a survey of the topics that Paul focuses on in different parts of his letter and b) shows where 1 Corinthians 15 fits in the broader context of the book, as the final section of the body of the book, wherein Paul argues for the reality of the resurrection of the dead.

2.1.2 The nearer context: 1 Corinthians 15 and 1 Cor 15:20-28. While Paul's main point in 1 Corinthians 15 is fairly clear—to counter those who deny the future resurrection of the dead—it is less clear who, exactly, Paul intends to counter.⁶⁸ Since the Corinthian church was evidently divided by schismatic factions (1 Cor 1:11-17) and Paul states that *"some (τινες)* of you say that there is no resurrection of the dead" (1 Cor 15:12), it is unclear whether all the Corinthian Christians denied the future resurrection of the dead, or if those who

---

⁶⁵ Marion L. Soards, *1 Corinthians* (NIBC; Peabody, MA: Hendrickson/Paternoster, 1999), 6-7.
⁶⁶ Adapted from Soards, *1 Corinthians*, 8-9.
⁶⁷ For example, Ben Witherington (*Conflict and Community in Corinth*) and Margaret M. Mitchell (*Paul and the Rhetoric of Reconciliation: An Exegetical Investigation of the Language and Composition of 1 Corinthians* [Tübingen: Mohr Siebeck, 1991]) understand 1 Corinthians to be structured in accord with formal rhetorical norms. Nevertheless, Witherington's and Mitchell's outlines still cohere somewhat with topical outlines such as the one proposed by Soards (*I Corinthians*, 8-9).
⁶⁸ For surveys of attempts to identify the opponents that Paul intends to counter here, see Joost Holleman, *Resurrection and Parousia: A Traditio-Historical Study of Paul's Eschatology in I Corinthians 15* (SNT 84; New York, NY: E. J. Brill, 1996), 35-37 and Garcialazo, *Corinthian Dissenters*, 79-125.

denied it all did so for the same reasons.[69] Furthermore, one must be careful to avoid crafting a highly developed hypothetical belief system around the notion of a "realized eschatology" wherein the Corinthians understood themselves to have already experienced a resurrection.[70] While it is impossible to rule out the possibility that some Corinthians had subscribed to some form of a realized eschatology,[71] Paul's argument in 1 Corinthians 15 does not seem to counter belief in a "premature" resurrection.[72] Rather, the primary motivation for rejecting the belief in a future resurrection seems to be an elevation of the spiritual over the physical in Greek thought, resulting in an aversion to the Jewish concept of a physical, bodily resurrection that Paul preached.[73]

Let us turn, then, to the development of Paul's argument for a future bodily resurrection in 1 Corinthians 15. Paul's use of rhetoric is advanced and skillful

---

[69] So Richard B. Hays, *1 Corinthians* (Interpretation; Louisville, KY: John Knox, 1997), 254. Frederick F. Bruce also seems to believe that only some of the Corinthians were denying the resurrection (*1 and 2 Corinthians* [NCBC; Grand Rapids, MI: Eerdmans, 1980], 137, 144). Fee, however, contends that "even though [Paul] mentions "some of you" (v. 12), nothing in Paul's response suggests that the Corinthians are divided among themselves on this matter" (*The First Epistle to the Corinthians*, 713).

[70] For a survey of the debate over the "realized eschatology" view, see David W. Kuck, *Judgment and Community Conflict: Paul's Use of Apocalyptic Judgment Language in 1 Corinthians 3:5-4:5* (NTSup 66; New York, NY: E. J. Brill, 1992), 16-25, and Holleman, *Resurrection*, 36-37.

[71] For cautious articulations of the possible influence of a "realized eschatology" on "some" Corinthians, see Witherington (*Conflict and Community*, 290-294) and Bruce (*1 and 2 Corinthians*, 137-157).

[72] Hays, *1 Corinthians*, 252-253. See also Holleman, *Resurrection*, 35-37 and Garland, *1 Corinthians*, 678. Moreover, even if some form of a realized eschatology does inform the Corinthians' thinking on this point, Bruce is correct to emphasize that it is as yet a nascent and inchoate set of beliefs, rather than a full-blown and carefully articulated Gnosticism (*1 and 2 Corinthians*, 21).

[73] Gerhard Sellin, *Der Streit um die Auferstehung der Toten: Eine religionsgeschichtliche und exegetische Untersuchung von 1 Korinther 15* (FRLANT 138; Göttingen: Vandenhoeck & Ruprecht, 1986); Garland, *1 Corinthians*, 678-679; Holleman, *Resurrection*, 36-40; Hays, *First Corinthians*, 252-253. See also idem, "The Conversion of the Imagination: Scripture and Eschatology in 1 Corinthians," *NTS* 45 (1999), 391-412, where Hays demonstrates that the Corinthians' claim to already possess spiritual maturity (1 Cor 4:8), often seen as proof of an over-realized eschatology, is in line with Stoic and Cynic claims to possess wisdom and perfection, independent of any eschatological understanding. Various proposals have been set forth concerning the precise nature of the Greek thought underlying the teaching that Paul counters in 1 Corinthians 15 (see Garcilazo [*The Corinthian Dissenters*], for the Stoic view, or Sellin for the "alexandrinisch-judischen Religionsphilosophie" view [*Der Streit um die Auferstehung der Toten*, 205]). It is unnecessary for our purposes, however, to settle the debate concerning the precise nature of the Greek philosophical system providing the primary impetus for the Corinthian's aversion to the concept of a physical resurrection.

and his argument here is nuanced and intricate.[74] Hays succinctly and lucidly outlines Paul's argument by dividing it into two main sections, as follows:

The resurrection of the dead is constitutive of the gospel. (vv. 1-34)
    The *kerygma* proclaims the resurrection of Christ. (vv. 1-11)
    Denial of resurrection of the dead negates the gospel. (vv. 12-19)
    Because Christ has been raised, all who belong to him will be raised (vv. 20-28)
    Otherwise, hope, suffering, and faithfulness are pointless. (vv. 29-34)
Resurrection means transformation of the body. (vv. 35-58)
    What kind of body is the resurrection body? (vv. 35-49)
    Both the dead and the living will be transformed. (vv. 50-57)
    Therefore, our labor is not in vain. (v. 58)[75]

As Paul makes his case for the future, physical resurrection of the dead, several Old Testament passages play a key rhetorical role. In fact, this chapter contains a higher concentration of Old Testament citations than any other part of the epistle.[76]

The citation of Psalm 8 comes towards the end of the first half of the chapter, where Paul makes the case that "because Christ has been raised, all who belong to him will be raised."[77] Verses 21-22 exhibit an almost poetic parallelism and verses 24-28 form an artful chiasm. Thus, in 1 Cor 15:20-28, Paul develops his argument across two interconnected units, as figure 2 shows.[78] The first thought unit argues that Christ's work will result in a resurrection because Christ has undone the death-producing damage done through Adam.[79] The second section, which culminates in the central claim that death will be annihilated (verse 26=X), argues that Christ's divinely ordained reign must result in a resurrection (=the annihilation of death). The two thought units are linked logically by an internal chronological development. The first unit (verses 20-23)

---

[74] For discussions of the way in which 1 Corinthians 15 follows classical rhetorical patterns, containing an *exordium, narratio, proposition, probatio/confirmatio,* and *peroratio,* see Witherington, *Conflict and Community*, 292, and Duane F. Watson, "Paul's Rhetorical Strategy in 1 Corinthians 15," in *Rhetoric and the New Testament: Essays from the 1992 Heidelberg Conference* (ed. Stanley E. Porter and Thomas H. Olbricht; JSNTSup 90; Sheffield, UK: Sheffield Academic, 2001), 231-249.
[75] Reproduced verbatim from Hays, *First Corinthians*, 254. Emphasis added to show the verses which contain the quotation of Ps 8:7.
[76] 1 Corinthians 15 references six Old Testament texts (verse 25=Ps 110:1; verse 27=Ps 8:7; verse 32=Isaiah 22:13; verse 45=Gen 2:7; verse 54=Isa 25:8; and verse 55=Hos 13:14). No other chapter has more than two clear references to the Old Testament (John P. Heil, *The Rhetorical Role of Scripture in 1 Corinthians* [SBL 13; Atlanta, GA: Society of Biblical Literature, 2005], 14-15).
[77] Hays, *First Corinthians*, 254.
[78] Adapted from Charles E. Hill, "Paul's Understanding of Christ's Kingdom in I Corinthians 15:20-28," *Nov T* 30 (1988), 300 and Heil, *The Rhetorical Role*, 212-213.
[79] See Garland, *1 Corinthians*, 706-707.

progresses from the primeval entry of death into the world via Adam, through the work of Christ to reverse the effects of death, and on to Christ's second coming. The second thought unit (verses 23-28) then describes "the end," when God will vanquish death itself (verse 26) and be "all in all" (verse 28).[80]

First Thought Unit:
20. But now Christ has been raised from the dead, the firstfruits of those who have fallen asleep.
21. (A) For as by a human (ἀνθρώπου) death came,
     (B) by a human (ἀνθρώπου) the resurrection of the dead has also come.
22. (A) For as in Adam all die,
     (B) so also in Christ shall all be made alive.
23. But each in its own order: Christ the firstfruits, then at his coming those who belong to Christ.

Second Thought Unit:
24. Then the end comes,
     (A) When he delivers the kingdom to God the Father
         (B) after destroying every rule and every authority and power.
25.   (C) For he must reign until he has put all the enemies under his feet (// Ps 110:1)
26.   (X) The last enemy to be annihilated is death.
27.   (C1) For "he has set all things under his feet" (Ps 8:7).
         (B1) But when it says that "all things are set under [him]," it is clear that he is excepted who put all things in subjection to him.
28. (A) When all things are subjected to him, then the Son himself will also be subjected to him who subjected all things under him, that God may be all in all.

Figure 2. The structure of 1 Corinthians 15:20-28[81]

Towards the heart of the second section (verse 27), Paul marshals Ps 8:7a in support of his argument. While Paul adapts the LXX version of the verse to fit the context of his argument (changing the second person "you have set/ὑπέταξας" to the third person "he has set/ὑπέταξεν") and to fit his preferred

---

[80] See Soards, *1 Corinthians*, 331. While, as Soards correctly notes, "Paul is probably not concerned here with a strict chronological ordering," 1 Cor 15:20-28 moves along a somewhat loosely developed internal chronological thrust from fall to final redemption.
[81] Adapted from Charles E. Hill, "Paul's Understanding of Christ's Kingdom in I Corinthians 15:20-28," *Nov T* 30 (1988), 300 and Heil, *The Rhetorical Role*, 212-213.

vocabulary (replacing the LXX's preposition "ὑποκάτω," which Paul never uses, with the synonym that Paul frequently uses "ὑπό"),[82] the explanatory gloss that follows the quotation, "for when it says," makes it clear that Paul is citing Ps 8:7 directly. Together with the parallel reference to Ps 110:1 in verse 25,[83] the citation of Ps 8:7 plays a key role in the rhetorical development of this argument.[84] In addition to positioning the two references to the book of Psalms in verses 25 and 27 in parallel with one another, Paul links Ps 110:1 and Ps 8:7 through the use of *gezirah sheva*.[85] *Gezirah sheva* is a rabbinic interpretive device wherein one clarifies the meaning of a text or verse (in this case, Ps 110:1) by finding another text or verse (Ps 8:7) that shares vocabulary with the first verse (πάντας and ὑπὸ τοὺς πόδας αὐτοῦ in verse 25 connect with πάντα and ὑπὸ τοὺς πόδας αὐτοῦ in verse 27).[86] Thus, "[a]ll (πάντας) the enemies" in 15:25 progresses in 15:27a to absolutely "all things" (πάντα), which embraces not just the negative, the enemies, but also the positive—everything in the universe."[87] These two citations make the point that God has planned all along to vanquish all of Christ's enemies; God has told us in the Scriptures of his eternal plan to vanquish death through the exaltation of the Messiah (1 Cor 15:26=the crux of the chiasm).

As the pericope concludes (1 Cor 15:27-28), the citation and explanation of Ps 8:7 transitions towards Paul's succinct summation of the *telos* of his argument, of salvation history, and of the messianic dominion described in Pss 8:7 and 110:1: "that God may be all and in all."[88] Thus, it is possible to summarize 1 Cor 15:20-28 as follows. The overarching goal of the pericope is "to demonstrate that Christ's resurrection, which both [Paul] and [his Corinthian audience] believe, has made the resurrection of the dead both necessary and inevitable."[89] The first part of the pericope (verses 20-23) argues from Christ's function as the second Adam, which can only be fulfilled if Christ's resurrection ultimately yields a corporate resurrection. The second section (verses 24-28) argues from

---

[82] See Christopher D. Stanley, *Paul and the Language of Scripture: Citation Technique in the Pauline Epistles and Contemporary Literature* (SNTSMS 69; New York, NY: Cambridge University Press, 1992), 206, and Heil, *Rhetorical Role*, 208-210.

[83] For 1 Cor 15:25 as a reference to Ps 110:1, see Heil, *Rhetorical Role*, 207-208 and Martin Hengel, "Psalm 110 und die Erhöhung des Auferstandenen zur Rechten Gottes," in *Anfänge der Christologie* (Stuttgart: KVW Verlag, 1972), 51-55. See also Fee, *First Epistle to the Corinthians*, 754-755.

[84] See Heil, *Rhetorical Role*, 221-229.

[85] Heil, *Rhetorical Role*, 210-211, Urassa, *Psalm 8*, 166-167.

[86] Heil, *Rhetorical Role*, 210. For the use of *gezirah shevah* in ancient and medieval Judaism, see Solomon Zeitlin, "Hillel and the Hermeneutic Rules," *JQR* 54 (1963), 167; and Michael Chernick, "Internal Restraints on *Gezerah Shawah's* Application," *JQR* 83 (1990), 253-282.

[87] Heil, *Rhetorical Role*, 210.

[88] See H. H. Drake Williams, "The Psalms in 1 and 2 Corinthians," in *The Psalms in the New Testament* (ed. Steve Moyise and Maarten J. J. Menken; New York, NY: T & T Clark, 2004), 172.

[89] Fee, *The First Epistle to the Corinthians*, 746.

Christ's function as God's exalted king. This function, too, can only be properly fulfilled if the last enemy of death is vanquished (verse 26), making God "all in all" (verse 28). To quote William Dykstra, then, "the strength of Paul's argument" does not "rest primarily on logic, but rather on his presentation of salvation history in connection with the person and the reign of Christ."[90] Having examined the citation of Ps 8:7 in its context, we are now in a position to look more closely at the way in which Paul interprets Ps 8:7.

2.1.3 The use of Ps 8:7 in 1 Corinthians 15:27. To the modern reader, Paul's employment of Psalm 110 to support and develop his teaching about the reign of Christ may seem straightforward and in need of little explanation; as a royal psalm speaking of the divine exaltation of the Davidic king, it does not require a fanciful imagination to see Psalm 110 as applying to Jesus the Christ, the Davidic Messiah. Yet, the modern reader may wonder what gives Paul the interpretive license to base his teaching about the reign of Christ upon Psalm 8, a hymn of creation praise that speaks about corporate humanity.

To understand the way in which Paul is interpreting Ps 8:7, one must begin by investigating the way in which he employs *gezirah sheva* to introduce his quotation. Neither of the two points of verbal linkage connecting verses 25 and 27 (πάντας and ὑπὸ τοὺς πόδας αὐτου) correspond directly to the LXX or MT version of Ps 110:1;[91] here, as elsewhere, Paul feels free to alter the wording of the text slightly in order to adapt its message to the situation that he is addressing.[92] Since these adaptations are most likely intentional, and not the result of Paul's reliance upon a now lost *Vorlage*,[93] one must ask why Paul adapted the text as he did. The addition of the modifier πάντας (all) to τοὺς ἐχθροὺς (the enemies) serves to strengthen Paul's argument that the reign of Christ must be universal.[94] Yet, it is hard to see how Paul's decision to replace the words "[as a] footstool for your feet/ὑποπόδιον τῶν ποδῶν σου" from Ps 110:1 LXX with

---

[90] "I Corinthians 15:20-28: A Central Part of Paul's Argument Against Those Who Deny the Resurrection," *CTJ* 4 (1969): 205.

[91] Where 1 Cor 15:25 reads "all the enemies" (πάντας τοὺς ἐχθροὺς), Ps 110:1 simply has "your enemies" (the LXX: τοὺς ἐχθροὺς σου, MT: איביך). Where 1 Cor 15:25 has "under his feet" (ὑπὸ τοὺς πόδας αὐτου), Ps 110:1 has "a (foot)stool for your feet" (the LXX: ὑποπόδιον τῶν ποδῶν σου, MT: הדם לרגליך). Whether or not one can still refer to Paul's reference to Ps 110:1 as a "quotation" after having undergone such drastic alterations (as per Heil, *Rhetorical Role*, 207-208) is beside the point. The coherences and divergences between 1 Cor 15:25 and Ps 110:1 are such that, 1) on the one hand, Paul is clearly referencing Ps 110:1 in such a way as to marshal the royal psalm as support for his description of Christ's reign, yet 2) on the other hand, Paul is clearly putting the ideas of Ps 110:1 into his own words for his own purposes within the broader context of his argument.

[92] See Stanley, *Paul and the Language*. For the ways in which Paul has adapted Ps 110:1 for his argument in 1 Cor 15:20-28, see Heil, *Rhetorical Role*, 207-208.

[93] See Stanley, *Paul and the Language*, 12-16, 350-360.

[94] So Heil, *Rhetorical Role*, 215-218.

"under his feet/ὑπὸ τοὺς πόδας αὐτου"[95] advances his argument, unless one considers the key role that the phrase ὑπὸ τοὺς πόδας αὐτου plays in the ensuing citation of Psalm 8. Thus, Paul is probably intentionally rephrasing Ps 110:1 in such a way as to enable him to introduce Ps 8:7 into his argument and connect both passages via *gezirah sheva*. If this is the case, then the rationale underlying the introduction of Ps 8:7 into the argument cannot be reduced to a mere word association, prompted by Paul's training in the method of *gezirah sheva*. Paul must have other reasons for bringing Ps 8:7 into his argument that go beyond the superficial verbal similarities shared between Ps 8:7 and Ps 110:1.[96]

Furthermore, although Paul employs exegetical techniques reminiscent of those found in the sectarian literature of Qumran,[97] he is not engaging here in an atomistic eisogesis, interpreting words and phrases in isolation from their broader context. While the precise nature of Paul's hermeneutic continues to be debated, good evidence exists indicating that Paul's biblical citations consistently evince an awareness of the broader context of the verse under consideration.[98] At the end of his thorough study of Paul's use of Scripture in 1 Corinthians, Heil concludes that "the significance of each scriptural quote or reference [in 1 Corinthians] derives not only from a particular context within the scriptures but from the global context of all the scriptures."[99] Similarly, Williams notes that "Paul seems to have paid strict attention to the types of

---

[95] Paul's decision to shift the pronoun from the second person (σου) to the third person (αὐτου) is unremarkable. Paul shifts grammatical elements of both Ps 110:1 and Ps 8:7 to fit his own context. Given the way in which Paul is using the material, such a shift "is virtually required" (Stanley, *Paul and the Language of Scripture*, 206 [speaking of 1 Cor 15:27=Ps 8:7]; see also Heil, *Rhetorical Role*, 207-210.

[96] Thus, it is somewhat misleading to simply state, as Garland does, that "[t]he exegetical principle of *gezerah shavah* . . . leads Paul to Ps 8:6 (8:7 Septuagint)" (*1 Corinthians*, 713).

[97] See Steve Moyise, *The Old Testament in the New: An Introduction* (New York, NY: Continuum, 2001), 83.

[98] Hays (*Echoes*; idem, *The Conversion of the Imagination: Paul as Interpreter of Israel's Scripture* [Grand Rapids, MI: Eerdmans, 2005]), J. Ross Wagner (*Heralds of the Good News: Isaiah and Paul In Concert in the Letter to the Romans* [SNT 51; Boston, MA: Brill, 2002]), Brian J. Abasciano (*Paul's Use of the Old Testament in Romans 9:1-9: An Intertextual and Theological Exegesis* [LNTS 301; New York, NY: T&T Clark, 2005]), and Shiu-Lun Shum (*Paul's Use of Isaiah in Romans* [WUzNT 2:156; Tubingen: Mohr Siebeck, 2002]) all conclude, after carefully examining part or all of Paul's Old Testament citations and allusions, that Paul's interpretation and application of the Scriptures demonstrates an awareness of the broader context of the text that Paul is citing. For diverse approaches to the question of the method of interpretation by New Testament writers and the question of the role of context in their hermeneutical method, see Gregory K. Beale, ed., *The Right Doctrine from the Wrong Texts? Essays on the Use of the Old Testament in the New* (Grand Rapids, MI: Baker, 1994), and Craig A. Evans, ed., *From Prophecy to Testament: The Function of the Old Testament in the New* (Peabody, MA: Hendrickson, 2004).

[99] Heil, *Rhetorical Role*, 261.

psalms that he used" in 1 and 2 Corinthians, such that the genre of the entire psalm cited (and not just the content of the citation in isolation from the rest of the psalm) is appropriate to Paul's broader rhetorical point.[100] Moreover, Williams concludes that "the context of the citations and allusions to these psalms [in 1 and 2 Corinthians] appears to influence or, at the very least, displays significant overlapping with Paul's ideas."[101]

In the case of Paul's citation of Ps 8:7 in 1 Cor 15:27, the broader context of Psalm 8 overlaps with the broader context of Paul's argument in three significant ways: 1) As already noted, Paul discusses Christ's function as the second Adam (1 Cor 15:20-23) immediately before discussing Christ's function as God's exalted ruler (1 Cor 15:24-28). Thus, just as Psalm 8 describes the way in which God maintains the created order through the reign of אדם ("humanity=a man=Adam") in idealized terms, 1 Cor 15:20-23 describes how the ideal ante-type of Adam/ Ἀδαμ, the human/ἀνθρώπου (verses 21-22), will maintain the created order in idealized terms; 1 Cor 15:20-23 and Psalm 8 both describe a perfect human ruler who does what Adam ought to have done, but failed to do.[102] 2) Both Psalm 8 and 1 Cor 15:20-28 delineate God's ordering of the cosmos in organized detail. Just as Psalm 8 presents a "top down" description of Genesis 1's created order, 1 Cor 15:20-28 describes how God will restore everything in its own order (ταγμάτος, verse 23), invoking a militant image of marshalling organization.[103] This description of restoration proceeds through a general chronological movement from "Adam" (verses 21, 22) to "the end" (verses 26-28). 3) Both Psalm 8 and 1 Cor 15:20-28 speak of a conflict between God and his "enemies" (צורר, אויב, and מתנקם, Ps 8:3 // ἀρχὴν, ἐξουσίαν, and δύναμιν, 1 Cor 15:24, and ἐχθροὺς, 1 Cor 15:25-26). In brief, then, Psalm 8 fits naturally within the context of Paul's argument in 1 Cor 15:20-28. Paul is describing Jesus here as a perfect ruler who will order creation by vanquishing his enemies; Psalm 8 describes just such a ruler. So, when Paul connects the second Adam with the ruling Christ in 1 Cor 15:20-28, Psalm 8 becomes a perfect *locus* for Paul to draw upon; for Paul, Ps 8:5-9 speaks both to Christ's function as the ante-type of Adam (verses 20-23) and to Christ's function as the perfect ruler whom God exalts (verses 24-28).

Even if identifying the human of Psalm 8 with the exalted Christ seems eisogetical to some modern interpreters, when viewed from within Paul's milieu, it is a natural interpretive move.[104] That early Christian tradition saw Jesus as

---

[100] Williams, "The Psalms in 1 and 2 Corinthians," 179-180.
[101] Williams, "The Psalms in 1 and 2 Corinthians," 180.
[102] Thus, while Garland is technically correct that "Paul interprets this psalm as applying to the Messiah, not to Adam or human beings in general" (*1 Corinthians*, 713), one must not forget that the Messiah to whom Paul applies Psalm 8 is a) the Second Adam (1 Cor 15:20-22, and b) the federal representative of humanity (see Romans 5) through whom all of redeemed humanity will be raised (1 Cor 15:23).
[103] See Hays, *First Corinthians*, 264-265.
[104] For the New Testament's interpretation of Psalm 8:5-7 as an example of midrashic exegesis, see Pickup, "Interpretation," 363-366. While I hesitate to apply the term

fulfilling the role of the בן־אדם/אנוש of Psalm 8 is evident from the use of Psalm 8 in Ephesians 1 and Hebrews 2.[105] The application of Psalm 8 to Jesus as a "last Adam" (1 Cor 15:51) may also have some affinities with "early Jewish apocalyptic portraits of 'The Exalted Adam' (4 Ezra and Bar. 2)."[106] Furthermore, Francis J. Moloney argues that the *Regia Targum* on Psalm 8 preserves evidence of a pre-Christian Jewish messianic interpretation of the "Son of Man" in Psalm 8.[107] Whether or not one agrees that Paul's description of Jesus as the ante-type of Adam (Rom 5:12-21, 1 Cor 15:21-22, 45-50) is consonant with contemporary non-Christian Jewish thought and messianic expectation,[108] it is unarguably an important aspect of Paul's christology.[109] Thus, if Paul reads Genesis 1-3 and sees therein a type of Christ, the "second Adam" (1 Cor 15:45) it is natural that Paul would read Psalm 8 and see therein a witness to Christ, the "second human/δεύτερος ἄνθρωπος" (1 Cor 15:47). Having addressed the way in which Paul has interpreted Psalm 8 and used Ps 8:6 in the context of his argument for a future, bodily resurrection, we may now turn to consider the level two question of the impact of 1 Corinthians 15:27 upon a canonical reading of Psalm 8.

2.2 Reading Psalm 8 in Light of 1 Corinthians 15:27

Paul makes three interconnected claims that impact upon a canonical reading of Psalm 8: 1) Jesus is a "second Adam" who brings new life. 2) Jesus is God's exalted ruler who will be fully exalted and will vanquish death in the eschaton. 3) As a result, the believer is to be assured that there will be a future, bodily resurrection. The following will address each claim, in turn: 1) Jesus is a "second Adam." This claim enables the reader of Psalm 8 to begin to see a resolution to two tensions already noted that are latent in a reading of Psalm 8 "in itself" (especially in the presence of the enemies in verse 3) and intensely

---

"midrash" to Paul's hermeneutic, Pickup's broader point stands: Paul's interpretive technique grows quite naturally out of his Jewish environment and training.
[105] For the way in which the concerns and interpretive moves of Hebrews 1 and 2 parallel those of 1 Cor 15:20-28, see Wilber B. Wallis, "The Use of Psalm 8 and 110 in I Corinthians 15:25-27 and Hebrews 1 and 2," *JETS* 15 (1972): 25-29.
[106] Urassa, *Psalm 8*, 187. See also ibid., 85-112.
[107] "The Reinterpretation of Psalm 8 and the Son of Man Debate," *NTS* 27 (1981): 656-672. For a thorough critique and firm rejection of Moloney's thesis, however, see Maurice Casey, "The Use of the Term (א)שנ(א) בר in the Aramaic Translations of the Hebrew Bible," JSNT 54 (1994), 105-109.
[108] So Casey, "Use," 105-109. For other points of connection between Paul's Adam-Christology and non-Christian Jewish thinking, see Menahem Kister, "'In Adam:' I Cor 15:21-22; 12:27 in their Jewish Setting," in *Flores Florentino: Dead Sea Scrolls and Other Early Jewish Studies in Honor of Florentino Garcia Martinez* (ed. Anthony Hilhorst, Emile Peuch, and Eibert Tigchelaar; Boston MA: Brill, 2007), 685-690; and idem, "Romans 5:12-21 Against the Background of Torah Theology and Hebrew Usage," *HTR* 100 (2007): 391-424; and Urassa, *Psalm 8*, 85-112.
[109] See Gordon D. Fee, *Pauline Christology: An Exegetical-Theological Study* (Peabody, MA: Hendrickson, 2007), 114-119, 271-272, 513-529.

actualized in a reading of Psalm 8 in the context of the Old Testament: A) the tension between "the apparent insignificance of man in the creation and . . . the place of honor which has been given him,"[110] and B) the tension between the idealized human of Psalm 8 and the anguished reality of the human experience in the world (Job 7:17-21). I do not claim that the Old Testament itself does not already speak to a future wherein such tensions are resolved, as though the witness of Israel to God's work in the world is the equivalent of a torso without a head.[111] Rather, the Old Testament already intimates a resolution to these tensions (see Isa 9:1-7; 12; 25:8 [=1 Cor 15:54c]; Jer 31; Joel 3:17-21, etc.), and Paul and the Church interpret such Old Testament hope in light of the person and work of Christ.

Nevertheless, in Paul's description of Jesus as the one who reverses the damage of Adam, the Christian canonical reader finds four pivotal insights for understanding Psalm 8: The Christian reader A) now has a clearer picture as to how the tensions of human existence can be resolved—in the life, death, and resurrection of Jesus, B) sees more clearly how he can read Psalm 8 as speaking to the resolution of such tensions without violating the discrete witness of Psalm 8, C) finds a way of reading the text that is in keeping with both Jewish and Christian theological exegesis,[112] and D) is now able to read Psalm 8 as simultaneously reflecting several stages of the salvation historical process whereby YHWH plans to maintain the created order. I have already shown that Psalm 8 can be understood to speak of YHWH's ideal maintenance of the created order in the "lost world" as well as his continuing maintenance of that order throughout all of history. In light of Paul's claim that Jesus is a new "Adam," Psalm 8 also speaks to the way in which God maintains the created order through Jesus's resurrection in the present life of those who are "in Christ" (2 Cor 5:17; Rom 8:10), and the way in which God will fully institute order at the eschaton by vanquishing the last enemy of death and placing all things under Christ's feet (Rom 8:18-25; 1 Cor 15:20-28).

2) Jesus is God's exalted ruler. Much of what was said concerning Jesus as a new Adam applies to Paul's depiction of Jesus as God's exalted ruler as well; the tensions in the status of humanity that emerge from reading Psalm 8 "in itself" and in the context of the Old Testament also apply both to the corporate human ruler and to the individual Davidic human monarch. When, with Paul, the Christian understands Jesus as the one whom God exalts to rule over other humans as well as every other created thing, this understanding clarifies how God has maintained, is maintaining, and will finally maintain the created order through a human vice-gerent. Moreover, Christ's role as exalted ruler enables corporate humanity to fulfill its role as ruler over the rest of the cosmos. The

---

[110] Brevard S. Childs, "Psalm 8 in the Context of the Christian Canon," *Interpretation* 23 (1969), 28.
[111] *Contra* Walther Eichrodt, *Theology of the Old Testament* (two volumes; J. A. Baker, trans.; Philadelphia: Westminster, 1961).
[112] See Pickup, "Interpretation," 366.

way in which 1 Cor 15:20-28 makes these claims informs a canonical reading of Psalm 8 in two significant ways.

First of all, the depiction of the exaltation of Christ in 1 Cor 15:24-28 differs subtly from the depiction of the exaltation of the human ruler in Ps 8:5-9 in one interesting way. The analysis of Psalm 8 in chapter two has already shown that, except for the mention of enemies in verse 3, the execution of the human's rule is described in Psalm 8 in predominantly pacific terms, with the emphasis upon the sub-human creatures as beneficiaries of humanity's rule, not as threats to that rule. By contrast, 1 Cor 15:20-28 describes Christ's exaltation using marshal imagery, depicting Christ as a conqueror vanquishing every foe.[113] Thus, when one reads Psalm 8 in light of 1 Cor 15:24-29, one is reminded that, on the one hand, even the last enemy, death, will be vanquished in the eschaton (verse 26). Yet, on the other hand, the eschaton has not come, and God is still in the process of subjugating the threats to his order. Such militant imagery may make some uneasy, as they fear the abuse of 1 Corinthians 15 by those who would institute a new Christian holy war. Yet, Jesus does not vanquish the enemy of death through holy war, but through humility and death on the cross. Paul is not calling for militant combat, "for," as one disputed Pauline epistle says, "our struggle is not against flesh and blood" (Eph 6:12, NIV). Nevertheless, when reading Psalm 8 in light of 1 Cor 15:20-28, one remembers that spiritual "enemies and avengers" (Ps 8:3) still exist, the greatest of which is death, and that humanity still struggles against such enemies until "the end" (1 Cor 15:24).

Secondly, the way in which Paul connects Ps 8:7 with the Davidic proclamation of Ps 110:1 is worth noting. Furthermore, while only 1 Cor 15:25-28 directly connects the two passages via *gezirah sheva*, all four of the New Testament authors present a citation of Psalm 8 in close proximity with a citation of Ps 110:1, possibly indicating a commonly held traditional association of the two texts.[114] A canonical reader interpreting Psalm 8 in light of its interpretation by New Testament authors, therefore, would do well to examine Psalm 110 and read Psalm 8 in light of Psalm 110. Thus, I will briefly offer two observations here derived from reading Psalm 8 in light of both Psalm 110 and 1 Cor 15:24-28.

The somewhat spiritualized marshal imagery of 1 Cor 15:23-28 is tame in comparison with the brutal declaration of Ps 110:5-6 that the Davidic king will "shatter kings," "fill [the nations] with corpses," and "shatter chiefs over the wide earth." Interpreting Psalm 8 in light of Ps 110 and 1 Cor 15, then, the canonical reader encounters a Davidic Messiah who engages his enemies (Ps 110:5-7) with furor, a second Adam who rules over his subjects with benevo-

---

[113] See Hays, *First Corinthians*, 264-265.
[114] So Wallis, "Psalms 8 and 110;" and William R. G. Loader, "Christ at the Right Hand: Psalm CX. 1 in the New Testament," *NTS* 24 (1978), 208-210. Psalm 110:1 is cited explicitly in Matt 22:44 and Heb 1:13, and is alluded to in Eph 1:20. For my part, however, I am less confident than Loader seems to be that it is possible to trace precisely trajectories of development shaping traditions of interpretation.

lence (Ps 8:7-9), and an exalted Christ who vanquishes spiritual enemies through the power of resurrection (1 Cor 15:20-28). It would be a mistake to allow any one of these images of Christ to override the other; rather, the appropriate response is humble trust in God and in Christ, who cannot be domesticated or distilled into convenient human categories.

Interestingly, Paul has chosen here to base his description of the exalted Christ upon Psalm 110, from the final book of the Psalter. If Wilson were correct that the shaping of the Psalter results in the muting of the Davidic hope,[115] one would not expect to find Paul making such an exegetical move. Yet, rather than giving up on the Davidic hope as a failed hope, Paul seems to see Christ as the one who both fulfills the Davidic hope and brings into reality the "kingdom 'not of this world'—the eternal kingdom in which YHWH alone is king."[116] In brief, when one reads Psalm 8, Psalm 110, and 1 Cor 15:20-28 in tandem, one begins to see the tension between king David, king Adam, and king YHWH resolved in the single person of Jesus the Messiah;[117] to use our Augustinian terminology once again, these texts working together push the reader towards an encounter with the divine reality revealed in the person of Jesus. The sections below treating the citations of Psalm 8 in Eph 1:15-23 and Heb 2:5-9 will explore the implications of reading Psalm 8 in light of the identification of Jesus as the exalted ruler further; both of these passages use Psalm 8 to make claims similar to those made in 1 Cor 15:20-28.

3) There will be a future, bodily resurrection. This claim impacts upon a canonical reading of Palm 8 by assuring the reader that the idealized human existence described in Psalm 8 will one day be a living, breathing, physical reality. Indeed, in that day, according to Paul, "πάντας τοὺς ἐχθροὺς/all enemies" will be vanquished (1 Cor 15:25), and the "enemy and avenger" will be fully and finally silenced (Ps 8:3). Meditating upon this claim is enough to motivate the reader to burst forth, with Paul, into doxology, saying "thanks be to God, who gives us the victory through our Lord Jesus Christ" (1 Cor 15:57). Yet, such exultation must wait, as we have yet to consider the broader scope of the rest of the New Testament. In the next section then, I turn to examine Eph 1:22, where the phrase "he has put all things under his feet" (Ps 8:3) is once again applied to Jesus.

---

[115] Gerald H. Wilson, *The Editing of the Hebrew Psalter* (SBLDS 76; Chico, CA: Scholars, 1985), 214-228.
[116] Gerald H. Wilson, "Shaping the Psalter: A Consideration of Editorial Linkage in the Book of Psalms," in *The Shape and Shaping of the Psalter* (JSOTSup 159; ed. J. Clinton McCann; Sheffield: JSOT Press, 1993), 81.
[117] See James L. Mays, *Psalms* (Interpretation; Louisville: John Knox, 1994), 67.

3. Ephesians 1:15-22 and Psalm 8

3.1 Reading Ephesians 1:15-22 "In Itself"

3.1.1 The broader context: The Epistle to the Ephesians. The question of the authorship of the book of Ephesians is a difficult one,[118] with a majority of scholars seeing the Epistle as being written by a later follower of Paul,[119] and a substantial minority viewing the book as written by Paul himself.[120] The ultimate goal of the present study is to understand the text as it stands, not to reconstruct the history behind the text, the question of authorship will not be in the fore in the following discussion. The more pressing question for our purposes is whether or not the theology of the portion of Ephesians under consideration differs substantially from that of Paul in such a way as to affect our canonical reading of Psalm 8. Thus, the following will attend to the question of the nature of the continuity and discontinuity between Eph 1:15-22 and 1 Cor 15:20-28, without attempting to resolve the question of whether or not Eph 1:15-22 comes from the pen of Paul.

Whoever wrote Ephesians, the letter contains several distinctive elements.[121] The message of Ephesians is the least situational of the putatively

---

[118] Andrew T. Lincoln delineates three major positions on the identity of the author of Ephesians: 1) Paul himself, 2) a secretary of Paul writing during Paul's lifetime on behalf of Paul, and 3) a later disciple of Paul carrying forward what he perceived to be the ideas of Paul (*Ephesians,* [WBC 42; Waco, TX: Word, 1990], lxii). In his brief, nuanced treatment, Charles H. Talbert delineates no less than six varieties of authorship in the ancient world that, either independently or combined one with another, might be said to characterize the authorship of Ephesians, depending upon the view that one takes: 1) an author has written "with his own hand," 2) an author has "dictated the writing," 3) "collaborators . . . functioned as coauthors," 4) "someone [that is, Paul] . . . authorized the writing," 5) something is written "'as if' by one individual but actually composed by a friend or disciple," and 6) a writing that is an "outright forgery" (*Ephesians and Colossians* [PCNT; Grand Rapids, MI: Baker Academic, 2007], 7-9).

[119] Talbert, *Ephesians and Colossians*, 10-11; Rudolf Schnackenburg, *Der Brief an Die Epheser* (EKKzNT 10; Neukirchen-Vluyn: Neukirchener Verlag, 1982); *idem, Ephesians: A Commentary*, Helen Heron trans. (Edinburgh, UK: T & T Clark, 1991); Lincoln, *Ephesians*; idem and A. J. M. Wedderburn, *The Theology of the Later Pauline Letters,* (New York, NY: Cambridge University Press, 1993).

[120] Markus Barth, *Ephesians*, 2 vols. (AB 34-34A; Garden City, NY: Doubleday, 1974); A. van Roon, *The Authenticity of Ephesians* (NTSSup 39; Leiden: E. J. Brill, 1974); Harold W. Hoehner, *Ephesians: An Exegetical Commentary* (BECNT; Grand Rapids, MI: 2002); Witherington, *The Letters to Philemon, the Colossians, and the Ephesians: A Socio-Rhetorical Commentary on the Captivity Epistles* (Grand Rapids, MI: Eerdmans, 2007). Bruce allows the possibility that a follower of Paul has written the letter, but argues that the book is thoroughly Pauline in its theology, describing Ephesians as "The Quintessence of Paulinism" *Paul: Apostle of the Heart Set Free* (Grand Rapids, MI: Eerdmans, 1977), 424-440.

[121] Lincoln and Wedderburn, *Theology*, 78-141; Talbert, *Ephesians and Colossians*, 9-11.

Pauline epistles.¹²² While the letter may assume situational concerns that influence its theological emphases, Ephesians does not directly identify those situational concerns,¹²³ making it well suited to serve as a circular letter; the omission of the words ἐν 'Εφέσῳ/in Ephesus in many early manuscripts likely indicate that the epistle did, in fact, serve as a circular letter.¹²⁴ Ephesians is striking in that it seems to draw on material from other Pauline literature, especially from its "companion letter," Colossians, pointing to a late date for the composition of Ephesians.¹²⁵ Ephesians is also written in a lofty rhetorical style, emphasizing the present tense,¹²⁶ and containing what Lincoln and Wedderburn call "traditional liturgical forms," especially in the first half of the book (chapters 1-3).¹²⁷

Theologically, while Ephesians revisits many themes found in other Pauline material, it does so in a distinctive way.¹²⁸ Ecclesiologically, the letter puts a

---

¹²² In the words of Lincoln and Wedderburn, Ephesians is "devoid of virtually all reference to particular circumstances which would enable the contemporary reader to reconstruct with any precision the setting of its addressees" (*Theology*, 78). Although, Clinton E. Arnold suggests that the epistle to the Ephesians addresses concerns arising from pagan magical practices in Ephesus (*Ephesians, Power and Magic: The Concept of Power in Ephesians in Light of its Historical Setting* [New York, NY: Cambridge University Press, 1989]).

¹²³ In addition to Arnold's view that Ephesians's theological messages militate against syncretistic magical beliefs in Asia minor (*Ephesians*), Thorsten Moritz takes up and modifies Arnold's view, arguing that Ephesians, unlike Colossians, simultaneously addresses Greek and Jewish believers (*A Profound Mystery: The Use of the Old Testament in Ephesians* [SNT 85; New York, NY: E. J. Brill, 1996], 216-220). While I find both contributions insightful and compelling, I have chosen to focus here upon the message of the text, rather than putative historical contexts behind the text.

¹²⁴ The NRSV (*contra* the RSV) may be correct to read the words ἐν 'Εφέσῳ as original. Yet, the fact that so many early manuscripts omit these words probably reflects the circular function that the letter served even at an early time. For the text critical problems associated with Eph 1:1, see Roon, *Authenticity*, 72-85; Ernest Best, "Ephesians 1.1 Again" in *Paul and Paulinism: Essays in Honour of C. K. Barrett* (London, UK: SPCK, 1982), 273-279. See also Barth, *Ephesians* 1:58-59; William J. Larkin, *Ephesians: A Handbook on the Greek Text* (BHGNT; Waco, TX: Baylor University Press, 2009), 2-3.

¹²⁵ The book of Ephesians also exhibits striking parallels to sections of the book of Romans at some points. For a discussion of the relationship between the book of Ephesians with Colossians and the rest of the Pauline corpus from the stand-point that Ephesians and Colossians are pseudo-Pauline, see Lincoln, *Ephesians*, xlvii-lviii, lxvi-lxvii. For a similar discussion urging Pauline authorship of Ephesians and Colossians, see Witherington, *Letters*, 12-19. See also Lincoln and Wedderburn, *Theology*, 87-89.

¹²⁶ See Witherington, *Letters*, 10-11, 14.

¹²⁷ Lincoln and Wedderburn describe Eph 1-3 as having a "liturgical flavour" (*Theology* 81, 87).

¹²⁸ In addition to the ecclesiological and eschatological emphases of Ephesians, the epistle's distinctive concerns are evident in the way that it emphasizes other theological themes, such as predestination, the lordship of Christ over all things and over the church, the work of the holy spirit, the mystery of salvation, and spiritual warfare (Max Turner,

distinctive emphasis upon the corporate and universal church, the need for unity within the Church, and reconciliation between Jews and Gentiles (2:11-19; 4:1-16).[129] The book also has a notable emphasis upon eschatology, and some have argued that the book of Ephesians parts company with Pauline theology by presupposing an over-realized eschatology.[130] The question of the relationship between the eschatology of Ephesians and the eschatology of the undisputed Pauline literature deserves special attention here at the outset; the way in which one understands this relationship will have a bearing upon the way in which one interprets both 1 Corinthians 15 and Ephesians 1.

In the case of 1 and 2 Corinthians, as I have already noted above, the Greek elevation of the spirit over the body, rather than Gnostic eschatology, is the primary motivation for the Corinthians' rejection of Paul's teaching of the resurrection. Furthermore, Paul makes statements throughout the undisputed letters indicating that he understands the church to have already experienced a transformation through the work of Christ,[131] and he describes eschatological realities that are not yet in effect as though they were already realized (Rom 8:29-30).

So also the book of Ephesians holds the Church's future hope and present blessing in tension.[132] Charles Talbert, admitting that "[t]he eschatology of Ephesians has been a difficult script to decipher," summarizes the tension with lucid brevity:

> Does the parallel [between Christ and Christians] . . . indicate an overrealized eschatology on the part of Ephesians? No, it does not. Ephesians does have references that indicate an inaugurated eschatology (e.g., sealed with the Holy Spirit who is the first installment, 1:3-14; raised and seated in dependence on him in the heavenlies, 2:5-6; access in one Spirit to the Father, 2:18; 3:11). But Ephesians also has a strong unrealized eschatological perspective (e.g., references to age or ages to

---

"Ephesians," in *Theological Interpretation of the New Testament: A Book-by-Book Survey* [ed. Kevin J. Vanhoozer, Daniel J. Treier, and N. T. Wright; Grand Rapids, MI: SPCK/Baker Academic, 2008], 126-130). See also Barth, *Ephesians* 1:33-36.

[129] See Hoehner, *Ephesians* 102-105. Barth seems to see the need for the Gentile Church to live out its unity with the people of Israel as the purpose underlying the epistle (see Markus Barth, "Conversion and Conversation: Israel and the Church in Paul's Epistle to the Ephesians," *Int* 17[1963], 3-4).

[130] Lincoln, *Ephesians*, lxxxix-xc.

[131] See 1 Cor 6:17-20 and 2 Cor 5:17. Paul even goes so far as to say that "the end of the ages (τὰ τέλη τῶν αἰώνων) has come/arrived (κατήντηκεν)" (1 Cor 10:11; see also Garland, *1 Corinthians*, 465). He also speaks of the believer's identification with Jesus as both a present reality and a future hope (Rom 6:1-14; Gal 2:17-21; Gal 5:24), and "the victory over the cosmic powers is also seen as having already taken place in Phil. 2:10, 11; 3:21b and Col. 2:15" (Lincoln, "The Use of the OT in Ephesians," *JSNT* 14[1982], 42).

[132] Turner, "Ephesians," 129-130; Talbert, *Ephesians and Colossians* 73-75.

come, 1:21; 2:7; 3:21; a future hope, 1:14, 18; 4:4; an incomplete process, 2:22; 3:19; 4:13, 15-16; the last judgment, 5:5-6; 6:8-9).[133]

Thus, it is best to describe the difference between the eschatology of Ephesians and the eschatology of undisputed Pauline literature as one of emphasis, rather than as betraying two irreconcilable theologies. In Ephesians, an emphasis upon the conquering, exalted Christ is fitting for the doxological and worshipful tenor of the epistle.[134]

Concerning the book's structure and development, the body can be divided into two halves. The first half (1:3-3:22) is worshipful and doctrinal (an "Extended Thanksgiving"), while the second (4:1-6:20) is didactic and ethical (a "Paraenesis").[135] The first half reflects upon "the knowledge of Christ" and his church (Eph 1:17). The second half emphasizes practice, exhorting the audience to live out the moral implications of that knowledge (chapters 4-6).[136] The quotation of Psalm 8 comes at the end of an extended prayer[137] that forms part of the first section of the doctrinal half of the epistle, in the context of a meditation upon the exalted status of the risen Lord (Eph 1:15-23).

3.1.2 The Nearer Context: Ephesians 1 and Ephesians 1:19-23. The first chapter introduces the doctrinal teaching of chapters 1-3 (=the opening exordium). Soaring with lofty rhetoric, it develops across three interconnected sections, as follows:

Address (verses 1-2)
A Hymn of praise (*Berakah*/eulogy, verses 3-14)
A prayer of thanksgiving (15-23).[138]

---

[133] Talbert, *Ephesians and Colossians*, 73.
[134] Moreover, in 1 Corinthians, Paul is arguing for a future, corporate, bodily resurrection; there, a discussion of the "already" realized effects of Christ's resurrection would serve little to advance his argument. In Ephesians, however, the emphasis upon Christ's present victory may advance the book's purpose to provide a "prophylactic against the danger [in the Lycus valley churches] of syncretistic veneration of angelic powers" (Turner "Ephesians," 125; following Arnold, *Ephesians*).
[135] Lincoln, *Ephesians*, xliii; Hoehner, *Ephesians*, 64-69. See also Edna Johnson, *A Semantic and Structural Analysis of Ephesians* (SSAS; Dallas, TX: SIL International, 2008), whose careful study supports dividing the body of Ephesians into two main sections. It is also possible to trace the development of the body of the book using the categories of Hellenistic epistolary rhetoric, as follows: A) Exordium (1:3-3:22): eulogy and extended thanksgiving; B) Narratio (chapters two and three); C) Exhortatio (4:1-6:9) and peroratio (6:10-20). See Witherington, *Letters*, 20, and Lincoln, *Ephesians*, xliii-xliv.
[136] See Hoener, *Ephesians*, 66-69.
[137] Or, more precisely, the author's summation of how he has been "remembering [the audience] in [his] prayers" (verse 18).
[138] Naymond H. Keathley, "To the Praise of His Glory: Ephesians 1," *RevExp* 76 (1976); see also Talbert, *Ephesians and Colossians*, 55.While Keathley and Talbert describe verses 3-14 using the Hebrew term, ברכה/*berekah*,others, using Latin rhetorical language,

After opening the book with a blessing, Paul prays for his audience in 1:15-23. In verses 19-23 "Die Fürbitte weitet sich zu einem christologisch-ekklesiologischen Exkurs"[139] which is so worshipful and poetic that some have suggested that it might be based upon a hymn.[140] The specific subject of this "christologisch-ekklesiologischen Exkurs" is τὴν ἐνέργειαν τοῦ κράτους τῆς ἰσχύος αὐτοῦ/the working of the strength of his (God's) might (verse 19), seen in God's exaltation of Christ, the head of the Church (verses 20-23). This meditation forms "the climax of the prayer . . . the understanding of God's mystery of redemption"[141] revealed in God's mighty exaltation of the Christ.

Eph 1:19-23 parallels 1 Cor 15:24-28 in striking ways. Both passages hermeneutically connect Pss 110:1 and Ps 8:7 together to construct a theology of the risen Christ in similar ways. While some attribute the similarities to the use of a common tradition, Moritz questions whether the evidence for such a widespread tradition is as strong as is often assumed.[142] In any event, the distinctive way in which 1 Corinthians 15 and Ephesians 1 connect Pss 110 and 8 and the other points of connection and resonance between the two passages cannot be adequately explained by an appeal to a common tradition.[143] Since these parallels deserve special attention for the purposes of the present study, it will be

---

describe this section as a "eulogy" (Lincoln, *Ephesians* xliii-xliv, Witherington, *Letters*, 20).

[139] Schnackenburg, *Der Brief an die Epheser*, 70.

[140] Reinhard Deichgräber reconstructs the original hymn as follows: "ἐγείρας αὐτὸν ἐκ νεκρῶν/καὶ καθίσας ἐν δεξιᾷ αὐτοῦ (ἐν τοῖς ἐπουρανίοις)/καὶ πάντα ὑπέταξεν ὑπὸ τοὺς πόδας αὐτοῦ/καὶ αὐτὸν ἔδωκεν κεφαλὴν ὑπὲρ πάντα (τῇ ἐκκλησίᾳ)"(*Gotteshymnus und Christushymnus in der frühen Christenheit* [Gottingen: Vandenhoeck & Ruprecht, 1967], 165). See also Jack T. Sanders ("Hymnic Elements in Ephesians 1-3"). See Lincoln, *Ephesians*, 50-51 for a survey and critique of proposals concerning possible hymnic origins for the passage, including the proposals of Deichgräber, Sanders, and Gottfried Schille.

[141] Urassa, *Psalm 8*, 221.

[142] Lincoln ("OT in Ephesians," 40-42) and Wallis ("Psalms 8 and 110") both see the author as drawing upon traditional material, and William R. G. Loader attempts to reconstruct the evolution of the tradition of interpreting Ps 110:1 Christologically, ("Christ at the Right Hand: Psalm 110:1 in the New Testament," *NTS* 24[1978], 199-217). Moritz points out that the other early Christian material connecting the two texts do not connect them as clearly and intricately as do Corinthians and Ephesians, do not seem to directly underlie Corinthians or Ephesians, and do not exhibit strong enough affinities with Corinthians and Ephesians to warrant the reconstruction of a common tradition (*Profound Mystery*, 9-22). Moreover, in the New Testament, only Heb 1:13 and 2:8 cites Ps 110:1 and Ps 8:7 in close proximity to one another, and there the two citations "are separated by six verses" and "form only part of a whole string of Psalm citations," with no clear indicator that the two psalms are hermeneutically intertwined (*Profound Mystery*, 12).

[143] Even if tradition came to associate Ps 110:1 and Ps 8:7 as a Christological textual nexus, the similarities between 1 Cor 15:24-28 and Eph 1:19-23 go beyond the mere Christological association of the two texts, as the following treatment will show. See also Moritz, *Profound Mystery*, 9-22.

helpful to examine the content and message of Eph 1:19-23 by focusing upon the similarities and differences between these verses and 1 Cor 15:24-28.[144]

The way in which Eph 1:21 draws upon Ps 110:1 has striking similarities with the use of Psalm 110 in 1 Cor 15:25 that seem to go beyond a traditional liturgical association of the two texts. Moritz delineates four aspects of the psalms' citation in Eph 1:21 that, he urges, illustrate its independence from other OT texts.[145] Yet, much of the language that Moritz uses to describe the "special features" of Eph 1:19-23 could also be used to describe 1 Cor 15:24-28.[146] In both passages, "the 'enemies' (see Ps 110:1) are clearly interpreted as evil powers and principalities" (Eph 1:21 // 1 Cor 15:24).[147] Also, "as in 1 Cor 15.25, Ephesians displays an interest in the time span envisaged in the Psalm [sic.]," and in both passages "the sitting motif is related to a heavenly scene" (see 1 Cor 15:38-42, where Paul describes the future resurrection as "celestial/ἐπουράνια").[148] Finally, both passages attend to "the subjection motif" wherein "Christ [is] over all things."[149]

In addition to the similarities in the way in which the two passages appropriate Ps 110:1, the passages contain some notable thematic and lexical similarities. In their broader contexts, both passages contemplate the effects of the way in which God has exalted Christ in the resurrection, both passages pray and plead for the audience to fully grasp these effects, and both passages emphasize the way in which these effects impact upon the broader, corporate church. Both passages use marshal imagery, and describe Christ as the victor of a conflict against his enemies.[150] Furthermore, both passages provide an orderly account of God's exaltation of Christ, enumerating in a list the enemies (=unwilling subjects) that Christ has conquered and will conquer (Eph 1:21, 1

---

[144] As I shall argue below, a consideration of the parallels can shine light upon an understanding of Eph 1:22 "in itself" by elucidating the way in which Ephesians is utilizing Ps 8:7. Furthermore, an intertextual reading of Psalm 8, 1 Cor 15:24-28, and Eph 1:19-23 will go far in clarifying this canonical exploration of Psalm 8, wherein I am using citations of Psalm 8 as entry points into the New Testament.

[145] Moritz, *Profound Mystery*, 10.

[146] To be fair, Moritz does see a strong relationship between the hermeneutic in 1 Cor 15:24-28 and the hermeneutic in Eph 1:19-23, and his case argues against a "pre-Pauline interpretative stratum" (*Profound Mystery*, 10). Yet, he characterizes Eph 1:20-23 as interpreting Pss 110 and 8 "independently" and argues for "considerably more exegetical activity" on the part of the author of Ephesians, whom he seems to assume is a disciple of a Pauline school (21).

[147] Moritz, *Profound Mystery*, 10.

[148] Ibid. See also Lincoln, "OT in Ephesians," 41-42.

[149] Moritz, *Profound Mystery*, 10.

[150] Concerning the marshal language of 1 Cor 15:20-28, see Hays, *First Corinthians*, 264-265. In the case of Eph 1:19-23, in addition to the militant implications involved in God subjecting all things to the Christ as per Pss 110:1 and Ps 8:7, the entire section is a meditation upon "τὸ ὑπερβάλλον μέγεθος τῆς δυνάμεως αὐτοῦ . . . κατὰ τὴν ἐνέργειαν τοῦ κράτους τῆς ἰσχύος αὐτοῦ/the immeasurable greatness of his power . . . according to the working of the strength of his might."

Cor 15:24-25)[151] and describing the implications of this exaltation for believers (=willing subjects, 1 Cor 15:22, 26, Eph 1:22-23). Other similarities exist in the way in which the two passages interpret and apply Psalm 8, including the prominence of the concept of totality and the key role of the word πάντα ("all") in both passages (see page 164 below). Finally, however one translates the final phrase of Ephesians 1, "τὸ πλήρωμα τοῦ τὰ πάντα ἐν πᾶσιν πληρουμένου" (NRSV: "the fullness of him who fills all in all"), the inclusion of the phrase "[τὰ] πάντα ἐν πᾶσιν/all in all" in Eph 1:23 and 1 Cor 15:28 is striking.[152]

Yet the two passages differ in one significant way: While Paul is discussing Christ's lordship in the broader context of a future resurrection that has not yet occurred in 1 Corinthians 15, Eph 1:19-23 emphasizes the current exalted reign of Christ.[153] Nevertheless, one must be careful to avoid overstating the differences between the two passages at this point.[154] What Talbert says of a related Pauline passage applies here: "Is there a difference in perspective between Rom 6 and Ephesians? Yes and no . . . [O]ne must attend to how the differing contexts result in differing arguments."[155] The concerns of 1 Cor 15:20-28 (and Romans 6) lead Paul to emphasize "the 'not yet;'" yet, as the following section

---

[151] See Lincoln, "OT in Ephesians," 41-42.

[152] Concerning the translation of πλήρωμα, some understand it to stand in apposition to "the body," or the Church, while others argue that it refers to "the head" (verse 22), or Christ (see Hoehner, *Ephesians,* 301-304). Concerning the function of πληρουμένου in the sentence, it is typically construed as an active middle, with Christ=the head, as the subject, but the middle of πληρόω does not have an active sense anywhere else in the New Testament. Thus some construe πληρουμένου here as a passive, translating the phrase to mean "the church is being filled" (Ignace de La Potterie, "Christ, Plérôme de l'Église," *Biblica* 58 [1977], 500-524). The exegete must also determine whether τὰ πάντα ἐν πᾶσιν is an adjective or substantive, and to what it refers (Roy Yates, "Reexamination of Ephesians 1:23," *ExpT* 83 [1972], 147; Hoehner, *Ephesians,* 294-301). While the present study does not seek to resolve the question, I follow the majority view here in understanding the entire phrase "the fullness of him who fills all in all" (so NRSV).

[153] See Lincoln, "OT in Ephesians," 42. Ephesians 1:19-23 describes Christ's exaltation with a string of aorist verbs: ἐνήργησεν(verse 20), ὑπέταξεν, and ἔδωκεν (verse 22), indicating completed action.

[154] I have already pointed out that the undisputed Pauline letters speak of the way in which the church already experiences the effects of the resurrection of Christ, and even 1 Cor 15:25 itself depicts Christ as already reigning. Furthermore, while Ephesians 1 affirms an as yet unexperienced eschatological hope for the Church (verses 10, 13-14, 18) one ought not interpret the author's use of the past tense in Ephesians 1 in a simplistic literal sense; Paul has elsewhere used aorist verbs in connection with a discussion on predestination to describe future glorification as though it were already experienced (Rom 8:29-30), and predestination also figures prominently in Ephesians 1 (verses 5, 11). Thus, the author of Ephesians, whether Paul or a follower of Paul, could very well use the aorist here in a way analogous to Paul's usage of the aorist elsewhere.

[155] Talbert, *Ephesians and Colossians,* 74.

will show, the concerns of Ephesians lead "'Paul'" to emphasize "the 'now.'"[156] Yet Ephesians 1 also speaks to a future hope, so that the "not yet" is noted even there.[157] Nevertheless, there is a marked difference in emphasis between the two passages. What, then, ought one to make of the similarities and differences between Eph 1:19-23 and 1 Cor 15:24-28? Before fully addressing this question, it is necessary to consider first the way in which Ephesians 1 interprets Ps 8:7 and applies it to Christ.

3.1.3 The use of Ps 8:7 in Ephesians 1:22. As already noted, several commentators understand Eph 1:20-22 as incorporating a hymnic tradition commonly known in the church that interprets Pss 110 and 8 Christologically.[158] While such a scenario is not impossible, it does not fully account for the way in which Eph 1:22 interprets Ps 8:7. To begin with, Eph 1:19-23 and Psalm 8 resonate strongly with one another, as though the author of Ephesians has reflected hermeneutically upon Psalm 8 in a way that goes beyond a mere mechanical recitation of traditional material. The two texts share a similarity of tone: Psalm 8 is a poem of praise, and Eph 1:19-23 is a digression of praise that is very poetic, though it may not be a poem, properly so called. The two contexts share a similarity of theme: The subject of Psalm 8 is the "glory of the Lord," and the theme of Eph 1:19-23 is "the strength of God's might;" Ps 8 is praising God for his self-exaltation by means of the exaltation of things in the created order, and Ephesians 1:19-23 is praising God for his self-exaltation by means of the exaltation of Christ. It is not surprising, then, that Paul would draw upon Ps 8:7 to illustrate his point in Eph 1:22.

Looking closely at the two passages, some specific elements point to a close thematic and lexical overlap between them. In the Septuagint version of Ps 8:2, God's magnificence is "raised up (ἐπήρθη)," (implicitly by God via the use of the divine passive), while in Eph 1:20-21, it is Christ whom God has "raised (ἐγείρας)" from the dead.[159] In Ephesians 1, after raising Christ from the dead, God seated him at his right hand in the heavenly realms (ἐν τοῖς ἐπουρανίοις) far above (ὑπεράνω) every ruler and authority, etc." (Eph 1:20-21). Similarly, Ps 8:2 (LXX) declares that God's "magnificence has been raised up (ἐπήρθη) above the heavens (ὑπεράνω τῶν οὐρανῶν)." Thus, in each passage, God raises

---

[156] Ibid.
[157] Ephesians emphasizes the Holy Spirit as a seal of things to come (verses 13-14) and praying that the audience "may know what is the hope to which" they have been called (verse 18). See Hoehner, *Ephesians*, 264-265. Thus, the strong language used here to describe Christ's exaltation as a present reality does not portray the story as over and Christ's work as fully accomplished. Rather, it encourages readers about the state of affairs "not only in this age, but also in the one to come (ἐν τῷ μέλλοντι, verse 21)."
[158] Lincoln, "OT in Ephesians," 41; *idem*, *Ephesians*, 50-51; Wallis, "Psalms 8 and 110."
[159] While there is no lexical parallel here, there is a conceptual parallel in the use of these verbs. See the definitions of ἐγείρω and ἐπαίρω in BDAG (Fredrick William Danker, et. al., *A Greek-English Lexicon of the New Testament and Other Early Christian Literature*, 3'rd ed. [Chicago, IL: University of Chicago Press, 2000], 271 and 357.

something to an exalted position "far above (ὑπεράνω)" something else, placing it in or above the heavens (τοῖς ἐπουρανίοις /τῶν οὐρανῶν).

Furthermore, the description of the position which the exalted Christ occupies in Eph 1:21b-23 parallels Psalm 8 in key ways. Both passages use the word "all/every" frequently; Ephesians uses the word every/all six times (verse 21: πάσης ἀρχῆς . . . παντὸς ὀνόματος, verse 22: πάντα ὑπέταξεν . . . πάντα τῇ ἐκκλησίᾳ, and verse 23: τὰ πάντα ἐν πᾶσιν πληρουμένου). As I have already shown, the psalmist also uses this word to describe what God has exalted at strategic points in Psalm 8: The inclusio repeats twice that the Lord's name is "excellent in *all* the earth (πάσῃ τῇ γῇ)," and verse 7, the center-point of the psalm, declares that God has exalted the son of humanity (υἱὸς ἀνθρώπου) by subjecting "all things" (πάντα) under his feet. Interestingly, when Paul Christologically interprets Ps 8:7 in 1 Cor 15:27, he includes a brief exegetical explanation of the word "all things/πάντα."[160]

Furthermore, Eph 1:21-23 describes Christ's exaltation with a list of things that Christ is over; so, too, a list of things which the child of humanity has authority over (LXX: πρόβατα καί . . . τὰ διαπορευόμενα τρίβους θαλασσῶν) in Ps 8:8, 9 follows the declaration of the exaltation of the בן־אדם/υἱὸς ἀνθρώπου in Ps 8:7. Interestingly, the description of Christ's exalted status begins in Eph 1:20 with Christ seated "in the heavenly places," and progresses through the list of Christ's subjects, both hostile and friendly: "the evil powers and the church."[161] Within the internal development of this progression, the author turns to address "die Heilsstellung Christi für die Kirche (V 22b)" that comes after "der Niederwerfung der Unheilsmächte."[162] The phrase "he has subjected all things under his feet" seems to occupy the point of transition from the evil powers to the Church who has Christ over it as a head. Thus, when the book transitions from considering the spiritual powers and authorities to addressing Christ's relationship with the Church, the author draws a line from Psalm 8 precisely where the psalmist has transitioned from a contemplation of heavenly things to the human's relationship to earthly things.[163] These observations strengthen Moritz's case for "attributing considerably more exegetical activity to

---

[160] "But when it says, 'all things are put in subjection,' it is plain that he is excepted who put all things (πάντα) in subjection under him. When all things (πάντα) are subjected to him, then the Son himself will also be subjected to him who put all things in subjection under him, that God may be all in all" (1 Cor 15:27).
[161] Talbert, *Ephesians and Colossians*, 57. For helpful discussions of the terms Paul uses to describe the various heavenly powers in Ephesians 1, see Arnold, *Ephesians*, 52-56 and Roon, *Authenticity* 219-227.
[162] Schnackenburg, *Der Brief an Die Epheser*, 71.
[163] The body of Psalm 8 begins with a meditation upon the heavenly bodies, within which is embedded a conflict involving God's enemies. It then addresses the role of humans (who are βραχύ τι παρ' ἀγγέλους) saying that God "has subjected all things under his feet/πάντα ὑπέταξας ὑποκάτω τῶν ποδῶν αὐτοῦ (Ps 8:5b)," and resolves into an orderly enumeration of creatures subjected to the human (Ps 8:8-9).

the author of Ephesians than has generally been assumed" and reinforce his claim that "Ephesians shows an awareness of the OT *Vorlage* which goes beyond the level of *Wirkungsgeschichte* and which extends to the level of the OT text itself."[164]

What, then, of the exegetical basis upon which the author of Ephesians grounds the connection between the human in Psalm 8 and the exalted Christ? To answer this question, it is necessary to return to the question of the implications of the parallels between Eph 1:19-23 and 1 Cor 15:24-28. Such strong similarities are not surprising in light of the tendency of the book of Ephesians to draw upon material not only from Colossians but also from the rest of the Pauline corpus.[165] Whether the author of Ephesians is Paul or an imitator of Paul, he or she seems to be intimately acquainted with the hermeneutical thought reflected in 1 Cor 15:24-28 and seems to have carried that thought forward in Eph 1:19-23.[166] Yet, along with carrying this exegesis of Psalm 8 forward, Eph 1:19-23 introduces a shift in emphasis from the eschatological "not yet" to the present reality of the "now."

Several factors may be involved in motivating the author to use Pss 8 and 110 to meditate upon the exaltation of Christ as the church already encounters it "now." Arnold makes a compelling case that the epistle is at pains to demonstrate that Christ is superior to the spiritual beings that new believers in Asia Minor would have feared.[167] Even if Arnold's thesis were to be proven false or unlikely, the exultant quasi-hymnic nature of the passage, the desire to encourage the believers at Ephesus (verse 18), and the exhortation to the Ephesians to live as a unified body here on earth (4:1-16) all provide adequate explanations for why the emphasis here is upon the present reign of the exalted Christ, rather than the future hope of resurrection.

Thus, the hermeneutical underpinnings for the Christological appropriation of Ps 8:7 in Eph 1:22 most likely derive primarily from the broader thought of Pauline Christianity, especially as found in 1 Cor 15:26, rather than from a reliance upon tradition or from the discrete concerns of the book of Ephesians (though both of these considerations may come into play as secondary factors).[168] Paul has already developed the Adam-Christ typology in Romans 5

---

[164] *Profound Mystery*, 21.

[165] Lincoln, *Ephesians*, xlvii-lviii, lxvi-lxvii; Witherington, *Letters*, 12-19; Lincoln and Wedderburn, *Theology*, 87-89.

[166] For a description of ancient authors writing "as if" they were someone else, closely mimicking the thought and ideas of another, see Talbert, *Ephesians and Colossians* 7-9; see also Lincoln, *Ephesians*, lviii. For the view that only Paul himself would feel free to reapply Pauline thoughts and ideas in new, seemingly divergent ways, see Barth, "Conversion," 3; Witherington, *Letters*, 12-19.

[167] Arnold, *Ephesians, Power and Magic*; Talbert, *Ephesians and Colossians*, 74.

[168] While I agree with Moritz that "Ephesians relates Christ implicitly to the man of Ps 8 within a framework of Adam-Christ typology," I disagree that one can detect such a move within the book of Ephesians itself. (Moritz, *Profound Mystery*, 20-21). Other than a brief note indicating the possible connection between the Pauline Adam-Christ

and, most importantly in 1 Corinthians 15, and it is taken up and assumed here by the author of Ephesians 1.[169] So, on the one hand, all that has been said about the connection between Christ, the second Adam, and the "child of humanity" of Ps 8:7 in the discussion of 1 Cor 15:27 above applies to the use of Ps 8:7 here insofar as it forms the theological underpinning for the appropriation of Psalm 8 in Ephesians 1. On the other hand, Ephesians 1 now freely utilizes Psalm 8 as Christological in its own right for the interrelated purposes of praising God's power (1:19), encouraging the church to hope (1:18) and not fear demonic forces, and challenging the church to live in unity (2:11-21; 4:1-11) under its head, Christ (1:10, 22). Having surveyed Eph 1:19-23 and the way in which the passage interprets Ps 8:7 and applies it to Christ (level one), we are now in a position to read Psalm 8 anew in light of Eph 1:19-23 (level two).

3.2 Reading Psalm 8 in Light of Ephesians 1:19-23

Since the use of Psalm 8 in Ephesians overlaps so substantially with the parallel passage in 1 Corinthians, I will limit my comments here to consider some of the distinctive contributions of Ephesians 1. Most prominent among these contributions, as I have shown, is the emphasis upon the way in which the resurrection and exultation of Christ is a spiritual reality that already has implications for the corporate Church in "this age" (ἐν τῷ μέλλοντι, verse 21). In light of these "already" claims, the Christian canonical interpreter of Psalm 8 may now understand the hope for the restoration of the lost world of Genesis 1, already generated within Psalm 8 itself, as coming to fruition here and now in the exaltation of Christ. Read in the light of Ephesians, "Ps 8 [is] a meeting point between protology and eschatology."[170] Thus, the contemporary reader and the contemporary corporate Church may be encouraged to hope. Reading, singing, or liturgically reciting Psalm 8 is not, then, an exercise in the denial of reality; rather, it is a celebration of the reality that God does order his cosmos through the exaltation of humble things, and that he is ordering the cosmos in a profound, transformative, and eschatological way in the exaltation of Christ over all things even now.

Such a celebratory reading of Palm 8, however, ought not become a source of arrogance for the reader. Rather, the letter to the Ephesians reminds its audience that it is Christ who is the head and who rules, and that the Church is part of the "all things" that are under Christ's feet (verse 21); read in this way, the reader ought not envision himself as the exalted human ruler placed over all things. In other words, when reading Psalm 8 in light of Ephesians 1, the

---

typology and the ἐν Χριστῷ formula as used in Ephesians (ibid., 21 note 59), Moritz does little to demonstrate how the book of Ephesians itself contains an Adam-Christ typology.
[169] Lincoln is nearer the mark than Moritz when he says that the Pauline interpretation of Psalm 8 in light of his Adam Christology "has been continued" in Ephesians 1 (Lincoln, "OT in Ephesians," 41).
[170] Moritz, *Profound Mystery*, 21.

believer sees himself in Ps 8:8-9, not in Ps 8:6-7. Furthermore, as a member of the body of Christ, the believer's role in ordering creation is now to a) humbly submit to Christ, the head, and b) strive for unity and reconciliation within the body (Eph 4:17-32) and walk in love with all humans (Eph 5:1-20). Thus, the interpretation of Psalm 8 in the book of Ephesians helps to guard against a militant misinterpretation of Psalm 8. Someone may identify quickly and arrogantly with the royal בן־אדם of Ps 8:5 and assume forthwith that he or she has the right, or even the mandate, to exploit the rest of creation or even other humans; such a reader, however, does not read the text in a way that is in keeping with the teaching of the book of Ephesians.

Finally, Eph 1:19-23's interpretation of Psalm 8 in the context of a meditation upon τὴν ἐνέργειαν τοῦ κράτους τῆς ἰσχύος αὐτοῦ/the working of [God's] great might (verse 19) in the resurrection of Christ can influence the way in which a canonical reader envisions that "majesty" of God's name in all the earth as described in Ps 8:2, 10. God's power in Ephesians 1 is mighty, militant, and subjugates enemies, to be sure. Yet God, not a human army, accomplishes this conquest through the resurrection and exaltation of the humble, crucified Christ, and through the vanquishing of death (read in connection with 1 Cor 15:26), rather than through military slaughter. Thus, in canonical perspective, the Christian reader begins to see just how far God will carry his counter-intuitive method of maintaining the creation order and making himself majestic through the exaltation of weak things. Neither domesticable and passive nor conventionally militant, God's majesty (Ps 8:2) and strength (Eph 1:19) subverts and eludes human conceptions. Perhaps a canonical exegesis of Psalm 8, then, is better served by focusing upon encountering and being transformed by God's majesty than in cognitively and exhaustively explaining it. With this humbling reminder of human limitations in mind, then, I turn now to consider one more New Testament quotation of Psalm 8, Heb 2:5-8, before returning to articulate an integrative understanding of Psalm 8 in light of the New Testament.

4. Hebrews 2:5-9 and Psalm 8

4.1 Reading Hebrews 2:5-9 "In Itself"

4.1.1 The broader context: The Epistle to the Hebrews. Despite many attempts to identify the author of the book of Hebrews,[171] it is impossible to know who the author was, and scholars now focus upon "the profile" of the author, rather than his or her identity. The author of the book, whoever she (or he) may be, has produced a remarkable and unique piece of epistolary literature.

---

[171] For a thorough survey of the history of reception and interpretation of the book of Hebrews, including the history of attempts at identifying the author, see Craig R. Koester, *Hebrews: A New Translation with Introduction and Commentary* (AB 36; New York, NY: Doubleday, 2001), 1-54. In a popular book, Ruth Hoppin revives the hypothesis that Priscilla wrote Hebrews (*Priscilla's Letter: Finding the Author of the Epistle to the Hebrews* [Fort Bragg, CA: Lost Coast, 2000]). See also Koester, *Hebrews*, 45.

The vocabulary and literary style of the book are highly sophisticated,[172] and the author uses literary devices to organize and arrange the material, such as bracketing sections with an inclusio and using hook-words to connect one section with another.[173] Nevertheless, despite Überlacker's attempts to trace the book's structures according to Greco-Roman conventions,[174] large sections of the book do not fit neatly into the categories of classical rhetoric. Rather, its structure develops according to its own creative line of thought.[175] The hortatory nature of Hebrews leads many to speak of the book as a sermon rather than a letter.[176]

On the one hand, finding an original audience for the epistle (or, perhaps better, homily) is fraught with difficulties, as the book itself does not identify any intended audience;[177] while the book seems to presuppose a specific

---

[172] Thomas H. Olbricht, "Hebrews as Amplification," in *Rhetoric and the New Testament*, 375-387; Timothy W. Seid, "Synkrisis in Hebrews 7: the Rhetorical Structure and Strategy," in *The Rhetorical Interpretation of Scripture: Essays from the 1996 Malibu Conference* (ed. S. E. Porter and D. L. Stamps; JSNTSup 180; Sheffield, UK: Sheffield Academic Press, 1999), 322-347; and Harold W. Attridge, *The Epistle to the Hebrews: A Commentary on the Epistle to the Hebrews* (Hermeneia; Philadelphia, PA: Fortress, 1989), 13-21. For a survey of the signs of the sophisticated literary techniques of the author of Hebrews (drawing from the works of Olbricht, Seid, and others such as Mitchell Cosby), see Guthrie, "Hebrews," 419-422.

[173] See Guthrie, *Structure*, 76-89, 94-104, for a detailed survey of the use of the *inclusio* and hook-words in Hebrews. See also *idem*, "Hebrews," 419-422 for a brief survey of studies examining various other literary devices used in the book of Hebrews.

[174] Walter G. Überlacker (*Der Hebräerbrief als Appell; Untersuchungen zu Exordium, Narratio, und Postcriptum Hebr 1-2 und 13 22-25* [Stockholm: Almquist & Wiksell Intl., 1989]).

[175] See Guthrie, *The Structure of Hebrews: A Text-Linguistic Analysis* (SNT 73; New York, NY: Brill, 1994); idem, "Hebrews," 422-424; Cynthia Long Westfall, *A Discourse Analysis of the Letter to the Hebrews: The Relationship between Form and Meaning* (LNTS 297; New York, NY: T & T Clark, 2005), 4-7; and David A. deSilva, *Perseverance in Gratitude: A Socio-Rhetorical Commentary on the Epistle to the Hebrews* (Grand Rapids, MI: Eerdmans, 2000), 46.

[176] See Lawrence Wills, "The Form of the Sermon in Hellenistic Judaism and Early Christianity," *HTR* 77 (1984): 277-299; C. Clifton Black, "The Rhetorical Form of the Hellenistic Jewish and Early Christian Sermon: A Response to Lawrence Wills," *HTR* 81 (1988):1-18; and George H. Guthrie, "Hebrews in its First-Century Contexts: Recent Research," in *The Face of New Testament Studies*, 430; Edgar McKnight and Christopher Church, *Hebrews-James* (SHBC; Macon, GA: Smyth & Helwys, 2004), 10-14. Guthrie gives a brief survey of works that have shown Hebrews to be a homily, including the works of Wills and Black, as well as earlier works such as the detailed study by Hartwig Thyen.

[177] For an extended discussion about the intended audience of the book, arguing that the audience consisted of Roman Christian house churches, see Lane, *Hebrews 1-8*, liii-lx. While various life settings for the epistle have been proposed, many would agree with William L. Lane that Hebrews is "a sermon in search of a life setting" ("Hebrews: A Sermon in Search of a Life Setting," *SwJT* 28[1985], 13-18).

audience facing some sort of persecution,[178] its doctrinal and ethical teachings have a universal quality about them. On the other hand, the book reflects the milieu of its provenance. As the title given to it by tradition suggests, the book of Hebrews also exhibits Jewish influences and founds its teaching firmly upon a Christological exegesis of various Old Testament passages (see Heb 1:1-2).[179] The book of Hebrews also has some similarities with the Dead Sea Scrolls, Paul, First Peter, and other Jewish and Christian writings.[180] It is reasonable, therefore, to situate the book of Hebrews within the context of the thought worlds of early Christianity and Hellenistic Judaism.[181]

The way that Hebrews extensively draws upon and interprets the Hebrew Scriptures is of special interest for understanding the book, and the Old Testament virtually permeates the homily.[182] The author exhibits a supreme ability to combine "the best of Jewish and Hellenistic thought" in her hermeneutical argument, and she also presupposes an almost equal degree of versatile sophistication on the part of her audience.[183] It is unnecessary for our purposes to take an emphatic position on the question of which context—Greek or Jewish— ought to be described as the primary soil from which the orator's hermeneutical

---

[178] See, for example, Koester, *Hebrews*, 64-79.

[179] Moyise, *Old Testament*, 98-108; Ronald E. Clements, "The Use of the Old Testament in Hebrews," *SwJT* 28 (1985): 36-45; Martin Kerrer, "The Epistle to the Hebrews and the Septuagint," in *Septuagint Research: Issues and Challenges in the Study of the Greek Jewish Scriptures* (Atlanta, GA: Society of Biblical Literature, 2006), 335-353; Beate Kowalski, "Die Rezeption alttestamentlicher Theologie im Hebräerbrief" in *Ausharren in der Verheissung: Studien zum Hebräerbrief* (SB 204; Stuttgart: Katholisches Bibelwerk, 2005), 35-62; and David Peterson, "God and Scripture in Hebrews," in *The Trustworthiness of God: Perspectives on the Nature of Scripture* (Grand Rapids, MI: Eerdmans, 2002), 118-138.

[180] See Guthrie, "Hebrews," 419-443. For Qumran, see Yigael Yadin, "מגילות ים המלח והאיגרת אל העברים," in *Essays on the Dead Sea Scrolls, in Memory of E. L. Sukenik* (ed. Chaim Rabin; Jerusalem: Hekhal Ha-Sefer, 1961), 191-208; Maxine L. Grossman, "Priesthood as Authority: Interpretive Competition in First-Century Judaism and Christianity," in *Dead Sea Scrolls as Background to Postbiblical Judaism and Early Christianity* (Boston, MA: Leiden Brill, 2003), 117-131. For Paul, see Koester, *Hebrews*, 54-55; Witherington, "The Influence of Galatians on Hebrews," *NTS* 37 (1991), 146-152. For I Peter, see Koester, *Hebrews*, 57-58; Guthrie, "Hebrews," 439-440.

[181] See Barnabas Lindars, *The Theology of the Letter to the Hebrews* (New York, NY: Cambridge, 1991), 21-25; William Lane, *Hebrews 1-8* (WBC 47a; Dallas, TX: Word, 1991), cxlvii-cl; and Guthrie, "Hebrews" 427.

[182] See Clements, "Old Testament in Hebrews," 36-45, and Dale F. Leschert, *Hermeneutical Foundations of Hebrews: A Study in the Validity of the Epistle's Interpretation of Some Core Citations from the Psalms* (NABPRDiss 10; Lewiston, NY: Edwin Mellen, 1994).

[183] Clements, "Old Testament in Hebrews," 37. Clements is here describing the rationale used by those who argue for an Alexandrian audience, without himself taking a position on the question.

thought springs,[184] and it suffices to emphasize that the author's interpretive approach exhibits affinities with a broad array of Greek, Jewish, and Christian interpreters. Among the diverse hermeneutical methods and motifs employed by the author of Hebrews, one motif dominates substantial portions of the book, including the section within which Psalm 8 is cited (Heb 1:5-2:18): the motif of Jesus's superiority in comparison with figures respected within Judaism.[185] It is also important to note that the book of Psalms figures prominently in the hermeneutical thought of the book of Hebrews.[186]

Various structural schemas for Hebrews have been proposed, focusing upon Greco-Roman hortatory patterns,[187] discourse analysis,[188] the comparisons between Jesus and other exalted beings that run throughout the book,[189] or a combination of factors.[190] Yet, Hebrews, more than many other biblical books, is structured in a way that resists schematization; outlines consisting of "a flat list" of section headings fail to "register the cumulative effect of sections tumbling one upon the other."[191] Nevertheless, by placing Stanley's outline (which considers the book's "literary genre, rhetorical character, and content") alongside the outline of Hughes (who organizes his outline around the theme "The Supremacy of Christ"), side-by-side, it is possible to adumbrate the structure of the book:[192]

---

[184] Seid, for example, argues that Greek conventions should be considered first, "and only when it [the Greek background] provides no satisfying points of similarity should one investigate other literary influences ("Synkrisis," 323-324. Cf, Überlacker, *Der Hebräerbrief* and Olbricht, "Hebrews as Amplification." For points of contact between Hebrews and Palestinian Judaism, see Koester, *Hebrews*, 61-63).

[185] Olbricht, "Hebrews as Amplification," 375-387; Lane *Hebrews 1-8*, cxxviii-cxxxv.

[186] See Leschert, *Hermeneutical Foundations*, Simon Kistemaker, *The Psalm Citations in the Epistle to the Hebrews* (Amsterdam: Wed. G. van Soest, 1961), and Harold W. Attridge, "The Psalms in Hebrews," in *The Psalms in the New Testament*, 197-212.

[187] Überlacker, *Der Hebräerbrief*.

[188] Westfall, *Discourse Analysis*; Lane, *Hebrews 1-8*, lxxx-lxxxiv.

[189] Olbricht, "Hebrews as Amplification."

[190] Steve Stanley constructs an outline of the book based upon the books "literary genre, rhetorical character, and content" ("The Structure of Hebrews from Three Perspectives," *TB* 45 [1994], 245-271). For a survey of attempts to determine a structural schema underlying the book, see Lane, *Hebrews 1-8*, lxxx-xcviii. For a sustained examination of the structure of the book of Hebrews, see Albert Vanhoye, *The Structure and Message of the Epistle to the Hebrews* (Rome: Editrice Pontificio Instituto Biblico, 1989).

[191] Fred B. Craddock, "The Letter to the Hebrews," in *The New Interpreter's Bible* (12 vols.; Nashville, TN: Abingdon, 1994-2004), 12:16.

[192] Adapted from Stanley ("Structure," 270-271) and Philip E. Hughes (*A Commentary on the Epistle to the Hebrews* [Grand Rapids, MI: Eerdmans, 1977], 3-4). In a way similar to Hughes, but more nuanced, Olbricht outlines the book as containing five exhortations embedded within four main sections demonstrating the superiority of Christ ("Hebrews as Amplification," 377).

Stanley:	Hughes:
Prologue (1:1-4)	I. Christ superior to the prophets (1:1-3)
I. The Sovereign Son as Superior Mediator (1:5-7:28).	II. Christ superior to the angels (1:4-2:18)
II. The Superior Ministry of the New Covenant Mediator (8:1-10:39).	III. Christ superior to Moses (3:1-4:13)
III. New Covenant Requirements for the People of God (11:1-13:19)	IV. Christ superior to Aaron (4:14-10:18)
Benediction and Epistolary Closing (13:20-25).	V. Christ superior as the new and living way (10:19-12:29)
	VI. Concluding exhortations, requests, and greetings (13:1-25).

Through the skillful employment of rhetorical techniques, the author/orator challenges his listeners to remain faithful in the face of persecution and temptation. The dramatic momentum of the book's argument builds as the author shows that Jesus is far superior to angels (1:5-2:18), Moses (3:1-4:16), and even the high priests and Melchizedek (10:1-18). The heightening rhetoric builds to a crescendo, as the orator challenges the members of his audience and encourages them to "hold fast" (11:1-12:29).

4.1.2 The nearer context: Hebrews 1:5-2:18 and Hebrews 2:5-9. After introducing both the book of Hebrews and the comparison between Jesus and the angels in 1:1-4, the author undertakes an extended comparison of Jesus with the angels in 1:5-2:18. The citation of Psalm 8 in Heb 2:6-8 comes towards the middle of this first comparison of the book, and the Septuagint's translation of the term אלהים as ἀγγέλους in Ps 8:6 seems, at least in part, to lead the orator to cite the psalm in this context.[193] The comparison moves from arguing that Jesus is superior to the angels 1:5-14) to discussing how and why Jesus became temporarily lower than the angels (2:5-18). Thus, Heb 1:5-2:18 consists of two major sections connected by a hortatory exhortation to the audience, as follows:

    A. 1:5-14, The Son Superior to Angels
    B. 2:1-4, Therefore, Listen Carefully
    C. 2:5-18, The Son Lower than Angels
        2:5-9, He Became as We Are
        2:10-18, A Faithful and Merciful High Priest[194]

---

[193] Attridge, "The Psalms in Hebrews," 204. The author of Hebrews seems to use a Greek text substantially the same as that of the Septuagint in his Scripture citations throughout. See Radu Gheorghita, *The Role of the Septuagint in Hebrews: An Investigation of its Influence with Special Consideration to the Use of Hab 2:3-4 in Heb 10:37-38* (WUNT 2/160; Tübingen: Mohr Siebeck, 2003), 44-46.

[194] Reproduced verbatim from Craddock, "Hebrews," 18.

The first section (1:5-14) contains a catena of Scripture citations joined together, with little explanation, in order to demonstrate the superiority of Christ and the relative inferiority of the angels.[195] After a brief interlude impressing upon the audience the importance of the message (2:1-4),[196] the author resumes the comparison between Jesus and the angels by introducing a citation of Ps 8:5-7.

In contrast with the rapid fire list of terse citations in chapter one, the citation of Psalm 8 in Heb 2:5-8 is followed by a more extensive exegesis wherein the text's application to Christ is explained.[197] As noted above, Moritz calls into question the assumption shared by some scholars that the concluding citation of the catena in chapter one (Heb 1:3=Ps 110:1) is connected to the citation of Ps 8:5-7 in Heb 2:6-8 and that this connection derives from a common traditional heritage shared by the authors of 1 Corinthians, Ephesians, and Hebrews.[198] Nevertheless, it is worth noting that the citation of Psalm 8 in Heb 2:5-8 gestures back towards the briefly interrupted argument of Heb 1:5-14 by a) resuming the conversation of the things "of which we are speaking" (Heb 2:5), and b) reiterating that God will subject things under the "feet" of Christ (Heb 1:13=Ps 110:1 and Heb 2:8=Ps 8:7).[199]

Rhetorical devices such as *inclusio* are used to set off Heb 2:5-18 as a pericope[200] and Heb 2:5-9 and 10-18 as sub-pericopes.[201] The first half of the

---

[195] See Attridge, "Psalms in Hebrews," 199-203, Moyise, *The Old Testament in the New*, 98-100. For a careful reading of the catena that is attentive to the problematic question of how Heb 1:5-14 relates with the broader argument of Hebrews, see Kenneth L. Schenck, "A Celebration of the Enthroned Son: The Catena of Hebrews 1," *JBL* 120 (2001), 469-485.

[196] As Lane comments, "from the fact that Christ is greater than the angels [1:5-14] it follows logically that the revelation delivered through the Son must be regarded with the utmost seriousness [2:1-4]" (*Hebrews 1-8*, 37; see also Westfall, who groups 1:1-2:4 together as a unity that declares "Let's Pay Attention to the Message of God's Ultimate Messenger" [*Discourse Analysis*, 89]).

[197] "While exegesis in the catena of ch. 1 was implicit," writes Attridge, "it is here explicit, and the verses immediately following the citation of the psalm constitute a brief midrash on the text" ("Psalms in Hebrews," 204).

[198] Moritz, *Profound Mystery*, 12.

[199] See George H. Guthrie, "Hebrews," in *Commentary on the New Testament Use of the Old Testament*, 946.

[200] Verses 5 and 16 contain similar phrases introducing the following discussions of privileges that the angels do not have, but Jesus does have ("οὐ γὰρ ἀγγέλοις ὑπέταξεν/now it was not to angels that he subjected" [verse 5], and "οὐ γὰρ δήπου ἀγγέλων ἐπιλαμβάνεται/for surely it is not angels that he helps" [verse 16]). See Lane, *Hebrews 1-8*, 44.

[201] Guthrie notes four correspondences between verses 10 and verses 17-18 that serve to bracket verses 10-18 as a unit by repetition, setting it apart from verses 5-9: 1) the use of the synonyms "Ἔπρεπεν/it was fitting" (verse 10) and "ὤφειλεν/he had to" (verse 17); 2) the discussion of the development of the son in both verses 10 and verse 17; 3) Jesus's help given to the "children" (verse 10) or "siblings" (verse 17); and 4) the discussion of the suffering of Jesus in verses 10 and 18. Verses 5-9 show an internal thematic balance and coherence in that verse 5 introduces the citation of Psalm 8, verses 6-8a quote the

first sub-pericope (verses 5-8a) contains the citation of the psalm. This section begins as a continuation of the consideration of the exaltation of Christ in "the world to come" (verse 5) already contemplated in chapter one's catena. This is followed by a vague introductory formula ("διεμαρτύρατο δέ πού τις/someone has testified somewhere," verse 6). This formula reflects "the strong emphasis throughout Hebrews on the oracular character of Scripture. Precisely because it is God who speaks in the OT, the identity of the person through whom he uttered his word is relatively unimportant."[202] This is followed by the quotation of Ps 8:5-7 in Heb 2:6-8a.[203]

The second half of the sub-pericope (verses 8b-9) turns the audience's attention to the "present" (verse 8b), when "we do not yet see everything in subjection to him" (the child of humanity, Heb 2:6=Ps 8:6). The second sub-pericope (verses 10-18) then goes on to fully explain why the Christ is not yet in the exalted state: he must be made perfect through suffering[204] so that he might be "a merciful and faithful high priest" (verse 17).[205] The transition of focus from "the world to come" (1:5-14; 2:5-8a) to "the present" (2:8b-18) is already anticipated within the citation of Ps 8:6 (Heb 2:6-8a). While the Hebrew version of Ps 8:6, in saying that God has made humans " a little less than divine," describes the exalted place of the child of humanity, "[o]ur homilist instead drives a wedge between the two parallel affirmations 'you have made him a little less than the angels' 'with glory and honor you have crowned him.' Instead, he reads these affirmations as two temporally discrete stages in the history of the Son."[206] Thus, the author/orator interprets Ps 8:5-7—with the Septuagint translation of the psalm as the starting point[207]—as relating the present state of affairs with the future exaltation of Jesus.

---

psalm, and verses 8b-9 explicate the psalm, with forms of the key word ὑποτάσσω/to subject running throughout verses 6-9 (once in verse 5 and three times in verse 8). Furthermore, as Marie E. Isaacs observes, Heb 2:7-9 inextricably interconnects the citation with the explication that follows in verses 8a-9 through the construction of a quasi-chiastic reiteration of the latter part of the psalms citation, as follows:
"a) Man's temporary subordination (v. 7a)
   b) His enthronement (v. 7b)
      c) His sovereignty (v. 8a)
      c1 His sovereignty (v.8b)
a1 His temporary subordination (vv. 8c-9a)
   b1 His enthronement (v. 9b)"
(*Reading Hebrews and James: A Literary and Theological Commentary* [Macon GA: Smythe and Helwys, 2002], 39).

[202] Lane, *Hebrews 1-8*, 46.
[203] The quotation follows the LXX version of Psalm 8, except that it omits the words "you have set him over the work of your hands."
[204] Craig R. Koester, *Hebrews*, 225.
[205] Craddock, "Hebrews," 18.
[206] Attridge, "The Psalms in Hebrews," 205.
[207] Gheorghita, *Role of the Septuagint*, 44-46.

Guthrie describes Heb 2:5-9 as a hinge transitioning from a focus upon "heaven" to a focus upon "earth."[208] Guthrie's construal is interesting in that he sees the progression of Heb 1-2 from heavenly to earthly as anticipating a parallel, reverse progression in Heb 5:1-10:18 from earthly to heavenly; the two sections work together to encourage the hearer to endure earthly suffering just as Jesus has endured suffering, as shown in figure 3. Read in this way, the citation of Psalm 8 has special importance for the book of Hebrews in that it a) serves as an interpretive hinge that explains the relationship between Jesus' earthly humiliation and his heavenly exalted status above the heavens, b) lays the groundwork for the preacher/author's later explanation of Jesus's high priestly function, and c) provides motivation for the audience to endure, just as Christ has endured.

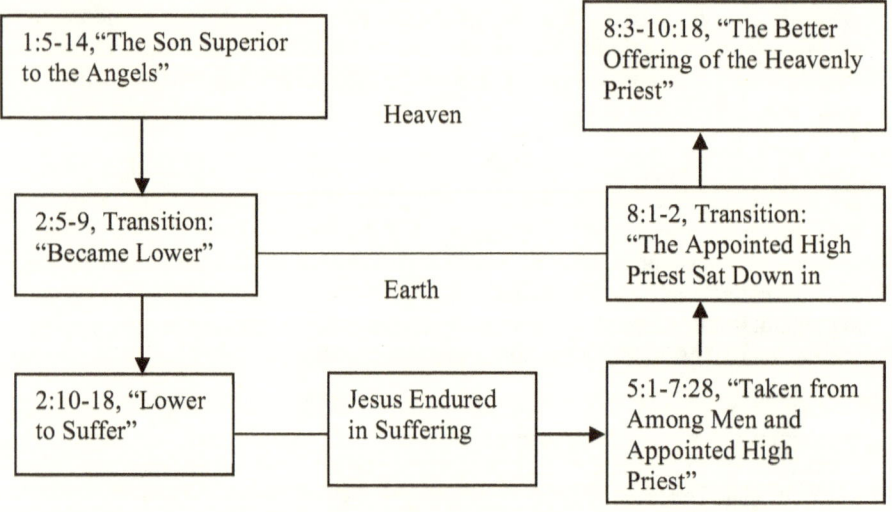

Figure 3. Internal movement within Hebrews 1:5-10:18[209]

Having surveyed the way that the citation of Ps 8:5-7 functions both in the nearer context of Heb 1-2 and in the broader context of the book of Hebrews, we may now turn to examine more closely the way in which the author of Hebrews interprets and applies Psalm 8.

4.1.3 The use of Psalm 8:5-7 in Hebrews 2:5-9. In order to properly understand the way in which the author of Hebrews interprets Psalm 8 in this context, one must address two interrelated questions: 1) Does the author understand the words ἄνθρωπος and υἱὸς ἀνθρώπου in Ps 8:5 (Heb 2:6) to speak of corporate

---

[208] Guthrie, *Structure*, 140-142.
[209] Condensed from Guthrie's more extensive flow chart (*Structure*, 142).

humanity (so NRSV, TNIV), an individual human (see RSV, NIV, NAB), or both? 2) On what logical and exegetical grounds, then, does the author relate the words of Ps 8:5-7 to the humbled and exalted Messiah? The two questions are inseparably connected, so that the way in which a reader answers one question will determine the way in which she answers the other question.

If one takes the terms ἄνθρωπος and υἱὸς ἀνθρώπου to speak of the human race corporately, then verses 5-8 speak of the idealized rule of humanity that does not exist now (Νῦν δε οὔπω ὁρῶμεν/ "at present, we do not yet see . . . ," verse 8b) but will exist in the eschaton ("τὴν οἰκουμένην τὴν μέλλουσαν/the world to come," verse 5).[210] A shift then occurs in verse nine ("τὸν δὲ . . . βλέπομεν Ἰησοῦν/but we see . . . Jesus"), where the orator "emphasize[s] that Jesus in a representative sense fulfilled the vocation intended for humankind."[211] If, however, the terms ἄνθρωπος and υἱὸς ἀνθρώπου speak of an individual, then the orator is interpreting Psalm 8 atomistically, identifying the term υἱὸς ἀνθρώπου (Ps 8:5) with the messianic term ὁ υἱὸς τοῦ ἀνθρώπου found elsewhere in the New Testament and early Christianity[212] and turning Ps 8:5 into a Christological "proof-text."[213] According to this view, the "him" of verse 8b ("οὔπω ὁρῶμεν αὐτῷ τὰ πάντα ὑποτεταγμένα/we do not yet see everything in subjection to him") is already speaking of Jesus, the "son of man."[214] A mere consideration of the term υἱὸς ἀνθρώπου is not enough to settle the issue. On the one hand the term ὁ υἱὸς τοῦ ἀνθρώπου is used Christologically widely in the New Testament and in early Christianity, and the author of Hebrews has already described the Messiah as a υἱός.[215] On the other hand, Psalm 8's υἱὸς ἀνθρώπου is anarthrous, and the author of Hebrews does not describe Christ with the phrase υἱὸς ἀνθρώπου elsewhere.[216]

Guthrie and Quinn have recently applied discourse analysis in an attempt to answer the question of the meaning of ἄνθρωπος/υἱὸς ἀνθρώπου in Heb 2:5-9.[217] They urge that, when read in light of "broader discourse concerns," it is clear that the author of Hebrews understands ἄνθρωπος/υἱὸς ἀνθρώπου Christologically, not anthropologically.[218] Three of the points that they make are quite strong, and significantly undermine the possibility of a thoroughgoing anthropological interpretation of ἄνθρωπος/υἱὸς ἀνθρώπου: 1) The introductory formula (2:5) in speaking of the eschatological "world to come" links the

---

[210] See Craig L. Blomberg, "Better Things in this Case: The Superiority of Today's New International Version in Hebrews," *BT* 55 (2004), 310-318; Lane, *Hebrews 1-8*, 46-47.
[211] Lane, *Hebrews 1-8*, 47.
[212] So George H. Guthrie and Russell D. Quinn, "A Discourse Analysis of the Use of Psalm 8:4-6 in Hebrews 2:5-9," *JETS* 49 (2006), 243; Childs, "Psalm 8," 25.
[213] Childs, "Psalm 8," 24-26.
[214] So Attridge, "Psalms in Hebrews," 204.
[215] Guthrie and Quinn, "Discourse Analysis," 243-244.
[216] Koester, *Hebrews*, 215-216.
[217] Guthrie and Quinn, "Use of Psalm 8:4-6."
[218] Guthrie and Quinn, "Use of Psalm 8:4-6," 246.

quotation of Psalm 8 with the discussion of the exalted son in Heb 1:5-14.[219] 2) the author's "rabbinic technique employed" to interpret the passage a) shows that the author interprets the psalm to speak of "the logical progression from [Christ's] incarnation to exaltation," and b) attends to the apparent contradiction occasioned by the depiction of Jesus' exaltation as already accomplished, yet lying in the future; such a contradiction does not exist unless the words ἄνθρωπος and υἱὸς ἀνθρώπου are interpreted messianically.[220] 3) Psalm 8 functions as a hinge within the broader context whereby the argument of Hebrews transitions from a consideration of the exalted son in the heavenly realm (Heb 1:5-14 // Ps 8:6b-7=Heb 2:7b-8a) to a consideration of the incarnate, humble son in the earthly realm (Heb 2:10-18 // Ps 8:6a=Heb2:7a).[221]

Yet, an overly thoroughgoing Christological understanding of the use of Ps 8:5-7 in Hebrews overlooks some evidence in the immediate context that the author also understands ἄνθρωπος/υἱὸς ἀνθρώπου as, in some sense, anthropological. First of all, when the person of Jesus is mentioned in verse 9, he is contrasted with the "him" of verse 8b. This contrast is not determinative, however, because the contrast is between an evidently future αὐτῷ whom "we do not yet see," and the present state of Jesus. Yet, the likelihood that this contrast between "him" (verse 8) and "Jesus" (verse 9) is more than merely temporal increases when one considers the way that verses 9-18 develop the relationship between Jesus and other humans.[222] At the outset of the second sub-pericope in verse 10, which is arguably an extension of the exegesis of Ps 8:5-7, the orator describes other humans as "πολλὺς υἱοὺς/many children" whom Jesus will lead into "δόξαν/glory" in the eschaton, thus echoing the declaration of Ps 8:5-6 that God will crown the "ἀνθρώπου" with "δόξῃ" in the eschaton (according to the orator's interpretation).

Verses 10-18 then go on to describe the earthly suffering and service of Christ in connection with its effects upon a corporate group of humans with whom Jesus closely identifies; "the sanctifier and the sanctified are all of one (ἐξ ἑνὸς, verse 11)," and Jesus "had to be made like his siblings" (verse 17). Furthermore, because of Christ's identification with the "children" (verse 14),

---

[219] Guthrie and Quinn, "Use of Psalm 8:4-6," 239-241.
[220] Guthrie and Quinn, "Use of Psalm 8:4-6," 241-243. I do not agree with Guthrie and Quinn, however, that this apparent contradiction lies almost exclusively with the apparent juxtaposition of Ps 110:1 with Ps 8:5-7. Rather, the apparent contradiction arises when a) one juxtaposes the entire chain of references demonstrating Christ's superiority to angels in 1:5-14 with Ps 8:6's claim that the human child is "for a little while lower than the angels" and b) one reads Ps 8:6a in connection with the exaltation of the human child that follows in Ps 8:6b-7, without understanding that there is temporal progression involved (thus motivating the author of Hebrews to clarify the temporal progression in verses 8b-9).
[221] Guthrie and Quinn, "Use of Psalm 8:4-6," 245. See also Guthrie, *Structure*, 142.
[222] Described as "many children" (verse 10), "those who are sanctified" (verse 11), "siblings" (verses 11 and 17), "the children" (verses 13-14), "the seed of Abraham" (verse 16), "people" (verse 17), and "those who are being tempted" (verse 18).

"the seed of Abraham" receive divine help that angels do not get (verse 16). This last declaration is especially noteworthy because it forms part of the inclusio that, via repetition, brackets verses 5-18 ("οὐ γὰρ ἀγγέλοις ὑπέταξεν/now it was not to angels that he subjected" [verse 5], and "οὐ γὰρ δήπου ἀγγέλων ἐπιλαμβάνεται/for surely it is not angels that he helps" [verse 16]).[223] Thus, even if the reader/auditor initially understands the contrast of verse 5 to implicitly speak of the exalted Christ, by the time the orator has completed the transition from the exalted Christ (chapter 1) to the earthly Christ (2:10-18), the audience will have come to understand that a corporate group of humans, too, can be "amplified" over and against angels.[224]

Thus, if one overemphasizes either the messianic or the universal anthropological dimension of the terms ἄνθρωπος and υἱὸς ἀνθρώπου, the resulting interpretation runs against the meaning of the text in its context. The passage as a whole and in context makes more sense when read as an explication of a double meaning involved in the text's description of the ἄνθρωπος/υἱὸς ἀνθρώπου. Even if the original audience (or, for that matter, the contemporary audience) would not have been aware of the double meaning when the citation was introduced, the point of the orator's explication of the passage is to elucidate the double meaning; Heb 2:8b-18 explains how Christ, the individual, fulfills what was described of the ἄνθρωπος/υἱὸς ἀνθρώπου in Psalm 8 and, in so doing, identifies with corporate humanity so that they, too, might fulfill the idealized reign described in Ps 8:5-7.[225] Thus, the citation of Psalm 8 in Heb 2:6-8 serves an additional transitional function unobserved by Guthrie: In the process of moving from the heavenly exaltation of Christ to the earthly ministry of Christ, the argument also moves from focusing exclusively upon Christ and his glory (Hebrews 1) to focusing on Christ, redeemed corporate humanity, and their shared glory (Hebrews 2).

This accounts for much of the exegetical logic underlying the orator's application of the passage to Christ. Other factors undoubtedly played a role in the way that the orator and his implied audience would have understood the relationship between Christ and Ps 8:5-7. These factors are subsidiary, however, to the main argument of the passage that drives the exegesis in context, namely, that Christ's humiliation and exaltation gives glory to corporate humanity. The connection between the citation of Ps 110:1 in Heb 1:13 and the citation of Ps 8:5-7 in Heb 2:6-8 may indeed reflect a common exegetical tradition, reflected in 1 Corinthians 15 and Ephesians 1. Yet, six verses are interposed between the two citations, including a hortatory digression. Furthermore, when the author/preacher resumes her Christological meditation by explicating Psalm 8, she does

---

[223] Lane, *Hebrews 1-8*, 44; Guthrie, *Structure*, 77-78.
[224] For the ancient rhetorical technique of amplification in Hebrews, wherein Jesus is compared favorably to other respected beings, see Olbricht, "Hebrews as Amplification."
[225] R. T. France expresses a similar view, wherein he sees the author of Hebrews using Ps 8:5-7 to speak simultaneously of corporate humanity and of the ideal "son of Man" ("The Writer of Hebrews as Biblical Expositor," *TynBul* 47 [1996], 262).

not resume discussing Ps 110:1, but rather pivots away from the enthroned one of Ps 110:1 to speak of the earthly, humble Christ.[226] Also, while Heb 1:13-2:9 certainly exhibits some parallels between the citation of the two texts in 1 Corinthians and Ephesians, the exegetical conclusions of the author of Hebrews are distinct and original. Thus, the hermeneutical moves in Heb 8:5-18 cannot simply be reduced to an appropriation of a tradition.

Similarly, the early Christological moniker ὁ υἱὸς τοῦ ἀνθρώπου may have informed the author's decision to apply Psalm 8 to Christ and made her audience more inclined to think of the passage Christologically. Yet, the Christological designation of Jesus as "the Son of Man" may also have generated some confusion for early Christians in terms of understanding Psalm 8; the term is anarthrous in the psalm, and the "υἱός" in Psalm 8 may have seemed to them to refer to corporate "children/υἱοί" (cf. Heb 2:10). The potential for confusion resulting from such differences between Ps 8:5 and the "Son of Man" Christology may underlie the orator's decision to break with the pattern of rapid-fire citations with little explication (1:5-14; 2:12-13) to give an extended explication of Psalm 8. Even if the author and audience identify the words υἱὸς ἀνθρώπου with the Christological Son of Man, this identification does not dominate the exegesis of the verses following the citation; when Hebrews goes on to explicate Ps 8:5-7, it does not focus upon the phrase "υἱὸς ἀνθρώπου" or explicitly connect the passage with any Christian or Jewish messianic discussions of a messianic "Son of Man." Rather, it discusses Jesus's temporary humiliation and future exaltation in connection with his identification with other humans, so that they can corporately become glorified "children" (Heb 2:10).

4.2 Reading Psalm 8 in Light of Hebrews 2:5-18

Of the four passages examined in this chapter, Hebrews 2 gives the most extended and detailed citation and exegesis of Psalm 8, especially if one considers the second sub-pericope (Heb 2:10-18) as carrying forward and clarifying the exegesis of Ps 8:5-7. What, then, are the resulting implications for a level two reading of Psalm 8? I will limit myself here to exploring three aspects of the discussion of Psalm 8 in Hebrews 2 that constitute the distinctive hermeneutical contribution of Heb 2:5-18: 1) the identification of Christ with believers and the resulting identification of the υἱὸς ἀνθρώπου both with Jesus and with redeemed corporate humanity; 2) the discussion of Ps 8:5-7 as a witness both to the "νῦν/present" (cf. Ephesians 1) and to "the world to come"

---

[226] Guthrie and Quinn ("Use of Psalm 8:4-6") make much of the connection between Ps 110:1 and Psalm 8:5-7 in these verses. They seem to think that, in fact, much of the exegetical rationale motivating the author's interpretation of Psalm 8 derives from a hermeneutical connection with Psalm 110. They overstate the case, however, in that much of what they see as being a direct meditation on Psalm 8 in connection with Ps 110:1 can more accurately be described as a meditation upon Psalm 8 in connection with the entire catena of citations in Heb 2:5-12.

(cf. 1 Corinthians 15); 3) the use of Ps 8:5-7 as a transitional hinge from the heavenly exalted Christ to the earthly, humble Christ.

1) While the author of Hebrews does not develop an Adam-Christ typology, Christ's identification with redeemed humanity in Heb 2:5-18 parallels the identification of Christ with Adam explicated in 1 Corinthians 15. Thus, Hebrews 2 reinforces the Adam-Christ identification discussed above, and much of what was said concerning the impact of such an identification could be reproduced here. The focus of Hebrews 2, however, is not upon the way in which Christ succeeds as a federal head where Adam, Christ's ante-type, has failed. Rather, the focus is upon the direct, intimate relationship between Christ and his "siblings" (verses 12 and 17); he has a common source (ἐξ ἑνὸς, verse 11) and common blood (verse 14) with them, so that he can identify with them "as a merciful and faithful high priest" (verse 17). While Christ's forensic and representative function as the "high priest (verse 17) and "founder of salvation" (verse 10) who "tastes death for everyone" (verse 9), figures prominently, the reality of the union between Christ and other humans gets more attention.

This close identification between Jesus and his "siblings" can inform one's reading of Psalm 8 in two ways. First of all, it encourages the reader to look to and identify with Jesus, the "founder of salvation" (verse 10; cf. 12:2) as the one through whom God will order the cosmos. Thus, the ordering of the cosmos and the restoration of the "lost world of Genesis 1" comes not from human effort or polity, but through identification with Christ the high priest. Moreover, as the "Lord" who "laid the foundation of the earth in the beginning" (1:10), and the perfect human who identifies with his siblings, Christ represents King David, King YHWH, and King Adam, simultaneously. Secondly, the close identification between Jesus and his "siblings" can inform one's reading of Psalm 8 by reminding the reader that her glorified status (Ps 8:6; Heb 2:10) is not an individual right, but a corporate blessing; the reader can receive glory through identification with Christ, and, by extension, identification with the rest of Christ's siblings.

2) The interpretation of the term βραχύ (Ps 8:6) in Heb 2:7, 9 derives from the Septuagint and not from the Hebrew form of the psalm;[227] this move enables the author of Hebrews to read Psalm 8 as a witness both to the present incarnation of Christ and to the future exaltation of Christ. On first blush, one might be tempted to insist that the canonical approach ought to reconfigure its understanding of the Hebrew Psalm 8 to conform strictly to the exegesis presented in Heb 2:9. According to such a view, since Heb 2:5-9 belongs within the hermeneutical circle both as Scripture and as exegetical tradition (insofar as it represents the oldest known extended quotation and exegesis of Psalm 8), then a translation of Psalm 8 ought to conform to Heb 2:5-9 by interpreting and understanding מעט in a strictly temporal sense, meaning "for a little while," in Ps 8:6, even if such a translation seems to run against the context of Psalm 8. All that has been said up until this point about Psalm 8 would have to give way to

---

[227] Gheorghita, *Role of the Septuagint*, 44-46.

Heb 2:5-9, and Psalm 8 would become a prophetic, programmatic prediction of the incarnation and exaltation of Christ.

Such an interpretation is not warranted, however, either by the hermeneutic of Hebrews or by a canonical approach. The vague introductory formula, as has already been noted, indicates that the author of Hebrews is concerned with a divine meaning, and is not treating the passage as a static prophetic oracle. Furthermore, insofar as the orator of Hebrews finds a double meaning in the ἄνθρωπος/υἱὸς ἀνθρώπου of Ps 8:5, the orator's interpretation leaves room for both a Christological interpretation and an anthropological interpretation. Also, as I have argued throughout, a canonical exegesis ought to seek to understand each text on its own and then to bring the two texts into dialogue rather than to flatten out the text.

How, then, does the orator's reading of Psalm 8 as speaking both to Christ's present humiliation and to his future exaltation inform a canonical understanding of Psalm 8? First of all, Heb 2:5-9 provides a median position between Ephesians 1, which emphasizes the "already," and 1 Corinthians 15, which emphasizes the "not yet." Thus, Psalm 8 becomes, in its canonical context, a witness to the way that God, through Christ, is in the process of ordering the cosmos now (Ephesians 1; Heb 2:9), an ordering which may be partial now (Heb 2:8) but will eventually be complete in the eschaton (1 Cor 15; cf. Heb 2:14; Rev 21-22). Furthermore, read in connection with the encouragement to endure in the suffering of the "now" as Christ has suffered (Heb 2:18; 12:3-17), the readers of Psalm 8 are encouraged to endure and resist enemies now (Ps 8:3) as they experience God's ordering (Ps 8:5-9) of the cosmos and anticipate a time when that ordering will be complete.

3) The use of Psalm 8 as a hinge from the heavenly (Heb 1:5-14) to the earthly realm (Heb 2:10-18)[228] parallels the internal movement of the MT version of Psalm 8; the psalm transitions from the heavenly realm (Ps 8:2-4) to the earthly realm (Ps 8:8-9), with the human serving as a hinge (Ps 8:4-7). Thus, reading Psalm 8 in light of the shift in Hebrews 2 reminds the reader that the top-down ordering of the cosmos in Psalm 8 is brought about through the humble anticipation of divine reversal. The descent of Christ from heaven to earth in his incarnation and humiliation brings glory to the saints (Ps 8:7; Heb 2:10); so, too, the ordering of the cosmos from the heavens down to the earth in Psalm 8 comes when humans humbly identify with Christ in his suffering and await a divine reversal that will destroy all enemies (Ps 8:4; Heb 2:14; 1 Cor 15:26). How, then, does this hope fit in with the broader witness of the New Testament and the Christian canon? Having surveyed all four of the New Testament passages that cite Psalm 8, I am now in a position to present a synthetic exegesis of Psalm 8 in the context of the New Testament, paying special attention to the way in which the texts bring one into an encounter with God and produce love in the reader.

---

[228] Guthrie, *Structure*, 140-142.

5. Psalm 8 in Dialogue with the New Testament: Encountering the res and engendering caritas

In the previous chapter, I described Psalm 8's place in the context of the Old Testament as representing the intersection of two main trajectories: the reversal motif of Psalm 8 and the plight of humanity that develops across the Old Testament. While both of these trajectories continue into the New Testament, they are taken up and expanded within a third trajectory: that of the redeeming Christ. In Christ we find the ultimate example of the reversal motif, wherein Jesus humbles himself in his incarnation, suffering, and death, and then experiences a divine reversal in his resurrection and exaltation. In Christ, the plight of the conflicting and conflicted human is addressed; Jesus suffers for, identifies with, and intercedes for corporate humanity, ensuring that death will one day be vanquished and the plight of humanity finally and fully addressed.

When one reads Psalm 8 and the New Testament together, the central question of Psalm 8, "what is the human/מה אנוש" and the central question of Matthew 21, "Who is this?/τίς ἐστιν οὗτος;" meet and become intertwined with one another. Moreover, in Christ we find both the divine *res* incarnate and ideal love for neighbor enacted; it is an encounter with this Christ that is the true object of a canonical exegesis. Thus, while our focus has been upon Matthew 21, 1 Corinthians 15, Ephesians 1, and Hebrews 2, all four of these passages, read in connection with Psalm 8, point beyond themselves to the rest of the New Testament and the Messiah to whom the New Testament points.

The application of Psalm 8 to the living Christ in Matthew 21 reminds the reader that Jesus and his disciples were a tool for God's ordering of the cosmos even during the earthly ministry of Christ. When the canonically minded reader encounters the gospel accounts of Jesus healing the blind and lame (Matt 21:14) and challenging the powerful (Matt 21:12-13) or of children recognizing the Messiah (Matt 21:15), he sees this as an instance of God using the insignificant and humble to order creation; such a reader is then motivated to emulate both Christ and the humble children; an encounter with the Christ of Scripture produces *caritas* in the reader.

Similarly, Ephesians 1 and Hebrews 2 provide entry points to the parts of the New Testament canon that speak of the present experience of the Church. Read in connection with Psalm 8, the work that God does in and through the Church is yet another instance of the ordering of the cosmos described in Psalm 8. This is especially true in that the Church is united with Christ, who alone has perfectly fulfilled the role of the human ruler envisioned by Psalm 8, and who then enables redeemed humanity to fulfill that role also. Thus, by reading these texts together, the community of faith today comes into a fresh encounter with the God who continues to maintain his created order through the work of Christ in the Church. In Augustinian fashion, this divine encounter can produce love for God and neighbor in today's Church by enabling the Church to understand its proper role in the process and identify with the humble and helpless (Ps 8:3) to find ways to act corporately on their behalf (see James 1:27).

Finally, Hebrews 2 and 1 Corinthians 15 serve as entry points to the eschatological hope that the New Testament testifies to, when Christ will have vanquished every enemy, including death (1 Cor 15:26), and God will be all in all (1 Cor 15:28, cf. Eph 1:23). Thus, when the third trajectory of the redeeming Christ intersects with the other two trajectories (of the reversal motif and the human's plight), they all drive together towards an event described in another New Testament passage: the restoration of creation in Rev 21-22. This realization produces a worshipful encounter with God in the reader who, filled with awe and wonder, is moved to worship God and confess with the psalmist, "Oh LORD, our LORD, how majestic is your name in all the earth!"

So, the divine ordering of creation described in Psalm 8 gestures towards the entire sweep of biblical history from Genesis 1 to Revelation 22. In describing God's program for maintaining the created order, Psalm 8 provides a lens through which to view the establishment of the created order (Genesis 1), the human plight that results from enemies threatening the order (Ps 8:3; Job 7; Gen 3-11; Psalm 144; etc.), the redemptive work of Christ to restore the created order (Matthew 21; Ephesians 1; Hebrews 2; etc.), and the future hope that creation will one day be in full order (1 Corinthians 15; Rev 21-22). Thus, the hope instilled in Psalm 8 points to the one who says "Behold, I am making all things new" (Rev 21:5) and motivates the Christian reader to pray "Amen! Come Lord Jesus!" (Rev 22:20).

6

SUMMARY AND CONCLUSIONS

Chapter one focused upon articulating the approach that the study was to take by examining, defending, and refining the canon-exegetical approach initially articulated by Brevard Childs and taken up by many others.[1] Three main emphases underlying the approach emerged: 1) A movement connecting description with theological reflection; 2) A desire to relate the text's ancient function with its function in the contemporary Church; 3) A commitment to the canon as the context for interpretation. The chapter then urged, *contra* Barr,[2] that the canonical approach presents a theologically satisfying basis for ecclesiastical exegesis, the faith claims of which are consonant with the historical data. Turning to Mark Brett[3] as a representative of a pluralist adoption of the canonical approach, Brett's insistence that the canonical approach must not marginalize all other approaches was affirmed. Yet I argued that the canonical approach must continue to maintain the text's status as normative within the approach itself.

The study then surveyed several representative proponents of the canonical approach since Childs in order to clarify the issues involved and locate the present work within the broader canon-exegetical school. In order to clarify some of the theological issues relevant to the approach and to set the stage for the way in which the approach would be implemented in this study, I brought the canonical approach into dialogue with Augustine's *De doctrina Christiana*.[4] Through this dialogue, I urged the adoption of three theological affirmations to guide the approach: 1) that exegesis aims at an encounter with God; 2) that the

---

[1] For some of Childs's more prominent works, see note 1 of chapter one. For some examples of others carrying forward the canonical approach, see Michael O'Neal, *Interpreting Habakkuk as Scripture* (SiBL 9; New York: Peter Lang, 2007), *Theological Exegesis: Essays in Honor of Brevard S. Childs* (ed. Christopher Seitz and Kathryn Green-McCreight; Grand Rapids, MI: Eerdmans, 1999), and other works mentioned in note 2 of chapter one.
[2] James Barr, *Holy Scripture: Canon, Authority, Criticism* (Philadelphia: Westminster, 1983).
[3] Mark G. Brett, *Biblical Criticism in Crisis? The Impact of the Canonical Approach on Old Testament Studies* (New York: Cambridge University Press, 1991).
[4] Saint Augustine, *Teaching Christianity: De Doctrina Christiana. The Works of Saint Augustine: A Translation for the 21'st Century, Part I, vol. 11* (Edmund Hill, O.P., trans.; Hyde Park, NY: New City, 2000).

exegete stands within a hermeneutical circle including Church teaching and Scripture; 3) that the Scriptures themselves set the interpretive boundaries.

The chapter concluded by surveying Psalm 8 to demonstrate that Psalm 8 is uniquely well suited to serve as a test case for a canonical approach and that the canonical approach is especially well suited for addressing questions concerning the interpretation of Psalm 8; an attempt to read Psalm 8 as Scripture must grapple with proposed pre-canonical forms of the text, the way in which other Old Testament passages relate with the psalm, and the relationship between the psalm and its interpretation by New Testament authors. Significantly, a canonical approach will pay special attention (in Augustinian fashion) to the way in which exegesis aims at an encounter with the divine *res* that engenders *caritas* in the reader.

Chapter two then began the study proper by offering an exegesis of Psalm 8 in its discrete context. After addressing various background issues from the standpoint of a canonical approach, the chapter traced the internal development of the psalm, as follows:

Inclusio: "how[מה] excellent your name in all [כל] the earth" (verse 2a)
    A. Reversals One and Two (verses 2b-4):
        Insignificant heavenly bodies (verses 2b, 4)
            Imbedded paradigmatic reversal: babes and infants/enemy and avenger (verse 3)
        Majestic heavenly bodies (verse 4)
    B. Reversal Three (verses 5-9):
        Insignificant human: "what [מה] is the human?" (verse 5)
        Majestic human: "you have placed all things [כל] under his feet" (verses 6-7)
        Denoument:
            Animals from creation day six (verse 8)
            Animals from creation day five (verse 9)
Inclusio: "how[מה] excellent your name in all [כל] the earth" (verse 10)[5]

Read in this way, the psalm presents a contemplation of the excellence of the name YHWH in creation (verses 1, 10), with the human's role in the created order occupying the central point of this contemplation (verse 5). The body of the psalm develops through three intertwined reversals wherein the psalmist contemplates how God has taken something that is relatively insignificant (the heavenly bodies [verses 2b, 4], babes and infants [verse 3], and humanity [verses 5-9]) and exalts them over and against seemingly superior things. Thus, I summarized the distinct theological message of Psalm 8 as a declaration that YHWH glorifies his name by maintaining the created order through the exaltation of inferior things, which is especially evident in YHWH's exaltation

---

[5] For the strategic positioning of the words כל and מה see Øystein Lund, "From the Mouths of Babes and Infants You have Established Strength," *SJOT* 11 [1997], 96-97.

of humanity. The artful depiction of this reversal motif in Psam 8 facilitates a worshipful encounter with the divine *res*, and readers who are able to find points of connection between the humble and weak in Psalm 8 and the humble and weak of their own experience will love their neighbor more as a result.

Chapter three then began the process of bringing Psalm 8 into dialogue with the rest of the canon by examining Psalm 8 in light of its immediate literary context, that is, the book of Psalms. The study traced the Psalter's development. The Psalter opens with the orienting introductory Psalms 1 and 2 that, taken together, emphasize Torah observance (Psalm 1), the LORD's anointed king (Psalm 2), the way of piety, and the vindication of the righteous and judgment of the wicked. The body opens with two sets of lament songs surrounding Psalm 8 (Pss 3-7, 9-14), and the rest of Book I oscillates between lament and praise. The rest of the Psalter was surveyed, which gradually moves from an emphasis upon the Davidic king and upon lament songs (especially in Books 1-III) to an emphasis upon king YHWH and upon hymns of praise (especially in Books IV-V). Despite these shifts in emphasis, themes from Books I-III are to be found in Books IV-V, and vice versa. This movement facilitates an encounter with the divine for those who apprentice themselves to the modes of prayer and praise modeled across the Psalter.

Within this context, I argued that Psalm 8 exerts a special influence upon the way in which one reads the rest of the Psalter as the first hymn of the Psalter. As the Psalter oscillates between lament and praise, the reader's constant expectation in light of Psalm 8 is that YHWH will intervene into a disordered world by means of insignificant and humble humans, and the silencing of the enemies in Ps 8:3 encourages the reader that the other enemies of the Psalter will ultimately be silenced. Furthermore, the royal human of Psalm 8 intersects with the Psalter's dual emphasis upon the Davidic king (Books I-III) and upon king YHWH (Books IV-V) to create a tension, the resolution of which the Psalter itself does not make clear. Nevertheless, Psalm 8 reminds the reader to identify with the weak and humble, the "babies and sucklings;" such humility will allow king YHWH to establish strength from the readers' "mouths," and, in so doing, to somehow exalt both corporate humanity and YHWH's anointed king.

Chapter four then moved on to consider Psalm 8 in the light of the rest of the Old Testament witness, selecting passages with notable verbal and thematic affinities with parts of Psalm 8 for entry points (Genesis 1, Job 7, and Psalm 144). While I argued that these affinities were due in each case to some sort of historical influence between Psalm 8 and each text, the question of literary relationship was secondary and the desire to interpret Psalm 8 in light of the Old Testament witness was in the fore. These texts were selected because they were specially well suited points of entry through which to bring Psalm 8 into dialogue with the rest of the Old Testament; insofar as these texts revisit the themes and language of Psalm 8 in new contexts, they open up the possibility for creating an inner-biblical dialogue exploring the topics of Psalm 8, and each of these texts can serve as a bridge connecting Psalm 8 with other parts of the Christian canon.

Using these texts as entry points, the chapter described the place of Psalm 8 as one that overlaps substantially with the ideal vision of the created order in Genesis 1, yet is distinct from Genesis 1 in that its focus is not on an ideal primeval state, but on YHWH's continuing activity in maintaining the created order. Job 7 stands in stark contrast with Psalm 8 in that Job sees God's constant attention to humanity as a nuisance, not as a blessing; Job 7 speaks of the world as it is at its worst, in disorder, while Psalm 8 speaks of the world as it ought to be at its best, in perfect order. Psalm 144, which prays for divine intervention on behalf of David and the nation, promising praise for the rescue that YHWH is sure to bring, stands somewhere between Job 7 and Psalm 8. Like Job 7, Psalm 144 honestly acknowledges present chaos, but, like Psalm 8, Psalm 144 confidently expects the LORD to intervene, restore order to the king, and silence the enemies.

Chapter four attempted to read all four of these texts together and situate them within the broader collection of the Old Testament corpus. In order to provide a coherent construct within which to synthesize the vast scope of material, the place of Psalm 8 in the Old Testament was summarized as representing the intersection of two trajectories: 1) the trajectory of the reversal motif, wherein YHWH maintains the created order through the exaltation of the weak and humble, especially in the case of humanity, and 2) the trajectory of the motif of the conflicted and conflicting human, wherein humans are depicted as beset by trials, failing to live righteously, and often even occupying the role of YHWH's enemies (Ps 8:3). One can read the Old Testament in light of these two trajectories; whether one looks to the account of the creation, fall and decline of humanity (Gen 1-11), the rise, decline, and fall of the Davidic monarchy (1 Samuel-2 Kings), or the trials and tortures of Job, one finds, on the one hand, the evidence of YHWH using seemingly weak things to establish the created order, and, on the other hand, humans who are beset by trouble, sin, and personal and corporate failure of some form or another. When the canonical reader is able to understand the intersection of these two trajectories and his or her place in relation to these two trajectories in the divine drama, he or she may be able to encounter God in a way that produces love for God and neighbor.

Chapter five went on to consider the New Testament, using four texts that cite Psalm 8 as entry points: Matt 21:1-17, 1 Cor 15:20-28, Eph 1:15-22, and Heb 2:5-9. This chapter paid special attention to the way in which each passage interpreted and applied Psalm 8 in its new context, and then briefly articulated how one might understand Psalm 8 in light of this new interpretation. Regarding Matthew 21, on the one hand, the rationale underlying Jesus's application of Psalm 8 to the children shouting "Hosanna" (verses 9, 15-16) is not extensively spelled out; Matthew's point, it was argued, is not to provide a detailed Christological exegesis of Psalm 8, but to bring the reader into an encounter with Christ. The reader is meant to ask and ponder, "who is this" Jesus? On the other hand, though, the citation of Psalm 8 in Matt 21:16 1) reinforces the various messianic claims made throughout the passage (especially that Jesus is the Son of David and a new Moses), and 2) seems to imply that, if the children of Matt 21:15 are the babies of Ps 8:3, then the religious leaders of Matt 21:12-15 are the enemies of Ps 8:3. Thus, Matt 21:1-17 encourages the canonically minded reader to see the life of Christ and his humble followers as an especially important enactment of the reversal motif summarized in Psalm 8.

1 Cor 15:20-28 and Eph 1:15-22 have much in common, yet also exhibit markedly different emphases. 1 Cor 15:20-28 applies the declaration that God has "placed all things under his feet" (1 Cor 15:27; Ps 8:7) to Christ for the purpose of convincing the audience that even death must ultimately be vanquished (1 Cor 15:26), so that all humanity will experience a future resurrection. The rationale underlying this hermeneutical move seems to be the identification of Christ as a representative second Adam (1 Cor 15:21-22, 45), so that Jesus has succeeded where Adam and humanity have failed (by silencing God's enemies, Ps 8:3, and reigning as a just vice-gerent, Ps 8:5-9). Although Eph 1:19-22 does not make this hermeneutical rationale explicit, the passage bears marked similarities to 1 Cor 15:25-27, and seems to presuppose and build upon the exegesis of 1 Corinthians 15. Eph 1:15-22 differs markedly from 1 Cor 15:20-27, however, in that the former emphasizes the present exalted state of Christ over his church, but the latter emphasizes Christ's future, complete exaltation at the eschatological resurrection. Thus, when one reads Psalm 8 in light of these two passages, several hermeneutical implications emerge. One begins to see how the tension between the conflicted human and the reversal motif resolves in the person of Christ, who succeeds in fulfilling the role of king Adam where other humans have failed. Ephesians 1 reminds the reader that the reversal motif is already being actualized in Christ's exaltation, while 1 Corinthians 15 reminds the reader that the final complete reversal which will maintain the created order will be realized in a future corporate resurrection.

Hebrews 2:5-9 quotes Ps 8:5-7 and is very similar to 1 Cor 15:20-27 and Eph 1:15-22. It was argued that the author of Hebrews interprets Psalm 8 as speaking simultaneously of a redeemed version of corporate humanity and of Christ himself. Heb 2:10-18 explains the rationale for this dual interpretation: Christ, in his incarnation and humiliation identifies with his fellow humans so that they too might come to glory (verse 9). Thus, Hebrews applies the words of Psalm 8 to Christ, presupposing a federal role for Christ similar to that articulated by Paul (Romans 5). Yet, through the close identification between Christ and his siblings, the author of Hebrews is also able to see how God can use corporate humanity to maintain order in creation, just as Psalm 8 describes.

Thus, bringing Psalm 8 into dialogue with the New Testament's message generates a third hermeneutical trajectory: That of the redeeming Christ. This third trajectory intersects with the other two hermeneutical trajectories in that it makes the redemption of the conflicted human possible, enabling God to establish order in creation through the exaltation of weak humans. As the reader ponders with the psalmist, "what is the human?" and with the ancient inhabitants of Jerusalem who marveled at Jesus, "who is this?" she may be drawn to an encounter with the divine reality incarnate in Jesus. Indeed, the redeeming

Christ is himself the divine reality of which the text speaks, and the Christian interpreter seeks a transformative encounter with him.

BIBLIOGRAPHY

Abasciano, Brian J. *Paul's Use of the Old Testament in Romans 9:1-9: An Intertextual and Theological Exegesis.* Library of New Testament Studies 301; New York, NY: T & T Clark, 2005.
Allen, Leslie C. *Psalms 100-150* Word Biblical Commentary 21. Waco, TX: Word Books, 1982.
Allison, Dale C. *A New Moses: A Matthean Typology.* Minneapolis, MN: Fortress Press, 1993.
———. and W. D. Davies. *A Critical and Exegetical Commentary on The Gospel According to Matthew in Three Volumes.* International Critical Commentaries. Edinburgh, UK: T & T Clark, 1988.
Anderson, A. A. *Psalms (1-72).* The New Century Bible Commentary. London, UK: Marshall, Morgan, and Scott, 1981.
Arnold, Bill T. *Genesis.* New Century Bible Commentary. New York: Cambridge, 2009.
Arnold, Clinton E. *Ephesians, Power and Magic: The Concept of Power in Ephesians in Light of its Historical Setting.* New York, NY: Cambridge University Press, 1989.
Arnold, Duane W. H. "To Adjust Rather than to Reconcile: *De doctrina Christiana* and the Oxford Movement." Pages 207-216 in *De Doctrina Christiana: A Classic of Western Culture.* Edited by Duane W. H. Arnold and Pamela Bright; Notre Dame, IN: University of Notre Dame Press, 1995.
Asensio, Felix "El Protagonismo del 'Hombre-Hijo del Hombre' del Salmo 8." *Estudios Biblicos* 41 (1983): 17-51.
Attridge, Harold W. "The Psalms in Hebrews." Pages 197-212 in *The Psalms in the New Testament.* New York, NY: T & T Clark, 2004.
———. *The Epistle to the Hebrews: A Commentary on the Epistle to the Hebrews.* Hermeneia; Philadelphia, PA: Fortress Press, 1989.
Auffret, Pierre. "Qu'est-ce que l'Homme que tu t'en Souviennes? Étude structurelle du Psaume 8." *Science et Esprit* 54 (2002): 25-35.
Augustine, Saint. *Expositions of the Psalms: 1-32. The Works of Saint Augusitne: A Translation for the 21'st Century, Part III, vol. 15.* Translated by Maria Boulding. Hyde Park, NY: New City Press, 2000.
———. *Teaching Christianity: De Doctrina Christiana. The Works of Saint Augustine: A Translation for the 21'st Century, Part I, vol. 11.* Translated by Edmund Hill, O. P. Hyde Park, NY: New City Press, 1996.
Ayres, Lewis. "Augustine on the Rule of Faith: Rhetoric, Christology, and the Foundation of Christian Thinking." *Augustinian Studies* 36 (2005): 33-49.
Bacon, Benjamin W. *Studies in Matthew.* New York, NY: Holt, 1930.
Balentine, Samuel E. "'What are the Humans that You Make so Much of Them?' Divine Disclosure from the Whirlwind: 'Look at Behemoth.'" Pages 259-278 in *God in the Fray: A Tribute to Walter Brueggemann.* Edited by Tod Linafelt and Timothy K. Beal. Minneapolis, MN: Augsburg, Fortress, 1998.
Barr, James. *The Concept of Biblical Theology: an Old Testament Perspective.* London, UK: SCM Press, 1999.
———. *Holy Scripture: Canon, Authority, Criticism.* Philadelphia:Westminster, 1983.

———. "Childs' Introduction to the Old Testament as Scripture." *Journal for the Study of the Old Testament* 16 (1980): 12-23.

———. "Man and Nature: The Ecological Controversy and the Old Testament." *Bulletin of the John Rylands University Library of Manchester* 55 (1972): 9-32.

Barth, Karl. *Fides Quaerens Intellectum: Anselm's Proof of the Existence of God in the Context of his Theological Scheme.* Translated by Ian W. Robertson. Richmond, VA: John Knox, 1960.

———. *Church Dogmatics.* Translated by G. W. Bromiley, O. Bussey, J. W. Edwards, J. L. M. Hare, W. B. Johnston, Henry Kennedy, Harold Knight, A. T. MacKay, John Marks, T. H. L. Parker, G. T. Thomson, and T. F. Torrance. Four Volumes. New York, NY: Charles Scribners, 1949-1962.

Barth, Markus. *Ephesians.* Two Volumes. Anchor Bible 34-34A. Garden City, NY: Doubleday, 1974.

———. "Conversion and Conversation: Israel and the Church in Paul's Epistle to the Ephesians." *Interpretation* 17 (1963): 3-24.

Bartholomew, Craig G. and Ryan P. O'Dowd. *Old Testament Wisdom Literature: A Theological Introduction.* Downers Grove, IL: IVP Academic, 2011.

Bartholomew, Craig G., Scott Hahn, Robin Parry, Christopher Seitz, and Al Wolters, editors. *Canon and Biblical Interpretation.* Scripture and Hermeneutics Series 7. Grand Rapids, MI: Zondervan, 2006.

Beale, Gregory K. and Don A. Carson. *Commentary on the New Testament Use of the Old Testament.* Grand Rapids, MI: Baker Academic, 2007.

———, editor. *The Right Doctrine from the Wrong Texts? Essays on the Use of the Old Testament in the New.* Grand Rapids, MI: Baker, 1994.

Bellinger, William H. "Reading from the Beginning (Again): The Shape of Book I of the Psalter." Pages 114-126 in *Diachronic and Synchronic: Reading the Psalms in Real Time: Proceedings of the Baylor symposium of the Book of Psalms.* Library of Hebrew Bible/Old Testament Studies 488. Edited by Joel S. Burnett, William H. Bellinger, and W. Dennis Tucker. New York: T & T Clark, 2007.

———. *Psalms: Reading and studying the Book of Praises.* Peabody, MA: Hendrickson, 1990.

Best, Ernest. "Ephesians 1.1 Again." Pages 273-279 in *Paul and Paulinism: Essays in Honour of C. K. Barrett.* London, UK: SPCK, 1982.

Beuken, William A. "Job's Imprecation as the Cradle of a New Religious Discourse: The Perplexing Impact of the Semantic Correspondences Between Job 3, Job 4-5, and Job 6-7." Pages 41-78 in *The Book of Job.* Edited by William A. M. Beuken; Louvain: Leuven University Press/Peters, 1994.

Beyerlin, Walter. "Psalm 8: Chancen der Überlieferungskritik." *Zeitschrift fur Theologie und Kirche* 73 (1976): 1-22.

Black, C. Clifton. "The Rhetorical Form of the Hellenistic Jewish and Early Christian Sermon: A Response to Lawrence Wills." *Harvard Theological Review* 81 (1988):1-18.

Blenkinsopp, Joseph. *The Pentateuch: An Introduction to the First Five Books of the Bible.* Anchor Bible Reference Library. New York: Doubleday, 1992.

———. *Prophecy and Canon: A Contribution to the Study of Jewish Origins.* Notre Dame, IN: Notre Dame University Press, 1977.

Blomberg, Craig L. "Better Things in this Case: The Superiority of Today's New International Version in Hebrews." *Bible Translator* 55 (2004): 310-318.

Blowers, Paul. "The Regula Fidei and the Narrative Character of Early Christian Faith," *Pro Ecclesia* 6 (1997): 199-228.

Bochet, Isabelle. "Le cercle herméneutique dans le *De doctrina christiana* d'Augustin." *Studia Patristica* 33 (1997): 16-21.
Bratcher, Robert G. and William D. Reyburn. *A Translator's Handbook on the Book of Psalms*. Helps for Translators Series. New York, NY: United Bible Societies.
Brennan, Joseph P. "Psalms 1-8: Some Hidden Harmonies." *Biblical Theology Bulletin* 10 (1980): 25-29.
Brett, Mark G. *Biblical Criticism in Crisis? The Impact of the Canonical Approach on Old Testament Studies*. New York: Cambridge University Press, 1991.
Briggs Charles Augustus and Emilie Grace Briggs. *Psalms*. Two Volumes. International Critical Commentary. New York: Scribners, 1906.
Brooks, Stephenson H. *Matthew's Community: The Evidence of His Special Sayings Material*. Journal for the Study of the New Testament Supplement Series 16. Sheffield, UK: Sheffield Academic, 1987.
Brown, William P. *Character in Crisis: A Fresh Approach to the Wisdom Literature of the Old Testament*. Grand Rapids, MI: Eerdmans, 1996.
———. *Structure, Role, and Ideology in the Hebrew and Greek Texts of Genesis 1:1-2:3*. Society of Biblical Literature Dissertation Series 132. Atlanta, GA: Scholars Press, 1993.
Bruce, Frederick F. *1 and 2 Corinthians* New Century Bible Commentary. Grand Rapids, MI: Eerdmans, 1980.
———. *Paul: Apostle of the Heart Set Free*. Grand Rapids, MI: Eerdmans, 1977.
Brueggemann, Walter. *Theology of the Old Testament: Testimony, Dispute, Advocacy*. Minneapolis: Fortress Press, 1997.
———. "A Shape for Old Testament Theology, II: Embrace of Pain." *Catholic Biblical Quarterly* 47 (1985): 395-415.
———. *The Message of the Psalms: A Theological Commentary*. Augsburg Old Testament Studies; Minneapolis, MN: Augsburg, 1984.
———. *Genesis: A Bible Commentary for Teaching and Preaching*. Interpretation; Atlanta, GA: John Knox, 1982.
Brunson, Andrew C. *Psalm 118 in the Gospel of John: An Intertextual Study on the New Exodus Pattern in the Theology of John*. Hemsbach: Mohr Siebeck, 2003.
Burkett, Delbert. *The Son of Man Debate: A History and Evaluation*. New York, NY: Cambridge University Press, 1999.
Buttenwieser, Moses. *The Psalms: Chronologically Treated with a New Translation* Chicago: The University of Chicago Press, 1938.
Calvin, John. *Commentary on the Book of Psalms I*. Translated by James Anderson. Grand Rapids: Eerdmans, 1949.
Casey, Maurice. "The Use of the Term (א)שנ(א) בר in the Aramaic Translations of the Hebrew Bible." *Journal for the Study of the New Testament* 54 (1994): 87-118.
Chapman, Stephen. "Reclaiming Inspiration for the Bible." Pages 167-200 in *Canon and Biblical Interpretation*. Craig G. Bartholomew, Scott Hahn, Robin Parry, Christopher Seitz, and Al Wolters, editors. Scripture and Hermeneutics Series 7. Grand Rapids, MI: Zondervan, 2006.
Charlesworth, James H. and Walter P. Weaver, editors. *The Old and the New Testaments: Their Relationship and the "Intertestamental" Literature*. Faith and Scholarship Colloquies. Valley Forge, PA: Trinity Press International, 1993.
Cheon, Samuel. "B. S. Childs' Debate with Scholars about His Canonical Approach," *Asia Journal of Theology* 11 (1997): 343-357.
Chernick, Michael. "Internal Restraints on *Gezerah Shawah's* Application," *Jewish Quarterly Review* 83 (1990): 253-282.

Childs, Brevard S. *The Canonical Shape of the Pauline Corpus: The Church's Guide for Reading Paul*. Grand Rapids: Eerdmans, 2008.

———. "Critique of Recent Intertextual Canonical Interpretation." *Zeitschrift für die Alttetestamentliche Wissenschaft* 115 (2003): 173-184.

———. *Isaiah: A Commentary*. Old Testament Library. Philadelphia: Westminster Press, 2001.

———. "Retrospective Reading of the Old Testament Prophets." *Zeitschrift für die Alttestamentliche Wissenschaft* 108 (1996): 362-377.

———. *Biblical Theology of the Old and New Testaments: Theological Reflection on the Christian Bible*. Minneapolis: Fortress Press, 1993.

———. *Old Testament Theology in a Canonical Context*. Philadelphia: Fortress Press, 1985.

———. *The New Testament as Canon: An Introduction*. Philadelphia: Fortress Press, 1984.

———. Review of James Barr, *Holy Scripture: Canon, Authority, Criticism*. *Interpretation* 38 (1984): 66-70.

———. "Response to Reviewers of the Introduction to the OT as Scripture." *Journal for the Study of the Old Testament* 16 (1980): 52-60.

———. *Introduction to the Old Testament as Scripture*. Philadelphia: Fortress Press, 1979.

———. "Canonical Shape of the Prophetic Literature," *Interpretation* 32 (1978): 513-522.

———. "The *Sensus Literalis* of Scripture: An Ancient and Modern Problem." Pages 80-93 in *Beiträge zur Alttestamentlichen Theologie: Festschrift für W. Zimerli*. Edited by Herbert Donner. Göttingen: Vandenhoeck und Ruprecht, 1977.

———. *The Book of Exodus: A Critical, Theological Commentary*. Old Testament Library. Philadelphia: Westminster Press, 1974.

———. *Biblical Theology in Crisis*. Philadelphia: Westminster Press, 1970.

———. "Psalm 8 in the Context of the Christian Canon." *Interpretation* 23 (1969): 20-31.

———. "Karl Barth as Interpreter of Scripture." Pages 30-39 in *Karl Barth and the Future of Theology: A Memorial Colloquium Held at Yale Divinity School January 28, 1969*. Edited by D. L. Dickerman. New Haven: Yale Divinity School Association, 1969.

———. "Interpretation in Faith: The Theological Responsiblity of an Old Testament Commentary." *Interpretation* 18 (1964): 432-49.

Clements, Ronald E. "The Use of the Old Testament in Hebrews." *Southwestern Journal of Theology* 28 (1985): 36-45.

Clines, David J. A. *Theme of the Pentateuch*. Journal for the Study of the Old Testament Supplement Series 10. Sheffield UK: Sheffield Academic Press, 1997.

———. *Job 1-20*. Word Biblical Commentary 17. Dallas TX: Word, 1982.

Coats, George W. "Self-Abasement and Insult Formulas." *Journal of Biblical Literature* 89 (1970):14-26.

Cole, Robert. "An Integrated Reading of Psalms 1 and 2." *Journal for the Study of the Old Testament* 98 (2002): 75-88.

Cope, O. L. *Matthew: A Scribe Trained for the Kingdom of Heaven*. Catholic Biblical Quarterly Monograph Series 5. Washington, DC: The Catholic Biblical Association of America, 1976.

Cotter, David W. *Genesis*. Berit Olam; Collegeville MN: Liturgical Press, 2003.

Bibliography

Craddock, Fred B. "The Letter to the Hebrews." Pages 1-174 in *The New Interpreter's Bible, Volume Twelve: Hebrews to Revelation*. Nashville, TN: Abingdon Press, 1998.
Craigie, Peter C. *Psalms 1-50*. Word Biblical Commentary: 19. Waco, TX: Word, 1983.
Creach, Jerome F. D. *The Destiny of the Righteous in the Psalms*. St. Louis, MO: Chalice, 2008.
──────. *Psalms*. Interpretation Bible Studies. Louisville: Geneva, 1998.
Crossley, James G. *The Solution to the 'Son of Man' Problem*. Library of New Testament Studies 343. New York, NY: T & T Clark, 2007.
Dahood, Mitchell. *Psalms I, 1-50*. Anchor Bible 16. Garden City: Doubleday, 1965.
Dailey, Thomas F. "Creation and Ecology—the 'Dominion' of Biblical Anthropology." *Irish Theological Quarterly* 58 (1992): 1-13.
Danker, Fredrick William, et. al. *A Greek-English Lexicon of the New Testament and Other Early Christian Literature*. Third Edition. Chicago, IL: University of Chicago Press, 2000.
DeClaissé-Walford, Nancy. *Reading from the Beginning: The Shaping of the Hebrew Psalter*. Macon, GA: Mercer University Press, 1997.
Deichgräber, Reinhard. *Gotteshymnus und Christushymnus in der frühen Christenheit*. Gottingen: Vandenhoeck & Ruprecht, 1967.
Delitzsch, Franz. *Biblical Commentary on the Psalms*. Foreign Biblical Library. London: Hodder and Stoughton, 1908.
Dempster, Stephen G. "Canons on the Right and Canons on the Left: Finding a Resolution in the Canon Debate," *Journal of the Evangelical Theological Society* 52 (2009): 47-77.
──────. "An 'Extraordinary Fact:' *Torah and Temple* and the Contours of the Hebrew Canon," *TB* 48 (1997) 23-53, 191-218.
deSilva, David A. *Perseverance in Gratitude: A Socio-Rhetorical Commentary on the Epistle to the Hebrews*. Grand Rapids, MI: Eerdmans, 2000.
Dion, Paul E. "Formulaic Language in the Book of Job: International Background and Ironical Distortions." *Sciences Religieuses* 16 (1987): 187-193.
Donnelly, Phillip J. *Rhetorical Faith: The Literary Hermeneutics of Stanley Fish*. English Literary Studies Monograph Series: 84. Victoria: English Literary Studies, 2000.
Driver, Daniel R. *Brevard Childs, Biblical Theologian: For the Church's One Bible*. Grand Rapids, MI: Baker Academic, 2012.
Dykstra, William. "I Corinthians 15:20-28: A Central Part of Paul's Argument Against Those Who Deny the Resurrection." *Calvin Theological Journal* 4 (1969): 195-211.
Eichrodt, Walther. *Theology of the Old Testament* Two Volumes. Translated by J. A. Baker. Philadelphia: Westminster Press, 1961.
English, Edward D., editor. *Reading and Wisdom: The De Doctrina Christiana of Augustine in the Middle Ages*. Notre Dame, IN: University of Notre Dame Press, 1995.
Enns, Peter. *Poetry and Wisdom*. Institute for Biblical Resaearch Bibliographies 3. Grand Rapids, MI: Baker, 1997.
Evans, Craig A., editor. *From Prophecy to Testament: The Function of the Old Testament in the New*. Peabody, MA: Hendrickson, 2004.
────── and James A. Sanders, editors. *Early Christian Interpretation of the Scriptures of Israel: Investigations and Proposals*. Journal for the Study of the New Testament Supplement Series 148/Studies in Scripture in Early Judaism and Christianity 5. Sheffield, UK: Sheffield Academic, 1997.

Fee, Gordon D. *Pauline Christology: An Exegetical-Theological Study*. Peabody, MA: Hendrickson, 2007.

———. *The First Epistle to the Corinthians*. New International Commentary on the New Testament. Grand Rapids, MI: 1987.

Fishbane, Michael. "Inner-Biblical Exegesis," Pages 33-48 in *Hebrew Bible/Old Testament: The History of its Interpretation I/1: Antiquity*. Edited by Magna Sæbø. Göttingen: Vandenhoek und Ruprecht, 1996.

———. "The Book of Job and Inner-Biblical Discourse," Pages 86-98 in *The Voice from the Whirlwind*. Edited by Leo G. Perdue and W. Clark Gilpin. Nashville, TN: Abingdon, 1992.

———. *Biblical Interpretation in Ancient Israel*. Oxford: Clarendon, 1985.

France, R. T. "The Writer of Hebrews as Biblical Expositor." *Tyndale Bulletin* 47 (1996): 245-276.

Freedman David N. with Jeffrey C. Geoghengan and Andrew Welch. *Psalm 119: The Exaltation of Torah*. Biblical and Judaic Studies volume 6. Winona Lake, IN: Eisenbrauns, 1999.

Frei, Hans W. *The Eclipse of the Biblical Narrative: A Study in Eighteenth and Nineteenth Century Hermeneutics*. New Haven: Yale University Press, 1974.

Fretheim, Terrence E. *God and World in the Old Testament: A Relational Theology of Creation*. Nashville: Abingdon Press, 2005.

———. *Creation, Fall, and Flood: Studies in Genesis 1-11*. Minneapolis, MN: Augsburg Publishing, 1969.

Garcialazo, Albert V. *The Corinthian Dissenters and the Stoics*. New York, NY: Peter Lang, 2007.

Garland, David E. *1 Corinthians*. Baker Evangelical Commentary on the New Testament. Grand Rapids, MI: Baker, 2003.

Garrett, Duane. *Rethinking Genesis*. Grand Rapids, MI: Baker, 1991.

Gerstenberger, Erhard S. *Psalms, Part 1, with an Introduction to Cultic Poetry*. The Forms of the Old Testament Literature 15. Grand Rapids, MI: Eerdmans, 1988.

Gheorghita, Radu. *The Role of the Septuagint in Hebrews: An Investigation of its Influence with Special Consideration to the Use of Hab 2:3-4 in Heb 10:37-38*. Wissenschaftliche Untersuchungen zum Neuen Testament 2/160. Tübingen: Mohr Siebeck, 2003.

Gilchrest, J. M. "Paul and the Corinthians: The Sequence of the Letters and Visits." *Journal for the Study of the New Testament* 34 (1988): 47-69.

Gillingham, Susan. "Through the Looking Glass." Pages 167-196 in *Diachronic and Synchronic: Reading the Psalms in Real Time: Proceedings of the Baylor Symposium on the Book of Psalms*. Library of Hebrew Bible/Old Testament Studies 488. Edited by Joel S. Burnett, William H. Bellinger, and W. Dennis Tucker. New York: T & T Clark, 2007.

———. *The Poems and Psalms of the Hebrew Bible*. Oxford Bible Series. New York: Oxford University Press, 1994.

Goldingay, John. *Psalms Volume 1: Psalms 1-41*. Baker Commentary on the Old Testament. Grand Rapids, MI: Baker, 2006.

———. Review of Brevard S. Childs, *Isaiah: A Commentary*. *Biblical Interpretation* 12 (2004): 331-333.

Görg, Manfred. "Königliche Eulogie. Erwägungen zur Bildsprache in Ps 8,2." *Biblische Notizen* 37 (1987): 38-47.

———. "'Alles hast Du Gelegt unter seine Füsse,' Beobachtungen zu Ps 8,7b im Vergleich mit Gen 1,28." Pages 125-148 in *Freude an der Weisung ders Herrn:*

Beiträge zur Theologie der Psalmen. Edited by E. Haag and F. L. Hossfeld. Stuttgart: Katholisches Bibelwerk, 1986.

———. "Der Mensch als königliches Kind nach Ps 8.3," *Biblische Notizen* 3 (1977): 7-13.

Gowan, Donald E. *From Eden to Babel: A Commentary on Genesis 1-11*. International Theological Commentary. Grand Rapids, MI: Eerdmans, 1988.

Grant, Jamie A. "The Psalms and the King." Pages 101-118 in *Interpreting the Psalms: Issues and Approaches*. Edited by David Firth and Philip S. Johnston. Downer's Grove, IL: IVP Academic, 2005.

———. *The King as Exemplar: The Function of Deuteronomy's Kingship Law in the Shaping of the Book of Psalms*. Academia Biblica 17. Atlanta, GA: SBL, 2004.

Grech, Prosper. "Hermeneutical Principles of Saint Augustine in *Teaching Christianity*." Pages 80-94 in *Teaching Christianity: De Doctrina Christiana. The Works of Saint Augustine: A Translation for the 21'st Century, Part 1, vol. 11*. Edited by John E. Rotelle, O.S.A. Hyde Park, NY: New City Press, 1996.

Grossman, Maxine L. "Priesthood as Authority: Interpretive Competition in First-Century Judaism and Christianity." Pages 117-131 in *Dead Sea Scrolls as Background to Postbiblical Judaism and Early Christianity*. Boston, MA: Leiden Brill, 2003.

Gundry, Robert H. *The Use of the Old Testament in Saint Matthew's Gospel, with Special Reference to the Messianic Hope*. Novum Testamentum Supplement 18. Leiden: Brill, 1975.

Gunkel, Hermann. *Introduction to Psalms: The Genres of the Religious Lyric of Israel*. Translated by James D. Nogalski. Mercer Library of Biblical Studies. Macon, GA: Mercer University Press, 1998.

Guthrie, George H. "A Discourse Analysis of the Use of Psalm 8:4-6 in Hebrews 2:5-9." *Journal of the Evangelical Theological Society* 49 (2006): 235-246.

———. "Hebrews in its First-Century Contexts: Recent Research." Pages 414-443 in *The Face of New Testament Studies: A Survey of Recent Research*. Grand Rapids, MI: Baker Academic, 2004.

———. *The Structure of Hebrews: A Text-Linguistic Analysis*. Supplements to Novum Testamentum 73. New York, NY: Brill, 1994.

———. and Russell D. Quinn. "A Discourse Analysis of the Use of Psalm 8:4-6 in Hebrews 2:5-9." *The Journal of the Evangelical Theological Society* 49 (2006): 235-246.

Habel, Norman C. *The Book of Job: A Commentary*. Old Testament Library. Philadelphia, PA: Westminster Press, 1985.

Hagner, Donald A. "Matthew: Christian Judaism or Jewish Christianity?" Pages 263-282 in *The Face of New Testament Studies: A Survey of Recent Research*. Grand Rapids, MI: Baker Academic, 2004.

Hamilton, Victor P. "אנוש." Pages 453-455 in vol. 1 of *The New International Dictionary of Old Testament Theology and Exegesis*. Edited by Willem A. VanGemeren. 5 vols. Grand Rapids: Zondervan, 1999.

———. *The Book of Genesis Chapters 1-17*. New International Commentary on the Old Testament 1. Grand Rapids: Eerdmans, 1990.

Harrisville, Roy A. "Paul and the Psalms." *Word and World* 5 (1985): 168-179.

Hartley, John E. *Genesis*. New International Biblical Commentary 1. Grand Rapids: Hendrickson, 2000.

———. *The Book of Job*. New International Commentary on the Old Testament. Grand Rapids, MI: Eerdmans, 1988.

Hauerwas, Stanley. *A Community of Character: Toward a Constructive Christian Social Ethic.* Notre Dame, IN: University of Notre Dame Press, 1981.

Hays, Richard B. *The Conversion of the Imagination: Paul as Interpreter of Israel's Scripture.* Grand Rapids, MI: Eerdmans, 2005.

———. "The Conversion of the Imagination: Scripture and Eschatology in 1 Corinthians." *New Testament Studies* 45 (1999): 391-412.

———. *I Corinthians.* Interpretation Commentary; Louisville, KY: John Knox, 1997.

———. *The Moral Vision of the New Testamet: Community, Cross, New Creation: A Contemporary Introduction to New Testament Ethics.* San Francisco: Harper, 1996.

———. *Echoes of Scripture in the Letters of Paul.* New Haven: Yale University Press, 1989.

Heil, John P. *The Rhetorical Role of Scripture in 1 Corinthians.* Society of Biblical Literature Monograph Series 13. Atlanta, GA: Society of Biblical Literature, 2005.

Hengel, Martin. "Psalm 110 und die Erhöhung des Auferstandenen zur Rechten Gottes." Pages 43-73 in *Anfänge der Christologie.* Stuttgart: KVW Verlag, 1972.

Hester, David C. *Job.* Interpretation Bible Studies. Louisville, KY: Westminster John Knox, 2005.

Hill, Charles E. "Paul's Understanding of Christ's Kingdom in I Corinthians 15:20-28." *Novum Tetamentum* 30 (1988): 297-320.

Hoehner, Harold W. *Ephesians: An Exegetical Commentary.* Baker Exegetical Commentary on the New Testament. Grand Rapids, MI: Baker, 2002.

Hollander, John. *The Firgure of Echo: A Mode of Allusion in Milton and After.* Berkeley: University of California Press, 1981.

Holleman, Joost. *Resurrection and Parousia: A Traditio-Historical Study of Paul's Eschatology in 1 Corinthians 15.* Supplement to Novum Testamentum 84. New York, NY: E. J. Brill, 1996.

Hoppin, Ruth. *Priscilla's Letter: Finding the Author of the Epistle to the Hebrews.* Fort Bragg, CA: Lost Coast Press, 2000.

Hossfeld, Franz Lothar and Erich Zenger. *Die Psalmen I, 1-50.* Die Neue Echter Bibel. Altes Testament: 29. Würzburg: Echter Verlag, 1993.

House, Paul R. *Old Testament Theology.* Downers Grove, IL: InterVarsity Press, 1998.

———. *The Unity of the Twelve.* Bible and Literature Series: 27. Sheffield, UK: Sheffield Academic, 1990.

Howard, David M. Jr. *The Structure of Psalms 93-100.* Biblical and Judaic Studies volume 5. Winona Lake, IN: Eisenbrauns, 1997.

Hübenthal, Sandra. "'Wer ist dieser?' Mt 21,1-17 in intertextueller Lektüre." Pages 260-277 in *Der Bibelkanonon in der Bibelauslegung: Methodenreflexionen und Beispielexegesen.* Edited by Egbert Ballhorn and Georg Steins; Stuttgart: Verlag W. Kohlhammer, 2007.

Hughes, Philip E. *A Commentary on the Epistle to the Hebrews.* Grand Rapids, MI: Eerdmans, 1977.

Isaacs, Marie E. *Reading Hebrews and James: A Literary and Theological Commentary.* Macon GA: Smythe and Helwys, 2002.

Isaak, Jon M. "Hearing God's Word in the Silence: A Canonical Approach to 1 Corinthians 14.34-35." *Direction* 24 (1995): 55-64.

Johnson, Alan F. *1 Corinthians* InterVarsity Press New Testament Commentary Series.Downers Grove, IL: InterVarsity Press, 2004.

Johnson, Edna. *A Semantic and Structural Analysis of Ephesians.* Semantic and Structural Analysis Series. Dallas, TX: SIL International, 2008.

Juel, Donald. *Messianic Exegesis: Christological Interpretation of the Old Testament in Early Christianity.* Philadelphia: Fortress, 1988.
Keathley, Naymond H. "To the Praise of His Glory: Ephesians 1." *Review and Expositor* 76 (1976): 485-493.
Keener, Craig S. *A Commentary on the Gospel of Matthew.* Grand Rapids, MI: Eerdmans, 1999.
———. *Matthew.* InterVarsity Press New Testament Commentary Series. Downers Grove, IL: InterVarsity Press, 1997.
Keener, Hubert James. "YHWH's Subversive Order: Reconsidering the Structure and Thematic Development of the Eighth Psalm." *Perspectives in Religious Studies* 40 (2013): 321–35.
Kerrer, Martin. "The Epistle to the Hebrews and the Septuagint." Pages 335-353 in *Septuagint Research: Issues and Challenges in the Study of the Greek Jewish Scriptures.* Atlanta, GA: Society of Biblical Literature, 2006.
Kilpatrick, George D. *The Origins of the Gospel According to Matthew.* Oxford, UK: Clarendon, 1946.
Kingsbury, J. D. *Matthew: Structure, Christology, Kingdom.* Philadelphia, PA: Fortress Press, 1977.
Kistemaker, Simon. *The Psalm Citations in the Epistle to the Hebrews.* Amsterdam: Wed. G. van Soest, 1961.
Kister, Menahem. "'In Adam:' I Cor 15:21-22; 12:27 in their Jewish Setting." Pages 685-690 in *Flores Florentino: Dead Sea Scrolls and Other Early Jewish Studies in Honor of Florentino Garcia Martinez.* Edited by Anthony Hilhorst, Emile Peuch, and Eibert Tigchelaar. Boston MA: Brill, 2007.
———. "Romans 5:12-21 Against the Background of Torah Theology and Hebrew Usage." *Harvard Theological Review* 100 (2007): 391-424.
Koester, Craig R. *Hebrews: A New Translation with Introduction and Commentary.* Anchor Bible 36. New York, NY: Doubleday, 2001.
Kowalski, Beate. "Die Rezeption alttestamentlicher Theologie im Hebräerbrief." Pages 35-62 in *Ausharren in der Verheissung: Studien zum Hebräerbrief.* Stuttgarter Bibelstudien 204. Stuttgart: Katholisches Bibelwerk, 2005.
Kraus, Hans-Joachim. *Psalms 1-59.* Translated by Hilton C. Oswald. Augsburg Continental Commentaries. Minneapolis, MN: Fortress, 1993.
———. *Theology of the Psalms.* Translated by Keith Crim, Minneapolis: Augburg, 1986.
Kruse, H. "Two Hidden Comparatives." *Journal of Semitic Studies* 5 (1960): 333 347.
Kuck, David W. *Judgment and Community Conflict: Paul's Use of Apocalyptic Judgment Language in I Corinthians 3:5-4:5.* New Testament Supplement 66. New York, NY: E. J. Brill, 1992.
Lane, William L. *Hebrews 1-8.* Word Biblical Commentary 47a. Dallas, TX: Word, 1991.
———. "Hebrews: A Sermon in Search of a Life Setting." *Southwestern Journal of Theology* 28 (1985): 13-18.
Larkin, William J. *Ephesians: A Handbook on the Greek Text.* Baylor Handbook on the Greek New Testament. Waco, TX: Baylor University Press, 2009.
Lawrie, Douglas. "How Critical is it to be Historically Critical? The Case of the Composition of the Book of Job." *Journal of Northwest Semitic Languages* 27 (2001): 121-146.
Leschert, Dale F. *Hermeneutical Foundations of Hebrews: A Study in the Validity of the Epistle's Interpretation of Some Core Citations from the Psalms.* NABPR Dissertation Series 10. Lewiston, NY: Edwin Mellen Press, 1994.

Lessing, Reed. Review of Brevard S. Childs, *Isaiah: A Commentary*. *Concordia Journal* 28 (2002): 470.

Lincoln, Andrew T. *Ephesians*. Word Biblical Commentary 42. Waco, TX: Word, 1990.

———. "The Use of the OT in Ephesians." *Journal for the Study of the New Testament* 14 (1982): 16-57.

——— and A. J. M. Wedderburn. *The Theology of the Later Pauline Letters*. New York, NY: Cambridge University Press, 1993.

Lindars, Barnabas. *The Theology of the Letter to the Hebrews*. New York, NY: Cambridge, 1991.

Lindbeck, George A. "Postcritical Canonical Interpretation: Three Modes of Retrieval." Pages 26-50 in *Theological Exegesis: Essays in Honor of Brevard S. Childs*. Grand Rapids: Eerdmans, 1999.

Loader, William R. G. "Christ at the Right Hand: Psalm CX. 1 in the New Testament." *New Testament Studies* 24 (1978): 199-217.

Lohfink, Norbert. "Der Messiaskönig und seine Armen kommen zum Zion: Beobachtungen zu Mt 21,1-17." Pages 179-200 in *Studien zum Matthäusevangelium: Festschrift für Wilhelm Pesch*. Stuttgarter Bibelstudien. Stuttgart: Katholisches Bibelwerk, 1988.

Löhr, Max. "Psalm 7 9 10." *Zeitschrift für die Alttestamentliche Wissenschaft* 36 (1916): 225-237.

Loretz, Oswald. "Die Psalmen 8 und 67, Psalmstudien V." *Ugarit-Forschungen* 8 (1976): 117-122.

Lucas, Ernest C. *Exploring the Old Testament, Volume Three: A Guide to the Psalms and Wisdom Literature*. Downer's Grove, IL: InterVarsity Press, 2002.

Lund, Øystein. "From the Mouths of Babes and Infants You have Established Strength." *Scandinavian Journal of the Old Testament* 11 (1997): 78-99.

Maloney, Les D. "Intertextual Links: Part of the Poetic Artistry within the Book I Acrostic Psalms," *Restoration Quarterly* 49 (2007): 11-21.

———. *A Word Fitly Spoken: Poetic Artistry in the First Four Acrostics of the Hebrew Psalter*. Ph.D. dissertation. Waco, TX: Baylor University, 2007.

Mann, Thomas W. *The Book of the Torah: The Narrative Integrity of the Pentateuch*. Atlanta, GA: John Knox, 1988.

Mays, James L. "The Self in the Psalms and the Image of God." Pages 27-43 in *God and Human Dignity*. Edited by Kendall Soulen and Linda Woodhead. Grand Rapids: Eerdmans, 2006.

———. *Psalms*. Interpretation: A Bible Commentary for Teaching and Preaching. Louisville: John Knox Press, 1994.

McCann, Jr., J. Clinton. *Great Psalms of the Bible*. Louisville, KY: Westminster/John Knox.

———. "Psalms." Pages 639-1280 in volume 4 of *The New Interpreter's Bible*. 12 vols. Nashville, TN: Abingdon Press, 1994-2004.

———. *A Theological Introduction to the Book of Psalms: The Psalms as Torah*. Nashville, TN: Abingdon, 1993.

———. "Books I-III and the Editorial Purpose of the Hebrew Psalter." Pages 93-107 in *The Shape and Shaping of the Psalter*. The Journal for the Study of the Old Testament Supplement Series 159. Edited by J. Clinton McCann. Sheffield: JSOT Press, 1993.

McKnight, Edgar and Christopher Church. *Hebrews-James*. Smith and Helwys Biblical Commentary. Macon, GA: Smyth & Helwys, 2004.

Mettinger, Tryggve N. D. *The Eden Narrative: A Literary and Religio-Historical Study of Genesis 2-3.* Winona Lake, IN: Eisenbrauns, 2007.
Millard, Matthias. *Die Komposition des Psalters, Ein formgeschichtlicher Ansatz.* Forschungen zum Alten Testament: 9; Tübingen: J. C. B. Mohr, 1994.
Miller, Patrick D. Review of Matthias Millard *Die Komposition des Psalters: Ein Formgeschichtlicher Ansatz. Journal of Biblical Literature* 116 (1997): 539-541.
———. "The Beginning of the Psalter." Pages 83-92 in *The Shape and Shaping of the Psalter.* Journal for the Study of the Old Testament Supplement Series: 159. Edited by. J. Clinton McCann. Sheffield: JSOT Press, 1993.
———. *Interpreting the Psalms.* Philadelphia, PA: Fortress, 1986.
Mitchell, David C. *The Message of the Psalter: An Eschatological Programme in the Book of Psalms.* Journal for the Study of the Old Testament Supplement Series 267. Sheffield, UK: Sheffield Academic, 1997.
Moberly, R. W. L.*The Theology of the Book of Genesis.* Old Testament Theology. New York: Cambridge University Press, 2009.
———. *From Eden to Golgotha: Essays in Biblical Theology.* SFSiHJ 52; Atlanta: Scholars, 1992.
Moloney, Francis J. "The Reinterpretation of Psalm 8 and the Son of Man Debate." *New Testament Studies* 27 (1981): 656-672.
———. "The Targum on Psalm 8 and the New Testament." *Salesianum* 37 (1975): 326-336.
Moritz, Thorsten. *A Profound Mystery: The Use of the Old Testament in Ephesians.* Supplements to Novum Testamentum 85. New York, NY: E. J. Brill, 1996.
Mowinckel, Sigmund. *The Psalms in Israel's Worship.* 2 vols. Translated by D. R. Ap-Thomas. Nashville, TN: Abingdon, 1979.
Moyise, Steve. *The Old Testament in the New: An Introduction.* New York, NY: Continuum, 2001.
———. and Maarten J. J. Menken, editors. *The Psalms in the New Testament.* New York, NY: T & T Clark, 2004.
Neumann-Gorsolke, Ute. *Herrschen in den Grenzen der Schöpfung: Ein Beitrag zur Alttestamentlichen Anthropologie am Beispiel von Psalm 8, Genesis 1 und verwandten Texten.* Wissenschaftliche Monographien zum Alten und Neuen Testament 101. Neukirchen-Vluyn: Neukirchener, 2004.
Newsom, Carol. "Re-Considering Job." *Currents in Biblical Research* 5 (2007): 155-182.
———. "Job." Pages 317-638 in *The New Interpreter's Bible*, volume 4. Nashville TN: Abingdon Press, 1994.
———. "Considering Job," *Currents in Research.* 1 (1993): 87-118.
Noble, Paul R. *The Canonical Approach: A Critical Reconstruction of the Hermeneutics of Brevard S. Childs.* Biblical Interpretation Series 16. New York: E. J. Brill, 1995.
Nolland, John. *The Gospel of Matthew: A Commentary in the Greek Text.* New International Greek Testament Commentary. Grand Rapids, MI: Eerdmans/Paternoster, 2005.
Novakovic, Lidija. "Matthew's Atomistic Use of Scripture: Messianic Interpretation of Isaiah 53.4 in Matthew 8.17." Pages 147-162 in *Biblical Interpretation in Early Christian Gospels Vol. 2: The Gospel of Matthew.* Library of New Testament Studies 310. Edited by Thomas R. Hatina. New York, NY: T & T Clark, 2008.
———. *Messiah, the Healer of the Sick: A Study of Jesus as the Son of David in the Gospel of Matthew.* Wissenschaftliche Untersuchungen zum Neuen Testament 2:170. Tübingen: Mohr Siebeck, 2003.

O'Donnel, James J. "*Doctrina Christiana, De.*" Pages 278-280 in *Augustine Through the Ages:An Encyclopedia*. Edited by Allan D. Fitzgerald, et. al. Grand Rapids: Eerdmans, 1999.

O'Neal, G. Michael. *Interpreting Habakkuk as Scripture*. Studies in Biblical Literature 9. New York: Peter Lang, 2007.

O'Regan, Cyril. "*De doctrina Christiana* and Modern Hermeneutics." Pages 217-243 in *De Doctrina Christiana: A Classic of Western Culture*. Edited by Duane W. H. Arnold and Pamela Bright; Notre Dame, IN: University of Notre Dame Press, 1995.

Olbricht, Thomas H. "Hebrews as Amplification." Pages 375-387 in *Rhetoric and the New Testament: Essays from the 1992 Heidelberg Conference*. Edited by Stanley E. Porter and Thomas H. Olbricht. Journal for the Study of the New Testament Supplement 90. Sheffield, UK: Sheffield Academic, 2001.

Otto, Eckart. "Myth and Hebrew Ethics in the Psalms." Pages 26-37 in *Psalms and Mythology*. Edited by Dirk J. Human. Library of Hebrew Bible/Old Testament Studies 462. New York: T&T Clark, 2007.

Overman, J. Andrew. *Matthew's Gospel and Formative Judaism: The Social World of the Matthean Community*. Minneapolis, MN: Fortress Press, 1990.

Parsons, Gregory W. "The Structure and Purpose of the Book of Job." *Bibliotheca Sacra* 138 (1981): 139-157.

Perdue, Leo G. *Reconstructing Old Testament Theology: After the Collapse of History* Minneapolis: Fortress, 2005.

———. *The Collapse of History: Reconstructing Old Testament Theology* Minneapolis: Fortress, 1994.

Peterson, David. "God and Scripture in Hebrews." Pages 118-138 in *The Trustworthiness of God: Perspectives on the Nature of Scripture*. Grand Rapids, MI: Eerdmans, 2002.

Peterson, Margaret Kim. *Psalm 8: A Theological and Historical Analysis of its Interpretation*. Ph.D. dissertation. Durham, NC: Duke University, 1998.

Phillips, Elaine A. "Speaking Truthfully: Job's Friends and Job." *Bulletin for Biblibcal Research* 18 (2008): 31-43.

Pickup, Martin. "New Testament Interpretation of the Old Testament: The Theological Rationale of Midrashic Exegesis." *Journal of the Evangelical Theological Society* 51 (2008): 353-381.

Plantinga, Alvin. *Warranted Christian Belief*. New York: Oxford University Press, 2000.

Pope, Marvin H. *Job*. Anchor Bible C15. New York: Doubleday, 1965.

Potterie, Ignace de La "Christ, Plérôme de l'Église." *Biblica* 58 (1977): 500-524.

Provan, Iain. "Canons to the Left of Him: Brevard Childs, His Critics, and the Future of Old Testament Theology." *Scottish Journal of Theology* 50 (1997): 1-38.

Rashi. *Rashi's Commentary on Psalms*. Translated by Mayer I. Gruber. The Brill Reference Library of Judaism 18. Boston: Brill, 2004.

Rendtorff, Rolf. "David in the Psalms," Pages 53-64 in *The Book of Psalms: Composition and Reception*. Vetus Testamentum Suppllement: 49:4. Edited by Craig A. Evans and Peter W. Flint. Boston: Brill, 2005.

———. *The Canonical Hebrew Bible: A Theology of the Old Testament*. Leiden: Deo, 2005.

Ringgren, Helmer. "Some Observations on the Text of the Psalms." Pages 307-309 in *Sopher Mahir: Northwest Semitic Studies Presented to Stanislav Segert*. Edited by Edward M. Cook. Winona Lake IN: Eisenbrauns, 1990.

Robertson, David. *The Old Testament and the Literary Critic*. Old Testament Studies. Philadelphia, PA: Fortress Press, 1977.

Roon, A. van. *The Authenticity of Ephesians*. New Testament Studies Supplement 39. Leiden: E. J. Brill, 1974.

Sailhamer, John H. *The Meaning of the Pentateuch: Revelation, Composition, and Interpretation*. Downers Grove, IL: IVP Academic, 2009.

———. *Introduction to Old Testament Theology: A Canonical Approach*. Grand Rapids, MI: Zondervan, 1995.

———. *The Pentateuch as Narrative: A Biblical-Theological Commentary*. Grand Rapids: Zondervan, 1992.

Saldarini, Anthony J. *Matthew's Christian-Jewish Community*. Chicago, IL: University of Chicago Press, 1994.

Sanders, James A. *Canon and Community: A Guide to Canonical Criticism*. Philadelphia: Fortress Press, 1984.

———. *From Sacred Story to Sacred Text: Canon as Paradigm*. Philadelphia, Fortress Press, 1987.

Sarna, Nahum M. *Songs of the Heart: An Introduction to the Book of Psalms*. New York: Schocken, 1993.

Scalise, Charles J. *From Scripture to Theology: A Canonical Journey into Hermeneutics*. Downer's Grove, IL: InterVarsity Press, 1996.

———. *Hermeneutics as Theological Prolegomena: A Canonical Approach*. Studies in American Biblical Hermeneutics 8. Macon, Georgia: Mercer University Press, 1994.

Schäublin, Christof. "*De Doctrina Christiana: A Classic of Western Culture?*" Pages 47-67 in *De Doctrina Christiana: A Classic of Western Culture*. Edited by Duane W. H. Arnold and Pamela Bright. Notre Dame, IN: University of Notre Dame Press, 1995.

Schedl, Claus. "Psalm 8 in ugaritischer Sicht." *Forschungen und Fortschritte* 38 (1964): 183-185.

Schenck, Kenneth L. "A Celebration of the Enthroned Son: The Catena of Hebrews 1." *Journal of Biblical Literature* 120 (2001): 469-485.

Schifferdecker, Kathryn. *Out of the Whirlwind: Creation Theology in the Book of Job*. Harvard Theological Studies 61. Cambridge: MA: Harvard University Press, 2008.

Schnackenburg, Rudolf. *Ephesians: A Commentary*. Translated by Helen Heron. Edinburgh, UK: T & T Clark, 1991.

———. *Der Brief an Die Epheser*. Evangelisch-kotholischer Kommentar zum Neuen Testament 10. Neukirchen-Vluyn: Neukirchener Verlag, 1982.

Seid, Timothy W. "Synkrisis in Hebrews 7: the Rhetorical Structure and Strategy." Pages 322-347 in *The Rhetorical Interpretation of Scripture: Essays from the 1996 Malibu Conference*. Edited by S. E. Porter and D. L. Stamps. JSNTSup 180; Sheffield, UK: Sheffield Academic Press, 1999.

Seitz, Christopher. *The Goodly Fellowship of the Prophets: The Achievement of Association in Canon Formation*. Acadia Studies in Bible and Theology. Grand Rapids, MI: Baker Academic, 2009.

———. "The Canonical Approach and Theological Interpretation." Pages 58-110 in *Canon and Biblical Interpretation*. Craig G. Bartholomew, Scott Hahn, Robin Parry, Christopher Seitz, and Al Wolters, editors. Scripture and Hermeneutics Series 7. Grand Rapids, MI: Zondervan, 2006.

———. *Word Without End: The Old Testament as Abiding Theological Witness*. Grand Rapids: Eerdmans, 1998.

Sellin, Gerhard. *Der Streit um die Auferstehung der Toten: Eine religionsgeschichtliche und exegetische Untersuchung von 1 Korinther 15*. Forschungen zur Religion und Literatur des Alten und Neuen Testaments 138. Göttingen: Vandenhoeck & Ruprecht, 1986.

Sheppard, Gerald T. "Barr on Canon and Childs: Can One Read the Bible as Scripture," *Theological Students Fellowship Bulletin* 7 (1983): 2-4.
Shum, Shiu-Lun. *Paul's Use of Isaiah in Romans*. Wissenschaftliche Untersuchungen zum Neuen Testament 2:156. Tübingen: Mohr Siebeck, 2002.
Sim, David C. *The Gospel of Matthew and Christian Judaism*. Edinburgh, UK: T & T Clark, 1998.
Smith, Mark S. "Psalm 8 2b-3: New Proposals for an Old Problem." *Catholic Biblical Quarterly* 59 (1997): 637-641.
Soards, Marion L. *1 Corinthians*. New International Biblical Commentary, New Testament Series. Peabody, MA: Hendrickson/Paternoster, 1999.
Soggin, Alberto J. "Textcritische Untersuchung von Ps 8:2-3 und 6." *Vetus Testamentum* 21 (1971): 565-571.
Speiser, E. A. *Genesis*. Anchor Bible volume C1. New York: Doubleday, 1963.
Stanley, Christopher D. *Paul and the Language of Scripture: Citation Technique in the Pauline Epistles and Contemporary* Literature. Society for New Testament Studies Monograph Series 69. New York, NY: Cambridge University Press, 1992.
Stanley, Steve. "The Structure of Hebrews from Three Perspectives." *Tyndale Bulletin* 45 (1994): 245-271.
Steck, Odil H. "Beobachtungen zu Psalm 8." *Biblische Notizen* 14 (1981): 54-64.
Steins, Georg. *Die Bindung Isaaks im Kanon, Gen 22: Grundlagen und Programm einer Kanonisch-Intertextuellen Lektüre: Mit einer Spezialbibliographie zu Gen 22*. Freiburg: Herder, 1999.
Subramanian, J. Samuel. *The Synoptic Gospels and Psalms as Prophecy*. Library of New Testament Studies 351; New York, NY: T & T Clark, 2007.
Sumney, Jerry L. "Studying Paul's Opponents: Advances and Challenges." Pages 7-58 in *Paul and His Opponents*. Pauline Studies 2. Edited by Stanley E. Porter; Leiden: Brill, 2005.
Talbert, Charles H. *Ephesians and Colossians* PCNT; Grand Rapids, MI: Baker Academic, 2007.
Talshir, Zipora. "Several Canon-Related Concepts Originating in Chronicles," *Zeitschrift für die alttestamentliche Wissenschaft* 113 (2001): 386-403.
Tate, Marvin. E. "An Exposition of Psalm 8," *Perspectives in Religious Studies* 28 (2001): 344-359.
Terrien, Samuel. *The Psalms: Strophic Structure and Theological Commentary*. Eerdmans Critical Commentary Grand Rapids, MI: Eerdmans, 2003.
Teuffel, Jochen "Fate and Word: The Book of Esther as Guidance to the Canonical Reading of Scripture." *Currents in Theology and Mission* 36 (2009): 26-31.
Tigay, Jeffrey H. "What is Man that You Have Been Mindful of Him?" Pages 169-17 in *Love and Death in the Ancient Near East: Essays in honor of Marvin H. Pope*. Edited by John H. Marks and R. M. Good. Guilford, CT: Four Quarters Publishing Co., 1987.
Todorov, Tzvetan. *Symbolisme et Interprétation*. Paris: Seuil, 1978.
Toom, Tarmo *Thought Clothed With Sound: Augustine's Christological Hermeneutics in De Doctrina Christiana*. New York: Peter Lang, 2002.
Topping, Richard. "The Canon and the Truth: Brevard Childs and James Barr on the Canon and the Historical-Critical Method." *Toronto Journal of Theology* 8 (1992): 239-260.
Tournay, Raymond J. "Le Psaume VIII et la Doctrine Biblique du nom." *Revue Biblique* 78 (1971): 18-30.

Tuckett, Christopher M. *Christology and the New Testament: Jesus and His Earliest Followers.* Edinburgh, UK: Edinburgh University Press, 2001.
Turner, Max. "Ephesians." Pages 124-133 in *Theological Interpretation of the New Testament: A Book-by-Book Survey.* Edited by Kevin J. Vanhoozer, Daniel J. Treier, and N. T. Wright. Grand Rapids, MI: SPCK/Baker Academic, 2008.
Überlacker, Walter G. *Der Hebräerbrief als Appell; Untersuchungen zu Exordium, Narratio, und Postscriptum Hebr 1-2 und 13 22-25.* Stockholm: Almquist & Wiksell Intl., 1989.
Urassa, Wenceslaus M. *Psalm 8 and its Christological Re-Interpretations in the New Testament Context: An Inter-Contextual Study in Biblical Hermeneutics.* Europäische Hochschulschriften/Publications Universitaires Européennes: 23: 577. New York: Peter Lang, 1998.
Van der Lugt, Pieter. *Rhetorical Criticism and the Poetry of the Book of Job.* Oudtestamentische Studiën xxxii. New York: Brill, 1995.
Van Fleteren, Frederick. "Principles of Augustine's Hermeneutic: An Overview," Pages 1-32 in *Augustine: Biblical Exegete.* Edited by Frederick Van Fleteren and Joseph Schnaubelt. New York: Augustinian Historical Institute at Villanova University, 2001.
Van Seters, John. *Prologue to History: The Yahwist as Historian in Genesis.* Louisville, KY: Westminster/John Knox, 1992.
———. *Abraham in History and Tradition.* New Haven, CT: Yale University Press, 1975.
VanGemeren, Willem. *Psalms.* Expositor's Bible Commentary 5. Grand Rapids: Zondervan.
Vanhoozer, Kevin J. *Is There A Meaning in This Text?* Grand Rapids: Zondervan, 1998.
Vanhoye, Albert. *The Structure and Message of the Epistle to the Hebrews.* Rome: Editrice Pontificio Instituto Biblico, 1989.
Van Leeuwen, Raymond C. "Psalm 8:5 and Job 7:17-18: A Mistaken Scholarly Commonplace?" Pages 205-215. in *The World of the Aramaeans I: Biblical Studies in Honour of Paul-Eugène Dion.* Journal for the Study of the Old Testament Supplement Series 324. Edited by P. M. Michèle Daviau, John W. Wevers and Michael Weigl. Sheffield, UK: Sheffield Press, 2001.
———. "Wealth and Poverty: System and Contradiction in Proverbs." *Hebrew Studies* 33 (1992): 25-36.
Vincent, M. A. "The Shape of the Psalter: An Eschatological Dimension?" Pages 61-82 in *New Heaven and New Earth: Prophecy and the New Millennium, Essays in Honour of Anthony Gelston.* Edited by P. J. Harland and C. T. R. Hayward. Vetus Testamentum Supplement Series 77. Leiden: Brill, 1999.
Wagner, J. Ross *Heralds of the Good News: Isaiah and Paul In Concert in the Letter to the Romans.* Supplements to Novum Testamentum 51. Boston, MA: Brill, 2002.
Wallis, Wilber B. "The Use of Psalm 8 and 110 in I Corinthians 15:25-27 and Hebrews 1 and 2." *Journal of the Evangelical Theological Society* 15 (1972): 25-29.
Waltke, Bruce K. with Charles Yu. *An Old Testament Theology: An Exegetical, Canonical, and Thematic Approach.* Grand Rapids, MI: Zondervan Academic, 2007.
———. "A Canonical Process Approach to the Psalms." Pages 3-18 in *Traditions and Testament: Essays in Honor of Charles Lee Feinberg.* Chicago: Moody, 1981.
Walton, John H. *Genesis.* New International Version Application Commentary. Grand Rapids, MI: Zondervan.

Watson, Duane F. "Paul's Rhetorical Strategy in 1 Corinthians 15." Pages 231-249 in *Rhetoric and the New Testament: Essays from the 1992 Heidelberg Conference*. Edited by Stanley E. Porter and Thomas H. Olbricht. Journal for the Study of the New Testament Supplement 90. Sheffield, UK: Sheffield Academic, 2001.

Wegner, Paul D. Review of Brevard S. Childs, *Isaiah: A Commentary*. *Journal of the Evangelical Theological Society* 45 (2002): 692-694.

Wenham, Gordon J. "Pondering the Pentateuch: The Search for a New Paradigm." Pages 116-144 in *The Face of Old Testament Studies: A Survey of Contemporary Approaches* Edited by David W. Baker and Bill T. Arnold. Grand Rapids MI: Baker, 2004.

———. *Genesis 1-15*. Word Biblical Commentary 1. Waco, TX: Word, 1982.

———. "The Coherence of the Flood Narrative." *Vetus Testamentum* 28 (1978): 336-348.

Weren, Wilhelmus J. C. "Jesus' Entry into Jerusalem: Mt 21, 1-17 in Light of the Hebrew Bible and the Septuagint." Pages 116-141 in *The Scriptures in the Gospels*. Edited by Christopher M. Tuckett. Bibliotheca Ephemeridum theologicarum Lovaniensium 81. Louvain: Leuven Universty Press, 1997.

Westermann, Claus. "אדם 'adam person." *The Theological Lexicon of the Old Testament, vol. 1*. Peabody, MA: Hendrickson, 1997.

———. *Genesis 1-11, A Commentary*. Translated by John J. Scullion. Minneapolis: Augsburg, 1984.

———. *Praise and Lament in the Psalms*. Translated by Keith R. Crim and Richard N. Soulen. Atlanta GA: John Knox Press, 1981.

Westfall, Cynthia Long. *A Discourse Analysis of the Letter to the Hebrews: The Relationship between Form and Meaning*. Library of New Testament Studies 297. New York, NY: T & T Clark, 2005.

White, Lynne. "The Historical Roots of Our Ecological Crisis." *Science* 155 (1967): 1203-1207.

Whybray, Roger N. *Reading the Psalms as a Book*. Journal for the Study of the Old Testament Supplement Series 222. Sheffield UK: Sheffield Academic, 1996.

———. *The Making of the Pentateuch: A Methodological Study*. Sheffield, UK: JSOT Press, 1987.

Wilfong, Marsha M. "Human Creation in Canonical Context: Genesis 1:26-31 and Beyond." Pages 42-53 in *God Who Creates: Essays in Honor of W. Sibley Towner*. Edited by William P. Brown and S. Dean McBride Jr. Grand Rapids, MI: Eerdmans, 2000.

Williams, H. H. Drake. "The Psalms in 1 and 2 Corinthians." Pages 163-180 in *The Psalms in the New Testament*. Edited by Steve Moyise and Maarten J. J. Menken. New York, NY: T & T Clark, 2004.

Wills, Lawrence. "The Form of the Sermon in Hellenistic Judaism and Early Christianity." *Harvard Theological Review* 77 (1984): 277-299.

Wilson, Gerald H. *Job*. New International Biblical Commentary 10. Peabody MA: Hendrickson, 2007.

———. *Psalms I*. New International Version Applied Commentary. Grand Rapids: Zondervan, 2002.

———. "Shaping the Psalter: A Consideration of Editorial Linkage in the Book of Psalms." Pages 72-81 in *The Shape and Shaping of the Psalter*. The Journal for the Study of the Old Testament Supplement Series 159. Edited by J. Clinton McCann. Sheffield: JSOT Press, 1993.

———. "The Shape of the Book of Psalms" *Interpretation* 46 (1992): 129-142.

———. "The Use of Royal Psalms at the 'Seams' of the Hebrew Psalter," *Journal for the Study of the Old Testament* 35 (1986): 85-94.

———. *The Editing of the Hebrew Psalter*. Society of Biblical Literature Dissertation Series: 76; Chico, CA: Scholars Press, 1985.

Witherington, Ben. *The Letters to Philemon, the Colossians, and the Ephesians: A Socio-Rhetorical Commentary on the Captivity Epistles*. Grand Rapids, MI: Eerdmans, 2007.

———. *Conflict and Community in Corinth: A Socio-Rhetorical Commentary on 1 and 2 Corinthians*. Grand Rapids, MI: Eerdmans, 1995.

———. "The Influence of Galatians on Hebrews." *New Testament Studies* 37 (1991): 146-152.

Wittstruck, Thorne. *The Book of Psalms, an Annotated Bibliography*. Two Volumes. New York, NY: Garland Publishing, 1994.

Yadin, Yigael. "מגילות ים המלח והאיגרת אל העברים׳." Pages 191-208 in *Essays on the Dead Sea Scrolls, in Memory of E. L. Sukenik*. Edited by Chaim Rabin. Jerusalem: Hekhal Ha-Sefer, 1961.

Yates, Roy. "Re-examination of Ephesians 1:23," *Expository Times* 83 (1972): 146-151.

Young, Frances M. "Augustine's Hermeneutic and Postmodern Criticism." *Interpretation* 58 (2004): 42-55.

Zeitlin, Solomon. "Hillel and the Hermeneutic Rules." *Jewish Quarterly Review* 54 (1963): 161-173.

Index of Biblical Citations

Gen			1 Chr		11
1		37, 45, 92-110, 127-28, 184, 187-88	2 Chr Job		11
			1-2		118-19
			1-3		112
			4-7		111
1-2		38, 127-29, 131, 144	5:17		112
			6-7		112, 114-15
1-3		32, 127	7		37, 61, 62, 92-93, 110-120, 126, 129, 184, 187-88
1-11		127-29, 188			
1:1		101			
1:1-2:3		92-110, 126			
1:2		128	7:17		117
1:6-8		102	7:17-18		92, 110-20, 128
1:8		102			
1:14		102, 107	7:17-21		38, 114-15, 117, 131, 155
1:16		102			
1:17		102			
1:26-31		103, 108	7:19-21		117
1:27		105	15:14		130
1:28-30		105	38-39		119
2		129	38-41		112-134
2:1		101			118-19
2:4-24		94, 127	40-41		119
3		130-31	40:3-5		
3-11		129, 184	40:4		112
3:24		130	40:15-41:34		119
Exod			42:1 6		113
15		141	42:6		112
15:1		141	42:7-8		112-13
Deut			Ps		
31:14-29		130	Book I		66, 73, 76-81
32:48-52		130			
II Sam			1		73-74, 76, 80, 82-84
7:9-16		129			
11		130			
12		130	1-2		76, 77, 79-80
22		123-24			
22:48		125	1-14		66, 73-76
24		130	1:1		77
II Kings			2		73-74, 76, 82-84
25		130			

Ps (cont.)		8:3 (cont.)	107, 117,
2:7-9	129		126, 130-
2:11	77		31, 136-
3-7	73-74, 76		45, 153,
3-14	73, 77, 79		182-84
5:11	79	8:4	48-49,
7	67-72, 80		102-3,
7-9	71, 74		106, 107,
7-10	66-73, 80		182
7:2-10	72	8:4-5	50
7:3	69	8:4-6	143
7:5-7	68	8:4-7	69, 182
7:15-16	129	8:4-9	50
7:15-17	68-72	8:5	69, 70,
7:18b	69		71, 73,
8	1-4, 11,		74, 76,
	22, 29,		88, 93,
	30, 33,		99, 110,
	34-38		115-17,
	39-65,		122-27,
	67-76,		136, 140,
	79-82,		143, 177
	85-91,	8:5-6	125-26
	92-94,	8:5-7	58, 103,
	98-111,		174, 176-
	115-21,		182
	122-31,	8:5-9	48, 72,
	132-33,		104, 107,
	135-45,		108, 124,
	149-57,		128, 131,
	162-63,		144, 153,
	165-69,		156, 182
	172, 176-	8:6	117, 173,
	184, 186-		181
	91	8:6-7	51, 169,
8-10	87		177
8:2	47-49,	8:6-9	69, 99,
	69, 101,		140
	107, 144,	8:7	149-57,
	165, 169		162-63,
8:2b	41-44,		165-69
	102, 106	8:7-9	50, 119,
8:2b-3	49, 104		105, 157
8:2-4	102, 182	8:8b	177
8:3	44, 48,	8:8-9	51, 58,
	52-57,		103, 166,
	58, 68,		169, 182
	70-72,	8:8	125
	74, 76,		
	102-3,		

Index of Biblical Citations

Ps (cont.)		110:1	149-52,
8:10	47-48,		156-57,
	51, 69,		162-63,
	101		165-67,
9	67, 69-		174, 178-
	72, 80		80
9-10	67, 78,	110:5-7	156
	79, 88	118:25	137
9-14	73-76	132	84
9:3b	69	138-43	87
9:4	69	144	37-38,
9:6-7	70, 85		83, 84,
9:7	69-70		85-89,
9:13	70		92-93,
9:14-15	72		120-27,
9:16-17	72, 79		130, 143,
9:17	70, 71		184, 187-
9:18	81		88
10	69-72	144:1-2	87, 121,
10:1-2	84		123
10:2	81	144:1-11	121, 125
10:16	70, 88	144:2	125
10:16-18	72	144:3	86, 87,
15-24	77, 79		88, 123
18	123-24	144:3-4	92, 120-
18:1	124		27, 122,
18:48	125		124, 126
25	78	144:3-11	86
25-34	77-79	144:4	89, 110-
34	78		11, 131
35-40	79	144:4-7	87
35-41	77	144:5-8	123, 126
37	78, 79	144:5-11	121, 126
37:14-15	79-80	144:7-8	89, 126
41	76-77,	144:8-9	87
	79-80	144:9-10	122
43-150	77	144:10-11	122
72	83	144:10-12	87
73	83	144:11	125-26
78:2	139	144:12-15	86, 121-
89	82, 83,		25
	85, 126,	144:13	121
	130	144:13-14	125
89:29	85	144:13-20	87
89:38-39	85	144:15	121
90	83	144:21	87
102	21	145	83, 86-88
110	149-52,	145:14	88
	162-67	146-50	87
		146:3-5	130

Prov		21:10-11	137-39
10-15	120	21:12-13	183
Isa		21:12-17	134-145
9:1-7	155	21:13	137
9:12	155	21:14	139, 140,
25:8	155		183
56:7	137	21:14-16	135
62:11	137	21:14-17	140, 144
Jer		21:15	136-40,
7:11	137		183
31	155	21:16	35, 38,
31:32	130		136-37,
Dan			139-45
7:13	143	21:17	136
Joel		22:43-45	139
3:17-21	155	24:30	140
Zech		26:1	134
9:9	136-37	26:64	140
Matt		27	135
1-2	135	27:9	139
1:1-4:16	134	28:16-20	135
1:1-8:1	136	Rom	
2:17	139	5	32, 167,
4:17-16:20	134		189
7:28	134	5:12-21	154
8:20	143	8:10	155
9:6	143	8:18-25	155
11:1	134	8:29-30	160
13:35	139	1 Cor	180
13:53	132	1:1-9	146
19:1	134	1:6	145
16:21-28:20	134	1:10-4:21	146
20:18	143	1:11-17	145, 146
20:29-21:22	135	3:4-8	145
21	132-145,	5-10	146
	183-84,	10:3	145
	188-90	11-14	146
21:1-3	136	12:12	145
21:1-6	135, 138	15	33, 132,
21:1-9	136		145-58,
21:1-11	135-36		160, 168,
21:1-16	137		181-84,
21:1-17	132-145		188-90
21:4	136	15:1-11	148
21:5	137	15:1-34	148
21:6	136	15:12	146
21:6-9	140	15:12-19	148
21:7-11	135	15:20-23	150, 153
21:9	136, 137	15:20-28	132, 145-
21:9-11	138		48, 158

Index of Biblical Citations

1 Cor (cont.)		1:18	161, 167-68
15:21-22	148, 153-54	1:19	162, 168
15:22	164	1:19-23	161-69
15:23	145	1:20	166
15:23-28	149	1:20-21	165
15:24	156	1:20-23	61, 162
15:24-28	153, 156, 162-65, 167	1:21	161, 163, 166
		1:21-23	166
15:25	157, 163	1:22	38, 140, 165-69
15:25-28	132, 145-48		
		1:23	184
15:26	149-51, 164, 169, 182, 184	2:7	121
		2:11-19	160
		2:11-21	168
15:27	38, 140, 149-58, 166, 168	2:18	160
		2:22	161
		3:11	160
15:27-28	150	3:19	161
15:28	149-51, 164, 184	3:21	161
		4-6	161
15:29-34	146	4:1-11	168
15:35-49	148	4:1-16	160, 167
15:35-58	148	4:4	161
15:38-42	163	4:13	161
15:45	154	4:15-16	161
15:45-50	154	4:17-32	169
15:47	154	5:1-20	169
15:50-57	148	5:5-6	161
15:54c	155	6:8-9	161
15:58	148	6:12	156
16	146	Heb	
16:22	145	1	178-79
2 Cor	145, 153, 160	1:1-4	173
		1:5-14	174-76, 178, 180
5:17	155		
Eph	180	1:5-2:18	172-76
1	132, 154, 158-69, 180, 182-84, 188-90	1:5-10:18	176
		1:10	181
		1:13	174, 179
		1:13-2:9	180
1-3	159, 161	2	62, 132, 154, 179, 183-84, 188-90
1:1-2	161		
1:3-14	160, 161		
1:10	168	2:1-4	174
1:14	161	2:5	174-75, 177
1:15-23	158-69		

Heb (cont.)		2:14	178, 181-
2:5-9	140, 169-83		82
		2:16	178
2:5-18	179-82	2:17	178, 181
2:6	175	2:18	182
2:6-8(a)	35, 38, 132, 169-83	3:1-4:16	173
		5:1-7:28	176
		5:1-10:18	176
2:7	181	8:1-2	176
2:8	174	8:3-10:18	176
2:8(b)-9	175, 178	10:1-18	173
2:8b-18	175	11:1-12:29	173
2:9	181, 182	12:2	142, 181
2:10	180-82	12:3-17	182
2:10-18	174, 176-80	James	
		1:27	183
2:11	178, 181	Rev	
2:12	181	21-22	182, 184
2:12-13	180	21:5	131, 184
		22	184
		22:20	184

INDEX OF AUTHORS AND SUBJECTS

Arnold, Bill T., 191
Abasciano, Brian J., 152, 191
Abraham, 95, 178, 179
acrostic psalms, 67, 69, 76-79, 86-88
Adam, 32, 33, 37, 102-3, 124-25, 129, 130, 144, 148-50, 153-57, 167, 168, 181, 189
all, 150, 151, 157, 162, 164, 166, 177
all in all, Christ as, 149, 151, 164, 166, 184
Allen, Leslie C., 86, 87, 121, 123, 125, 191
Allison, Dale, 134, 135, 136, 138, 141, 142, 191
Alter, Robert, 48, 49, 58, 59, 101, 102
analogy of Scripture, 24
Anderson, A. A., 43, 45, 46, 98, 191
angels, 173-79
anointed one, 79
Anselm, 9
anthropology, biblical concet of, 126
Arnold, Bill T., 94, 166, 167
Arnold, Clinton E., 159, 161, 167, 191
Arnold, Duane W. H., 24, 191
Asensio, Felix, 35, 37, 45, 47, 62, 191
Attridge, Harold W., 170, 172, 173, 174, 175, 177, 191
Auffret, Pierre, 36, 51, 54, 55, 58, 191
Augustine, St., 3, 17, 21, 23-35, 44, 50, 59, 62, 129, 142, 185, 191
Augustinian, 23, 38, 59, 90, 127, 157, 183, 186
avenger, *see* enemies
Ayres, Lewis, 25, 26, 27, 191
babes and sucklings, 30, 40, 48, 49, 52-55, 58, 90, 102, 103, 110, 125, 140-42, 186-87
Babylonian mythology and ideology, 96, 106, 141
Bacon, Benjamin W., 134, 191
Balentine, Samuel E., 119, 191
Barr, James, 2, 5-12, 15, 20, 22, 27, 28, 32, 63, 108, 185, 191, 194
Barth, Karl, 1, 3, 9, 61, 192, 194
Barth, Markus, 158, 159, 160, 167, 192

Bartholomew, Craig G., 1, 120, 192, 203
Bauckham, Richard, 19
Bellinger, William H., 57, 66, 67, 68, 69, 73, 74, 75, 76, 77, 78, 79, 80, 81, 192, 196
Best, Ernest, 159, 192
Beyerlin, Walter, 46, 51, 54, 55, 56, 192
Black, C. Clifton, 170, 192
Blenkinsopp, Joseph, 10, 94, 95, 192
Blomberg, Craig L., 139, 142, 177, 192
Bochet, Isabelle, 26, 192
Bratcher, Robert G., 43, 192
Brennan, Joseph P., 67, 68, 69, 71, 72, 193
Brett, Mark, 1, 5, 6, 10, 11, 13, 14, 15, 16, 22, 24, 185, 193
Briggs, Charles Augustus and Emilie Grace, 42, 46, 99, 100, 102, 103, 193
Brooks, Stephenson H., 133, 193
Brown, William P., 96, 97, 108, 113, 114, 193,
Bruce, Frederick F., 147, 158, 193
Brueggemann, Walter, 22, 46, 47, 66, 67, 84, 95, 105, 106, 108, 109, 119, 120, 191, 193
Brunson, Andrew C., 98, 104, 193
Burkett, Delbert, 143, 193
Buttenwieser, Moses, 41, 193
Calvin, John, 32, 33, 43, 61, 62, 68, 193
Canaanite mythology, 36, 52-54, 119
canon-critical, 4, 76
caritas, 38, 59-60, 90, 127, 131-132, 183, 186
Casey, Maurice, 154, 193
chaos, 36, 70, 73, 88, 91, 103, 109, 118-20, 126, 128, 130, 131, 188
Chapman, Stephen, 17, 18, 19, 193
Charlesworth, James H., 132, 193
Cheon, Samuel, 5, 193
Chernick, Michael, 150, 193
chiastic structure,
　in I Cor 15:24-28, 148-50

in Matt 21:1-17, 137-38
in Psalm 7:5-7, 68
in Psalm 8:2b-4, 102-6
in Psalms 15-24, 77
child of humanity, 40, 86, 116, 122, 123, 140, 143, 166, 168, 175
Childs, Brevard, 1-10, 12-17, 19-22, 24, 31-34, 37, 38, 44, 46, 49-50, 56, 57, 59, 60, 64, 73, 76, 81, 84, 86, 87, 93, 94, 96, 99, 100, 106, 108, 117, 127, 128, 130, 142, 155, 177, 185, 194
Christ, 22, 26, 27, 32, 34, 35, 62, 91, 135, 143, 145, 148-57, 159-69, 172-84, 188-89
see also Jesus
as head of the Church, 162, 164, 166, 168
as high priest, 175, 176, 181
as second Adam/identified with Adam, 153, 154, 168, 181
exalted, 153, 157, 161, 163, 166, 167, 176, 179, 181
identification with humanity, 180
lordship of, 164
under the feet of, 150-152
Christological, 162, 165, 166, 177, 180
Christology, 22, 25, 35, 37, 38, 124, 132, 134-36, 141-44, 154, 162, 167, 168, 171, 177, 178, 180, 182, 188,
Church, the, 1, 4, 7, 8, 10, 11, 12, 15, 20, 22, 25, 26, 29-34, 42, 44, 59, 60, 93, 99, 144, 145, 155, 159-62, 163-68, 183, 189, 192,
authority of, 22, 25
Clements, Ronald E., 171, 194
Clines, David J. A., 95, 114, 115, 117, 194
closing phenomena, 10
Coats, George W., 110, 115, 116, 122, 123, 194
Cole, Robert, 84, 194
community of faith, 4, 12, 14, 16, 32, 34, 90, 99, 101, 128, 183
Cope, O. L., 133, 194
cosmos, ordering of, 153, 181, 182, 183
Craddock, Fred B., 172, 173, 175, 195
Craigie, Peter C., 37, 40, 41, 44, 46, 47, 49, 55, 56, 61, 71, 72, 92, 99, 104, 118, 140, 144, 195

Creach, Jerome, 37, 62, 66, 73, 74, 76, 77, 80, 119, 122, 126, 194
created order, 35, 41, 47-51, 56-63, 69-71, 73, 80-90, 92, 99, 102, 104, 105, 107, 109, 110, 117, 119, 124-26, 129, 131, 144, 153, 155, 165, 183, 184, 186, 188, 189
humanity's place in, 41, 47, 49, 51, 62, 107, 125, 126
YHWH's maintenance of, 29, 48, 62, 71, 99, 119, 125, 127, 129, 130, 144, 153, 155, 169, 181-84
creation, 11, 30, 35, 37, 45-51, 56, 58, 60-63, 66, 71, 75, 77, 87, 93-110, 117, 119, 120, 122, 125-29, 144, 151, 153, 155, 169, 183-86, 188, 189
creation account, 94, 96, 99, 100-2, 109
day four, 102-105, 107
day six, 58, 103-105, 107, 186
creation tradition, 46, 98
crisis of exile, 82
Crossley, James G., 143, 194
Dahood, Mitchell, 40, 41, 43, 55, 67, 195
Dailey, Thomas F., 37, 195
David, 35, 36, 39, 45, 63, 72, 80, 81-88, 90, 121, 123, 124, 126, 129-30, 134-36, 139-44, 157, 181, 188,
Jesus as "Son of", 134-36, 139-44, 188
Davidic covenant, 83-85, 89-90, 93, 129
Davidic frame of the Psalter, 83
Davidic monarchy, 87, 126, 129, 130, 143
Davies, W. D., 134, 135, 136, 138, 141, 142, 191
De doctrina Christiana, 3, 18, 21-28, 30, 34, 185, 191
death, 72, 134, 135, 148-51, 154-56, 169, 181, 183, 184, 189
DeClaissé-Walford, Nancy, 70, 74- 77, 81-83, 86, 87, 90, 195
Deichgräber, Reinhard, 162, 195
Delitzsch, Franz, 41, 42, 43, 46, 49, 50, 121, 195
Dempster, Stephen G., 10, 195
demythologization, 106
deSilva, David, 170, 195

Index of Authors and Subjects

Dion, Paul E., 114, 115, 117, 195
disorientation psalms, 67, 76, 79, 80, 84
divine reversal, 51, 58-60, 64, 68-73, 76, 79, 80, 88-91, 104, 106, 117, 126, 128, 129, 131, 142, 182-84, 186-89
Documentary Hypothesis, 96
Donnelly, Phillip J., 24-26, 28, 31, 195
Driver, Daniel, 1, 3, 5-7, 14, 19-22, 59, 93, 195
Dykstra, William, 151, 195
Egypt, 36, 45, 141
Egyptian mythology and ideology, 36, 45, 53, 54, 63, 96, 101
Eichrodt, Walther, 155, 195
Eliphaz, 111-114, 118, 120, 130
enemies, 30, 36, 40, 44, 48-50, 52-58, 62, 68-72, 74, 76, 77, 81, 85, 88, 89, 110, 117, 118, 124-28, 130, 131, 140, 143, 144, 149-51, 153-57, 163, 166, 169, 182, 184, 186-89
enlightenment, 8-9, 12
Enns, Peter, 76, 82, 195
Enuma Elish, 96
Ephesians, Epistle to
   authorship of, 158-59
eschatology, 147, 160, 161, 168
   (over)realized, 147, 160
evangelical canonical exegesis, 19
Evans, Craig A., 36, 132, 152, 195, 202
Eve, 102, 103, 130
Fee, Gordon D., 145, 147, 150, 154, 196
fides quaerens intellectum, 9, 24
final form of the text, 4-7, 14, 19, 20, 22, 29-33, 42, 45, 53, 66, 67, 70, 82-86, 88, 90, 95-96, 111-12, 121, 123
Fishbane, Michael, 92, 93, 110, 115-17, 122, 195
foes, *see* enemies
France, R. T., 179, 196
Freedman, David N., 78, 80, 196
Frei, Hans, 13, 14, 32, 196
Fretheim, Terrence E., 63, 128, 196
fulfillment, 130, 139, 144, 155, 179, 183
Gadamer, Hans-Georg, 8, 13, 14
Garcialazo, Albert V., 145, 146, 196

Garland, David E., 145, 147, 148, 152, 153, 160, 196
Garrett, Duane, 19, 95, 196
Gentiles, 160
Gerstenberger, Erhard, 45, 52, 57, 196
gezirah sheva, 150, 151, 156
Gheorghita, Radu, 173, 175, 181, 196
Gilchrest, J. M., 145, 196
Gillingham, Susan, 35, 62, 67, 196
Gnostic, 160
Goldingay, John, 39, 40, 42, 53, 61, 196
Görg, Manfred, 36-37, 45, 53, 55, 63, 196-97
Gosnell, Kermit, 60
Gowan, Donald, 128, 197
Grant, Jamie A, 83, 84, 88, 197
Grech, Prosper, 24, 197
Greco-Roman, 170, 172
Grossman, Maxine L., 171, 197
Gundry, Robert H., 133, 140, 197
Gunkel, Hermann, 45, 46, 67, 121, 197
Guthrie, George H., 37, 170, 171, 174, 176-80, 182, 197
Habel, Norman C., 115, 117, 119, 197
Hagner, Donald A., 133, 197
hallel, 87, 143
Hamilton, Victor P., 40, 94, 197
Harrisville, Roy A., 37, 197
Hauerwas, Stanley, 30, 198
Hays, Richard, 29, 30, 124, 132, 147, 148, 152, 153, 156, 163, 198
heavenly bodies, 46, 48, 49-52, 58, 99, 100, 102-7, 109, 166, 186
Hebrew Old Testament Text Project, the, 43
Hebrews, Epistle to
   anthropological interpretation of Psalm 8, 177-179, 182
   authorship of, 169
   as sermon, 170
   Jewish influences, 171
Heil, John P., 148, 149, 150, 151, 152, 198
Hellenistic thought, 161, 170, 171
Hengel, Martin, 150, 198
hermeneutical circle, 26, 28-30, 33-34, 90, 181, 186
Hester, David C., 113, 198

Hill, Charles E., 3, 148, 149, 185, 191, 198
Hoehner, Harold W., 158, 160, 161, 164, 165, 198
Hollander, John, 104, 198
Holleman, Joost, 146, 147, 198
Hoppin, Ruth, 169, 198
Hosanna, 135, 137, 138, 140, 141, 188
Hossfeld, Franz Lothar, 37, 51, 68, 71, 92, 196, 198
House, Paul, 2, 19, 198
Howard, David M., 83, 84, 198
Hübenthal, Sandra, 134, 137, 138, 140, 142, 198
Hughes, Philip E., 172, 173, 198
human
    conflicted and conflicting, 130, 131, 142, 143, 188
    human ruler, 59, 89, 91, 106-7, 109-10, 153, 155, 156, 168, 183
iconography, 110
illegitimate totality transfer, 140
in Christ, 25, 27, 62, 149, 155, 157, 183, 189
inclusio,
    bracketing Heb 2:5-18, 174, 179
    bracketing Psalm 8, 46, 47, 51, 58, 69, 101, 102, 104, 166
    in Hebrews, 170
inspiration, 18-19
intentionality in the text, 17, 28
Isaacs, Marie E., 175, 198
Isaak, Jon M., 21, 198
Jerome, St., 33, 34, 37, 43, 66, 73, 74, 119, 125, 126
Jesus, 21, 35, 37, 61, 91, 126, 131-45, 151, 153-57, 160, 172-81, 183-84, 188, 189, 204
    see also Christ
Johnson, Alan F., 145, 198
Johnson, Edna, 161, 198
Judaism, 90, 133, 150, 170-72
Juel, Donald, 132, 199
Karen people group, 60
Keathley, Naymond H., 161, 199
Keel, Othmar, 110
Keener, Craig, 134, 136, 143, 144, 198
Kerrer, Martin, 171, 199
kerygma, 148
Kilpatrick, George D., 133, 199

King Adam, 85, 87, 125, 181
King David, 72, 73, 81, 82, 85, 88-90, 121, 124-26, 151, 156, 181, 187
King YHWH, 72-74, 82, 85, 88-90, 130, 143, 157, 181, 187
Kingsbury, J. D., 134, 199
Kistemaker, Simon, 172, 199
Kister, Menahem, 154, 199
Koester, Craig R., 169, 171, 172, 175, 177, 199
Kompositionsbögen, 74
Kowalski, Beate, 171, 199
Kraus, Hans J., 46, 47, 61, 67, 68, 79, 121, 122, 123, 199
Kruse, H., 40, 199
Kuck, David W., 147, 199
lament, 55, 67, 70-71, 73-76, 79-80, 82-85, 87-90, 114-5, 117-8, 121, 187
Lane, William L., 170-72, 174, 175, 177, 179, 199
Larkin, William J., 159, 199
Lawrie, Douglas, 111, 199
Leschert, Dale F., 171, 172, 199
Lessing, Reed, 6, 200
level one canonical meaning, 33, 59, 63, 93, 94, 100, 115, 132, 142, 168
level two canonical meaning, 33, 60, 72, 93, 100, 132, 139, 154, 168, 180
levels of canonical meaning, 33
Leviathan, 119
Lincoln, Andrew T., 158-65, 167-68, 200
Lindars, Barnabas, 171, 199
Lindbeck, George, 5, 13, 14, 200
Loader, William R. G., 156, 200
Lohfink, Norbert, 134, 137, 138, 200
Löhr, Max, 67, 71, 200
Loretz, Oswald., 35, 45, 53, 200
love, 25, 26, 38, 59, 60, 90, 91, 127-31, 169, 182, 183, 187, 188
Lucas, Ernest C., 67, 200
Lund, Øystein, 36, 40, 44, 49, 51, 54-56, 58, 70, 72, 186, 200
LXX., *see* Septuagint
MacDonald, Nathan, 21
Maloney, Les, 78, 79, 80, 86, 200
Mann, Thomas W., 95, 127, 200
marshal imagery, 156, 163
Masoretes, 41, 42

Index of Authors and Subjects

Masoretic Text, 29, 33, 34, 36, 39-44, 53, 56, 66, 84, 96, 97, 125, 140, 143, 151, 182
Matthew, Gospel of
    Christology of, 134
    Jesus in, 135, 136, 139, 140
    Jewish characteristics of, 133
    Structure of, 134
Mays, James L., 37, 40, 47, 48, 55, 61, 62, 66, 72, 73, 75, 86, 88, 91, 99, 103, 108, 128, 157, 200
McCann, Jr., J. Clinton, 51, 58, 67, 70, 73, 75, 76, 81-83, 157, 200
McKnight, Edgar, 170, 200
Mesopotamian mythology and ideology, 36, 45, 54, 63, 106
Messiah, 91, 131, 134, 138, 139, 142-44, 150-51, 153, 156-57, 177, 183
messianic, 40, 125, 135, 136, 138, 140, 141, 143, 144, 150, 154, 177, 179, 180, 188
messianic interpretation, 140, 154
Mettinger, Tryggve N. D., 127, 201
midrash, 20, 154, 174
Millard, Matthias, 36, 74, 75, 77, 201
Miller, Patrick D., 67, 69, 72-77, 81, 201
Moberly, R. W. L., 21, 93, 95, 127, 201
Moloney, Francis J., 37, 154, 201
Moritz, Thorsten, 159, 162, 163, 166, 167, 168, 174, 201
Moses, 95, 130, 134, 136, 141, 142, 173, 188, 191
motifs of Psalm 8, 47
mouth(s), 40, 44, 52, 53, 55, 57, 72, 80, 85, 90, 125, 140, 187
Mowinckel, Sigmund, 45, 46, 201
Moyise, Steve, 132, 139, 150, 152, 171, 174, 201, 206
Neumann-Gorsolke, Ute, 37, 63, 92, 97, 103, 105, 108, 110, 201
Newsom, Carol, 111, 114, 119, 201
Noble, Paul, 1, 2, 5, 13, 16-18, 22, 23, 32, 38, 130, 201
Nolland, John, 133, 135, 136, 201
norma normans and norma normata, 30, 33, 35, 42
Novakovic, Lidija, 134, 138, 139, 140, 201
O'Donnel, James J., 23, 24, 26, 27, 202

O'Dowd, Ryan P., 120, 192
O'Neal, G. Michael, 1, 5, 16, 185, 202
O'Regan, Cyril, 24, 201
Olbricht, Thomas H., 148, 170, 172, 179, 202, 205
orientation psalms, 15, 24, 67, 72, 76, 79, 84, 128, 129, 143
Otto, Eckart, 63, 202
Overman, Andrew J., 133, 202
pagan ideology, 145
Parsons, Gregory W., 112, 202
Paul, 132, 145-67, 171, 189
Perdue, Leo G., 12, 13, 110, 195, 202
Peterson, David, 171, 202
Peterson, Margaret Kim, 35, 62, 202
Phillips, Elaine A., 112, 113, 202
Pickup, Martin, 132, 153-55, 202
Plantinga, Alvin, 53, 202
Pope, Marvin H., 36, 45, 104, 111, 114, 115, 119, 202, 204
Potterie, Ignace de La, 164, 202
pre-canonical form of a text, 2, 7, 22, 29, 30, 33, 36, 38, 124, 186
primacy effect, 74, 80, 89
primeval history, 77, 127
Provan, Iain, 6, 8, 11, 12, 15, 202
Psalm 8
    as democratizing, 35, 63, 88, 124
    Juxtapositional pairings in, 48, 51
Psalter, 29, 30, 33, 36, 38, 53, 55, 58, 64-70, 72-93, 118, 120, 124, 126-30, 134, 143, 157, 187, 192
Quinn, Russell D., 177, 178, 180, 197
Qumran, 81, 139, 152, 171
Rash Shamra, *see* Ugarit
Rashi, 202
regula fidei, see rule of faith
Rendtorff, Rolf, 21, 36, 202
res, 15, 21, 26, 28, 59, 66, 80, 90, 127-29, 131-32, 142, 183, 186, 187
resurrection, 62, 134-35, 146-50, 154-55, 157, 160-61, 163-64, 167-69, 183, 189
reversal motif, 59, 60, 64, 68, 70, 90, 91, 128, 131, 142, 183, 184, 187-89
Reyburn, William D., 43, 192
rhetoric, 147, 161, 170, 173
Ringgren, Helmer, 42, 202
Robertson, David, 9, 113, 117, 202
Roon, A. van, 158, 159, 166, 203

royal psalms, 73, 74, 77, 82, 83, 85, 121, 124, 151
royalty, 72, 73, 81, 85, 86, 106
rule of faith, 14, 20, 24-27, 29, 44
Sailhamer, John, 2, 10, 19, 203
Saldarini, Anthony J., 133, 203
salvation history, 150, 151, 155
Sanders, James, 4, 5, 76, 132, 162, 203
Sarna, Nahum M., 40, 41, 43, 203
Satan, 118
Scalise, Charles J., 1, 5, 16, 23, 203
Schäublin, Christof, 24, 27, 203
Schedl, Claus, 40-43, 45, 52-55, 203
Schenck, Kenneth, 174, 203
Schifferdecker, Kathryn, 112, 203
Schnackenburg, 158, 162, 166, 203
Seid, Timothy W., 170, 172, 203
Seitz, Christopher, 1, 4-7, 12, 15, 17-20, 22, 33, 34, 59, 185, 203
Sellin, Gerhard, 147, 203
sensus literalis, 14, 32
Septuagint, 29, 37, 40, 42-44, 52, 59, 62, 96-97, 136-37, 140-41, 143, 149-51, 165-66, 171, 173, 175, 181
Sheppard, Gerard T., 21, 204
Shum, Shiu-Lun, 152, 204
Sitz im Leben, 32, 45
Smith, Mark S., 30, 36, 40, 41, 45, 52-55, 103, 203
Soards, Marion L., 146, 149, 204
Soggin, Alberto J., 36, 40-43, 45, 52, 53, 56, 204
Son of God, 134
Son of Man, 37, 126, 134, 140, 142-44, 154, 177, 180
Song of the Sea, the, 141
Speiser, E. A., 94, 96, 204
Stanley, Christopher D., 150-2, 204
Stanley, Steve, 172-73, 204
status of the human, 50, 109, 142
Steck, Odil H., 46, 55, 204
Steins, Georg, 5, 6, 13-16, 135, 137, 198, 204
subjection motif, 163
Subramanian, J. Samuel, 139-41, 204
Sumney, Jerry L., 145, 204
Symacchus, 43
synagogue, 15, 34, 45
Syriac, 42, 43, 125

Talbert, Charles, 158, 160, 161, 164, 166, 167, 204
Talshir, Zipora, 10, 204
Tate, Marvin E., 63, 108, 109, 204
Terrien, Samuel, 39, 40, 42, 43, 58, 61, 68, 120-22, 124, 204
Teuffel, Jochen, 21, 204
theodicy, 112, 118, 119
Tigay, Jeffrey H., 36, 45, 53, 104, 106, 107, 204
Todorov, Tzvetan, 26, 204
Toom, Tarmo, 25, 204
Topping, Richard, 6, 8, 204
Torah, 4, 10, 11, 19, 70, 74, 77-79, 82-84, 88, 89, 93, 95, 127, 128, 154, 187
Tournay, Raymond J., 35, 45, 204
tradents of Scripture, 24, 29, 34, 42, 43, 54, 63
trajectories for interpretation, 60, 64, 106, 108, 120, 129, 137, 183, 184, 188, 189
triumphal entry, 135, 136
Tuckett, Christopher M., 134, 137, 205, 206
Turner, Max, 159, 160, 161, 205
typology, 38, 130, 136, 167, 181
Überlacker, 170, 172, 204
Ugarit, 45, 52, 57, 200
Unger, Merril F., 19
Urassa, Wenceslaus, 35, 37, 38, 45, 124, 135-38, 140, 142-44, 150, 154, 162, 205
Van der Lugt, Pieter, 114, 205
Van Fleteren, Fredrick, 23, 205
Van Leeuwen, Raymond C., 115, 116, 120, 123, 205
Van Seters, John, 95, 205
VanGemeren, Willem, 41, 42, 46, 52, 56, 72, 87, 103, 197, 205
Vanhoozer, Kevin, 14, 15, 17-19, 23, 28, 160, 204, 205
Vanhoye, Albert, 172, 205
vice-gerent, 56, 63, 71, 85, 88, 105, 119, 125, 131, 144, 155, 189
Vincent, M. A., 81, 83, 85, 205
Wagner, J. Ross, 152, 205
Wallis, Wilber B., 154, 156, 162, 165, 205
Waltke, Bruce, 19, 33, 59, 97, 205

Walton, John H., 102, 128, 205
Watson, Duane F., 148, 206
Wedderburn, J. M., 158, 159, 167, 199
Wegner, Paul D., 6, 206
Wellhausen, Julius, 94
Wenham, Gordon J., 95-97, 104-6, 205
Weren, Wilhelmus J. C., 37, 137, 142, 206
Westermann, Claus, 74, 75, 79, 94-97, 101, 105-7, 127, 206
Westfall, Cynthia Long, 170, 172, 174, 206
what is the human, 86, 88, 108, 110, 113, 120-23, 126-27, 129, 132, 183, 189
White, Lynne, 109, 206
Whybray, Roger N., 81-83, 95, 206
Wilfong, Marsha, 108, 109, 125, 206
Williams, H. H. Drake, 9, 150, 152, 153, 206
Wills, Lawrence, 170, 192, 206
Wilson, Gerald, 36, 48, 50-52, 69-70, 73, 76-77, 80-84, 87, 112, 115, 118, 143, 157, 206-7

Wilson, Robert Dick, 19
Wisdom, 24, 67, 73-77, 79, 82-88, 93, 113, 120-21, 134, 141, 146, 147
Wisdom frame of the Psalter, 83
Wisdom psalms, 73, 74-75, 82-85
Witherington, Ben, 145-48, 158-59, 161, 162, 167, 171, 206
Wittstruck, Thorne, 45, 53, 122, 207
Wolf, Herbert, 19
world to come, the, 175, 177, 181
Yadin, Yigael, 171, 207
Yates, Roy, 164, 207
YHWH, name of, 37, 39, 41, 47, 48, 50-51, 56-58, 59-61, 68, 69, 71, 101, 105, 107, 109, 118, 144, 166, 169, 184, 186
Young, E. J., 19
Young, Frances M., 24, 207
Youngblood, Ronald, 19
Zeitlin, Solomon, 150, 207
Zenger, Erich, 51, 68, 70, 71, 92, 198

www.ingramcontent.com/pod-product-compliance
Lightning Source LLC
Chambersburg PA
CBHW030316080526
44584CB00012B/586